S0-CDO-191

Adobe® InDesign® 2

Introduction to Electronic Documents

Prentice
Hall

Upper Saddle River, NJ 07458

Library of Congress Cataloging-in-Publication Data

Adobe InDesign 2: Introduction to Electronic Documents/Against The Clock
    p. cm. — (Against The Clock series)
Includes Index
ISBN 0-13-048697-3
1. Adobe InDesign. 2. Desktop Publishing.
    I. Against The Clock (Firm). II. Series.

Z253.532. A34 A37 2003
686.2'25445369 — dc21

2002070006

Editor-in-Chief: Stephen Helba
Director of Production and Manufacturing: Bruce Johnson
Executive Editor: Elizabeth Sugg
Managing Editor – Editorial: Judy Casillo
Editorial Assistant: Anita Rhodes
Managing Editor – Production: Mary Carnis
Production Editor: Denise Brown
Composition: Diana Van Winkle, Van Winkle Design
Design Director: Cheryl Asherman
Design Coordinator: Christopher Weigand
Cover Design: LaFortezza Design Group, Inc.
Cover Icon Design: James Braun
Sidebar Icon Design: Bill Morse
Prepress: Photoengraving, Inc.
Printer/Binder: Press of Ohio

The fonts utilized in these training materials are the property of Against The Clock, Inc., and are supplied to the legitimate buyers of the Against The Clock training materials solely for use with the exercises and projects provided in the body of the materials. They may not be used for any other purpose, and under no circumstances may they be transferred to another individual, nor copied or distributed by any means whatsoever.

A portion of the images supplied in this book are Copyright © PhotoDisc, Inc., 201 Fourth Ave., Seattle, WA 98121. These images are the sole property of PhotoDisc and are used by Against The Clock with the permission of the owners. They may not be distributed, copied, transferred, or reproduced by any means whatsoever, other than for the completion of the exercises and projects contained in this Against The Clock training material.

Against The Clock and the Against The Clock logo are trademarks of Against The Clock, Inc., registered in the United States and elsewhere. References to and instructional materials provided for any particular application program, operating system, hardware platform, or other commercially available product or products do not represent an endorsement of such product or products by Against The Clock, Inc. or Prentice Hall, Inc.

InDesign, Photoshop, Acrobat, Adobe Type Manager, Illustrator, PageMaker, Premiere, and PostScript are trademarks of Adobe Systems Incorporated. QuarkXPress is a registered trademark of Quark, Inc. Macintosh is a trademark of Apple Computer, Inc. Macromedia Flash, Generator, FreeHand, Dreamweaver, Fireworks and Director are registered trademarks of Macromedia, Inc. CorelDRAW!, Painter, and WordPerfect are trademarks of Corel Corporation. FrontPage, Publisher, PowerPoint, Word, Excel, Office, Microsoft, MS-DOS, and Windows are either registered trademarks or trademarks of Microsoft Corporation.

Other product and company names mentioned herein may be the trademarks of their respective owner.

Pearson Education LTD.
Pearson Education Australia PTY, Limited
Pearson Education Singapore, Pte. Ltd
Pearson Education North Asia Ltd
Pearson Education Canada, Ltd
Pearson Educación de Mexico, S.A. de C.V.
Pearson Education – Japan
Pearson Education Malaysia, Pte. Ltd
Pearson Education, Upper Saddle River, New Jersey

Copyright © 2003 by Pearson Education, Inc. , Upper Saddle River, New Jersey 07458. All rights reserved. Printed in the United States of America. This publication is protected by copyright and permission should be obtained from the publisher prior to any prohibited reproduction, storage in a retrieval system, or transmission in any form or by any means, electronic, mechanical, photocopying, recording, or likewise. For information regarding permission(s), write to: Rights and Permissions Department.

10 9 8 7 6 5 4 3 2 1

ISBN 0-13048697-3

Contents

Purpose

The Against The Clock series has been developed specifically for those involved in the field of computer arts — and now animation, video, and multimedia production. Many of our readers are already involved in the industry in advertising and printing, television production, multimedia, and in the world of Web design. Others are just now preparing for a career within these professions.

This series provides you with the necessary skills to work in these fast-paced, exciting, and rapidly expanding fields. While many people feel that they can simply purchase a computer and the appropriate software, and begin designing and producing high-quality presentations, the real world of high-quality printed and Web communications requires a far more serious commitment.

The Series

The applications presented in the Against The Clock series stand out as the programs of choice in professional computer-arts environments.

We use a modular design for the Against The Clock series, allowing you to mix and match the drawing, imaging, and page-layout applications that exactly suit your specific needs.

Titles available in the Against The Clock series include:

Macintosh: Basic Operations
Windows: Basic Operations
Adobe Illustrator: Introduction and Advanced Digital Illustration
Macromedia FreeHand: Digital Illustration
Adobe InDesign: Introduction and Advanced Electronic Documents
Adobe PageMaker: Creating Electronic Documents
QuarkXPress: Introduction and Advanced Electronic Documents
Microsoft Publisher: Creating Electronic Mechanicals
Microsoft PowerPoint: Presentation Graphics with Impact
Microsoft FrontPage: Creating and Designing Web Pages
HTML & XHTML: Creating Web Pages
Procreate Painter: A Digital Approach to Natural Art Media
Adobe Photoshop: Introduction and Advanced Digital Images
Adobe Premiere: Digital Video Editing
Adobe After Effects: Motion Graphics and Visual Effects
Macromedia Director: Creating Powerful Multimedia
Macromedia Flash: Animating for the Web
Macromedia Dreamweaver: Creating Web Pages
Preflight and File Preparation
TrapWise and PressWise: Digital Trapping and Imposition

You will see a number of icons in the sidebars; each has a standard meaning. Pay close attention to the sidebar notes where you will find valuable comments that will help you throughout this book, and in the everyday use of your computer. The standard icons are:

The Hand-on-mouse icon indicates a hands-on activity — either a short exercise or a complete project. The complete projects are located at the back of the book, in sequence from Project A through D.

The Pencil icon indicates a comment from an experienced operator or trainer. Whenever you see this icon, you'll find corresponding sidebar text that augments the subject being discussed at the time.

The Key icon is used to identify keyboard equivalents to menu or dialog box options. Using a key command is often faster than selecting a menu option with the mouse. Experienced operators often mix the use of keyboard equivalents and menu/dialog box selections to arrive at their optimum speed of execution.

The Caution icon indicates a potential problem or difficulty. For instance, a certain technique might lead to pages that prove difficult to output. In other cases, there might be something that a program cannot easily accomplish, so we present a workaround.

If you are a Windows user, be sure to refer to the corresponding text or images whenever you see this Windows icon. Although there isn't a great deal of difference between using these applications on a Macintosh and using them on a Windows-based system, there are certain instances where there's enough of a difference for us to comment.

For the Reader

On the CD-ROM, you will find a complete set of Against The Clock (ATC) fonts, as well as a collection of data files used to construct the various exercises and projects. The ATC fonts are solely for use while you are working through the Against The Clock materials.

A variety of resource files are included. These files, necessary to complete both the exercises and projects, may be found in the RF_Intro_InDesign folder on the Resource CD-ROM.

For the Trainer

The Trainer's CD-ROM includes various testing and presentation materials in addition to the files that are supplied with this book.

- **Overhead presentation materials** are provided and follow along with the book. These presentations are prepared using Microsoft PowerPoint, and are provided in both native PowerPoint format and Acrobat Portable Document Format (PDF).

- **Extra free-form projects** are provided and may be used to extend the training session, or they may be used to test the reader's progress.

- **Test questions and answers** are included on the Trainer's CD-ROM. These questions may be modified and/or reorganized.

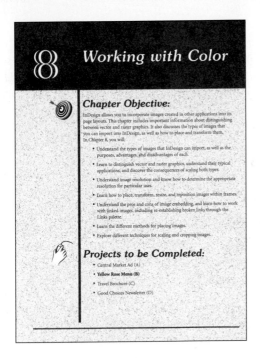

Chapter openers *provide the reader with specific objectives.*

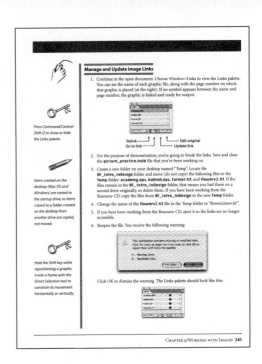

Sidebars and hands-on activities *supplement concepts presented throughout the book.*

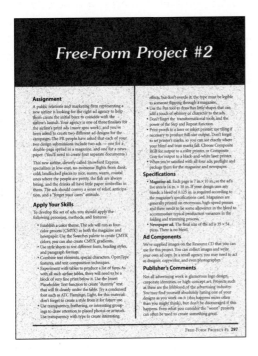

Free-form projects *allow readers to use their imagination and new skills to satisfy a typical client's needs.*

Step-by-step projects *result in finished artwork — with an emphasis on proper file-construction methods.*

Against The Clock books have been constructed with two primary building blocks: exercises and projects. Projects always result in a finished electronic layout — digital imagery built from the ground up (for the most part), utilizing photographic-quality images, vector artwork from illustration programs, and type elements from the library supplied on your CD-ROM.

This book, InDesign 2: An Introduction to Electronic Documents, includes several projects that you will work on during your learning sessions. You will find finished, full-color examples of the finished projects displayed on the inside covers of this book. Here's a brief overview of each:

Project A: Central Market Ad

This project helps you apply the skills you have learned in the first four chapters — an overview of design, working with the variety of palettes, and working with text. Beginning with a pre-designed template, you will create text frames, compose a headline, insert and format text, and import and format a block of body text, managing its flow across the ad and around an image. This project will introduce the combination of text and graphics for a clean, striking design.

Project B: Yellow Rose Menu

This is a document that you create from scratch, following exact typographic specifications. You'll create an eye-catching, colorful menu using the powerful text formatting features in InDesign, adding accent art along the way. Primarily, you'll create and work with paragraph and character styles to simplify and speed your progress with the menu. Finally, you'll add a finishing touch using the versatile Pen tool. When you've finished with this project, you'll have the knack for composing complex type layouts effectively and efficiently.

Project C: Travel Brochure

This project is similar to work that's performed in design bureaus day in and day out. You'll set up a 6-panel brochure, complete with folds. Establishing your color scheme will take some work, as will the demanding job of creating style sheets. Each pictorial element requires exacting placement in this project, and you'll be dropping your pictures in "by the numbers," to ensure that they interact well with the surrounding text. This project allows you to rotate text and images, to bleed elements off the page, and to allow your type and background to interact with one another.

Project D: Good Choices Newsletter

So, how hard can a two-page newsletter be? You'll find out when you create this "final exam" project. We help you stretch your skills as you set up this document. You'll place a variety of photos and graphics at varying percentages to create a newsletter that screams "read me!" You'll also insert and format text using style sheets, apply new and familiar techniques, and use InDesign's powerful text-management tools to ensure that the document not only looks good, but is also accurate from a spelling perspective. Finally, you'll prepare this document for printing, so the whole world (or at least the mailing list) can enjoy it.

ACKNOWLEDGMENTS

I would like to give thanks to the writers, illustrators, editors, and others who have worked long and hard to complete the Against The Clock series. And special thanks to Gavin Nagatomo, Project Manager, for his hard work and dedication to our team.

Special thanks to Caron Gordon of Caron Gordon Graphics for her art and project contributions. And a big thanks to Dennis Kelly Photography for his contribution.

A big thank you to the dedicated teaching professionals whose comments and expertise contributed to the success of these products, including Janet Frick of Training Resources, Jamie McKee of Kellogg Community College, and Doris Anton of Wichita Area Technical College.

Thanks to Angelina Kendra, copy editor, and final link in the chain of production, for her help in making sure that we all said what we meant to say.

A big thanks to Denise Brown and Kerry Reardon, for their guidance, patience, and attention to detail.

— *Ellenn Behoriam, April 2002*

Our History

Against The Clock (ATC) was founded in 1990 as a part of Lanman Systems Group, one of the nation's leading systems integration and training firms. The company specialized in developing custom training materials for such clients as L.L. Bean, *The New England Journal of Medicine*, the Smithsonian, the National Education Association, *Air & Space Magazine*, Publishers Clearing House, the National Wildlife Society, Home Shopping Network, and many others. The integration firm was among the most highly respected in the graphic-arts industry.

To a great degree, the success of Lanman Systems Group can be attributed to the thousands of pages of course materials developed at the company's demanding client sites. Throughout the rapid growth of Lanman Systems Group, founder and general manager Ellenn Behoriam developed the expertise necessary to manage technical experts, content providers, writers, editors, illustrators, designers, layout artists, proofreaders, and the rest of the chain of professionals required to develop structured and highly effective training materials.

Following the sale of the Lanman Companies to World Color, one of the nation's largest commercial printers, Ellenn embarked on a project to develop a new library of hands-on training materials engineered specifically for the professional graphic artist. A large part of this effort is finding and working with talented professional artists, authors, and educators from around the country.

The result is the ATC training library.

About the Authors

David Broudy has written a variety of books and articles on color management and various publishing applications. He currently works for Jostens, Inc. as an R&D engineer.

David holds a Master of Science degree (1999) from the Rochester Institute of Technology. A native of Dana Point, California, David now lives in a renovated tire factory in St. Paul, Minnesota.

Robin McAllister is a writer educator, and consultant to the graphic arts industry. He has been speaking about and teaching others to create effective pages and to manage their graphics businesses since the early 1980s. Rob is the team leader for America Online's Applied Computing Community. He is also a technical editor for Electronic Publishing, a contributing editor for Printing News and senior project manager for Against The Clock.

Getting Started

Platform

The Against The Clock series applies to both Macintosh and Windows platforms. On the Macintosh, InDesign 2.0 requires Mac OS 9.1 or higher, and runs natively in Mac OS X 10.1 or higher. The Windows version runs on Windows 98, Windows NT, Windows 2000, and Windows XP. There are separate reader files for Macintosh and Windows readers on the CD-ROM.

Prerequisites

This book is based on the assumption that you have a basic understanding of how to use your computer.

You should know how to use your mouse to point and click, as well as to drag items around the screen. You should be able to resize and arrange windows on your desktop to maximize your available space. You should know how to access drop-down menus, and understand how check boxes and radio buttons work. Lastly, you should know how to create, open, and save files. It doesn't hurt to have a good understanding of how your operating system organizes files and folders, and how to navigate your way around them.

If you're familiar with these fundamental skills, then you know all that's necessary to utilize the Against The Clock courseware library.

The CD-ROM and Initial Setup Considerations

Before you begin using your Against The Clock book, you must set up your system to have access to the various files and tools to complete your lessons.

Resource Files

This book comes complete with a collection of resource files, which are an integral part of the learning experience. They are used throughout the book to help you construct increasingly complex elements. These building blocks should be available for practice and study sessions to allow you to experience and complete the exercises and project assignments smoothly, spending a minimum of time looking for the various required components.

All the files that you need to complete the exercises and projects in this book are located on your Resource CD. You can either work directly from the Resource CD or copy the files onto your hard drive before beginning the exercises.

These steps assume you aren't using a font management utility such as Suitcase, Font Reserve, Master Juggler, or ATM Deluxe. If you have one of these font managers installed, refer to the documentation that came with it for font installation instructions.

You must install Adobe Type Manager (ATM) or ATM Deluxe to use PostScript Type 1 and OpenType fonts with Mac OS 9, Windows 98, and Windows NT. You can download the free "Light" version of ATM from the Adobe Web site (http://www.adobe.com/products/atmlight/main.html). TrueType font support is built into Mac OS 9 and X, and Windows 98, NT, 2000, and XP, so you don't need any extra software to use this font format.

The Work in Progress Folder

Before you begin working on the exercises or projects in this book, you should create a folder called "Work_In_Progress", either on your hard drive or on a removable disk. As you work through the steps in the exercises, you will be directed to save your work in this folder.

If your time is limited, you can stop at a logical point in an exercise or project, save the file, and later return to the point at which you stopped. In some cases, the exercises in this book build upon work that you have already completed. You will need to open a file from your Work_In_Progress folder and continue working on the same file.

Locating Files

Files that you need to open are indicated by a different typeface (for example, "Open **file.indd**.") The location of the file also appears in the special typeface (for example, "Open **document.indd** from your **Work_In_Progress** folder.")

When you are directed to save a file with a specific name, the name appears in quotation marks (for example, "Save the file as 'new_file.indd' to your **Work_In_Progress** folder.")

In most cases, resource files are located in the **RF_Intro_InDesign** folder, while exercises and projects on which you continue to work are located in your **Work_In_Progress** folder. We repeat these directions frequently in the early chapters, and add reminders in sidebars in the later chapters. If a file is in a location other than these two folders, the path is indicated in the exercise or project (e.g., "Open the file from the **Images** folder (**RF_Intro_InDesign>Images**)."

File Name Conventions

Files on the Resource CD are named according to the Against The Clock naming convention to facilitate cross-platform compatibility. Words are separated by an underscore, and all file names include a lowercase three- or four-letter extension. You see the three extension characters as part of the file name.

The Windows version of InDesign 2.0 automatically appends the four-letter file extensions for InDesign documents (.indd) and templates (.indt) to the file names. The Macintosh versions (both Mac OS 9 and Mac OS X) do not add these extensions to filenames, unlike other Adobe applications, so you need to add them manually if you plan to exchange files with Windows users.

When your Windows system is first configured, the views are normally set to a default that hides these extensions. This means that you might have a dozen different files named "myfile," all of which may have been generated by different applications and may consist of completely different types of files. This can become very confusing.

On a Windows system, you can change this view. Double-click "My Computer" (the icon on your desktop). Select View>Folder Options. From Folder Options, select the View tab. Within the Files and Folders folder is a check box: Hide File Extensions for Known File Types. When this is unchecked, you can see the file extensions.

It's easier to know what you're looking at if file extensions are visible. While this is a personal choice, we strongly recommend viewing the file extensions.

Fonts

You must install the ATC fonts from the Resource CD to ensure that your exercises and projects will work as described in the book. These fonts are provided on the resource CD-ROM, in the ATC Fonts folder. Specific instructions for installing fonts are provided in the documentation that came with your computer.

We assume that most people using this book have an extended keyboard and can use the function and modifier keys and numeric keypad. If you are using a laptop computer, or other computer with an abbreviated keyboard, some of the key commands discussed in this book may not be available.

Key Commands

There are three keys generally used as modifier keys — they don't do anything by themselves when pressed, but they either perform some action or type a special character when pressed along with another key or keys.

We frequently note keyboard shortcuts. A slash character indicates that the key commands differ for Macintosh and Windows systems; the Macintosh commands are listed first, then Windows. If you see the command "Command/Control-P", for example, Macintosh users would press the Command key and Windows users would press the Control key.

The Command/Control key is used with another key to perform a specific function. When combined with the "S" key, it saves your work. When combined with "O", it opens a file; with a "P", it prints the file. In addition to these functions, which work with most Macintosh and Windows programs, the Command/Control key can be combined with other keys to control specific functions. At times it is also used in combination with the Shift and/or Option/Alt keys.

The Option/Alt key, another modifier key, is often used in conjunction with other keys to access special typographic characters. On a Windows system, the Alt key is used with the number keys on the numeric keypad. For example, Alt-0149 produces a bullet (•) character. The Alt key can be confusing because not only do you use it to type special characters, you can also use it to control program and operating-system functions. Pressing Alt-F4, for example, closes programs or windows, depending on which is active. On a Macintosh computer, the Option key is often used with a letter key to type a special character.

The function keys on the top row of the keyboard, F1–F15, accomplish specific tasks in a given application. In InDesign, pressing "F1" will bring up the Help menu. "F6" and Shift-F6 will move elements to the front or the back of a "stack" of text and graphic objects. These function keys do different things in different applications. Some keyboards such as those included with older iMac and G3/G4 computers don't have "F13" through "F15" keys, but InDesign doesn't use those keys for anything.

The Shift key is the third modifier key. While you're used to using this key to type uppercase letters and the symbols at the top of the number keys, it's also used with Command/Control and Option/Alt in a number of contexts.

InDesign will work if your monitor resolution is lower than 1,024 × 768 pixels, but your screen area will become cluttered and messy very quickly.

Function Keys

You can use function ("F") keys as shortcuts for accessing many of the application commands and palettes. These shortcuts are extremely useful and timesaving. We note many of the function-key shortcuts throughout this book, indicating the relevant key enclosed in quotation marks (for example, "Press 'F12' to open the Colors palette.")

On a Macintosh system, you may need to configure your computer properly before using the F-key shortcuts. If you open the Keyboard control panel, the Function Keys button opens the Hot Function Keys dialog box. You have to deselect the Enable Hot Function Keys check box before you can use the built-in shortcuts.

System Requirements for InDesign

For the Macintosh, you need the following:

- PowerPC G3 or G4 processor
- Mac OS 9.1 or later, or Mac OS X 10.1 or later
- 128 MB of RAM using virtual memory
- Monitor with a resolution of 1,024 × 768 pixels
- PostScript Level 2 printer
- CD-ROM drive
- 240 MB of free hard drive space is required for software installation

For a Windows environment, you'll need the following:

- Pentium II, III, or IV processor (or equivalent)
- Windows 98 Second Edition, Windows NT Workstation 4.0 with Service Pack 6, Windows 2000 with Service Pack 2, or Windows XP
- 128 MB RAM
- Monitor with a resolution of 1,024 × 768 pixels
- PostScript Level 2 printer
- CD-ROM drive
- 105 MB of free hard drive space is required for software installation

InDesign needs to be installed by a user with Administrator privileges when using Mac OS X and Windows NT, 2000, and XP.

On all platforms, Adobe recommends an available Internet connection to run the Adobe Online automatic update system, but this is not a requirement. A printer is nice for looking at a printed page, but it's not a requirement. For best performance on all platforms, we recommend at least 256 MB of RAM, and 512 MB is better. InDesign works best if you have lots of memory.

Introduction

Adobe InDesign is a powerful, design-oriented publishing tool. It lets you integrate text and graphics into finished layouts, and produces files that may be printed to local or networked printers, taken to commercial service providers, or published to the World Wide Web.

It is our goal to first demonstrate that you can create "cool stuff" quickly and easily using InDesign's built-in features. Then we build on those principles, going beyond the basics to let you to work even more quickly and with less repetition; an example of this is using the power of InDesign's text styles. Becoming an expert is hard work, but it should also be fun and fulfilling.

As you progress through this book, we encourage you to pay attention not only to the details — how to do the tasks associated with the exercises and projects — but also to the principles behind them. While some projects and exercises require careful attention to each detail, many give you more latitude. We encourage you to experiment, rather than to limit yourself solely to ideas that we found interesting. The goal is to expand your creative vision, and to be able to look at the "big picture" of what you're actually creating. You should make decisions based on your needs at the moment, rather than establishing blanket rules for production.

Our goals are to:

- Build on your existing knowledge of the graphic-arts industry.
- Expand your vision of creative and production techniques.
- Temper creative technique with production reality.
- Explore expanded uses of Adobe InDesign.

This course is targeted toward design and print production techniques and functions. We also recognize the limitations of InDesign, and you'll note a number of cautions in the sidebars (look for the "warning hand" icon). You'll also find useful tips, tricks, and other information in our commentary sidebars.

InDesign is only two years old, but it is an evolving product with enormous potential in the graphic-design industry. We believe you will enjoy working and playing with it as you master its features.

1 The Process of Document Production

Chapter Objective:

This chapter takes a brief look at the history of publishing, from its origins with hieroglyphs through the development of the computer and desktop publishing as we know it. We introduce terms and ideas you will hear in the industry, as well as the basic process of publishing from initial concept to delivered file. In Chapter 1, you will:

- Explore the major innovations in the history of publishing, including key inventions, improvements on systems and media, and some of today's possibilities through computers and software.

- Review the stages of the design process, from initial thumbnail sketches and comps to the delivered electronic document.

- Distinguish between the various roles performed by the members of a design, content, or production team.

- Understand the differing requirements posed by print and electronic media.

- Differentiate the components of electronic documents: text, graphics, and pages.

- See examples of file and job management.

- Learn about intellectual property concepts as they pertain to the publishing process and industry.

Projects to be Completed:

- Central Market Ad (A)
- Yellow Rose Menu (B)
- Travel Brochure (C)
- Good Choices Newsletter (D)

The Process of Document Production

Electronic page layout is a result of the evolution of the publishing process. The printing and publishing industry has developed its own unique rules, protocols, and language. The publishing process has expanded to include electronic publications in addition to printed documents, presenting us with a variety of new communication methods, including CD-ROM production and the Internet.

This chapter provides a short history of publishing, and acquaints you with the basics of creating documents for publication. Its purpose is to get you off to a good start, so the terms we use will make sense, rather than simply being new words you must memorize.

A History of Publishing

From earliest times, even in the most primitive cultures, humans have had a history of publishing. Ancient communications with gods or other people appear on cave walls, preserving for posterity the story of the artists and the culture of their day.

Over the centuries, the human race developed many formalized systems of writing. Egyptian hieroglyphs were not only pictorial representations of ideas but phonetic symbols. Cuneiform, the writing of Sumerians and others in ancient Mesopotamia, used wedge-shaped characters to represent both ideas and syllabic sounds. Writing systems developed by one culture were often used and adapted by others. Eventually alphabets were developed, using symbols representing consonants and later vowels to correspond to the sound of the language, rather than to ideas.

In the East, the Chinese written language evolved quite differently as a logographic system. In this system, a word is represented by two graphs: one represents the meaning and the other indicates pronunciation. Because Chinese has so many words that sound the same, an alphabet sound-based system would not be as efficient as it is for Western languages. Each system works well for the languages and dialects it represents.

The media evolved too — from earliest rock carvings and paintings to writing on animal skins, clay tablets, vellum, fine papyrus, and eventually the high-quality papers (and low-quality newsprint) we have today. Media have been created to fulfill specific needs, including coated papers that give superior presentation of photographs and textured papers (often used by commercial and fine artists to create a specific effect) as they interact with the medium being applied (charcoal, watercolors, or ink, for example). Other media include plasticized substrates suitable for outdoor advertising, papers that can withstand the elements to preserve an image, and even clothing that is screened with images or corporate logos.

Documents also developed greater portability and ease-of-use. The scroll was portable, but required great skill to turn to the exact spot to resume reading. *Leaved* publications, forerunners of today's books, made such reading and the production of documents much easier.

Written language was often limited to priests, bureaucrats, and scribes — the first publishing professionals — who became the writers and readers of the written word. In those days, the rules for writing were relatively simple — the words had to be captured, and captured accurately.

In some cultures, these people had great power as the writers and sole readers of the recorded word. They often acted as spokespeople and interpreters for the gods of that society, thereby controlling the people. Limited literacy and access to written material throughout the centuries also often restricted the spread of ideas to only the privileged and wealthy.

For thousands of years, books and other documents were painstakingly written and copied by hand, character by character, making them extremely valuable. A revolution occurred in the mid-1400s that would make large-scale publishing a reality. The documents would become public, in the sense that they could be produced in sufficient quantity to be distributed to larger groups of people, and could be afforded by other than the very wealthy.

Automating the Publishing Process

In 1450, Johannes Gutenberg invented a printing press that used movable type, hand-carved from small pieces of wood or soft metal, changing forever the way people communicate. Multiple copies of documents could be made with relative ease with Gutenberg's invention. Once the type was set to form a page, the typeforms were inked with a roller, and then pressed against the paper with tremendous pressure, achieved primarily with human muscle power amplified with a lever or screw. The inked sheet was removed, and the process started again for the next copy.

Over the next five centuries, the basic concept of printing did not change. Ink was applied to a raised surface, and then impressed onto the paper. The term *impression* is still used in printing. There were, however, a number of improvements to that original approach.

One such improvement had to do with the letterform. Prior to Gutenberg, scribes typically wrote in a style called "blackletter", so Gutenberg fashioned his original type to emulate that lettering style. If you've ever tried to read anything set in a blackletter typeface, you know how difficult this style can be to read in long passages.

An example of Blackletter type.

The Linotext typeface, an example of a blackletter typeface.

Emulating the writings of scribes continued for about 50 years, until Nicholas Jensen designed the first roman typeface. The following year, Aldus Manutius designed the first italic typeface. The results of those changes are reflected in all our type libraries — there are literally thousands of typefaces to choose from today.

Roman Type
Italic Type

More than just the look of type changed over the years. In a variety of ways, the process of printing became automated. As a result of the industrial revolution, presses were driven by steam and by electricity, making them faster and capable of printing larger sheets of paper, and publications became less expensive to produce.

One of the most extraordinary changes came about in 1890. For over 400 years, type was handpicked and literally set in place (hence, typesetting) one letter at a time. In 1890,

Moveable type, reusable elements employed to compose and print text, was developed in China in the 11th century, but written Chinese is so complex, with thousands of distinct characters, that this printing innovation was impractical at the time.

All movable type had to be carved or cut in a mirror image of the final letter. Imagine the difficulty of doing this by hand, which is how it was done for centuries.

Ottmar Mergenthaler invented the *typecaster*, a machine that would set an entire line of type at one time. He called it, appropriately, the "Linotype."

The Linotype automated the process of preparing typeset pages.

The Linotype created a complete line of metal type (hence the name, Line-o-Type) by setting the entire line of type with pre-cut brass matrices. An operator typed the copy on a huge keyboard, and as each character was typed, a brass matrix (with a mirror-image mold form for that letter and typeface) was released from a case and set with the other matrices used to create the line. Molten lead was squirted into the mold created by the brass matrices, and the cooled, finished line of type was dispensed through a chute. The brass matrices were automatically sorted and returned to their storage case. The lead *slugs* were placed with other lines of finished metal type into the final page layout and then clamped into place in a frame called a "chase." After use, the lead type forms were usually tossed back into the pot to be melted and used again. Other hot-metal typesetting machines such as the Monotype produced a single letterform at a time and dispensed a line made up of individual pieces of type, which made assembling the final page a very disaster-prone process.

Some printing processes used the finished chase as the image carrier; others used image carriers created from the chase in the final printing process. For example, in rotary letter-press printing, a process still used in newspaper printing, a mold is made from the chase then used to make a reverse raised plate that's mounted on a rotary cylinder. This process is called "stereography". The now-common lithographic process requires a flat plate as an image carrier; prior to modern typesetting systems, chases were used to manually print a sheet, which was then photographed with high-contrast film to produce a suitable lithographic printing plate.

At about the same time, the modern typewriter emerged (the Underwood, 1897), which used the familiar QWERTY keyboard developed by Remington in 1873. Mergenthaler

The process of typesetting with molten lead is referred to as "hot metal" or "hot type".

The Linotype did not have a backspace key, and there was no way to correct anything if the operator made a mistake. An operator who noticed an error would cancel the rest of the line by running a finger down the first two columns of keys on the keyboard — which was arranged ETAOIN SHRDLU — eject the slug, and start over. This helped galley composers see the bad line and throw it away, but it was still pretty common to see ETAOIN SHRDLU appear in print.

The Photon was a photo-typesetter — a machine that printed directly to photosensitive paper by exposing it to negatives of type with a very bright lamp. Phototypesetters are often referred to as "second-generation type-setters" to distinguish them from earlier machines that created type with metal.

used a completely different keyboard for the Linotype, with the keys arranged in a vertical order by the letter frequency; subsequent developers of typesetting machines created their own (often very complex) keyboard layouts.

Gradual changes brought typesetting and typing increasingly closer. In 1928, the TTS system (which generated a punched paper tape) was introduced, using a standard type-writer keyboard. Using this system, three Linotypes operated by paper tape could produce the same amount of type as seven Linotype operators banging away on keyboards. In time, the first commercially viable typesetting machine resembling a typewriter emerged (the Photon, 1953).

A Merger of Two Cultures

In the early 1950s, Varityper and Compugraphic corporations each introduced reasonably priced (compared to other systems of that time) stand-alone photocomposition systems. The keyboards and monitors of these systems were directly wired to the imaging devices; a turret of lenses or a zoom lens would project light through a filmstrip or disk onto photosensitive media. On those early terminals, you could view only two lines of type: the one you were working on and the one that you just finished typing. These machines evolved into powerful, text-based dedicated machines that were, until the late 1980s, the standard of the publishing industry.

A true merger of the print and office environment occurred in 1964 when the IBM MT/ST (Magnetic Tape Selectric Typewriter) was introduced in Germany. A functional word-processing system with video display terminal wasn't available until 1972.

Word processing made it feasible for typists with limited training to do most of the work necessary to convert word-processed files to typesetting. This was still a far cry from what we know as desktop publishing today. Still, it represented a vast improvement over machines that required all text to be composed only on the attached keyboard, and that could not accept text from an outside source.

By the late 1970s, two system standards were emerging: Apple-DOS and CP/M. In August 1981, the IBM personal computer and MS-DOS entered the market. Hewlett-Packard also introduced the LaserJet, raising the standard of printing quality for both office and professional printing environments.

Apple introduced the Macintosh in 1984, which revolutionized the desktop computer world with its *graphical user interface* (GUI). At about the same time that Apple intro-duced the first Macintosh, Adobe introduced the PostScript page description language, Aldus released PageMaker, and Apple released the LaserWriter printer.

Merged Text and Graphics

Until the introduction of the Macintosh operating system and the first versions of page-layout software, merging text and graphics into a document was a manual, time-consuming process. If you examine early newspapers, you'll note that they are almost entirely devoid of graphics, especially photographs. This was because every element in a publication other than type had to be manually inserted. In the days of hot metal, this meant literally engraving the lead with a stylus to produce such simple elements as rules. More complex graphics were painstakingly etched in metal, included with the type, and plated.

When lithography became the printing technology of choice, layout elements (including type and photographs) were pasted onto a stiff board called a "mechanical." The finished mechanical was photographed with a large graphic arts camera (hence

The "QWERTY" keyboard, so called from the first six letters in the top letter row of the typewriter (and now the computer), was used in the early prototypes for a commercial typewriter. It was thought to be more efficient than an alphabetic arrangement. Keys were placed in combinations less likely to hit each other and stick during rapid typing.

Throughout this book, we will refer to service providers. These are typically professionals and companies who operate high-end imaging devices and sometimes printing presses. No job should be undertaken without consulting the service provider who will image or print the job. Typically, a service provider is a printer, a prepress shop, or a bindery, but the service provider concept can also extend to typesetters, color separators, fabric printers, suppliers of CD-ROMs and DVDs, and many more.

the term "camera-ready art"). These graphic arts cameras produced film, which was used to expose a lithographic printing plate. It was still a laborious process, but photographs could be incorporated into a layout more easily than with the earlier processes.

The introduction of desktop-publishing programs such as PageMaker, Ventura Publisher, QuarkXPress, and now InDesign, afforded publishers the ability to combine text and graphics quickly and easily — provided that all elements were in electronic form. Drawing programs (such as Adobe Illustrator, Macromedia FreeHand, and CorelDRAW!) are now used to create vector-based illustrations. Painting programs (such as MetaCreations Painter, Deneba Canvas, and Adobe Photoshop) are used to create raster-based images. Desktop scanners can import picture data into a computer so it can be manipulated and incorporated into documents.

Understanding the Design Process

Design involves creating the look of a document. Technically speaking, design has little or nothing to do with content, and everything to do with the way that content speaks to its audience. As publishing migrated to the computer, the need for individual skills increased. Designers today also handle page-layout responsibilities, although they'd often rather leave those mundane operations to production artists. As documents produced on the desktop have become more complicated and desktop-publishing software has added more features, users are able to make more serious and expensive mistakes.

Desktop publishing promised greater control over documents and lower prices; those benefits, though, can be realized only if the documents are prepared with the technical requirements of reproduction in mind.

The Design/Content/Production Team

Publishing has always been a team effort. We may wish that we could do it all, but there are very few twenty-first century Renaissance people out there. In addition, those who are very good at one thing usually prefer to do what they're good at and have been trained to do. Of course, there's often some overlap, particularly with today's publishing technology. Let's look at the team in its purest sense.

- **Content providers** include writers, editors, illustrators, photographers, and others who provide the information contained in a document. As an example, writers provide the words and the hierarchy of elements (such as Headline 1, Headline 2); designers then determine the appearance of those words and headlines.

- **Designers** determine the overall look of a document; they select fonts and make decisions about art and color. They are usually responsible for bringing the document through the comprehensive sketch phase; they often work with illustrators and photographers to ensure that their ideas are implemented. They generally approve the final product before it is sent to the client.

- **Page-layout specialists** quickly assemble the pages, using the *comp* (comprehensive sketch) as a guide. They create masters so elements that will appear on every page do not have to be recreated each time. They prepare style sheets to make consistent application of character and paragraph features quick and easy. They position text onto the pages, position artwork, and fine-tune the details. When the page-layout specialists are finished, there should be no more changes to the document; such changes are very expensive to make after the document passes

The cost of producing a publication is extremely important to most clients. Authors' alterations (AAs) are defined as any changes made to the original specifications or content (for example, the correction of spelling or grammatical errors, replacement of copy or graphics, and changes made to the layout). AAs made late in the process add substantially to the cost of the job. Avoid them whenever possible by planning carefully and proofing thoroughly before sending finished work out. Printers love chargeable AAs.

Although this thumbnail sketch doesn't look like much, award-winning campaigns have been created with scrawls on the backs of bar napkins.

through this stage, because even a minor change can affect the flow of text throughout the entire document. Additionally, changes made after pages have been assembled may require that other elements be changed. It is not difficult to double the cost of a project by making a change at this stage.

- **Production professionals** have technical knowledge of numerous computer programs, as well as an understanding of the printing process (or the intricacies of the Web). There must be a close interaction between production professionals and designers to ensure that the document can be reproduced efficiently and that the client will be happy with the result.

As the process of document production evolved, the power structure became divided. Content providers produce text, illustrations, and photographs. Production artists combine these elements in electronic documents. Prepress technicians color-correct scans and otherwise prepare the electronic document for printing. At the printing house, press, bindery, and other specialists complete the process. Today, some of us do perform more than one of these functions.

Sketches from Thumbnail to Comp

Designing a document requires creativity and imagination, in addition to a thorough understanding of the advantages and limitations of the media used. We recommend creating initial sketches (or *thumbnails*) with paper and pencil, not a computer. This is the way designers have traditionally created their designs, and it's still the best way. Many designs still originate on cocktail napkins or restaurant placemats. The computer is a wonderful production tool, but it is not particularly efficient as a design tool. (You can take a pencil and paper anywhere and allow inspiration to strike; you probably won't carry your computer around everywhere you go.)

This thumbnail sketch shows a section opener, a chapter opener, and a standard page.

An object that prints to the edge of the page is said to "bleed," because when it is created, it actually goes beyond (bleeds off) the edge of the page. Notice how these images do this.

After the basic idea has been sketched, your design will probably progress to the stage known as the "comprehensive sketch" or "comp." This stage refines the thumbnail by providing graphic information about the following issues:

- Trim size of the finished piece, bleeds, and folds
- Number of pages
- Balance of pages, margin size, and number of columns
- Picture placement and cropping
- Type specifications
- Colors to be used

The comp (top) and finished product (bottom) created from the thumbnail of the section opener shown earlier.

Comps (left) and finished pages (right) for chapter openers and inside text pages. Note that the comp for the text page shows a variety of features (levels of headlines, body text, bulleted text, and caption formats), but does not attempt to show a full-page layout.

The comp is often the first proof that a client approves. For documents that have a number of types of pages, or a number of styles, the comp includes samples of each. Comps should include specific styles for tables, sidebars, footnotes, and each level of headline. This allows the client to approve or alter specific elements at this preliminary stage, rather than when the document is completed.

In the past, designers often prepared comps with colored markers and rubdown letters. Today, they typically prepare comps with computers, sometimes using nonsense type (called "greeking" or "lorem text") at the appropriate size and line spacing. Pictures may be low-resolution *for-position-only* (FPO) versions of the actual images; more often, they are images from stock libraries that approximate the look and feel of the final image that will be used.

After the client approves the comp, the job is ready to move into production. Creative professionals, prepress production staff, and printers must work together closely to avoid costly mistakes, which can easily hide in a digital layout. The advantage of the digital mechanical is that changes can be made in text, images can be replaced, and colors can be changed, up to the very last minute when the file is sent off to the service provider.

Repurposing Documents

Today's documents often perform double or even triple duty. A magazine ad may be featured on a company's Web page, and also be included with sales kits. It may even be screen printed on T-shirts or enlarged to wall size for use at trade shows. Because of such *repurposing*, it is important to know in advance how each graphic element will be used, and to determine how it should be produced for maximum flexibility.

Although many programs claim to be able to repurpose a document designed for print to the Web, the results are seldom acceptable unless the document has been prepurposed for multiple uses.

Understanding the Medium

Even experienced designers often forget that the first consideration in designing a document should be the medium in which it will be reproduced. Are you designing a newspaper ad? Will the ad appear in a magazine on glossy paper? Will it be photocopied and stuck under windshield wipers? Will it be displayed on a Web page? A document may even be intended for use in multiple media. Such cases require even more planning — one size does not fit all, so understanding the goal is of paramount importance.

There are a number of technical considerations related to the various reproduction processes. The designer must know the required resolution, format, structure, and appropriate file type for each graphic. Designers must make decisions about the number of colors to use, and the color mode in which a job will be presented. If, for example, a design will be screen printed on a t-shirt, six specific colors of ink would be desirable instead of the four process-ink colors commonly used for lithographic printing. Your service provider or printer is always the best source for information regarding the requirements of the output process.

Designing for Print and the Web

There are substantial differences between documents prepared for print and electronic (especially Web) publication.

Element	Print	Web
Format	Anything; 8.5 x 11 in. is standard	Usually horizontal (to fit monitor), 640 x 480 pixels (approx. 9 x 6.7 in.)
Type	Fixed; what you produce is what is seen	Variable; depends on fonts installed on the readers' computers.
Graphics	High-resolution CMYK or spot color TIFF or EPS format	Low-resolution RGB color JPEG or GIF format
Color Display	Fixed; what you produce is what is seen	Variable; depends on the color depth of the viewer's monitor, and on how color is calibrated on the viewer's system
Interaction	May be read	Users can read, link to other documents, or enter information in variable fields
Modification	Cannot be modified, except at substantial expense	May be modified at will, even automatically updating itself from a database

Issues such as display, interaction, and modification are as important as issues surrounding format, type, and graphics representation.

Although the difficulties in designing for both print and the Web are not insurmountable, these design issues must be addressed at the time a project is defined. Far too frequently, a document is prepared for print, and only then does somebody decide to "adapt" the same document for the Web. This is not only impractical, but it also results in documents that do not work well, and that get poor results.

When designing for both media, a document should be produced in two distinct formats, often using different fonts. Different graphics files will be needed. Although color is critical for print documents, it is far less important on the Web because color depends on the viewer's monitor, which the designer cannot control. One of the greatest benefits of Web documents is that there can be a great deal of interaction with the viewer, as opposed to a static print page.

Components of an Electronic Document

Electronic layouts, like their physical predecessors, comprise text and images. Although we have become an increasingly picture-oriented society, text still makes up the majority of information in documents. And, believe it or not, text is much more difficult to manage than graphic elements.

The Page

The page provides the background for text and images. It is comprised of the *live area* (where text and images are placed), margins, and gutters. Informational text or graphics called "running heads" or "running footers" may be placed in top or bottom margins. When an image is to print to the edge of the page, it must actually overlap the edges of the page into what is called the "bleed" area. No printing process is accurate enough to print a bleed without actually cutting the excess parts off.

Text

While pictures help us demonstrate our point, text is an extension of speech. Thus, we have a responsibility to present text in our documents in a highly readable form. We should take advantage of technology, but it is more important to understand how we can make the text in our documents best perform its task of communication. We will discuss text more fully in Chapter 4, *Working with Text*.

Graphics

As you are aware, creating attractive publications involves more than using text wisely. InDesign's images can come from a variety of sources. Some will be computer-generated from programs such as CorelDRAW!, Adobe Illustrator, or Macromedia FreeHand. Others will be scanned from photographs, traditionally produced sketches, line art, or illustrations. Still others may be created within InDesign.

It is critical to understand the benefits and limitations of different types of graphic files. Ultimately what is important is whether the picture is appropriate for the intended display medium (for example, print, Internet, or CD-ROM). For printed results, EPS and TIFF formats are best; for the Web, JPEG and (to a lesser extent) GIF or PNG formats are preferable. We will discuss graphics in more detail in Chapter 7, Working with Graphic Elements, and Chapter 9, *Working with Images.*

Managing a Variety of Files

Especially when you are creating long documents, you will have many files to manage on your computer. Text may originate in word-processing documents; graphics can come from a variety of sources. Organizing these files is often a challenge for busy designers.

The best way to manage your files is to store them in clear, logically labeled directories or folders. So, while

[My Computer\Images\WSS003.tif]

may be an appropriate file name and location for a photo from West Side Story, it would be better to file it as

[My Computer\SRT\Plays\WSS\WSS003.tif]

where "SRT" is a unique code for a particular client.

This may seem like overkill, but once you have accumulated hundreds or thousands of images, the value of clear, systematic labeling will become apparent. It's also a good idea to keep every graphic file's name in the job jacket in case you need to reference it later. In fact, InDesign has a utility that will keep track of all files associated with a specific document.

Designing an efficient system for organizing your publication files at the outset is mandatory. If you number your jobs sequentially, and if you name files and sort them by job number alone, you will simply end up with have a long list of numbers. Without descriptive file names, it can be difficult to locate the correct version of a file. Without logical directories, you may not even be able to find the files associated with a particular client. That can create havoc when a client asks you to "just do it like the last time, with these changes" — particularly if "the last time" was several months ago.

Adding a file description to each job, and filing it by job type, will be a great help. If, for example, you create your company's newsletters, brochures, and product sheets, those are three ready-made directories that you can use to file your jobs. A newsletter could reasonably be filed as:

[My Computer\Newsletters\Jan01NL.indd]

It's also a good idea to use (and, if you're using Windows or Mac OS X, to display) file extensions so you can easily recognize the type of file that you're looking for.

Intellectual Property

No discussion about publishing would be complete without commenting on issues of intellectual property. At the heart of this issue is the matter of copyright, and the right of the creator of a document, photo, illustration, program, font, or other element to be paid for the work they created. Just because it's easy to grab an image from the Web doesn't mean it's legal or ethical to do so.

Copyright is a form of protection provided by law. In the United States, it protects intellectual property expressed in a tangible way for the lifetime of the creator plus 50 years. Even if the work is unpublished, it is still protected by copyright.

In general, the creator of a work owns the copyright. The exception to this is when the work performed is a "work for hire." A work for hire occurs if you create something while in the employ of another (you're an employee), or if you agree that the work is "for hire." In that case, the one who has hired you owns the copyright — not the person who has commissioned your services. Copyright owners may sell specific rights, or assign rights for a specified time, at their option.

As you begin to inventory larger numbers of graphics, you'll probably want to investigate software specifically designed for archiving graphics files. Initially, though, the methods we've outlined here will be adequate.

When should you obtain permission to use an image?

- When an image will be copied in whole or in part
- When an image will be published
- When an image will be used for reference by an artist, illustrator, or photographer
- When an image will be used for presentation

A safe rule to follow is "always ask first." Some people (or their estates) make a very good living suing people who violate copyright.

In addition to respecting the rights of other creative professionals, it is important to adhere to the law with respect to software — including fonts. Sometimes people believe that they purchased the software, so they can give it to others as long as they don't realize any commercial gain. This belief is problematic for two reasons:

- Software is not purchased, it is licensed. That license stipulates how many copies of the software may be made. Generally, the principle is "one license, one computer."
- Although the person giving away the software may realize no commercial gain, the developer of the software realizes a commercial loss, which is clearly unacceptable.

As a result, it is our responsibility to adhere to licensing agreements, take precautions against software piracy, and prevent illegal copying and borrowing of software.

Fonts are a special category of software of great importance in publishing. People who would never consider loaning out their illustration or page-layout programs often blithely give away or trade fonts. The only time this is considered acceptable is when you include them when sending a job to your service provider so they will have the same fonts that you do; even then, you need to verify that your font-licensing agreement allows this kind of transfer. The Adobe Acrobat PDF format lets you embed your fonts into the finished layout, which eliminates the need to hand over your fonts and complies with most type vendors' licensing agreements. Regardless of our personal beliefs, we are governed by the license agreements that take effect when we open any software package.

Summary

So far, you've learned about the historical origins and the progress of publishing through the centuries, following it from its scribal beginnings through the Renaissance and into the computer age. Understanding the history will be of value when we discuss some of the terms used today.

We've considered the process of publishing, from thumbnail sketch to digital mechanical. We've also compared files designated for print with files designated for the Web, and have seen distinct differences in the parameters for each.

We have addressed issues of managing files and have discussed legal and ethical issues that designers regularly face. These intellectual property issues include concern for the rights of creative artists, photographers, and software developers.

As you continue with this book, you'll discover even more facets of publishing, and how you can effectively create documents for both print and the Web.

2 *Getting Started with InDesign*

Chapter Objective:

The InDesign work environment revolves around a series of menus, palettes, and windows that allow you to create and modify elements in your document layout. Most of the application tools can be accessed in a number of different ways. This chapter introduces the different features that you will use as you create an InDesign document. In Chapter 2, you will:

- Become familiar with InDesign's windows, tools, menus, and palettes.

- Learn how to move from page to page, and how to change page views.

- Explore the contents of the toolbox, learn the functions of each tool, and review the keyboard shortcuts for choosing these tools.

- Practice grouping and arranging palettes, and minimizing and maximizing palette size, to suit your work environment.

- Review menu basics, and learn to use contextual menus.

Projects to be Completed:

- Central Market Ad (A)

- Yellow Rose Menu (B)

- Travel Brochure (C)

- Good Choices Newsletter (D)

Getting Started with InDesign

InDesign, like many other page-layout applications, offers a variety of ways to perform tasks. For now, we'll break them into three categories — tools, menus, and palettes. Don't try to memorize the information that follows; we just want you to be aware of some of your available options.

In this chapter we present various tools and features available in InDesign. Learning which tool to access for a particular task is key to increased productivity. Time is money, and your ability to streamline the production cycle of any project will bring you one step closer to meeting your deadlines.

The Document Window

A new or existing InDesign document is restricted visually by the available screen space. The toolbox, palettes, and document page quickly fill the document with task-specific items.

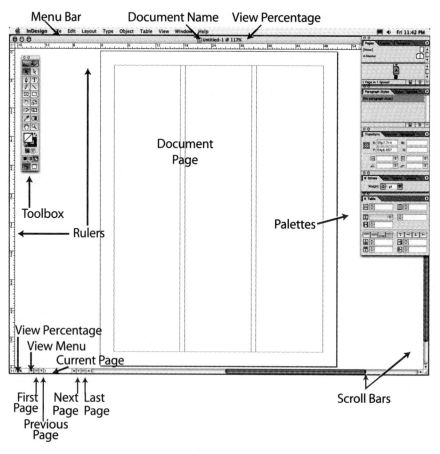

The Mac OS X document window. The Mac OS 9 and Windows windows are similar.

*Shortcuts for accessing
the toolbox tools:*

Selection tool – "V"

Direct Selection tool – "A"

Pen tool – "P"

*Add Anchor Point tool –
   "=" (equal sign)*

*Delete Anchor Point tool –
   "-" (hyphen)*

*Type on a Path tool –
   Shift+T*

Type tool – "T"

*Convert Point
Direction tool –
   Shift+C*

Pencil tool – "N"

Line tool – "\" (backslash)

Rectangle tool – "M"

Rectangle Frame tool – "F"

Ellipse tool – "L"

Rotate tool – "R"

Scale tool – "S"

Shear tool – "O"

Free Transform tool – "E"

Eyedropper tool – "I"

Gradient tool – "G"

Scissors tool – "C"

Hand tool – "H"

Zoom tool – "Z"

Toggle Fill and Stroke – "X"

*Swap Fill and Stroke –
   Shift-X*

*Default Fill and Stroke –
   "D"*

Apply Color – "," (comma)

*Apply Gradient –
   "." (period)*

Apply None – "/" (slash)

Toggle View Mode – "W"

- **View Percentage.** ...
  ment displays. In ...
  percentage of ma...
- **View.** Next to the ...
  choose from a va...
- **First Page.** This l...
- **Previous Page.** T...
- **Current Page.** Th...
  page by highligh...
  Return/Enter to ...
- **Go To Page.** You ...
  that appears nex...
- **Next Page.** This ...
- **Last Page.** The I...

Note that m...
means th...
butto...
alo...

If you've used QuarkXPress
before, then you've had
some experience with
frames. InDesign fram...
are similar to tho...
QuarkXPress.

The Toolbox

The toolbox contains tools that serve a particular function; no other menu or palette contains tools that are able to create the same effect in the same manner. The tools included in the toolbox are used for selecting objects, creating transformations, modifying paths, painting, and moving the page. Moving the pointer over each and pausing briefly will show the tool's name, along with its keyboard shortcut if there's one available.

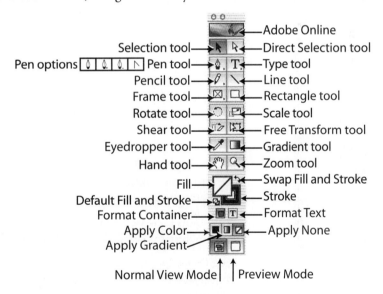

The InDesign toolbox.

…any of the tools have a little black triangle in the lower-right corner. This …at there's more than just one tool hiding there. If you hold down your mouse … while the cursor is positioned over the tool icon, you can see all of the other tools, …ng with their keyboard shortcuts.

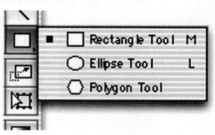

The Ellipse and Polygon tools are hidden behind the Rectangle tool.

- **Adobe Online.** Clicking this tool activates Adobe Online, which provides you with available news and software updates from Adobe Systems. You must have Internet access, be online, and have a Web browser to use this feature.

- **Selection ("V").** With this tool, you can select an object or group of objects by clicking it or by dragging a selection marquee around it. QuarkXPress users will recognize this as the Move tool.

- **Direct Selection ("A").** This tool directly isolates and selects specific parts of an object or path. It can also be used to select groups of objects and nested groups of objects. It is similar to the Content tool in QuarkXPress.

- **Pen ("P").** The Pen tool is the primary drawing tool; you can use it to create straight or curved vector paths. The pop-up menu of the Pen tool offers three optional tools: Add Anchor Point, Delete Anchor Point, and Convert Anchor Point.

- **Type ("T").** This tool enables you to type text directly into a text frame. The Selection tool adjusts the handles of text frames. The pop-up menu accesses the Path Type tool, which can be used to set type on a Bézier path. This is the only tool that, when active in a text frame, cannot be switched to another tool by pressing a shortcut key, because you'll just type the key's letter instead of activating the command.

- **Pencil ("N").** With this tool, you can draw free-form paths. The Smooth and Erase tools (accessed from the Pencil tool pop-up menu) enable you to smooth out rough paths or erase parts of them.

- **Line ("\").** Dragging and releasing the Line tool creates a single, straight line with no internal Bézier points. You can constrain lines to 45° increments by holding down the Shift key as you drag the Line tool.

- **Rectangle Frame ("F").** You can use this tool to create frames into which type is flowed or graphics are placed. You can access the Ellipse Frame and Polygon Frame tools from the Rectangle Frame pop-up menu.

- **Rectangle ("M").** This tool is used to draw rectangles, which may be constrained to squares by holding down the Shift key when dragging. The Ellipse and Polygon tools are also accessed with this tool by holding down the mouse button until they appear in the pop-up menu.

Double-clicking the Line tool icon displays the Stroke palette.

Double-clicking the Polygon tool icon displays the Polygon Settings dialog box, which can then be used to modify the polygon.

You can create a perfect circle by holding the Shift key while dragging the Ellipse tool.

In most cases, you activate the Hand tool by pressing the Spacebar. If you try to activate the Hand tool while the Type tool is active in a text frame, however, you will type a bunch of spaces. In this case, you need to press the Option/Alt key to activate the Hand tool.

- **Rotate ("R").** The Rotate tool is a transformation tool that enables you to spin a selected object (or objects) around a set origin point.
- **Scale ("S").** With this tool, you can enlarge or reduce an object around a set origin point. To constrain the object's proportions, you can hold Command/Control-Shift when dragging the Scale tool on the object.
- **Shear ("O").** Shearing an object skews (slants) an object along a horizontal axis or rotates the object along horizontal and vertical axes.
- **Free Transform ("E").** This tool allows you to perform a variety of transformations — moving, scaling, reflecting, rotating, and shearing — on an object without changing tools.
- **Eyedropper ("I").** With this tool, you can copy and apply type, fill, stroke attributes, and color from one element to another.
- **Gradient ("G").** The Gradient tool works in conjunction with the Gradient palette to change the angle, direction, and type of gradient that fills the selected object.
- **Scissors ("C").** When you click a vector path with the Scissors tool, the path splits at the selected point, providing separate anchor points that can be moved or deleted. It is located under the Gradient tool pop-up menu.
- **Hand ("H").** The Hand tool moves the document around within the document window. This is useful for viewing a page, a spread, or specific items, especially at higher magnifications.
- **Zoom ("Z").** This tool enlarges or reduces a document's view to preset percentages. Clicking without holding a complementing key enlarges the view. Holding the Option/Alt key while clicking reduces the view. When the Zoom tool is dragged around an object, the selected area enlarges to fill the center of the screen.
- **Fill ("X").** If you click the Fill box, you can quickly apply a chosen color, gradient, or pattern to the interior of an object. It works with the Color palette, which has a Fill box as well.
- **Swap Fill and Stroke (Shift-X).** This tool reverses the two, allowing an object's fill to acquire the current stroke color, and the stroke to acquire the current fill color.
- **Default Fill and Stroke ("D").** This tool returns the Fill and Stroke tools to their defaults: a fill of None, and a black stroke.
- **Stroke ("X").** The stroke is the defining outline of a vector path. The Stroke tool in the toolbox applies color to the stroke of a selected object. Attributes of the stroke are defined in the Stroke palette.
- **Formatting Affects Container/Text.** If a frame containing text is active, clicking either of these tools toggles the fill/stroke application between the frame and the text. These two tools are also available in the Color palette.
- **Apply Color (";").** Clicking with this tool applies its set color to either the fill or stroke of a selected object, determined by whichever tool (Fill or Stroke) is active. The Color palette appears if this tool is double-clicked.
- **Apply Gradient (".").** Clicking this tool applies its set gradient to the fill or stroke of a selected object. Double-clicking this icon activates the Gradient palette.

- **Apply None ("/").** Do not be misled by the appearance of a white fill within an object; because the page is white, looks can be deceiving. A fill of "None" is the same as a transparent setting. An object with a fill or stroke set to None has no color applied to it.
- **View Mode ("W").** Margins, guides, grids, and frame edges are all visible in Normal View mode. In Preview mode, these features are hidden but still active.

Palettes and Screen Space

No matter how large your monitor is, it will soon be cluttered up with InDesign's many palettes and you won't be able to see the page very well. The fastest way to hide all palettes is to press the Tab key. The Tab key toggles back and forth between hiding and showing the palettes. To toggle all the palettes except for the toolbox, you can press Shift-Tab. You can also show or hide individual palettes by choosing their names from the Window menu, which lists any available keyboard shortcuts for palette access.

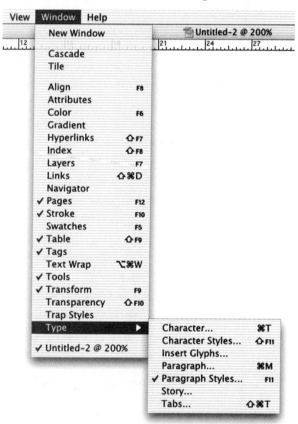

The Window menu in Mac OS X.

You should leave open only the palettes you need. Some palettes are needed almost all the time, and sending them away then bringing them back again with the Tab key can become tedious. Palettes can be manipulated to occupy less screen space, yet still be available for instant access. In the following section, we describe the functions for grouping, docking, and minimizing/maximizing palettes.

*A **palette** is a collection of related commands or operations in a floating window; the group of commands is used to help monitor and modify your work. By default some palettes are grouped together into a panel, and some palettes reside in their own panel.*

To move or rearrange palettes, you can drag their tabs to another panel; you can drag a tab away from a panel to create a stand-alone palette.

The default palette groupings when you first start InDesign 2.0 are: Pages, Layers, Navigator; Paragraph Styles, Character Styles, Swatches; Transform, Character, Paragrap; Stroke, Color, Gradient, Transparency; Table

Grouping

If a panel contains multiple palettes, then there is a series of tabs across the top that enables you to select a particular palette to work with. You can also use these tabs to move individual palettes by dragging them to another panel. *Grouping* is accomplished by moving a palette's tab to a different panel to create a new combination panel. Many individual palettes can be grouped together, or a single palette can be dragged from a group to become a stand-alone, individual palette.

One example of this is the default grouping of the Paragraph Styles and Character Styles palettes, which are grouped with the Swatches palette into a single panel. They are all visible, accessible with a single click, and yet out of the way.

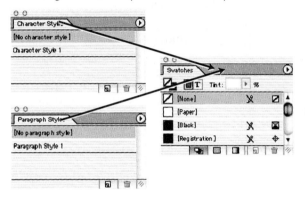

To create this palette arrangement, the Paragraph Styles and Character Style palettes were separated; they can easily be regrouped with the Swatches palette.

Docking

You can attach an individual palette or grouped panel of palettes to the bottom of any other panel, creating a sort of "super-panel" with multiple, visible palettes. To dock a palette, you simply drag its tab to the bottom of a panel until a thick black line appears. If you move the tab too high, the inside of the destination panel will show a black border, and the source palette will be grouped instead of docked.

Docking a palette to a panel. Notice the black line at the bottom of the panel.

The Transform palette docked with other palettes.

Minimize/Maximize

By clicking the Minimize/Maximize button on the right (Windows, Mac OS 9) or left (Mac OS X) of a panel's title bar, you can collapse a palette. In its minimized state, the palette folds up like a window shade, leaving only the title bar and the name tabs visible.

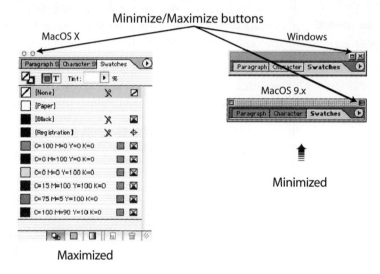

Maximised and Minimized views of the Swatches palette.

Palette Options

The arrow at the upper right of the palette reveals a submenu of available options (called the "Options pop-up menu") associated with that palette. These include the ability to create a new element, duplicate, edit, and delete a palette element, plus other, palette-specific options.

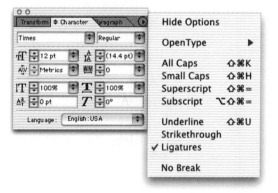

The Options pop-up menu for the Character palette.

The Minimize/Maximize button toggles the palette sizes. If the palette is in its truncated state, the Minimize/Maximize button will toggle between truncated and minimized sizes, ignoring the full size.

Double-Clicking Name Tabs

By double-clicking a palette's name tab, you can change the palette into one of three sizes. When a palette is first accessed and shown on your monitor, it is at its default size, but some palettes, such as the Swatches palette, contain more items than are usually shown. If you resize the Swatches palette to show everything (as in the Full Size example below), and then double-click the palette tab, the palette will be truncated. If you double-click the tab again, the palette will be minimized.

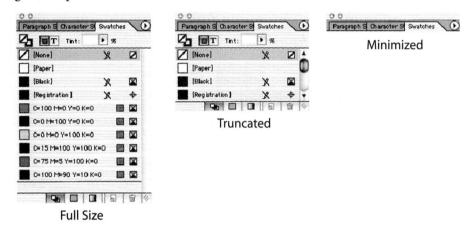

Minimized

Truncated

Full Size

Full, truncated, and minimized views of the Swatches palette.

Resetting Palettes

To reset all of the palettes to their original state, as if you'd just installed InDesign, you need to quit InDesign, delete the InDesign Defaults file, and then restart InDesign. If you want to do this, you can find the InDesign Defaults file in the following locations:

- **Mac OS 9.** System Folder>Preferences>Adobe InDesign>Version 2.0>InDesign Defaults
- **Mac OS X.** (user home)>Library>Preferences>Adobe InDesign>Version 2.0>InDesign Defaults
- **Windows NT, 2000, and XP.** Documents and Settings>(user home)>Local Settings>Application Data>Adobe>InDesign>Version 2.0>InDesign Defaults
- **Windows 98.** Windows>Local Settings>Application Data>Adobe>InDesign>Version 2.0>InDesign Defaults

Menus

The main InDesign menus are critical for accessing certain features not found in either the toolbox or palettes. As the features of InDesign are showcased, the menu options will be illustrated. Some menus have nested, pop-up menus that offer additional choices.

These are marked by the triangle symbol; the other options show when you rest the cursor on the triangle. Note that the Preferences and Quit options are both located in the InDesign menu when running Mac OS X; under Mac OS 9, Quit is in the File menu, and Preferences is in the Edit menu.

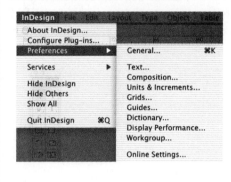

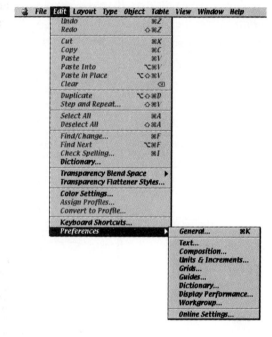

Mac OS X InDesign menu.   *Mac OS 9 Edit menu.*

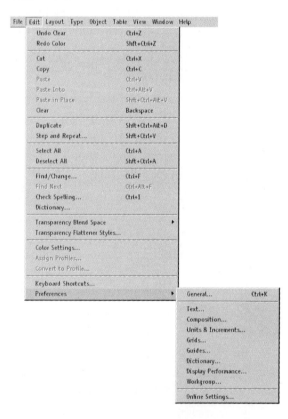

Windows Edit menu.

Contextual Menus

If you Control-click (Macintosh) or right-click (Windows), you can access a *contextual menu*, the contents of which depend on the context of what you're doing at the time. In other words, the type of object selected determines the items included on a contextual menu; there is even a contextual menu available if no object is selected. Contextual menus pop up from the cursor wherever it is located.

The contextual menus change context based on the type of object that they are referencing.
Top row: Text Frame, Text. Bottom row: Nothing selected, Object, Object Frame.

- **Text Frame selected.** With a text frame selected, you may access the Text Frame options. You can fill the frame with placeholder text, change the content of the frame, or affect the frame's properties, such as stroke weight, corner effects, arrangement, drop shadow, feathered edge, and position.

- **Text selected.** This menu becomes available when the text cursor is active within a text frame. It provides options for text size, finding and changing text, checking spelling, setting text frame options, inserting special characters and white space, changing text to outlines, filling the text frame with placeholder text, defining a path (if the text is bound to a path), inserting a break character, changing case, and showing hidden characters.

- **Nothing selected.** This menu appears if you click an area of the document page or pasteboard where no objects are placed. It enables you to change document settings such as guide and grid visibility, zoom percentage, or view options.

- **Object or Object Frame selected.** This properties menu pops up when you click objects such as placed graphics, frames, paths drawn with the Pen tool, or graphic objects drawn with the Ellipse, Rectangle, Polygon, or Line tools. The pop-up menu enables you to arrange objects from front to back, group or lock objects, change the fitting options, set stroke weight and corner effects to graphics drawn with the InDesign tools, and add drop shadows and feathered edges. The only real difference between these two tools is the Paste Into command, which only appears in the Object Frame properties menu if you have cut or copied something to the clipboard. The Arrange command appears in the menu only if the frame is overlapping another object (Mac OS only).

Explore the InDesign Tools

1. From the File menu, select New to create a new document. At the Document Setup window, set the number of pages to 8. Set the Margins to 3p0, leaving all other settings at default. Click OK.

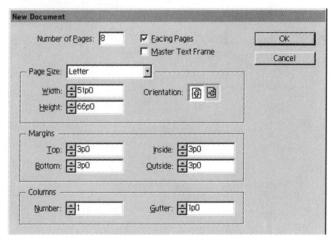

The Selection and Direct Selection tools' cursors respond visually when the tool is poised over an object. Both tools' cursors display a dot next to them when positioned over an unselected object, which lets you know that a click there will select it. The Selection tool's cursor changes to a single arrowhead when positioned over an object that's already selected, letting you know that dragging will move the object.

2. The document will open to Page 1.

3. Press Shift-Tab to hide all palettes except the toolbox. Press Shift-Tab again to show the palettes again.

4. From the View menu, select Zoom Out for a better view of the page. Look at the View Percentage box to see the percentage of the page view. It may be set at 50%, 75%, or 100%, depending upon the size at which you started and the size of your display.

5. In the toolbox, select the Hand tool and drag anywhere on the document page. Notice how you can change the location of the view for more precise work.

6. From the View menu, select Fit Page in Window. The page reverts to its original size.

7. Press Command/Control-R a few times to hide and show the page rulers in the document. Leave the rulers activated.

8. Click the Transform palette's tab to bring it to the front of the panel. Select the Rectangle tool in the toolbox. Drag the tool cursor diagonally on the page, drawing a rectangle approximately 18 picas wide, referring to the rulers or the Transform palette as you drag.

9. Click the Default Fill and Stroke icon in the toolbox to give the rectangle a black outline.

10. Now click the Selection tool in the toolbox. The rectangle you made is still selected. Notice that the Selection tool cursor turns into a single arrowhead when you move it over the rectangle's outline or its center point. This indicates that the object is selected and ready to be moved. Drag the rectangle to the center of the page.

11. Click the Zoom tool in the toolbox. Drag around the rectangle to draw a marquee. The area you select will fill the document view.

12. Leave the document open for the next exercise.

Navigate the Document

1. In the View Percentage box at the lower left of the document window, highlight the number and type "90". Press the Enter/Return key to view the document at 90%. Press the Delete/Backspace key to remove the rectangle.

2. To the right of the View Percentage box is the Current Page box showing the number of the page you are working on. Highlight the number "1" and type "6". Press Return/Enter to go to this page.

3. You will be on Page 6, but Page 7 adjoins it. The two pages together are called a "spread." You want to see both of these pages centered in the screen, so choose View>Fit Spread in Window. Both pages move to the center of the screen.

4. Look at the Current Page box. It will read 7, though both pages are visible.

5. Click the Next Page button, which is to the right of the Current Page box. Notice how the Current Page changes to the next page number, 8, and that the page is centered in the window.

6. Click the Previous Page button. The previous page, 7, centers in the window. Press the Previous page button again and you will be on Page 6.

The pasteboard is an area the width of a page, to the left and right of a spread when the Facing Pages option is selected, and to the left and right of a single page when a single-page layout is selected. You can use the pasteboard to temporarily store InDesign objects, but be sure to remove them when you've finished with a layout to prevent any confusion.

7. Go to Page 4 by selecting it from the Go To Page pop-up menu on the right side of the Current Page box. Page 4 is centered in the view. Press Next Page to center Page 5 in the view.

8. Choose View>Entire Pasteboard. The view changes to show smaller pages in the document window, so the entire pasteboard is visible.

9. Click the Last Page button to the right of the Next Page button. The document view moves up to show the last page — Page 8.

10. Click the First Page button, to the left of the Previous Page button. The screen jumps back to Page 1 in the document.

11. Press Command/Control-0 (zero) to activate the Fit Page in Window view setting. Page 1 will now fill the document screen.

12. Leave the document open for the next exercise.

Work with the Palettes

1. Locate the Pages palette, which appears in the same panel as the Layers and Navigator palettes. Locate the Transform palette, which is grouped with the Paragraph and Character palettes.

2. Click and hold the Navigator palette's tab, then drag it to the left away from the Pages palette. Release the mouse button. You've separated the palettes.

3. Click the Paragraph palette's tab and drag it out to separate it. Do the same with the Character palette.

4. Drag the Layers palette from its grouping. Drag the Character and Paragraph palettes back into the grouping with the Transform palette.

5. Click the title bar (the strip across the top of the palette) of the Navigator palette. Drag it below the Layers palette and dock it. Remember to look for the thick black bar at the bottom of the Layers palette. The two palettes seem to snap together when they come close to each other. This feature helps you arrange your palettes tidily.

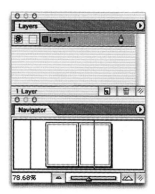

The Pages palette can be resized to a vertical orientation, handy for those with experience using QuarkXPress, as shown at right. You can also specify whether master pages are shown on the top or bottom of the palette with the Palette Options item on the pop-up menu.

Sometimes it might look like a palette's tab disappears after you drag it to another panel. This happens because the last palette dragged into the panel goes on top, and all others get pushed to the back. You can reset the stacking order by dragging the palettes out and back in again.

6. Drag the Transform palette out and dock it under the Navigator palette.

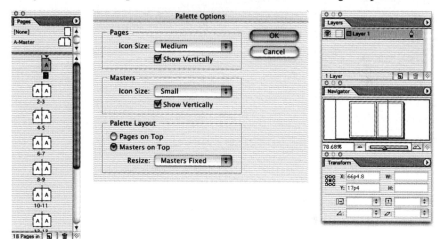

7. In each palette, click the Minimize button so the palette disappears, leaving only the title bar.

8. Drag the title bars of each palette and move them so they are all stacked against each other. This gives you more working area. Drag the Transform palette last.

9. Click the Minimize button of the Navigator palette. This will toggle the palette to maximize it. Now you can see the Navigator palette, but it's behind the Transform palette. That's because the Transform palette is still active from being moved in Step 8. Click the Minimize button on the Navigator palette again to make it small. Now double-click the Navigator tab, and notice that it comes right to the front, because now it's the active palette. Double-click the Navigator tab again to reduce it.

10. Drag the Navigator and Layers tabs back into the Pages palette, next to the Pages name tab. You have grouped the Pages, Layers, and Navigator palettes back together.

11. Now make a big docked super-palette. Drag the two panels containing the Pages, Layers, and Navigator palettes, and the Character, Paragraph, and

Transform palettes out to the middle of the screen. Separate the Character and Paragraph palettes. Group the Transform palette with the Pages, Navigator, and Layers palettes.

12. Drag the Character palette's tab to the bottom of the grouped palette, aligning the outline of the dragged palette to the bottom of the grouped one, until you see a black bar across the bottom of the grouped palette. This means you can dock the dragged palette.

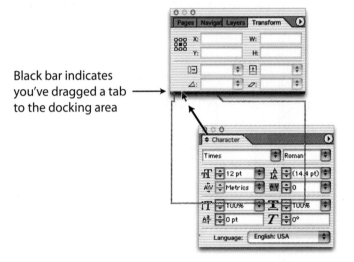

Black bar indicates you've dragged a tab to the docking area →

13. Repeat this process with the Paragraph palette. You should now have a set of grouped and docked palettes (the actual order of the palette tabs may be different from the example shown below). You can move and minimize this super-palette like any other.

14. Close the document without saving, and quit InDesign.

15. Locate and delete the InDesign Defaults file as described on page 9 to reset the palettes back to their default locations.

Summary

In this chapter, you have become acquainted with the toolbox, windows, menus, and palettes of InDesign. You have learned to manage a number of palettes to maximize your available screen space, and to navigate within an InDesign document. You are now ready to begin working with InDesign.

NOTES

3 Working with Documents

Chapter Objective:

By simplifying the management of the many parts of a document, InDesign makes it easy to turn creative design ideas into effective layouts. You can even define your own customized settings to use as you work with InDesign. This chapter discusses InDesign's default settings, procedures for customizing the work environment, and the basic anatomy of a document page. In Chapter 3, you will:

- Explore InDesign's numerous preferences and default settings, and how they can be set for a single document or for all new documents.

- Review the basics of opening, closing, and saving documents in Windows, Mac OS 9, and Mac OS X.

- Become familiar with the structural elements of a page, including live areas, bleeds, gutters, and margins.

- Learn how to create new documents and work with InDesign's initial settings.

- Explore multiple-page documents, and see how you can use master pages to build multiple-page documents quickly.

- Discover how the Hand tool and the Navigator palette make it easy to move around a document page.

- Learn how to reduce and enlarge page views.

Projects to be Completed:

- Central Market Ad (A)
- Yellow Rose Menu (B)
- Travel Brochure (C)
- Good Choices Newsletter (D)

*Press Command/
Control-K to show the
General Preferences.*

Working with Documents

The key to creating effective pages with a minimum of effort is understanding how InDesign manages the document file and its many parts. This section helps you understand preferences and default settings, and guides you through the basics of document structure and management.

Working with Preferences and Defaults

Many InDesign properties can be set to function as program defaults, or as document defaults or preferences. Setting an InDesign preference when no document is open establishes that setting as an InDesign default, and affects all documents you create afterwards. For example, if you always want new documents to use picas as your preferred measurements, you could set the InDesign preferences to use picas when no documents are open. If you set or change preferences when a document is open, those settings affect that document only. Preferences are found on the Edit menu (Mac OS 9, Windows) or the InDesign menu (Mac OS X).

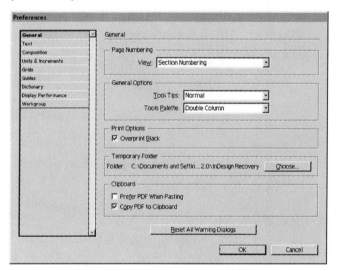

General Preferences pane (Windows).

There are nine preferences *panes* available. We recommend leaving the default settings unchanged while you're getting used to InDesign, but you should still understand the functions of the different settings.

General Preferences

The General Preferences pane is a sort of catch-all for options that aren't related to the others in the Preferences panes.

Page Numbering
You can view page numbers in the Pages palette and Go To Page pop-up menu by *section* or by *absolute numbers.* If you choose Section Numbering, then any customized page numbers are shown; for example, if the document contains pages numbered with Roman numerals, those pages show in the Pages palette with Roman numerals. Similarly, if a chapter begins on Page 61, it numbers the chapter with the user-defined numbers. The Absolute Numbering option, in contrast, displays the pages in a document as 1–x, regardless of any custom user definitions. Section Numbering is the default.

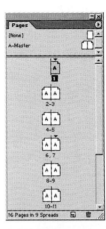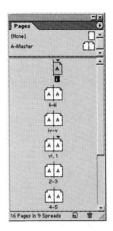

The same layout using Absolute Numbering (left) and Section Numbering (right).

General Options

General Options include settings related to the tool tips and Tools palette. Tool tips display the tool's name when the cursor is over the icon. The Normal and Fast settings prompt InDesign to display tool tips after various lengths of time; the None setting deactivates tool tips.

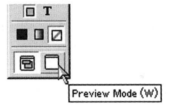

An example of a tool tip.

The Tools palette (also referred to as the toolbox) may be displayed as a double column, single column (both vertical), or single (horizontal) row.

Print Options

The Overprint Black setting causes black ink to print on top of all colors. In general, you should always leave this setting activated. You can turn it off where appropriate later.

Temporary Folder

InDesign keeps copies of open documents in this temporary folder; although you can specify a different temporary folder, there's really no reason to do so. The temporary folder's contents are used to automatically re-create any open documents if InDesign or your operating system crashes.

Clipboard

These options allow you to specify how InDesign should handle objects that you want to copy into InDesign or paste out of InDesign from other programs, especially Adobe Illustrator 9 or 10. If you choose Prefer PDF When Pasting, then any artwork pasted into InDesign from Illustrator is formatted as a single, non-editable PDF object. Typically, you should paste Illustrator art as PDF for the highest quality. You can choose the Copy PDF option when pasting InDesign objects into other Adobe applications.

Reset All Warnings Button

Some InDesign functions may display a warning dialog with a "Don't ask again" option. Clicking this button resets the "Don't ask again" status to Off.

Text Preferences

You will find that setting text preferences requires serious thought and attention to detail. All typefaces are unique, so setting text defaults is not a one-size-fits-all solution. These preferences should be adjusted on a document-by-document basis as necessary.

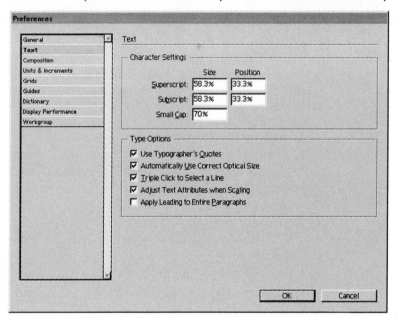

Text Preferences pane.

Character Settings

The size and position of superscript and subscript characters is based on the size of the standard letter and a percentage of the size of the letter above and below the baseline. (A superscript, 36-pt. letter with a size of 50% and a position of 33.3% is the size of an 18-pt. letter and has its baseline 12 pts. above the baseline.)

Ideally, the top of an uppercase superscript letter aligns with the top of an uppercase base letter. Sometimes you need to play with the adjustment to achieve this. Subscripts are not as precise. In many cases it is necessary to determine what size and position the author wants the character to occupy. When setting mathematical type, superscript and subscript numbers must work together.

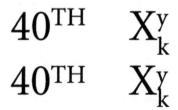

Be careful when determining the size and offset of superscript and subscript numbers. An offset of 33% is too great for the raised "TH," which should be at the same position as the cap height. It is needed, however, when superscript and subscript letters are used together in equations.

To switch between typing typographer's quotes and typing straight quotes, press Command-Option-Shift-" (Macintosh) or Control-Alt-Shift-" (Windows). This won't affect any quotes you've already typed.

Most word processors and page-layout applications have the ability to convert quotes as you type. The latter also converts quotes when importing text.

Mac OS X does not natively support Multiple Master type, but you can use Multiple Master fonts with Adobe applications in Mac OS X by copying them to the Library>Application Support>Adobe>Fonts directory.

In the Small Cap field, you can define small-cap letters as a percentage of the size of a standard uppercase letter. Whenever possible, though, you should select a font designed with built-in small caps. When you create small caps by reducing the point size, the strokes become narrower than those of the standard typeface, and the characters look a little spindly. If you have an OpenType font on your computer that contains a set of true small caps, InDesign automatically swaps out the artificially generated small cap in place of the true or *cut* small cap. The percentage size you specify is automatically overridden and cut small caps are used instead.

TIMES ROMAN ADOBE MINION

Times Roman set in artificial small caps (left) suffers a visible reduction in size of its strokes. Adobe Minion set in true small caps (right) offers better symmetry, fit, and spacing of the small caps with the uppercase letters.

Type Options

The Use Typographer's Quotes option automatically substitutes typographer's quotes (sometimes called "curly quotes" or "smart quotes") when you type an apostrophe (') or quotation mark ("). This option should be left on.

Automatically Use Correct Optical Size is for use with Multiple Master type. It uses a font mastered for a smaller text size for small type, and type mastered for a larger text size for display type to achieve a clean letterform. Adobe has discontinued its line of Multiple Master typefaces, but they will remain around for some time to come. This option is activated by default and should be on when using Multiple Master type. You can tell if you're using a Multiple Master font if it has "MM" at the end of its name.

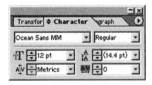

Example of a Multiple Master typeface.

The Triple-click to Select a Line option enables you to control how to select a line of text. When this option is off, triple-clicking selects an entire paragraph. When it is on, triple-clicking selects only a single line; in this case, you need to click four times to select a whole paragraph.

Adjust Text Attributes When Scaling determines whether text attributes, such as point size, leading, and tab stops, are scaled along with the text if you enlarge or reduce a text frame. For example, text set at 10 points with a 2-pica tab stop that is scaled to 200% reformats to 20 points with a 4-pica tab stop. This is what you'd probably expect to happen, but earlier versions of InDesign did not do this, and it was confusing. The text looked like it was twice as big, but retained its attributes in the Character palette.

Apply Leading to Entire Paragraph allows you to specify leading as a character attribute or a paragraph attribute. When deselected, you can apply different leading values to characters in a line of type, but only the largest is applied. When selected, leading is applied consistently throughout a paragraph. We suggest leaving it selected.

Composition Preferences

You can define Composition preferences to show you any layout problems that occur when InDesign can't resolve them automatically. With these options, you can instruct InDesign to show missing fonts that have been substituted, lines that break against any Keep Options, and instances of custom kerning and tracking. Glyph substitution may occur if you set a special or foreign character in one font, then change the font to another that doesn't include the character.

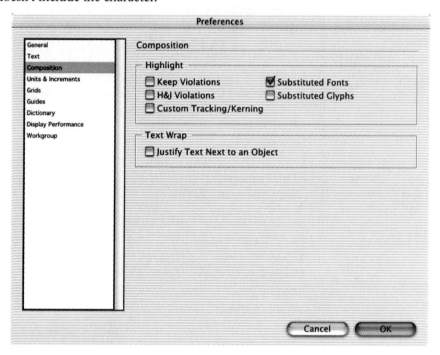

Composition Preferences pane.

Highlight

Keep Violations are instances when the Keep with Next Line rules are not enforceable; text that causes a Keep Violation is highlighted in purple. When hyphenation and justification rules can't be followed, an H&J Violation occurs, and the text is highlighted in yellow. The H&J Violation highlight option varies the shade of the yellow highlight color, depending on how severe the problem is. Custom Tracking and Kerning highlights any text that has had these attributes applied. If a font is missing, InDesign substitutes a font and highlights the substitution in pink if you've turned on Highlight Substituted Fonts. Glyph substitution can occur if you've set a glyph in one font, then changed it to a different font that doesn't contain that glyph, or has it in a different character position. You can set the Substituted Glyphs option to alert you when this occurs.

Text Wrap

The Justify Text Next to an Object option turns on justification when type approaches an image or other object on a page. This option affects text justification for an entire document and is turned off by default. If text justification is desired next to an object, you can turn it on as needed. Justification near some objects can result in strange line breaks and hyphenation.

A spread is two or more pages that would face each other in a publication. InDesign considers all pages to be part of a spread, even those that are stand-alone, so be aware of this terminology.

Units & Increments Preferences

The options in this section determine which units of measurement are displayed in your documents. Ruler units may be defined in points, picas, inches fractional, inches decimal, millimeters, centimeters, ciceros, and a custom option that lets you use points to specify the unit of measure. Keyboard increments define how much movement or change occurs when keyboard shortcuts are used to adjust the position or size of an element.

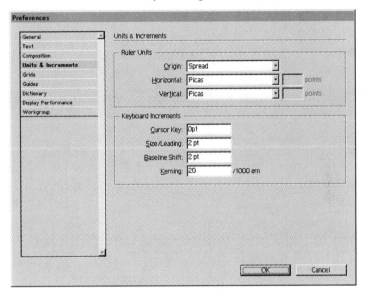

Units & Increments Preferences pane.

Ruler Units

The origin of the ruler may be defined as Spread, Page, or Spine. When defined as Spread, the width of the entire spread is used and the origin is the upper-left corner of the spread. When defined as Page, each page has its own origin (zero point) in the upper-left corner. When defined as Spine, the measurement begins in the upper-left corner, but if there are multiple pages that originate from the binding spine, such as might be the case in a fold-out, the measurement continues across the width of the pages on that side of the binding spine.

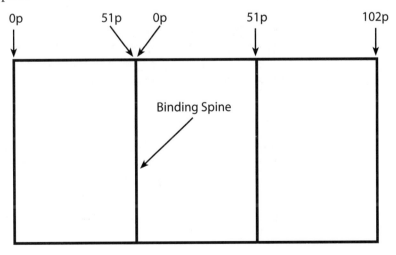

When Spine is selected, the horizontal units are cumulative across the spread.

*Command/Control-Shift->
increases the point size of
selected characters and
Command/ Control-Shift-<
decreases their point
size by the Size/Leading
increment. Adding the
Option/Alt key increases
or decreases the point size
by five times the amount.*

*Option/Alt-[Up Arrow key]
increases the leading and
Option/Alt-[Down Arrow
key] decreases the leading
by the Size/Leading
increment of a paragraph.
Adding the Command/
Control key increases or
decreases the leading by
five times the amount.*

*Option/Alt-Shift-[Up
Arrow key] shifts the
baseline up and
Option/Alt-Shift-[Down
Arrow key] shifts the
baseline down the by
Baseline Shift increment.
Adding the Command/
Control key increases or
decreases the baseline
shift by five times
the amount.*

Although the United States typically uses the Imperial or English measurement system (inches, feet, etc.) and the rest of the world uses the metric system, the graphic arts industry generally uses *picas* for horizontal measure and picas or *points* for the vertical unit. We use points for the vertical unit throughout this book.

There are 72 points per inch, with 12 points to a pica. A notation of "3p6" indicates a measurement of 3 picas and 6 points, or 3.5 picas. The following chart shows the conversions between inches, inches decimal, picas and points, and standard points:

Inches	Decimal	Picas	Points
1/16	0.0625	0p4.5	4.5
1/8	0.125	0p9	9
3/16	0.1875	1p1.5	13.5
1/4	0.25	1p6	18
5/16	0.3125	1p10.5	22.5
3/8	0.375	2p3	27
7/16	0.4375	2p7.5	31.5
1/5	0.5	3p	36
9/16	0.5625	3p4.5	40.5
5/8	0.625	3p9	45
11/16	0.6875	4p1.5	49.5
3/4	0.75	4p6	54
13/16	0.8125	4p10.5	58.5
7/8	0.875	5p3	63
15/16	0.9375	5p7.5	67.5
1	1	6p	72

The Keyboard Increments section of this window determines the distance an element moves when an action is performed. You can enter the settings in these fields using any units of measurement, but they are automatically converted to the units specified above. For example, if you enter "0.5 in". in the Baseline Shift field, but your Units Preferences are set to picas, InDesign converts your entry to 3p0.

The Cursor Key field determines how far a selected object moves when you press the Up, Down, Left, or Right Arrow key. If you hold down the Shift key along with one of the arrows, the object moves 10 times that distance. Size/Leading, Baseline Shift, and Kerning settings apply to highlighted text when you press the appropriate key combination.

Grids Preferences
There are two different grids used in documents. The Baseline Grid is used to align columns of text. The Document Grid is used to align objects. These grids cannot be assigned to an individual master page or to individual layers.

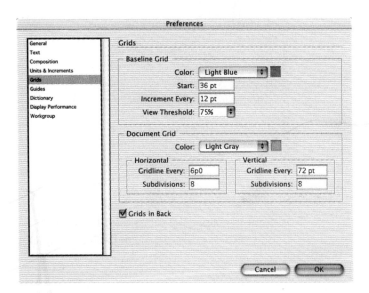

Grids Preferences pane.

Baseline Grid

The baseline grid looks like lined paper, and interacts with each paragraph's Indents and Spacing command. Paragraphs that align to the baseline grid always jump to the next grid line, regardless of how the spacing or leading is defined. In other words, if the grid is incremented every 12 pts., and the paragraph is set with 12-pt. leading and 6 pts. of space between paragraphs, it advances an additional 6 pts. to the next available grid line. Using the baseline grid is very useful for balancing columns of text across a page, especially if any images or headlines are inserted into a column, which tends to throw off column balance. When you use this feature, you should set the baseline grid's Increment Every value to the same leading value used in body copy, and turn on Align to Baseline Grid for the body text. We'll discuss the baseline grid further in Chapter 4, *Working with Text*.

Alice was beginning to get very tired of sitting by her sister on the bank, and of having nothing to do: once or twice she had peeped into the book her sister was reading, but it had no pictures or conversations in it, 'and what is the use of a book,' thought Alice 'without pictures or conversation?'	Alice was beginning to get very tired of sitting by her sister on the bank, and of having nothing to do: once or twice she had peeped into the book her sister was reading, but it had no pictures or conversations in it, 'and what is the use of a book,' thought Alice 'without pictures or conversation?'
So she was considering in her own mind (as well as she could, for the hot day made her feel very sleepy and stupid), whether the pleasure of making a daisy-chain would be worth the trouble of getting up and picking the daisies, when suddenly a White Rabbit with pink eyes ran close by her.	So she was considering in her own mind (as well as she could, for the hot day made her feel very sleepy and stupid), whether the pleasure of making a daisy-chain would be worth the trouble of getting up and picking the daisies, when suddenly a White Rabbit with pink eyes ran close by her.
There was nothing so very remarkable in that; nor did Alice think it so very much out of the way to hear the Rabbit say to itself, 'Oh dear!	There was nothing so very remarkable in that; nor did Alice think it so very much out of the

You should take care with baseline grid settings, because they can strongly affect the appearance of text. The text block on the left is specified identically to the one on the right, with 12-pt. leading and a 6-pt. space between paragraphs. The only difference is that the paragraphs in the right text block have the Align to Baseline Grid feature activated. This setting overrides inter-paragraph spacing that does not exactly equal the space between grids.

A grid may appear on your screen in any color that you choose. When setting up grids, it's best to pick a color that is not used in the document.

The Start position of the grid should be one grid increment above the position of the first baseline of text. The grid always starts at the upper-left corner of the page, regardless of where the zero point is set.

The View Threshold setting is the page magnification at or below which the grid does not show, even if it is turned on in the View menu.

The document grid resembles graph paper. Like the Baseline Grid, it aligns itself to the upper-left corner of the page. The default grid structure puts a main grid line every 6 picas (1 inch), and divides that into 8 subdivisions. When working with picas, you may want to change the subdivisions to 6 or 12 — or turn the grid off completely. Horizontal and vertical grids may be defined individually.

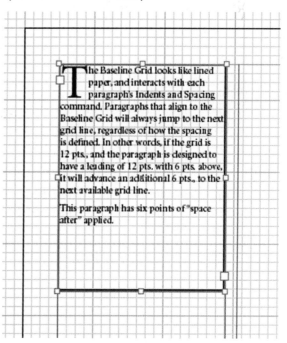

The document grid.

If you activate the Grids in Back option, the grids won't be visible if you place opaque objects (such as images or filled rectangles) on the page. Turning off this option means that the grids always show in front of everything on the page, which is handy when building a page.

Guides Preferences

Guides are designed to provide placement for columns and other page-related elements. The colors may be adjusted to your taste, and should be selected to minimize confusion between them and any colored printing elements on the page. Unlike grids, guides may be assigned to layers and master pages.

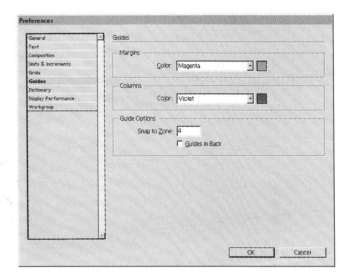

Guides Preferences pane.

The Snap to Zone is defined in pixels. This means when you have guides turned on, anything you move within the number of pixels to the guide "snaps" to the guide. This is really useful when precision layout is required. A Macintosh monitor usually has 72 pixels per inch; a Windows monitor usually has 96 pixels per inch. The default setting of four pixels is usually sufficient.

Guides, by default, are placed in front of all objects on the page. Some people think this gets in the way, and would rather be able to use the snap-to effect of guides but not have them clutter up their view. To send the guides to the back, you can click the Guides in Back box.

Dictionary Preferences

As we mentioned in the introductory chapter, InDesign supports multiple languages and includes spelling and hyphenation dictionaries for many western European languages, as well as specialized dictionaries for medical and legal uses.

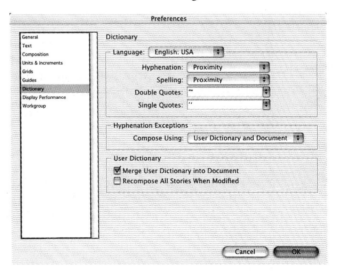

Dictionary Preferences pane.

You can also specify the type of quotation marks to use when the Use Typographer's Quotes option in the Text Preferences pane is activated. Some languages use different styles of quotation marks, or different symbols completely, than those used in American English. For example, British style generally dictates a reversal of style for quotation marks from the style used in North American English, German reverses the opening and closing marks, and puts the opening mark on the baseline, and French and Russian use characters called "guillemets".

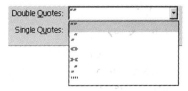

Choosing the default quotation marks.

Most of the time you don't need to change the style of quotation marks here. Instead, you can easily switch a selection of text to another style for quotation marks and hyphenation by assigning another language to it, if you've installed the optional language dictionaries.

Language

InDesign provides dictionaries for spelling and hyphenation in a number of languages. A default dictionary is selected for the document, but individual paragraphs, or even individual words, may be assigned a different dictionary. For example, you may need to create a manual in English, Spanish, French, and German. Each language is supported by its own dictionary. The language you choose here is the default language for spelling and hyphenation.

Choosing the default language.

Hyphenation Exceptions

Exceptions allow composition employing a user-defined hyphenation dictionary, changes made in the document only, or both, using the options in the Compose Using menu. A *user dictionary* is one you create with customized hyphenations for specific words. The user dictionary may be merged into the document, so the exceptions do not alert another user's spell check. When a change is made to the user dictionary, all stories may be recomposed using the new dictionary exceptions.

When you install InDesign, the dictionaries for your localized version of InDesign (for example, English: USA and French: Canadian) are the only ones installed. If you want additional dictionaries, you can either select them when you install InDesign, or you can use the Custom Installer to install additional dictionaries later. Be sure not to select "Install InDesign."

User Dictionary

In most cases you'll want to use the default setting, Merge User Dictionary into Document, so any custom hyphenation you've made in the past is incorporated into your documents. This isn't a good idea in an environment where you receive InDesign files from other users, however, so in such cases you should deactivate this option. The Recompose All Stories When Modified option is off by default; if enabled, it can cause text to reflow, which is a bad idea in a production environment where finished documents are submitted for processing.

Display Performance

These preferences control how images and other page components are displayed on your computer. When working with large images, you generally need to choose between high-quality image representation and performance. High-quality image displays require more processing power from your computer.

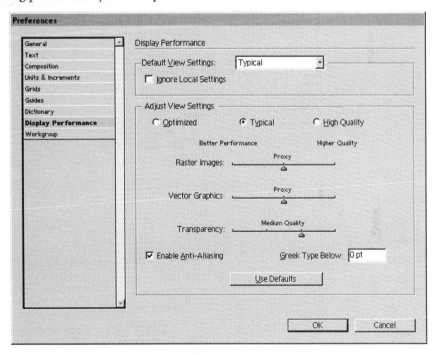

Display Performance Preferences pane.

Default View Settings

Images and graphics may be viewed as Optimized, Typical, or High Quality. Images in the High Quality mode can take a long time to draw, so it is usually best to use the Typical view setting. The Optimized View setting simply shows a gray box for images and imported graphics, which speeds up screen performance but obviously can make arrangement of page items a little tricky. The Typical setting suffices in most cases. The Ignore Local Settings option overrides any image display properties of individual images. You can change the display settings for any image in a document to suit your viewing needs, but if the Ignore Local Settings option is checked, then these settings are ignored and the view setting specified in Default View Settings is used instead.

Adjust View Settings

You can customize each setting further with the sliders in this part of the Preferences pane for each view setting. In most cases, you don't need to change these, but if, for example, you want raster images to be displayed as Typical, and vector graphics displayed as High Quality, then you can fine-tune the Typical setting to reflect that preference. The "proxy" value in the sliders means that the image is displayed at a low resolution.

Workgroup Preferences

InDesign supports the WebDAV protocol for sharing documents and other data across the Internet. WebDAV stands for "Web-based Distributed Authoring and Versioning." WebDAV is a set of extensions to the HTTP (HyperText Transfer Protocol) data transmission method, which is used to communicate between Web servers and Web browsers. This extension of HTTP allows users to collaboratively edit and manage files on remote Web servers, as long as their applications support the WebDAV protocol. Adobe products that support WebDAV at the time of publication include InDesign 2.0, Illustrator 10.0, GoLive 6.0, Photoshop 6.0, InCopy 2.0, InScope 1.0, and Acrobat 5.0.

Using WebDAV lets you share InDesign documents, text, graphics, and other types of data with other users who have access to the server. A WebDAV server may be a simple file repository, such as Apple's iDisk, or it can be an industrial-strength collaboration product. You can "check out" a file from the server, which locks it so nobody else can make changes to it; when you save your changes, the file is updated and unlocked so others can open it. Other users can get a copy of a checked-out file, but you are the only user who can save changes to the file while it is checked out.

The Apple iDisk only supports simple WebDAV file sharing, and cannot be used to check in or check out a document.

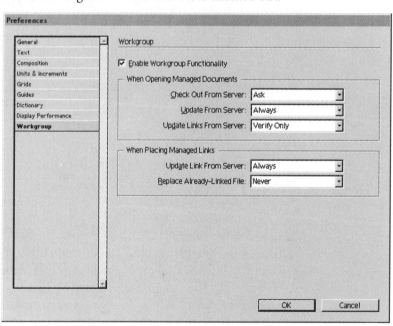

Workgroup Preferences pane.

We cover the uses of and preferences for the Workgroup feature in *Adobe InDesign 2.0: Advanced Electronic Composition*. Generally, the default settings should be fine for non-critical uses of a WebDAV server, but in a production or collaborative environment, your system administrator should configure these settings, or at least be able to tell you how they should be set up.

Set the Preferences

Close any open documents. You are going to customize a few of InDesign's default preferences, so the program will behave consistently throughout this book's exercises and projects.

1. Choose Edit>Preferences>General (Mac OS 9, Windows) or InDesign>Preferences>General (Mac OS X).

2. In the Page Numbering field, the choices are Absolute Numbering or Section Numbering. Leave the default of Section Numbering. Click the Tool Tips pop-up menu. The options are Normal, None, or Fast. These options affect whether (and the speed at which) tool tips display once you move the cursor over the tool. Leave it at the default of Normal. Leave the Tools Palette option set to Double Column.

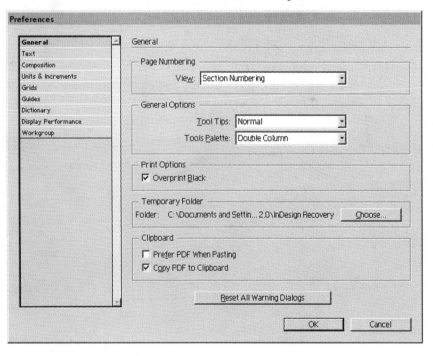

3. Leave the text preferences at the default settings. Select Composition from the list. In the Highlight section, make sure that only the Substituted Fonts check box is selected.

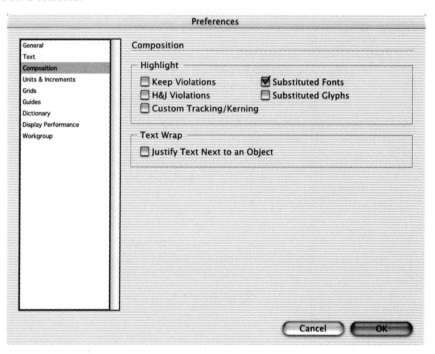

4. Select Units & Increments from the list. Set the Origin field to Page, the Horizontal field to Picas, and the Vertical field to Points. Leave the Keyboard Increments fields at their default settings.

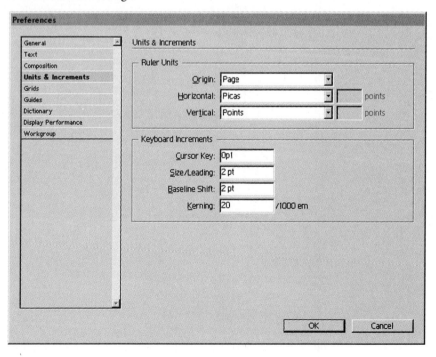

5. Select Grids. Review the options available and leave the preferences at their default settings.

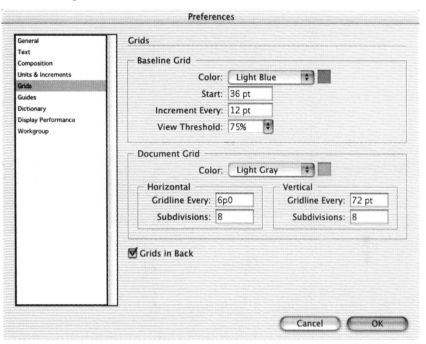

6. Select Guides. Review the options available and leave the preferences at their default settings.

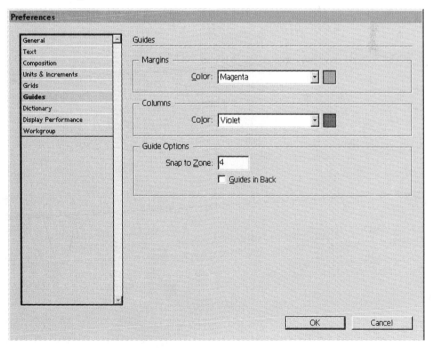

7. Select Dictionary. Click the Language drop-down menu to see if any optional dictionaries are installed. If they aren't, you'll probably only see English: USA. Remember that if you didn't choose additional languages during the initial instal-

lation, you can install them later with a custom installation. Leave the dictionary preferences at their default settings.

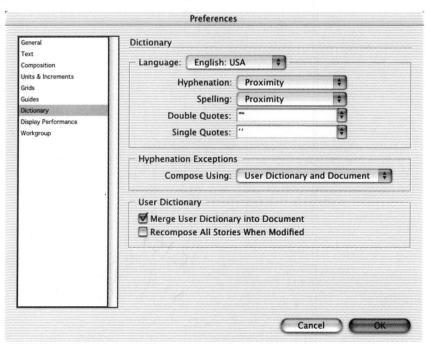

8. Select Display Performance from the list. Your display choices are Optimized, Typical, and High Resolution. Check that the default of Typical is selected, and that the Ignore Local Settings option is unchecked.

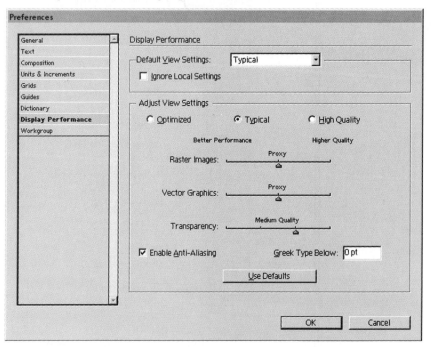

9. Click OK.

10. You're going to set one more preference — one that is not included in the Preferences menu. If the Pages palette is not already open, select Window>Pages.

11. Click the arrow on the top right of the palette and select Palette Options from the submenu that appears.

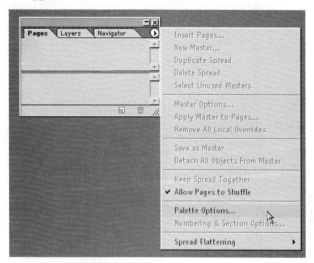

12. In the Palette Options window that appears, set the Page Icon Size field to Medium and the Masters Icon Size to Small. Be sure that Show Vertically is checked for both. In the Palette Layout section, select the Masters on Top radio button and set the Resize field to Masters Fixed.

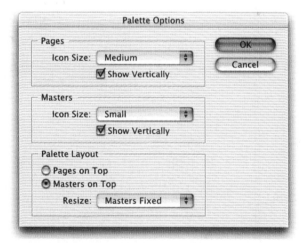

13. Click OK.

14. Leave InDesign running.

Opening, Closing, and Saving Documents

These actions become automatic with experience — and you may have performed these functions many times with other programs. They are all performed from the File menu.

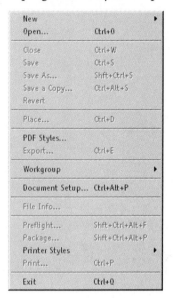

InDesign's File menu.

To open a document, you simply choose File>Open. You'll be presented with a number of options and icons.

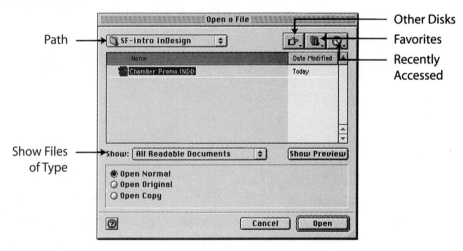

The Mac OS 9 Open a File dialog box.

Command/Control-O invokes the Open File dialog box.

Command/Control-W closes the current document.

At the top of the menu are navigation features. The bar at the left provides the familiar path navigation. On the Macintosh, the pointer icon allows direct access to other disks on the network. The next icon is used to save a file as a Favorite, immediately accessible from the Favorites menu. The clock icon is a connector to recently accessed files (which may not be InDesign documents).

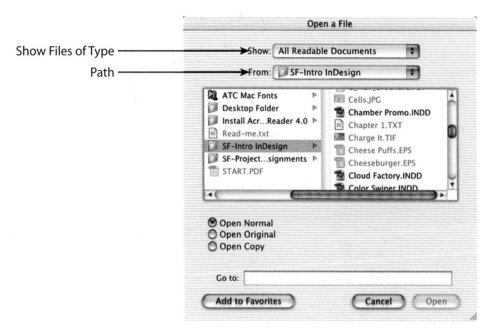

Show Files of Type ——————→ Show: All Readable Documents

Path ——————→ From: SF-Intro InDesign

The Mac OS X Open a File dialog box.

The main field (the large white box in the center of the window) lists all documents in the current folder. You can choose which type of files to display in the list. Your options are InDesign, PageMaker 6.5–7.0, QuarkXPress 3.3–4.1x, All Readable Documents (Macintosh only), or All Formats (Windows only). If the document has been saved with a preview, the first page of the document may be displayed by clicking the Show Preview button (Macintosh only).

An alternate method of opening a file is to double-click the file's icon.

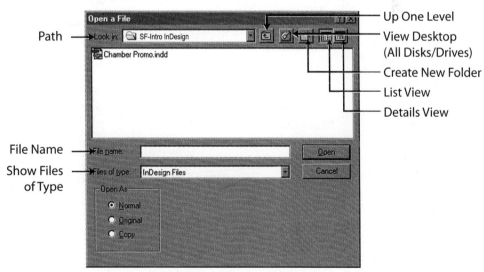

Path →
Up One Level
View Desktop (All Disks/Drives)
Create New Folder
List View
Details View
File Name →
Show Files of Type →

The Windows Open a File dialog box.

In a Windows environment, you can access a parent folder by clicking the Up One Level icon. View Desktop provides a view of all disks and drives. Create New Folder allows you to create a new folder from within the Open or Save dialog boxes. List View and Details View show these optional file window views in the dialog box.

When presented with the Save Changes? dialog on the Macintosh, pressing Command-S is the same as clicking Save or pressing Return, Command-D is the same as clicking Don't Save, and pressing Esc is the same as clicking Cancel. On Windows, you can press "Y" or Enter to accept changes, "N" to close without saving changes, and Esc to cancel.

You can open documents created with prior versions of InDesign (1.0 and 1.5) and save these in the 2.0 format, but you can't save a 2.0 document in a format that the older versions can read.

Even though a page includes space around it for bleeds, we usually set up a document in a page-layout program such as InDesign to the actual, finished page size. The bleed area is usually set when you print the document.

Your choices are to Open Normal, Open Original, or Open Copy. You almost always want to Open Normal. Open Original lets you open an InDesign template file; if Normal is chosen, a copy is always made of a template file. The Copy option lets you open a copy of a regular InDesign file instead of opening the original file.

To close a document, you can simply select File>Close or press Command/Control-W. If no changes have been made, the file closes immediately. If you have made any changes to the document, you are presented with the following warnings:

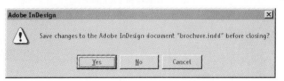 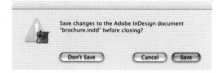

Save warnings in Windows and Mac OS X.

When you see this warning, you should not automatically press the Return/Enter key. Doing so saves the document with any changes you have made. It's best to take a second to think about whether you made those changes intentionally (it's not that hard to accidentally move an object, and that counts as a change), and if you want to save them. If you do want to save the changes you made, you can then click the Save button (or press Return/Enter). If you do not wish to save your changes, you can either click Don't Save to close the document without saving changes, or click Cancel to leave the document open.

There are three options for saving a document. Choosing File>Save is the one you'll use most of the time, and it saves the document's current state to the same location on your computer. Choosing File>Save As allows you to rename the file or to save the current version of the file to a different location; the renamed file is left open. The File>Save a Copy command is similar to Save As, except the original file is left open instead of the copy; the file name of the original document is preserved, and the word "copy" is appended prior to the file extension of the new file.

Page Anatomy

A typical page is made up of a number of standard elements. Good designers employ these to enhance the readability of the document and to guide readers from one element to another.

A typical page of a magazine or newsletter that uses a facing-pages layout. The facing pages, together, make up a spread.

Pages that come off a printing press are almost always larger than the finished page size. A typical 8.5 × 11-in. page has at least an extra 1/8 in. all around to allow for *bleed*, which occurs when a graphic element (such as a line or photo) prints to the very edge of the page. A printing press or laser printer typically can't print right to the edge of a page, so the element must extend beyond the page boundaries. In the final finishing process, the extra paper is trimmed off with a large cutter to create the finished page size; any bleed then appears to print right to the edge.

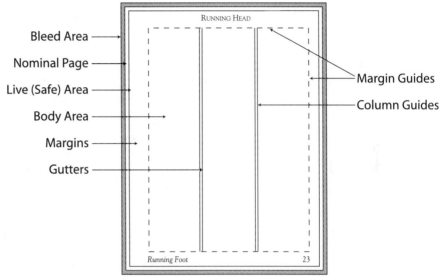

Page area definitions.

When designing documents, keep in mind the physical characteristics of the finished product. Things to consider are the thickness, how it will be bound, and any special sizing requirements.

InDesign remembers exact path names when identifying linked files. As you work through the exercises and projects in this book, you may encounter the Fix Links dialog box. If this occurs, just click the Fix Links button to automatically update the file links (unless the linked files have been moved to a different folder).

The area containing non-bleeding elements is called the "live area" or "safe area." This area is generally at least 1/8 in. inside the actual page boundary and gives printers more latitude when running the job through the press.

The majority of text and graphics are placed within the *body* of the page. Surrounding this area are *margins*. Margins may all be the same size, or they may vary, depending upon the document's structure and what is to be placed in them. For example, a document with facing pages may require a larger inside margin than an ad. Thick books usually need larger inside margins than outside margins because text tends to get buried in the spine area if the margins are too tight. Books may have elements such as *running heads* and *running footers* in the top and bottom margins. These are elements such as chapter names, page numbers, or section headings.

If a page has more than one column, there is a space between each column referred to as a "gutter." It should be wide enough so columns of type do not appear to touch, but if space is at a premium, one trick is to place a vertical line or *rule* in the gutter to act as a "stopper" for the eye.

The *Zero Point* is an element that is used to establish relative page positions. By default, it is positioned in the upper-left corner of the first page of a spread, but you can move it as the need arises. To move it, you can click the Zero Point icon and drag it to a new position. To return the Zero Point to its original position, you just double-click the Zero Point icon.

Zero Point ——————→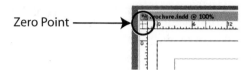

The Zero Point is at the top left of the screen, where the two rulers meet.

Explore a Document

1. From File>Open, navigate to the **RF_Intro_InDesign** folder on the Resource CD-ROM, and open the file **chamber_promo.indd**. You might see the warning below:

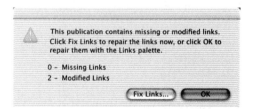

If you see this warning, click Fix Links.

2. The file should open to the spread of Pages 2–3. Open the Pages palette (Window>Pages) if it's not visible. If the file didn't open to the Pages 2–3 spread, double-click the numbers "2, 3" below the page icons in the Pages palette.

3. Note in the Pages palette that there are three sections (the pages beginning each section have an arrow above them). The two sections for the covers of the booklet (using the C-Master) are numbered 1, 2, 3, and 4. The pages that will hold booklet content (using the A-Master) are numbered 1–8.

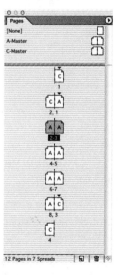

*Press Command/
Control-H to show
or hide frame edges.*

4. In the View menu, be certain Hide Frame Edges is shown. Viewing the frames helps you identify the page geometry. If Show Frame Edges appears in the View manu, select it.

5. Identify the following on Pages 2–3 (refer to the diagram on page 23):

   Bleed Area
   Live Area
   Body Area
   Margins
   Columns
   Gutters
   Running Feet (Footers)

6. Select File>Save As. Navigate to your **Work_In_Progress** folder and click Save to save the document, leaving the name the same.

7. Close the document.

Now that you've looked at some real document pages, it's time to create your own document. We'll start with the basics, and by the time you're finished with this chapter, you'll be able to effectively structure the underlying document.

Creating New Documents

New documents are created using the File>New>Document command. When the New Document window appears, you are presented with a number of options.

*Press Command/
Control-N to show
the New Document
window.*

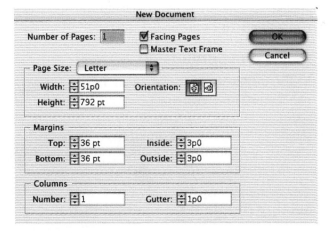

The default sizes in the Page Size pop-up menu are shown at right.

In the Number of Pages field, you may enter either a starting number or the actual number of pages the document will contain. Some people leave the default at one and simply add pages as needed. Check boxes offer options to create a Facing Pages view, where the page margins are mirrored, or to select single pages. When the Master Text Frame box is checked, a single text frame is created for each page. You may type text into this frame by pressing Command/Control-Shift and clicking the frame.

The page may be defined as a standard North American paper size (such as Letter, Legal, Tabloid, Letter-Half, or Legal-Half) or a metric paper size (such as A4, A3, A5, or B5). You can type in a specific width and height to create a custom page size. You have the option of selecting a portrait (vertical) or landscape (horizontal) orientation for your page.

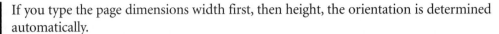

If you type the page dimensions width first, then height, the orientation is determined automatically.

InDesign displays the unit of measurement that you defined in the Preferences window. You may override that preference by typing in the appropriate abbreviation. If you designated picas as your unit preference but you wish to set up an 8.5 × 11 in. page, you can simply type "8.5 in" and "11 in" in the Width and Height fields. InDesign automatically converts these values to 51p0 and 66p0.

Millimeters and centimeters are measurements typically used outside of the United States. Ciceros are rarely used outside of France. You should, however, be prepared to receive and work with InDesign documents that use these measurement systems.

System	Type As	Comment
Picas	#p#	the first "#" is the number of picas and the second is the number of points (up to 11)
Points	#pt	
Inches	#in	
Millimeters	#mm	
Centimeters	#cm	
Ciceros	#c#	the first "#" is the number of ciceros and the second is the number of cicero points (up to 11)

The margins are defined in the next section. You may either type in the widths manually or use the up and down arrows. When the Facing Pages option is specified, the Left and Right margin fields change to Inside and Outside because the pages are horizontally mirrored.

Finally, you can specify the number of columns and the gutter width. All of this information is displayed on the underlying master.

Pages and Spreads

Earlier, we discussed the makeup of individual pages. When you design a multi-page publication, however, a single page is only half the view. The entire spread must be appealing to the eye and we usually view the facing pages simultaneously. The two pages should work together as a unit. The arrangement of columns should complement one another. In addition, the placement of elements on the spread should be pleasing, so as not to present a lopsided appearance.

Set Up a Newsletter
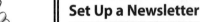

1. Choose File>New>Document and create a new document with facing pages. Be sure the Master Text Frame box is unchecked.

2. Make the Page Size "Letter" (8.5 × 11 in., or 51p0 × 792 points if you've set your Units and Increments as directed above) with a Portrait orientation.

3. The margins should be as follows:

   Top: 36 pt   Inside: 3p6
   Bottom: 48 pt   Outside: 3p0

Picas and Points — there are 12 points to a pica, and six picas to an inch. This system of measurement is peculiar to the printing industry and is fairly old, but many designers, agencies, and others will expect you to understand how this system works. Once you do, it's a much easier system for specifying size and locations than inches because there are no pesky fractions to deal with. Use the notation #p#, where the first "#" is the number of picas and the second "#" is the number of points.

4. Set the Column Number field to 3; set the Column Gutter field to 1p3.

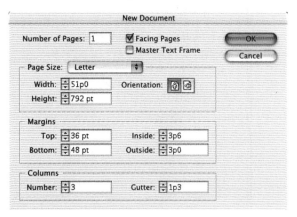

5. Click OK or press the Return/Enter key.

6. Choose File>Save, and save the document to your **Work_In_Progress** folder. Name the file "newsletter_master.indd", and click Save.

7. Leave the document open for the next exercise.

Master Pages

Master pages are the foundations of your InDesign documents. If you ignore the opportunity to tailor them to the document, you make your work harder than it needs to be.

Every element that you want to repeat on document pages can be included in a master page. Elements you want to repeat on spreads in your document may be included in the master spread (which can be one or more pages). These elements may include guides, running heads and feet, automatic page numbering, and graphic elements.

You can have several different masters per document, so long documents can be created by applying different masters to specific types of document pages. For example, you may have a section title, a chapter opener, and a text page, all with different parameters. Applying masters to pages, even if a different one has already been applied, is very easy.

Set the Foundation of the Document

1. Continue in the document you just created.

2. Be sure the Pages ("F12") and Transform ("F9") palettes are visible, and that Show Frame Edges is turned on (Command/Control-H toggles this option on or off).

3. You should see two sections in the Pages palette. The upper section is for master pages, and the lower section holds the document pages, based on the preference settings you made earlier.

4. Double-click the left page of the master-page spread labeled "A-Master" to select it. The left master page should display in your window.

5. Click the Type tool in the toolbox.

6. Below the three-column box in the left master page, drag to create a text frame. The resulting text box appears outlined in blue. It doesn't really matter where you start the text box, nor what size you make it, because you're going to use the Transform palette to precisely size and position it.

7. Click the Selection tool. The new text box is automatically selected.

8. If it is not highlighted, click the Transform tab, then click the upper-left proxy reference point. (It will turn black).

Proxy Icon

The page proxy allows you to define the object's axis from nine distinct reference points.

9. Type the following dimensions into the Transform palette:

X: 3p0   W: 44p6
Y: 756 pt H: 18 pt

Press Return/Enter to apply these settings and exit the menu.

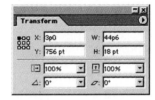

Notice how the text box is resized and repositioned after you press Return/Enter.

10. Double-click the right master-page icon and create another text frame using the Type tool. Choose the Selection tool, and in the Transform palette set the following dimensions:

X: 3p6   W: 44p6
Y: 756 pt H: 18 pt

Press Return/Enter to apply these settings.

11. Select the Type tool, and click in the frame you created first on the left master page.

12. Type the word "Page" and press the Spacebar.

13. Select Type>Insert Special Character>Auto Page Number. An "A" appears in the text frame after the word "Page." The "A" is a marker for InDesign's automatic page numbering system.

14. Click the Paragraph palette to select it. Click the Align Center icon to center the page number in the text box.

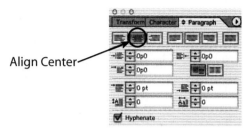

Align Center

15. Position the Type tool in the text frame you created in the right master page.

16. Type the word "Page" and press the Spacebar.

17. Place an automatic page number marker after the word "Page."

18. Center this text as you did on the left master page.

19. Double-click Page 1 in the Pages palette. You'll notice that the items placed on A-Master appear on Page 1. The "Page A" that resulted from inserting the automatic page number is now "Page 1."

20. Save the document (Command/Control-S), and leave it open for the next exercise.

We commented earlier that a document could have multiple master pages or spreads. Each master may be created from scratch, or it may be built from information contained on another master. You are going to base the next two masters on the one you've already created.

Add Multiple Masters

1. Continue in the open document. Be sure the Pages ("F12") and Transform ("F9") palettes are visible.

2. From the Pages palette Options menu, select New Master.

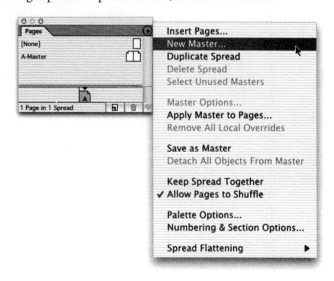

Many documents don't display a page number on the first page.

Text frames on a master page that's made from another master always require you to press Command/Control-Shift and click once to make any changes to their contents. This is to prevent inadvertent changes to master-page text. After you do this the first time, you don't need to do it again.

Mac OS X displays a large file icon in the right-hand preview pane when you select a file in the Place dialog. Some applications include a small preview of the file contents in the file icon, but others don't.

3. Name the new master "Nameplate", based on A-Master. Leave the number of pages at 2 and click OK.

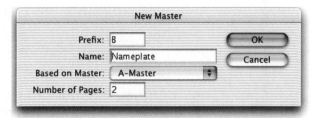

Once you click OK, you can see the new B-master spread. (InDesign automatically assigns the new master the prefix of "B.") This is the master for Page 1 of the newsletter. You're going to remove the page number and add the nameplate.

4. Choose the Selection tool. On the right-hand Nameplate (B) master, press Command/Control-Shift and click the text frame containing the page number placeholder. (Simply clicking a master text frame does not unlock the frame.)

5. Choose Edit>Cut (or press Command/Control-X) to remove it.

6. From File>Place, choose the file **jw_nameplate.eps** from your **RF_Intro_InDesign** folder. Uncheck the Show Import options box. Click Choose/Open, or simply double-click the file icon.

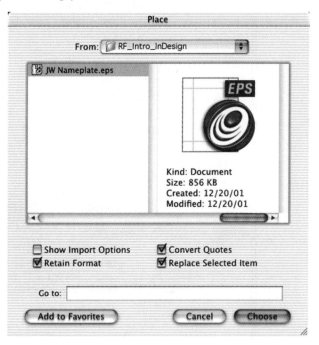

7. When the "loaded" image placement pointer appears, click in the upper-left corner of the live area (inside the margin guide) of the right master page to place the nameplate image. Notice how the little black triangle of the loaded pointer turns white when you get within the snap distance of the margin guides (set in the Guides Preferences).

8. Check the Transform palette and make any necessary changes. The upper-left corner of the image you just placed should be at X: 3p6, Y: 36 pt. Remember to check the proxy reference point; it should be set to the upper-left corner.

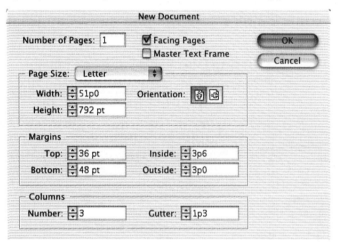

9. You have one more master to create. This one is for Page 2 of the newsletter, which will carry the masthead. Select New Master from the Pages palette Options menu.

10. Name this page "Masthead", and base it on A-Master. Leave the number of pages at 2. (To see this master in the Pages palette, you may need to increase the size of the palette window or scroll down.)

11. From File>Place, choose the file **jw_masthead.eps** from your **RF_Intro_InDesign** folder. Click Choose or double-click the file name.

12. When the paintbrush icon appears, click the lower part of the third column on the left page.

13. Using the Transform palette, adjust the position of the upper-left corner of the image to X = 33p6, Y = 560 pt. Don't forget to check your proxy.

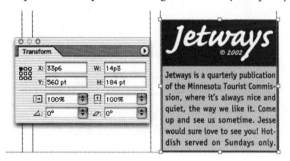

14. Save the document and leave it open for the next exercise.

Document Pages

Once the masters are constructed, the document can take shape. Longer documents are usually based on masters, while shorter documents such as one-page ads are frequently built interactively with frames for text and graphics. This allows for a smooth workflow from design through the finished document stage.

Basing Document Pages on Masters

New pages are added to the document either by clicking the page icon at the bottom of the Pages palette, by selecting Insert Pages from the Pages palette Options menu, or by dragging a master into the document pages section of the Pages palette. When a page is added by clicking the page icon, it uses the same master as the page immediately previous to it. When you use the drop-down menu, you can specify the number of pages to be added, the master to be used, and the position of the new page(s) in the document.

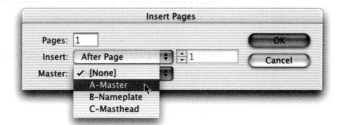

To apply a master to a document page, you can click the master icon, drag it on top of the document page icon (which has a heavy border around it), and release the mouse button. To apply a master to a single spread, you can click the *name* of the master, drag it to the spread, and release the mouse button. Alternately, you can select Apply Master to Pages from the Options menu. You may specify a single page, a spread, or a larger range of pages. To apply a master to noncontiguous pages, you separate the pages with a comma.

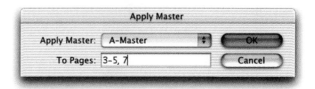

In this example, A-Master is being applied to Pages 3-5 and Page 7.

While master elements appear on all pages to which the specified master is applied, these master elements may be altered or overridden, as appropriate. To do so, you can Command/Control-Shift-click the element. It then becomes a "live" object and may be altered.

If you discover that you have accidentally overridden a master element and wish to undo your override, you can select the overridden element and choose Remove Selected Local Overrides from the Pages palette Options menu. To remove overrides from all master elements, select Remove All Local Overrides from the Pages palette Options menu with no master elements selected.

Allow Pages to Shuffle is checked by default. This option allows pages to be added as spreads. If it's turned off, single pages are added.

If a master is modified, those modifications affect all pages to which the master has been applied, except in instances where master elements have been altered on the document page.

It's usually desirable to create a series of frames on the master page, either frames that will contain graphics or text frames linked to other text frames, to create a specific text flow. We'll explore the many text flow options available to you in the next chapter.

Apply Masters to Your Document

1. Continue in the open document. Double-check that the Pages and Transform palettes are visible.

2. From the Pages palette Options menu, select Insert Pages.

3. Insert seven pages after Page 1, based on the A-Master. Click OK.

   Now apply information from the masters.

4. In the Pages palette, click the B-Nameplate master icon and drag it on top of Page 1. Release the mouse button.

5. Click the C-Masthead master icon and drag it on top of the Page 2 icon. Be certain only Page 2 is highlighted. Your Pages palette should look like this.

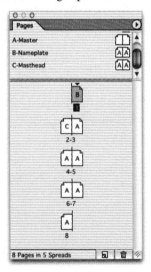

Now you will learn what modifying a master does.

6. In the Pages palette, double-click the left-hand C-Masthead master icon.

7. Select the Rectangle Frame tool and draw a frame with the following definition:

   X: 3p0   W: 29p3
   Y: 36 pt H: 708 pt

8. From the Object menu, select Content>Text.

While you can reapply a master to a page that's already based on the same master, all this does is place the master elements underneath the other elements on the page. It won't undo any changes you made to the document page. If you've removed any master elements from the page, though, reapplying the same master brings them back.

9. Select View>Hide Guides. Double-click the Page 2 icon to view the change.

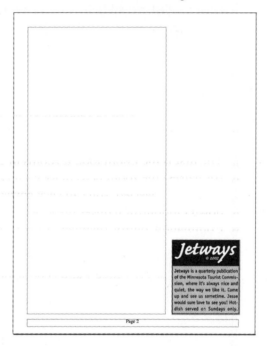

This example shows the result of the Display Performance preference set to High Quality. If set to Typical, the preview of the masthead looks a bit ragged.

10. Now alter the frame on Page 2. Choose the Selection tool, press Command/Control-Shift, and click the new frame. Shorten its height to 500 pt.

11. Click the C-Masthead icon in the Pages palette and drag it over the Page 2 icon. Note that the original 708-pt. master-page frame has been applied beneath the frame you altered.

12. The frame you altered should still be selected. If it is not, click it with the Selection tool.

13. Display the Pages palette menu. Note that Remove All Local Overrides is grayed out and unavailable (if it isn't grayed out, you haven't reapplied the C-Masthead master). Because the master was reapplied, the altered frame is no longer regarded as a master element. Press Command/Control-X to delete it.

14. Press Command/Control-Shift, click the frame with the reapplied master, and shorten its height to 600 pt.

15. From the Pages palette Options menu, choose Remove Selected Local Overrides to return the master elements to their original specifications.

16. Save the document. From the File menu, select Close.

Basing Document Pages on Frames

Text and graphics are placed in frames in InDesign. It is not necessary to predraw the frame, as is the case with some other programs, but it is often useful to do so. When you place a graphic, or enter or flow text, the graphic or text automatically creates its own frame, or you can create frames using the Ellipse, Rectangle, Polygon, Frames, Pen, or Pencil tools.

As we noted earlier, frames smooth the workflow from design through production because they provide continuity. As with frames on masters, text frames on document pages can be linked to create a specific text flow. For example, text may be linked from a frame on Page 3 to a frame on Page 6. We will discuss frames in the context of text and graphics in upcoming chapters.

Viewing and Controlling the Page

It is often necessary or advisable to change the page view. InDesign provides a number of ways to do so.

The first is the Zoom tool. It zooms in 25% increments from 25% to 100% and doubles (or halves) the zoom percentage each time it is clicked from 100% to 4000%. With the Zoom tool selected, you can click anywhere in the document to enlarge the view. Holding down Option/Alt reduces the view. Pressing Command/Control-[equal sign] or Command/Control-[hyphen] accomplishes the same functions.

Think of the zoom in and out functions as "plus" and "minus" when using the Command/Control key shortcuts for zooming in or out.

To zoom to a specific view percentage, you can simply click the View Percent box in the lower left of the window and choose the desired view percentage from the pop-up menu. You can also type the view percentage you want into the little text entry area of the pop-up menu.

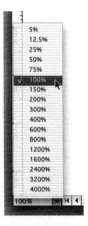

Zoom options in the View Percent pop-up menu.

To toggle between the last two views, press Command-Option-2 (Macintosh) or Control-Alt-2 (Windows). You must use the "2" key on the first row of the standard keyboard, not the numeric keypad.

When the Type tool is active in a text frame, pressing the Spacebar simply types a bunch of spaces at the text cursor. To use the Hand tool while the Type tool is active, press the Option/Alt key instead of the Spacebar. You can use the Spacebar to access the Hand tool while the Type tool is active, but only if you haven't clicked the tool in a text frame.

Other features that help you maneuver the page effectively are the Hand tool, the Navigation palette, and the ability to have multiple views of the document open simultaneously.

The Hand tool allows you to "grab" the entire page and move it so you can better see the specific area that you are working on. To use it, simply choose the Hand tool from the toolbox, click anywhere on the page, and drag. To temporarily switch to the Hand tool while you are working with another tool, just press the Spacebar then drag the page.

When you are working on a small area of a page, it's helpful to get a picture of the entire page structure. For that, you can use the Navigator palette. To use it, just position the red box in the Navigator palette's proxy image of the current page over the portion of the page you wish to view, and enlarge as needed. You will still have a feel for how the overall page looks, even when you are zoomed into a very small area. You can quickly shift your view of a page area by moving the red box over the miniature page proxy in the Navigator palette.

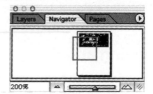

The Navigator palette.

A total of 28 (Macintosh) or 60 (Windows) windows may be open at one time. You can, for example, open additional windows of the same document to see how changes affect different pages of the document, compare different spreads, or work on details. You can observe how the changes you make affect the entire layout, which may be displayed at a smaller view percentage, while you work on a much-magnified view in another window.

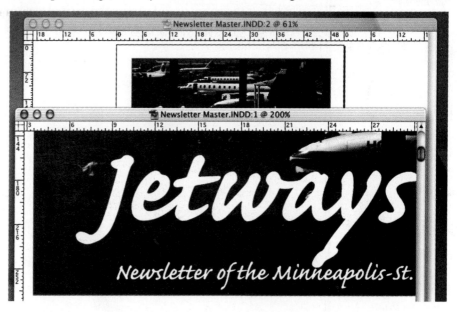

Here, the foreground is the original window, and the background is a new window of the same page.

To close all open windows for a single document, you can press Command/Control-Shift-W. To close all open document windows, just add the Option/Alt key.

You can create new window views by choosing Window>New Window. All windows opened after the original one are titled [document name]:x where "x" is a number from 1 to the number of new windows opened. You can also choose whether document windows overlap or appear side-by side by choosing Window>Cascade to stack all windows, or Window>Tile to arrange all open windows equally without any overlap.

Summary

In this chapter, you have learned the basic structure of electronic documents, and have explored the settings you will use to control your documents. You learned how to open, close, and save documents, and how to build on the document's structure with master pages and master elements. You also learned how to maneuver around the page quickly and easily.

4   *Working with Text*

Chapter Objective:

Successful communication is the goal of all printed and electronic documents. Formatting text appropriately can be the key to achieving that goal — if readers can't easily distinguish individual letters, words, or sentences, then you can't expect them to spend time reading the content of your documents. InDesign offers myriad features for enhancing the readability of text. In Chapter 4, you will:

- Learn how to create text frames. Understand how to navigate through text frames, how to edit text, and how to work with overset text.

- Use the Character palette to define text attributes such as font, font size, leading, tracking, and more.

- Learn about special characters and keyboard shortcuts.

- Learn about other, generally invisible, characters used for spacing and line breaks, and how to use them appropriately.

- Learn about ligatures, oldstyle numbers, superiors, inferiors, the Glyph palette, and other features of InDesign's OpenType support.

- Use the Paragraph palette to define paragraph attributes, such as text alignment, indents, hyphenation, paragraph rules, and inter-paragraph spacing.

- Discover how to set and use tabs, and how to format tabular material.

- Understand the process of importing and exporting text files, including the word-processing formats that InDesign supports.

- Learn how to place and thread text between multiple frames.

Projects to be Completed:

- **Central Market Ad (A)**

- Yellow Rose Menu (B)

- Travel Brochure (C)

- Good Choices Newsletter (D)

One of the more difficult things to understand about InDesign is the inconsistency between scaling or resizing objects with the Selection tool, the Direct Selection tool, and the Transform palette. InDesign cannot scale text with the Selection tool, nor does it notice if you scale objects with the Selection tool. For example, if you adjust the size of a frame with the Selection tool, the Transform panel still says "100%". If, however, you perform the adjustment with the Direct Selection tool or the Transform panel, every measurement reflects the new size of the frame and its contents. To confuse the matter even more, if you use the Scale functions in the Transform palette on a text frame, then type is scaled in only one direction; the dimensions always read "100%".

Working with Text

In Chapter 1, you learned about the evolution of type and typography. We also discussed a number of text terms that we will use throughout the rest of the book. Text makes up approximately 70%–80% of printed matter, so it is important to learn to handle it well. This book will help you learn ways to handle text most efficiently and to set it attractively.

In InDesign, text is always contained in frames, which you can think of as containers for text. You may create a text frame with the Type tool, or any of the frame-creation tools, or InDesign can create the frame for you when you type or place text into your document. A text frame is identified by the ports on the upper left (In port) and lower right (Out port) of the frame. The ports indicate whether text in the frame is part of a stream coming from and going to other frames in the document. The Type tool is used to insert text into the frame or to edit it. To position and size the text frame, you can use the Selection tool or Transform palette. To alter the shape of the frame, you can use the Direct Selection tool, sometimes in conjunction with elements of the Pen tool. You can resize a frame with the Selection tool, although the contents will not scale along with it. Text *will* resize if you scale the frame with the Transform palette's Scale functions.

This text frame shows the In and Out ports. Notice that the Out port has a plus sign in it, which indicates that there is more text contained in the frame. This is known as "overset" text — you can adjust it by enlarging the frame, flowing the text to another frame, or resetting the text to fit within the frame.

Setting Text Frame Properties

When you create a text frame, the default property is one column containing no text. Columns and frames can be modified with the Text Frame Options after you create them. You can access the Text Frames dialog by selecting Object>Text Frame Options, Control-clicking>Text Frame Options (Macintosh), right-clicking>Text Frame Options (Windows), or simply pressing Command/Control-B.

Press Command/Control-B to access the Text Frame Options dialog.

You can also specify the number of columns and the gutter space in the New Document dialog.

It's traditional to set nonsense Latin "dummy" text when creating page layouts at the beginning of the design stage. InDesign has a built-in dummy text generator (Type>Fill with Placeholder Text), which is available whenever a text frame is selected. This function completely fills the selected text frame with meaningless Latin text, with no overset text. Later in the production process you can replace this text with the actual copy to be used in the job.

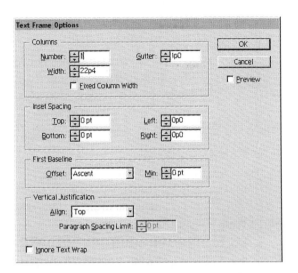

Default Text Frame Options settings.

Columns

When you change the number of columns or the gutter width, the column width changes as well. If the Fixed Column Width box is checked, the overall width of the text frame changes if the number of columns is changed.

Inset Spacing

With rectangular frames, you can adjust the text inset for each of the frame edges independently. If the frame isn't rectangular, you can only adjust an overall inset. It's better, however, to use paragraph margins to control text offset from frame sides because inset spacing can cause some confusion when you start defining margins, tabs, and text frame positions.

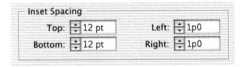
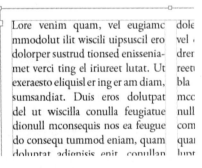

The Inset Spacing settings on the left produce the "keepaway" effect shown on the right. The inset area shows as a thin line inside of the text frame.

First Baseline

This option shifts the first line of text up or down according to the type of offset specified. The default value is Ascent (the height of the lowercase ascenders of the typeface). The other options you can choose from are:

- **Cap Height.** The height of the capital letters of the typeface
- **Leading.** The leading value of the paragraph, exclusive of any Space Before values

- **x Height.** The height of the "x" character, generally the body height of lowercase letters
- **Fixed.** Sets a fixed distance between the baseline of the first line and the top inset value defined for that frame

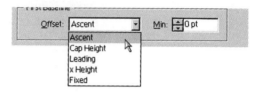

Baseline Offset options.

Vertical Justification

The Vertical Justification options are Top, Center, Bottom, and Justify. These options change the position of text in the frame, allowing empty space to occupy the balance of the frame.

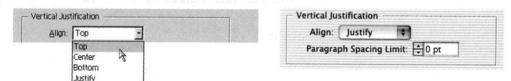

Vertical Justification options.

The Justify option adds space between lines to completely fill the frame with text. The value in the Paragraph Spacing Limit field defines how much extra space is allowed between paragraphs, in addition to any space already assigned. InDesign first tries to fill the frame by putting extra space between paragraphs, up to the maximum you specify in Paragraph Spacing Limit. After the limit has been reached, it adds space between lines to fill the frame. You can only specify vertical justification for rectangular frames.

Ignore Text Wrap

If the Ignore Text Wrap box is checked, text wrap values of an image placed in the paragraph are ignored, and the text overprints the graphic. You should probably leave this deactivated in most cases.

Editing Text

Almost as important as getting text into a frame is modifying it once it's there. You can cut, copy, paste, and move text, or modify the properties of text.

Viewing Hidden Characters

A number of characters in a story aren't normally visible, including the space, the tab, and the return. These are items that you wouldn't ordinarily consider to be characters at all, but they are. It is often useful to view these when editing text, particularly if you are working with text someone else has entered. To view them, you can either select Type>Show Hidden Characters or, when the Type tool is active, select Properties>Show Hidden Characters. The now-visible characters appear in the same color as the guides and text frame (the default is light blue).

InDesign defines all of the text within a frame, or a series of threaded frames, as a story. You can have many stories in a document, but only one story per frame, or one story per series of threaded frames.

Lorer sum acidunt aliquipis exer sit aliquis non-sequam, velese tat.¶
Duipit il euguercilit nim quamcon llumsandre etum vent acipit praesto consed tem veliquat, commy nummy nisim quation equatum dolut ea cons dolor susto odoloreet utatem dolor sent ilit alit lore vero eui endre facidunt volorem quate ex el ulluptatin veliqui blaoreetum deliqui cipis non henim nim nibh eu facipit, volorting ex ero dolutpat alis el dignis dolore vullutat, conulla facip exerat.¶
Dui et, sum doloreet, sit aci te consequatue exero dolore consequat ut dolore magnibh essi#

Text frame with Show Hidden Characters enabled. Spaces are shown with a dot (·), and returns are shown with a pilcrow (¶), which is the name of the character representing the return or paragraph mark character. The end of the story is marked with an octothorp (#) symbol, also called the number or pound sign. Not shown are tab characters, which are represented by a closing guillemet (») symbol. These symbols may appear differently depending on the chosen font.

Selecting Text

InDesign offers several methods for selecting text. You can double-click to select the word under the cursor, along with the space following that word. If Triple Click to Select a Line is turned off in the Text pane of the InDesign Preferences, a triple-click selects the entire paragraph; otherwise it takes four clicks to select an entire paragraph.

Another way to select text is to click once within the paragraph, then hold down the Shift key and click another location. All text between the two clicks is selected.

InDesign defines a paragraph as a section of text that is terminated with a return (or pilcrow), created by pressing Return (Macintosh) or Enter (Windows).

You can use the keyboard to select text. With the Type tool active, simply position the cursor at the beginning of the text to be selected, then hold the Shift key and use the arrow keys to select the text. If you press Command/Control along with Shift, then pressing the Up and Down Arrow keys selects the entire paragraph before or after the insertion point. Each time you press an arrow key, another paragraph is selected. You can use the Shift key along with Command/Control and the Left or Right Arrow keys to select multiple words.

To select all of the text in a text stream or story, you can select the Type tool and click once within the text frame, then choose Edit>Select All or press Command/Control-A. This selects all text in the story, whether all of the text is contained in a single frame or threaded across multiple frames.

Using Cut, Copy, Delete, and Paste Commands

To move text, you can select it and press Command/Control-X. The selected text is *cut* from the text frame and placed onto the Clipboard. You can then place the Type tool at a new insertion point where you want the text to be repositioned and press Command/Control-V to paste.

Similarly, to copy text, you can select it and press Command/Control-C. The selected text is copied into the Clipboard, but the original remains in the text frame. You can then position the insertion point at a new location and press Command/Control-V to paste the text.

The Clipboard is a temporary holding area for objects that you have cut or copied. In InDesign, the Clipboard only holds one object or selection of text at a time, and it is cleared of its contents if you cut or copy something else.

To delete text, you simply select it and press the Delete/Backspace key. You can also cut the text, so it remains on the Clipboard until you cut or copy something else.

The Paste command places all information currently on the Clipboard at the current cursor location. If the Type tool is active, the Clipboard contents are pasted into a text frame; if any other tool is active, the Clipboard is pasted as a new object on the current page. InDesign treats any non-text objects pasted (as inline graphics) into text frames as any other character.

Navigating through Text Blocks

A paragraph is defined as any text that is followed by a paragraph mark, resulting from pressing the Return/Enter key. If you press Return/Enter twice after typing something to create a blank line, then continue typing, the blank line is still considered a paragraph, even though there's no text in it. If you have Show Hidden Characters turned on, any text followed by a ¶, or a ¶ on a line by itself, is a discrete paragraph. Headings, bulleted items, and captions are examples of paragraphs. Each time you press the Return/Enter key, you create a paragraph.

As you've learned, you can navigate through blocks of text using the arrow keys or the mouse. The commands below help you edit text more efficiently:

- Command/Control-Left/Right Arrow moves the insertion point one word in the direction of the arrow.
- Command/Control-Up/Down Arrow moves the insertion point to the beginning of the paragraph preceding or following the insertion point.
- Command/Control-Home moves the insertion point to the beginning of a story.
- Command/Control-End moves the insertion point to the end of a story.

These commands may be used with the Shift key to select text. For example, if you press Command/Control-Shift-Home, all text from the insertion point to the beginning of the story is selected. If you begin typing when any text is selected, the selected text is deleted and replaced with the new text.

Text Overflow

You don't want to see an overflow icon in a text frame. A simple paragraph return can create an overflow state; although an extra hidden character won't print, it still serves as a warning. You should take action when you discover that your document contains text that's not in view. Consider making the frame larger, making the type smaller, deleting the text, or linking the text to another frame.

When there is too much text to fit the frame, an overflow icon alerts you to the problem. If this happens, the Out port of the text frame shows a small, red plus sign (+). This condition is also known as *overset* text. We showed an example of an overset text frame at the beginning of this chapter. If the text were flowing into another frame, the plus sign would turn to a blue arrow.

Here is an example of a frame where the overflowing text has been linked to another frame. This allows the overset text to flow into the linked frame. You need to choose View>Show Text Threads to see the link-line between the Out ports and In ports of linked frames.

Press Command-Option-Y/ Control-Alt-Y to turn Show Text Threads on and off.

Formatting Text

Controls that affect the appearance of s[...] are located on the Character palette and[...]

The Character Palette

The Character palette is divided into fo[...] font and style. The second describes for[...] pertain to the spacing of letters and lin[...] physical attributes, such as vertical or h[...] defines which language dictionary is us[...] a drop-down menu from which to sele[...] directly type values into the appropriat[...] apply those values.

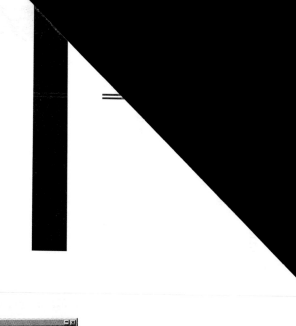

InDesign's Character palette.

Font and Style

The *font* is the name of the family of type (typeface) selected from the drop-down menu. Within font families there are various weights, such as Regular, Semibold, Bold, and Ultra, and style variants, such as Italic, Oldstyle, and Roman. Typically, professional typefaces include a full family of weights and style variants, such as those included with Adobe Garamond Pro:

Adobe Garamond Regular

Adobe Garamond Semibold

Adobe Garamond Bold

Adobe Garamond Italic

Adobe Garamond Semibold Italic

Adobe Garamond Bold Italic

Six different weights and style variants of the Adobe Garamond Pro typeface.

A specific type variant must be installed on the computer for InDesign to recognize it as valid. For example, if you set a headline in ATC Daiquiri, which only has a Regular (or Roman) variant, you can only select that variant, because a bold variant of ATC Daiquiri doesn't exist. QuarkXPress and PageMaker both let you apply a Bold style to any font, even if the actual style variant isn't installed. Both of these programs artificially bloat up selected type to imitate a true bold style or artificially slant selected type to imitate a true italic style which. If such type actually gets through prepress without causing an error, it looks ugly and amateurish.

This example shows the variants available in the selected typeface, Adobe Caslon Pro. Unlike some other page-layout applications, InDesign does not let you create "fake" italic or bold styles, which prevents potential trouble at press time.

Size, Leading, Kerning, Tracking

The *font size* is the height of a typeface, measured in points. This distance refers not only to the visible size of the character, but also includes the distance from the bottom of the descender to the clearance allowance above the ascender.

This 72-pt. example in Minion Regular shows the different height specifications in a typeface. Notice that the cap height is different from the ascender height of some lowercase letters; also notice the small clearance allowance above the ascender. True small caps are the same height as the x height of the standard font.

Leading is the space between lines of type, measured in points. If Auto leading is selected, the value of the leading (by default 120% of the point size) appears in parentheses. Be careful that the leading values you choose ensure good readability of the text. Leading that is tight conserves space but can impair readability; open leading can sometimes be effective as a design tool, but can also impair readability. Optimal leading values vary depending on the typeface used and on the context of the document. A "big" typeface such as ITC Bookman requires more leading for better legibility than a more compact typeface such as Times, and pages of solid text such as you would find in a novel benefit from more leading than dense material such as dictionary listings.

Typographers specify the size of the type with the leading by separating them with a slash. "10/12" means the type should be 10 points with 12 point leading. This is also referred to as "10 over 12."

Loreet, quamconumsan volor
sum aliqui elit praesenim
zzriure exero dolorti cipsusto
delit irilissenit in voloreet
ullute dolortin vel ute feuguer
uscil duis eu feugiam, si eum
volore dolesti nsectet alis nit
landre vullandiat. Duisci blan

Loreet, quamconumsan
volor sum aliqui elit
praesenim zzriure exero
dolorti cipsusto delit
irilissenit in voloreet
ullute dolortin vel ute
feuguer uscil duis eu
feugiam, si eum volore

The function of the printed piece and the chosen typeface dictates the proper leading. Notice that even though both type samples are set at 12 points with "auto" leading, the Bookman sample (right) appears much larger than the Times sample (left). Both are 12 points in size, but Bookman has a larger x height and set size (width) than Times. Bookman can benefit from extra leading.

10-pt. Minion Regular with 10-pt. leading is what many people call "tight" line spacing. Too little line spacing creates dark, uninviting "color" that causes the eye to take in other lines.

10-pt. Minion Regular with a 12-pt. leading is what many people call "normal" line spacing. A proper amount of line spacing allows the eye to travel easily from one line to the next.

10-pt. Minion Regular with 15-pt. leading is what many people call "open" line spacing. Too much line spacing creates disruptive jumps from line to line.

Examples of tight, normal, and open leading.

ATC typefaces are created without kerning pairs because they aren't intended for commercial use. Many commercial fonts have a large number of built-in kerning pairs, so in most cases you don't need to alter the kerning much when using these fonts. This is called "robust kerning," and is one reason these fonts are more expensive than shareware fonts; it takes an enormous amount of time and effort to create kerning pairs.

The default spacing between two letters is defined by most well-designed typefaces and is called a "kerning pair." Typefaces designed for professional typesetting typically have several hundred kerning pairs built into them; some typefaces have several thousand kerning pairs.

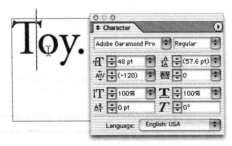

If you place the insertion point between two letters, the built-in kerning value for that letter pair displays in the Kerning field of the Character palette.

Kerning is defined in thousandths of an *em*. The three kerning options available to InDesign users are Metrics, Optical, or Manual. In body text, it is usually best to use the Metrics setting if you are working with a typeface with robust kerning pairs. You can also apply optical kerning for typefaces that lack robust kerning pairs, or if you simply don't like the appearance produced by metric kerning. With the Optical setting applied,

An em is a unit of measure that is always the same size as the point size of the type. An em in 10-point type is 10 points wide. In 24-point type it is 24 points wide. An em dash (—) is one em wide, and an en dash (–) is half an em wide. Most typefaces include em and en dashes; many also have em and en spaces.

InDesign examines the shapes of paired letters and applies a general tightening or loosening of the kerning of the letter pairs.

WATCH YOUR WHITESPACE
WATCH YOUR WHITESPACE
WATCH YOUR WHITESPACE

In the first line above, all kerning has been removed; the vertical lines indicate that one letter begins at the end of the preceding letter's set width. The second line uses only the built-in font metrics. The third line is kerned more heavily, to maintain even amounts of white space throughout the entire line. When kerning headlines, pay attention to the white space created between letters; it should be relatively even throughout.

Tracking is the spacing between a range of letters and is defined in thousandths of an em. Kerning and tracking are cumulative in InDesign, so a word might be tracked −10 and a kerned pair could have an additional −35/1000 of kerning. Tracking applies the same amount of spacing to a range of letters, while kerning applies a variable amount of space between specific letter pairs. You can apply tracking to a single word, a line, a paragraph, or an entire story.

When manually kerning letter pairs, exercise restraint. Too much kerning is worse than none at all.

When tracking lines of text is it best to track the entire paragraph, rather than a single line. Tracking just one line, either to make it tighter, or to make it looser, simply calls attention to the line. At any rate, tracking, like kerning, should be exercised with discretion.

Proper letterspacing depends on many factors, such as the typeface, the amount of copy, line spacing, size, and weight of the type, as well as individual taste.

When letterspacing is set at its optimum, text has enhanced readability. The tighter the letterspacing, the darker the lines of type become; the looser, the grayer they are.

When letterspacing is set at its optimum, text has enhanced readability. The tighter the letterspacing, the darker the lines of type become; the looser, the grayer they are.

In this example, the third line in the upper-left paragraph is tracked to force the word "just" up. Notice how tracking a single line makes it stand out. The paragraph at lower left is tracked normally, the one at upper right is tracked to −35, and the one at lower right is tracked to +35. Notice how the legibility and color of the type change with different tracking settings.

Scaling, Baseline Shift, Skew

Even though InDesign gives you the tools to do it, you should not make transformations such as Scale and Shear/Skew to type. The appearance of the typeface is usually destroyed, as you can see in the following example:

$$\mathrm{E}\ _{\mathrm{E}}\ \mathrm{E}$$

$$a\ \mathit{a}\ \mathit{a}$$

*Here are letters set in Adobe Minion Regular: respectively, an "E" with no scaling applied,
an "E" vertically scaled to 50%, and an "E" horizontally scaled to 50%. Notice how the thick
and thin strokes are radically altered. Below are a Minion Regular lowercase "a", a skewed italic "a",
and a true italic "a". Many characters change their shapes when true italics are applied.*

*Type is often said to have
"color," but this use of the
word has nothing to do
with type being green or
blue. Instead, it refers to
the overall blackness or
grayness of a section of
type when viewed as an
object instead of as words.
A designer's goal is to
achieve an even balance
of typographic color by
adjusting type size, word
spacing, letter spacing,
and leading. One typogra-
pher's trick to evaluate
typographic color is to
view the text upside-
down, which eliminates
any biases introduced by
the tendency to read the
words rather than view
the words as graphical
elements.*

The effect of vertically scaling type is to keep the vertical stroke width the same and to
compress or expand the horizontal stroke. The effect of horizontally scaling type is to
keep the horizontal stroke width the same and to compress or expand the vertical stroke.
Either modification can destroy the integrity of a typeface. Use these functions as little as
possible. If you need condensed or expanded type, you should use a typeface that includes
a condensed or expanded style variant, or one that is designed from the start as a
condensed or expanded typeface. As a last resort for a copyfitting problem, apply horizontal scaling only; you should never apply scaling more than 3% in either direction.

Skewed type may be used for special effects, but should never be substituted for italics.
It is simply a distortion of the letterform and should not be used for body and headline
text. This effect is only appropriate when using small amounts of type as a design element.

The imaginary line on which letters sit is called the "baseline." Moving the baseline of
letters up or down is called "baseline shift." A baseline shift may be useful in a number of
instances. For example, it may be used to create fractions in fonts that lack pre-built or
cut fractions, or to alter a character that should be superscripted.

Some OpenType fonts include some cut characters for superscripting and subscripting,
known as superiors and inferiors. We will discuss this in greater detail in the OpenType
Menu section of this chapter.

Language

The final section in the Character palette allows you to select a specific language for punctuation, hyphenation, and spelling when these features are needed. This is particularly
useful when more than one language is used within a publication. You should always
change the language specification when working with languages other than English if the
language is supported in InDesign. For example, the German word for sugar, "Zucker," is
hyphenated as "Zuk-ker" in traditional German when it is broken between lines, or as
"Zuc-ker" in reformed German. It won't be hyphenated at all, however, if you forget to
change the language setting to either set of German rules, because the word "Zucker" isn't
in the English hyphenation dictionary.

$$\text{«Allons-y!»}$$
$$\text{„Schnell!"}$$

*This example shows the results of changing the language to French and then to German.
InDesign applies the punctuation and hyphenation rules specific to the chosen language.
Although it correctly hyphenates words and checks spelling in the specified language,
InDesign does not retroactively change punctuation such as quotation marks if
you apply a different language to text that you've already typed.*

Character Palette Options Menu

The pop-up Options menu on the Character palette has four sections. The first deals with the display of the palette itself. The second concerns the case and position of text. The third has to do with text styling, and the fourth allows you to specify words that should never hyphenate.

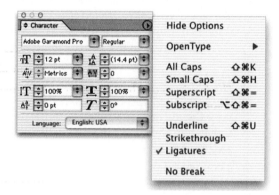

Most of the formatting commands on the Character palette's Options menu have keyboard shortcuts.

Hide/Show Options hides or shows the vertical and horizontal scale, baseline shift, skew, and language features. It shrinks the size of the palette to include only the most commonly used features.

When characters are highlighted, the All Caps, Small Caps, Superscript, and Subscript styles may be applied. The size (and position in the case of super- and subscript) is determined by the character settings defined in the Text Preferences pane. When the Small Caps option is selected, InDesign uses cut small caps if they're installed in the form of an Expert typeface, an "SC-OsF" set, or included in an OpenType font set, such as some of the new Adobe Pro typefaces. If these aren't available, InDesign shrinks uppercase letters to simulate true cut small caps, superiors, and inferiors.

The styling options — Underline, Strikethrough, and Ligatures — can be a little confusing. Underline and strikethrough characters are always available in any font, although underlining is discouraged and strikethrough is only appropriate for financial and legal documents.

Ligatures are specially-built characters that provide aesthetically pleasing alternates for letter pairs that ordinarily collide. The two most common ligatures are those for the "fi" and "fl" letter pairs, though some fonts include ligatures for a number of other pairs such as "ff," "ffi," "ffl," "fj," and "Th." A ligature eliminates the "crash" between, for example, the crossbar of "f" and the dot of "i."

ff fi fj fl ffi ffj ffl Th

ff fi fj fl ffi ffj ffl Th

Ligatures enabled (top) and disabled (bottom) in Adobe Warnock Pro.

Most serif typefaces include ligatures, and most sans serif ones don't, but there are exceptions to both rules. The Palatino and Aldus fonts are serif typefaces that were designed to not need ligatures; Adobe Cronos is a sans serif typeface that includes ligatures.

Underlined text is an old-fashioned legacy of the typewriter and should not be used. Use italics instead.

Ligatures are available only if they are supported in a particular font. If you're using a Macintosh to work on a document that will be opened on Windows computers, be aware that ligatures are not always included in the Windows versions of fonts. If an "fi" ligature is broken into separate "f" and "i" characters, the difference may be substantial enough to force the text to rewrap; different availability of ligatures when crossing platforms can cause major problems in print production. InDesign includes functions to mitigate this type of event and is more capable in this regard than other layout applications, but you should be aware that moving documents across platforms can introduce subtle errors such as text reflow that won't be caught without careful proofing.

The last item on the Character palette menu, No Break, forces a selected word to never hyphenate.

Enter Text

1. Select File>New>Document. Create a letter-size document, using the default margins. The Facing Pages and Master Text Frame options should not be checked.

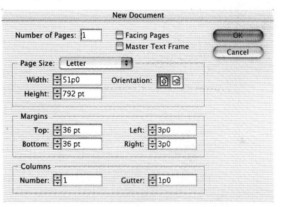

2. Make sure Hide Frame Edges appears in the View menu. If Show Frame Edges appears, that means that they're currently hidden, so choose Show Frame Edges to turn this option on. From the Type menu, select Show Hidden Characters.

3. The Transform palette should be open. If it isn't, select Window>Transform.

4. Select the Type tool, then drag to create a text frame on the page's live area. Make sure the proxy reference point is set to the upper-left square. Click the Transform palette's tab to activate it, then enter these values to position and size the text frame exactly:

X: 3p0   Y: 36 pt   W: 22p0   H: 220 pt

Press Command-Option-I (Macintosh) or Control-Alt-I (Windows) to show or hide hidden characters. Press Command/Control-H to show and hide frame edges.

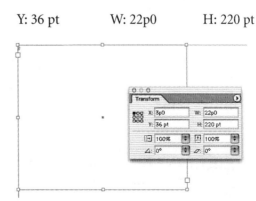

As you fill the text frame with copy, you can either stretch the frame to make it taller or wider to fit the text, or you can link two text frames. Alternately, you can change the type size to fit it to the frame.

Typically, capitalized words should not hyphenate, nor should headlines.

The default proxy reference point is the center. If you forget and enter a frame's specifications with the proxy reference set to the center point, select the upper-left proxy reference point and re-enter the X and Y values.

5. Click the Character palette tab.

6. Click in the text frame, and type "Alice's Adventures in Wonderland".

7. Select all of the text, and in the Character palette, change the typeface to ATC Plantation Regular, 36 pt.

8. Click the insertion point right before the word "Adventures" (but after the space following "Alice's"), then hold down the Shift key and press Return/Enter. This inserts a *soft return*, or forced line break, while not ending the paragraph. This wraps the word "Adventures" to the next line.

9. Type another soft return in front of the word "in." This forces the word to the next line.

10. The type looks OK now, but it looks a little loose. Select all of the text, and in the Tracking field type "–20".

11. Now kern the "Wo" letter pair. Place the insertion point between the "W" and "o". In the Kerning field of the Character palette, enter the value –75.

12. Kern any other letters that look poorly spaced (for example, the "Ad" pair in "Adventures" could be tightened up).

The effects of soft returns and manual kerning.

13. Change to the Selection tool, and move the text frame to the right side of the page.

14. Create a new text frame with a width of 12p and a height of 144 pt. below the text frame containing "Alice's Adventures in Wonderland".

15. With the Type tool selected, choose as the typeface ATC Cabana Normal, 12 pt.

16. Click in the text frame and press Command/Control-D to place the file **alice.txt** from **RF_Intro_InDesign**. Reapply the formatting from Step 15 if necessary.

17. Notice the red overset text icon in the lower right of the text frame. This icon indicates that the text frame is not large enough to display all the text in the story.

18. Hold down the Command/Control key to temporarily switch to the Selection tool, then click the edge of the frame once to select it. Resize the text frame so all text entered in Step 16 fits, then release the Command/Control key to revert back to the Type tool.

19. Double-click the word "bank" in the first sentence, and replace it with "fence". Notice how any selected text is replaced by whatever you type.

20. Select the first word, "Alice". In the Character palette, click the arrow in the upper right to reveal the Options menu. Select the Small Caps text style. Notice how the lowercase letters became small capitals, but the capital letter was unaffected.

21. Save the document to your **Work_In_Progress** folder as "working_text.indd" and leave the document open for the next exercise.

Inserting Special Characters

Special characters are those that cannot be typed directly from the keyboard by pressing a letter or number key, but are produced by typing a letter or number key along with the Option or Alt key, and sometimes along with the Shift key. You can use the Type>Insert

Special Character menu, or the Type>Insert White Space menu, to insert a number of characters or types of spaces at an active text insertion point.

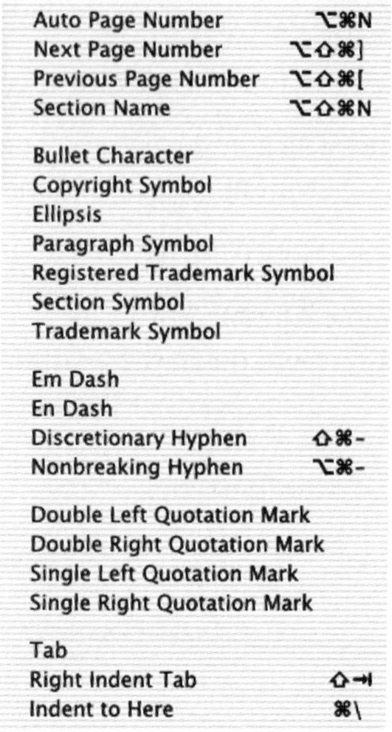

Auto Page Number	⌥⌘N
Next Page Number	⌥⇧⌘]
Previous Page Number	⌥⇧⌘[
Section Name	⌥⇧⌘N
Bullet Character	
Copyright Symbol	
Ellipsis	
Paragraph Symbol	
Registered Trademark Symbol	
Section Symbol	
Trademark Symbol	
Em Dash	
En Dash	
Discretionary Hyphen	⇧⌘-
Nonbreaking Hyphen	⌥⌘-
Double Left Quotation Mark	
Double Right Quotation Mark	
Single Left Quotation Mark	
Single Right Quotation Mark	
Tab	
Right Indent Tab	⇧→|
Indent to Here	⌘\

The Insert Special Character menu.

Windows users might be accustomed to entering special characters by holding down the Alt key and typing a zero followed by three numbers on the numeric keypad. InDesign offers Windows users some easier shortcuts to these characters; for example, to type an em dash, you can press Alt-Shift-[hyphen] instead of having to type Alt-0151 as required in most other programs. Macintosh users access these characters by holding down the Option or Option-Shift keys in combination with another character. The character typed with the modifiers is the same for both Macintosh and Windows platforms, as the following chart shows:

Special Characters

Character/Result	Macintosh Keystroke	Windows Keystroke
Auto Page Number	Command-Option-N	Control-Alt-N
(inserts an automatic page number marker; only for master pages)		
Previous Page Number	Command-Option-Shift-[	Control-Alt-Shift-[
(inserts page number where story is continued from; only for master pages)		
Next Page Number	Command-Option-Shift-]	Control-Alt-Shift-]
(inserts page number where story continues; only for master pages)		
Section Name	Command-Option-Shift-N	Control-Alt-Shift-N
(inserts the section marker, if defined for current section)		
Bullet •	Option-8	Alt-8
Copyright ©	Option-G	Alt-G
Ellipsis …	Option-;	Alt-;
Paragraph (pilcrow) ¶	Option-7	Alt-7
Registered Trademark ®	Option-R	Alt-R

Character/Result	Macintosh	Windows
Section §	Option-6	Alt-6
Trademark ™	Option-2	Alt-2
Em Dash —	Option-Shift-[hyphen]	Alt-Shift-[hyphen]
En Dash –	Option-[hyphen]	Alt-[hyphen]
Discretionary Hyphen	Command-Shift-[hyphen]	Control-Shift-[hyphen]
Nonbreaking Hyphen	Command-Option-[hyphen]	Control-Alt-[hyphen]
Quote, Double " or "	Option-[or Option-Shift-[	Alt-[or Alt-Shift-[
Quote, Single ' or '	Option-] or Option-Shift-]	Alt-] or Alt- Shift-]
Tab	Tab	Tab
Right Indent Tab	Shift-Tab	Shift-Tab

(Inserts right-aligned tab at right indent)

Indent to Here	Command-\	Control-\

(Indents all subsequent text in the paragraph to that point)

Spaces

These different types of spaces are available by selecting Type>Insert White Space.

Em Space	⇧⌘M
En Space	⇧⌘N
Flush Space	
Hair Space	⌥⇧⌘I
Nonbreaking Space	⌥␣
Thin Space	⌥⇧⌘M
Figure Space	⌥⇧⌘8
Punctuation Space	

The Insert White Space options.

These spaces differ in their widths, but only when used without justification. Justification requires that spaces be "elastic" and not fixed. The font designer determines the width of a standard space in a font.

Type of Space	Macintosh Keystroke	Windows Keystroke
Em Space/En Space	Command-Shift-M or -N	Control-Shift-M or -N

(em spaces are one em wide; en spaces are one en — half an em — wide)

Flush Space	(no keyboard equivalent)	

(all text following this character is set flush with the right margin, also known as "quad middle")

Hair Space	Command-Option-Shift-I	Control-Alt-Shift-I

(a hair space is 1/24 of an em)

Nonbreaking Space	Option-Spacebar	Alt-Spacebar

(words around this space will not break)

Thin Space	Command-Option-Shift-M	Control-Alt-Shift-M

(a thin space is 1/8 of an em)

Figure Space	Command-Option-Shift-8	Control-Alt-Shift-8

(a space usually equal to the width of the number zero in the font at a given font size; in fonts with only oldstyle numbers, it is the same as a normal space)

Punctuation Space	(no keyboard equivalent)	

(a space equal to the width of the period in the font at a given font size)

Special Formatting (Break) Characters

The first five of these break characters cause any text that follows them to flow to the next text frame that is threaded to the current frame. The cursor is also repositioned to the next frame.

Column Break	↗
Frame Break	⇧↗
Page Break	⌘↗
Odd Page Break	
Even Page Break	
Forced Line Break	⇧↵
Paragraph Return	

The Insert Break options.

Type of Break	Macintosh Keystroke	Windows Keystroke
Column Break	Enter	Enter
(flows text and cursor to next column)		
— this is the Enter key on the numeric keypad		
Frame Break	Shift-Enter	Shift-Enter
(flows text and cursor to next threaded frame, disregarding column settings)		
— this is the Enter key on the numeric keypad		
Page Break	Command-Shift-Enter	Control-Shift-Enter
(flows text and cursor to next threaded page)		
— this is the Enter key on the numeric keypad		
Odd Page Break	(no keyboard equivalent)	
(flows text and cursor to next odd-numbered page)		
Even Page Break	(no keyboard equivalent)	
(flows text and cursor to next even-numbered page)		
Forced Line Break	Shift-Return	Shift-Enter
(same as a soft return)		
Paragraph Return	Return	Enter
(a normal return)		

The OpenType Menu

InDesign 2.0 fully supports the features and glyphs present in OpenType fonts and is currently the first major application that does so (InDesign 1.0 and 1.5 did not fully exploit all of the features of OpenType). A *glyph* is broadly defined as any type of symbol, including letters and numbers, and it encompasses forms that are typically thought of as pictographs, such as Japanese or Chinese words. A *character* is a specific, coded entity that usually represents the smallest discrete unit of a language or alphabet, which is typically a letter. Glyphs are the specific forms that those characters can take in a given font; for example, the character "a" can have a number of different forms, such as lowercase, lower-case with swash, uppercase, small cap, and more. An OpenType font can contain glyphs for many different languages and alphabets; some only include glyphs for languages that use discrete alphabets, such as English, Russian, Thai, or Hebrew, and some can include glyphs for languages that use pictographs, such as Japanese, Chinese, and Korean.

OpenType fonts are the next generation of computer type. Prior to OpenType, most fonts existed as either TrueType or PostScript Type 1 format, and these required separate versions for Macintosh and Windows computers. OpenType developed as a cooperative venture between Adobe and Microsoft; the format is cross-platform, and each font can contain over 65,000 glyphs. You can use the same OpenType font files on a Macintosh and a Windows computer, which wasn't possible in the past without a lot of conversion work.

The following OpenType fonts are included on the InDesign installer CD. They are located in the Adobe OpenType Fonts folder inside the Goodies folder. There are also PDF type specimen documents within each font's folder. You need to install these on your computer before you can use them, because they are not installed automatically:

- Adobe Garamond Pro

- Adobe Caslon Pro

- Adobe Caflisch Script Pro

- Kozuka Gothic & Kozuka Mincho

If you have not already installed these fonts, please install the first three before continuing. The Kozuka fonts are Japanese and are not needed for the material in this book. If you use Mac OS 9 these fonts require Adobe Type Manager 4.6, or you can move them to the "private" InDesign fonts folder (Macintosh HD>Adobe InDesign 2.0>Fonts). Mac OS X and Windows 2000 and newer support OpenType fonts natively, without a font manager. Font managers such as Suitcase and Font Reserve work with OpenType fonts, but do not allow their use with operating systems that do not support them.

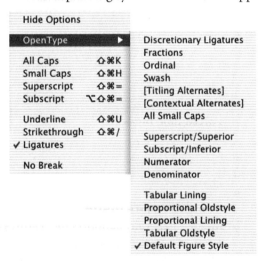

The OpenType menu.

From the OpenType menu, available from the Character palette Options menu, you can access any special OpenType typographic features that are present in an OpenType font. If an option on this menu is enclosed in brackets [like this], then that feature is not available for the currently selected font. A checkmark indicates that the option is currently enabled. A dash next to an option means it's enabled in parts of a text selection, but not throughout the entire selection. When an OpenType option is enabled, certain letters or expressions you type are replaced with the corresponding OpenType glyph; these options can be applied to text you've already typed or placed.

Discretionary ligatures are additional ligatures that may be present in a font. The standard Ligatures option replaces the "fi" and "fl" letter pairs with correct ligatures in nearly all fonts, and replaces other standard letter combinations if their ligatures are defined in the font. The Discretionary Ligatures option, if enabled (and if they are defined in the font), replaces any other pairs or triplets with a ligature.

Cast·the·first·stone.#

Discretionary "st" ligatures in the Adobe Warnock Pro font.

The Fractions option replaces typed fractions with a typographically correct fraction as long as it exists in the current font. For example, typing "1/2" with this option enabled produces the correct symbol if it's in the font; otherwise it's left unchanged.

Use·½·cup·of·sugar,·¼·cup of·coffee,·and·a·smidge·of· cinnamon.#

Use·1/2·cup·of·sugar,·1/4· cup·of·coffee,·and·a·smidge· of·cinnamon.#

Fractions enabled (left) and disabled (right).
Notice how much better the correct fraction symbols look; the numbers don't jump off the page.
Also, notice the "ff" pair in "coffee" is replaced with the correct ligature in both samples.

The Ordinal option sets ordinal numbers such as 1st, 2nd, and the Spanish 1a, 2o, and No (numeró) as correct superscripted characters. This option does not set ordinals for French (1er).

1st,·2nd,·and·4th.·1^a,·2°,·№·13.·#

Ordinals used with oldstyle numerals.

If swash characters are defined in a font and this option is enabled, decorative swash characters replace the standard characters. Swash characters typically have a leading or trailing "tail" and can be uppercase or lowercase. Some fonts include a large number of swash characters, including different swash styles for the same letter, but these usually need to be set manually.

a·d·e·g·h·l·m·n#

Swash characters in Adobe Warnock Pro.

Titling alternatives are only available in a few fonts. If available, specially cut uppercase titling capitals are substituted for standard uppercase letters. These tend to be slightly lighter than standard uppercase letters, and are best suited for use at large sizes (for example, in headlines). This option doesn't affect lowercase letters, but it should not be used in lines of mixed case, because the apparent weight of the titling caps is less than that of the lowercase letters.

TITLING·CAPS#   TITLING·CAPS#

Titling alternatives on (left) and off (right) in Adobe Garamond Pro.
Notice that the titling caps are slightly lighter in weight than the standard caps.

Contextual alternatives, if available in the font, are contextual ligatures and alternative characters that change shape according to the letters around them. The font designer has the option of creating different letter shapes to fit specific adjacent letters when creating an OpenType font.

object obtuse·inject·#

Contextual alternatives in Adobe Caflisch Script Pro. Notice the different versions of the letters "b," "j," and "e," which change according to the letter before or after them.

The All Small Caps option forces all letters to small caps regardless of their case. This differs from the Small Caps option on the Character palette Options menu, which only affects lowercase letters; uppercase letters remain at their standard size.

The Superscript/Superior and Subscript/Inferior options substitute pre-built superior or inferior characters for the selected letters. Not every letter or number is available as a superior or inferior. These two choices differ from the Superscript/Subscript options on the Character palette Options menu in the position and the weight of the letter or number relative to the surrounding characters. If the letter or number isn't in the font as a pre-built superior or inferior, nothing happens to it; you must use the Superscript/Subscript option from the Character palette Options menu.

$$X^3·+·Y_1·=·?\# \qquad\qquad X^3·+·Y_1·=·?\#$$

Superior/Inferior (left) and Superscript/Subscript (right) options. Notice that the characters in the second example are optically reduced, and look lighter than the pre-built characters in the first example. They're also placed at different distances from the baseline.

Press Option-Shift-1 (Macintosh) to type a solidus between a numerator and a denominator in custom fractions. There is no keystroke to type a solidus in Windows — you'll have to use the Insert Glyphs palette, described shortly, instead.

The Numerator and Denominator options let you create custom fractions in case the fraction you want isn't already pre-built in the current font. You can tell if a pre-built fraction isn't in the font because if you select the Fraction option on the OpenType menu for the selected text, nothing happens. To achieve the look of a proper fraction you need to assign the appropriate numerator/denominator option to each part of the fraction, and replace the slash with a *solidus*. A solidus is a special character that is designed to separate the numerator and denominator. You could use a standard slash (or *virgule*), but the solidus looks a lot better.

$$99·^{44}\!/_{100}·\%·\text{pure}\#$$

"44" is set as the numerator, "100" as the denominator. The standard slash has been replaced with a solidus, which has a steeper slope than a standard slash and is deeply kerned on each side. You can use a standard slash for unformatted fractions such as 3/4.

There are four possible types of numbers or numerals in an OpenType font, but not every OpenType font contains all of them. Oldstyle numerals are also called "non-lining" or "lowercase" numerals. They are designed to be used when set within lines of text, as they are much less obtrusive than the usual "lining" numerals, so-called because these are always above the baseline. Non-lining numerals can be above or below the baseline.

1 2 3 4 5 6 7 8 9 0

1 2 3 4 5 6 7 8 9 0

This example shows the difference between standard "lining" numerals (top), and oldstyle "non-lining" numerals (bottom) in the Aldus typeface.

The·course·included·students·from·the·classes·of·2001,·2002,·and·2004.#

The·course·included·students·from·the·classes·of·2001,·2002,·and·2004.#

Oldstyle numerals look much better when set in lines of text, because they more closely match the style of lowercase letters and don't jump out at the reader.

Within oldstyle and lining numerals there can be two types of each: proportional and tabular. Proportional numerals behave like letters and are variable in width, while tabular numerals have a fixed width. As the name implies, tabular numerals are intended for use in tables or wherever else numbers need to line up from one line to another. A font's default figure style is almost always Tabular Lining. Proportional numerals are intended for use within text.

24,982·11,943·4,195¶

24,982·11,943·4,195¶

24,982·11,943·4,195¶

24,982·11,943·4,195#

This example shows, from top to bottom, the same numbers set as Tabular Lining, Proportional Lining, Tabular Oldstyle, and Proportional Oldstyle. The difference in spacing is much more apparent with oldstyle numbers.

These options for numerals may be selected only when OpenType fonts are used. Although some non-OpenType Adobe typefaces include oldstyle figures (typically labeled "<typeface

name> SC-OsF" or "<typeface name> Expert"), InDesign does not automatically substitute these for lining numerals; you'll have to change the numbers to the oldstyle font yourself.

The Glyph Palette

The Glyph palette (Type>Insert Glyphs) enables you to insert any available character or symbol into a text frame at the insertion point.

If you use Mac OS X, you probably already have a number of Asian fonts installed; these generally don't appear in most applications' font menus because they are not supported, but you can use them with InDesign. Windows 2000 includes several Unicode fonts that, although not specifically OpenType fonts, include a vast array of glyphs for many languages. These fonts include Arial Unicode and Lucida Sans Unicode. You can use the Glyph palette with any installed font, not just OpenType or Unicode fonts.

You can access any installed font through the Glyph palette.

Asian fonts installed on Western operating systems are generally unusable for typesetting more than a few words, but they can be used to display documents that were created with an Asian version of InDesign. If you like, you can install the Kozuka fonts from the InDesign installer CD and experiment with Japanese typesetting on your own.

You can use the Insert Glyph palette to "type" characters that aren't on your keyboard but which are contained in a given font. For example, if you know Russian and have the Adobe Warnock Pro font installed, you can use this palette to enter Russian text. You can also mix different alphabets (for example, Roman, Cyrillic, and Greek) within the same text frame.

Cyrillic letters in the Adobe Warnock Pro Regular font, accessible from the Glyphs palette.

Some OpenType typefaces generally include glyphs for the Roman, Cyrillic, and Greek alphabets, along with a number of special glyphs used in specific languages, such as Icelandic, Lapp, Vietnamese, and Polish. You can also enter Asian glyphs if they're available.

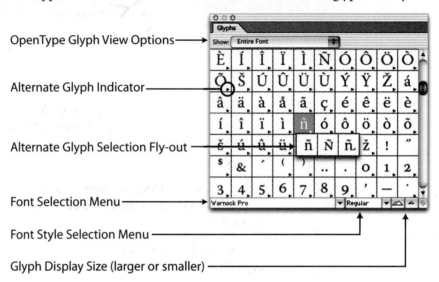

OpenType Glyph View Options

Alternate Glyph Indicator

Alternate Glyph Selection Fly-out

Font Selection Menu

Font Style Selection Menu

Glyph Display Size (larger or smaller)

The Glyph palette features.

If alternate glyphs exist for a character, this is indicated with the little black triangle in the character's box in the palette. You can click and hold the character's box to display the available alternates.

To insert a glyph at the active insertion point, you can double click the desired glyph, or select an alternate from the pop-up menu. To make the palette's display larger or smaller, just click one of the sizing buttons.

Format Characters

1. Open the document **working_text.indd** from your **Work_In_Progress** folder, if it is not already open.

2. After the word "Wonderland" in the headline, insert the text cursor and press Return/Enter to make a hard return.

3. Change the font to 12-pt. ATC Mai Tai Normal. Set the tracking to 0.

4. Type the following on two lines, separated by a soft return:

   "—by Lewis Carroll <hold Shift key to make a soft return>© [Public Domain]"

   You may use either the keyboard shortcuts from the chart above or the Insert Special Characters menu to find the em dash and copyright characters.

Alice's
Adventures
in Wonderland
—by Lewis Carroll
© [Public Domain]

5. Switch to the Selection tool and press Command/Control-0 to fit the view to the window, then press Command/Control-C to copy the text frame to the Clipboard. Press Command/Control-V to paste it. Move the copied frame to the lower part of the page.

6. Switch to the Type tool (or press "T"), then select all of the text in the copied frame. Press Delete/Backspace to delete it. The insertion point moves to the top left of the frame.

7. Change the font to Adobe Garamond Pro, 12 point, auto leading, zero tracking. Type the following sentences, separated with returns:

"Sift 1/2 cup of flour."

"24 = 16" (it will after this exercise)

"The 1st Pitch."

Alice's
Adventures
in Wonderland
—by Lewis Carroll
© [Public Domain]

8. Select the characters "1/2" and choose "Fractions" from the OpenType menu. Select the "4" in the second line and choose "Superscript/Superior" from the OpenType menu. Then select the "st" after the "1" in the third line, and choose "Ordinal" from the OpenType menu. Your type should look like this now:

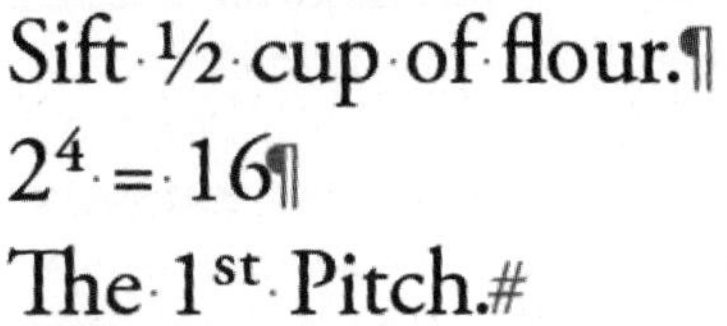

Sift $\frac{1}{2}$ cup of flour.¶

$2^4 = 16$¶

The 1st Pitch.#

9. Save the file and close it.   *Print*   *Name Chp. Page*

Formatting Paragraphs

The appearance and style applied to text influence the tone and type color of a page. In addition, the formatting applied to entire paragraphs affects how your page looks and reads.

Paragraph formatting issues you should consider include:

- Alignment of text (left, right, centered, or justified)
- Indents (left, right, and first line)
- Spacing above and below paragraphs
- Drop caps (if any)
- Hyphenation and justification
- Widow and orphan control
- Paragraph rules (or lines)

The manner in which text is aligned affects its readability.

To apply paragraph formatting, you first need to place the Type tool anywhere in the paragraph that you want to be affected. Because paragraph formatting affects the entire paragraph, all the text does not have to be manually selected. The Paragraph palette is initially found in the same panel as the Transform and Character palettes, or it may be activated by selecting Type>Paragraph or pressing Command/Control-M.

This paragraph is formatted with the Align Left setting. The left margin is in a constant position. Its value lies in the fact that there are consistent spaces between words and a consistent spot to which the eye returns.

The Paragraph Palette

The Paragraph palette is divided into four primary sections. The first manages the overall justification of the paragraph. The second section controls indentations and determines whether the paragraph aligns with the underlying baseline grid. The third controls space before and after the paragraph, and drop cap specifics. The fourth section determines whether the paragraph is hyphenated.

This paragraph is set to the Justified option. Left and right margins are even, but spaces between words are uneven. This style gives documents a formal, finished look.

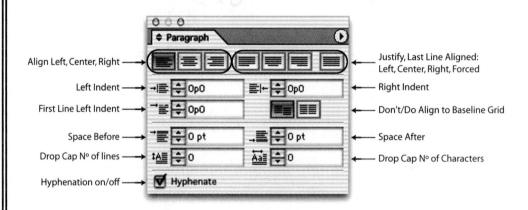

The Paragraph palette.

This paragraph is set to Align Right, which should be used sparingly (perhaps for special uses such as picture captions). This style is difficult to read because there is no consistent spot for the eye to return to.

The first section, justification options, is grouped into three subsections. The first is for *unjustified text* — text that is aligned to the left or right margins, or is centered on the page. The second section determines how the last line of paragraphs of justified text is addressed — right, left, or centered. The third forces all lines of text in the paragraph, including the last line, to justify to both margins.

Align Center is generally used for invitations, captions, and headlines. It is pretty, but hard to read, especially when multiple lines are centered.

The top two boxes in the next section are for setting a left or right indent for the entire paragraph. A first-line indent is added to any existing paragraph indent. So, if a paragraph is indented one pica from the left margin, with a first-line indent of one pica, the first line is indented two picas from the margin. Additionally, the first line may be given a negative

In justified text, the character spacing and the spaces between words are adjusted to align both margins of the text. Good justification is a result of choosing an appropriate typeface and font size, and a column width that's not too narrow. Bad justification leaves unsightly white spaces between words.

is indented two picas from the margin. Additionally, the first line may be given a negative indent or *outdent* by typing a hyphen (minus) in front of the indent amount; this is also called a "hanging indent."

The Don't/Do Align to Baseline Grid icons determine, on a paragraph-by-paragraph basis, whether the baselines of each line in the paragraph align with the underlying baseline grid. In most cases, aligning to the baseline grid is not a good idea.

The Space Before and Space After fields allow you to place a specific amount of space before or after a paragraph. Fixed spaces between paragraphs are usually used between elements in a bulleted list, between headlines and text, and between paragraphs that do not have first-line indents, in lieu of a double return or blank line. The body paragraphs of this book, for example, have 6.5 points of spacing applied after each one.

Drop Cap Number of Lines and Drop Cap Number of Characters are reasonably self-explanatory. When paragraphs have a drop cap, these dialog boxes control the number of lines a paragraph drops and the number of characters to include in the drop. If a quotation opens a section, it is appropriate to include both the quotation mark and the first character of the quote as a two-character drop cap. Dropping more than two caps can look awkward.

Example of a single, initial drop cap, dropped three lines.

The Hyphenate check box turns hyphenation on or off for that paragraph. Generally, callouts, headlines, and captions have hyphenation turned off.

Behind the triangle at the top right of the Paragraph palette is the "behind the scenes" power of paragraph controls. Most of these are advanced features and are considered in the book *Advanced InDesign: Creating Electronic Documents*, but we'll give an overview here.

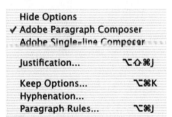

The Paragraph palette Options pop-up menu.

You'll almost always want to use the Adobe Paragraph Composer, which is the most advanced desktop text composition system ever designed. The Single-Line Composer only considers single lines when making hyphenation and justification (H&J) decisions and behaves like the composition system in other page-layout applications such as PageMaker or QuarkXPress. The Paragraph Composer considers all lines in a paragraph when making H&J decisions, identifies all possible combinations of word breaks, then makes intelligent decisions for applying breaks based on a weighting of the evenness of letter spacing, word spacing, and hyphenation. Although this system produces the best quality text composition, you may occasionally wish to use the Single-Line Composer if you are setting type with exact specifications.

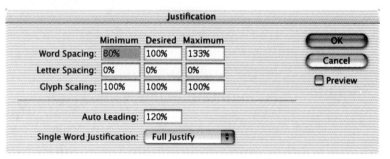

Justification options dialog box.

Justification rules take effect when the text alignment is justified to both margins. They control the word spacing, letter spacing, and glyph (character) scaling that is used to force a paragraph to justify. InDesign uses the parameters, in the order that they appear, to justify a paragraph correctly. The minimum and maximum fields let you specify the minimum and maximum inter-word spacing to apply when setting justified text. In ideal situations, InDesign uses 100%, but if necessary it applies word spacing up to the limits you define when composing justified text.

> Alice was beginning to get very tired of sitting by her sister on the bank, and of having nothing to do; once or twice she had peeped into the book her sister was reading, but it had no pictures or conversations in it, and what is the use of a book, thought Alice, without pictures or conversation?

> Alice was beginning to get very tired of sitting by her sister on the bank, and of having nothing to do; once or twice she had peeped into the book her sister was reading, but it had no pictures or conversations in it, and what is the use of a book, thought Alice, without pictures or conversation?

These otherwise identical columns of text use different minimum and maximum word-spacing values. The sample on the left uses a restrictive 95-100-105 setting, and the example on the right uses the default setting of 80-100-130, which results in tighter word spacing and better overall fit.

Non-justified text, which is any text set to align left, centered, or right, does not require any word spacing; all three parameters are always 100%. Letter spacing should be avoided, because it puts extra space between letters and results in loose-appearing text. It is better to adjust tracking instead of letter spacing.

Glyph scaling shrinks or enlarges the font-defined width of characters, and as we've mentioned already, altering the shapes of letters is a bad idea. But used in small amounts, no more than ± 3%, glyph scaling can help solve copyfitting problems without causing a visible change in appearance.

Auto Leading is expressed as a percentage based on the point size. A paragraph set in 10-pt. type has a leading value of 12 pts. if the Auto Leading value is 120%. The Single Word Justification menu offers the same functions as the Justification buttons in the Paragraph palette.

Orphans are generally acceptable, but widows are not. You should avoid both when possible, but it's better to create an orphan than to leave the widow. You might also consider recomposing the paragraph to either add another line to the widow, or to move the widow back to the page containing the rest of the paragraph.

Some people might call a single word or the end of a hyphenated word that sits alone on the last line of a paragraph a widow, but it's not. Still, it's a good idea to avoid leaving the "stub" of a hyphenated word, or a word shorter than 4–5 letters, by itself on the last line.

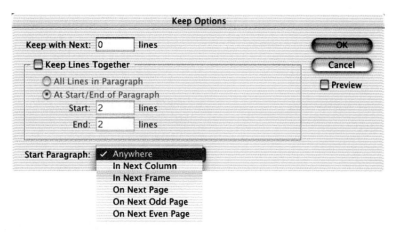

Keep Options dialog box showing Start Paragraph options.

Keep Options can be very useful in some situations. They can prevent some unattractive composition errors, but can introduce others, so it's best to use these settings with care. Keep with Next forces a paragraph (such as a headline) to stay with the number of lines stipulated in the following paragraph. Keep Lines Together refers to a single paragraph. It protects against the first line of a paragraph falling at the bottom of a page or column (known as an "orphan"), or the last line being forced to the next page or column (known as a "widow"). Paragraphs may start anywhere, or they may be forced to the next column or the next threaded frame. They may also be forced to the next page, the next odd page, or the next even page. These functions replicate the various Break characters described earlier.

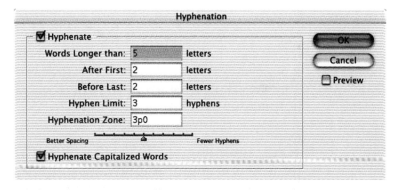

Hyphenation options dialog box, showing the hyphenation slider near the bottom.

Automatic hyphenation is controlled on a paragraph-by-paragraph basis through the Hyphenation options, but you may manually override any automatic hyphenation decisions. The minimum length of words that will hyphenate is controlled here, as is the number of letters allowed after and before hyphens. You can also limit the number of hyphens in successive lines — more than three is generally unacceptable. The Hyphenation Zone can be set, although this only affects non-justified text composed by the Single-Line Composer. A Hyphenation Zone is the distance from the right margin or indent in which hyphenation can occur. The hyphenation slider offers you some control over the way the Adobe Paragraph Composer considers hyphenations when composing a paragraph. The Better Spacing option creates more hyphens but generally produces better composition, and the Fewer Hyphens option gives the Composer fewer options because it limits flexibility in composing a paragraph. You can control automatic hyphenation of capitalized words; capitalized words are not usually hyphenated because they are often proper nouns, but this option is turned on by default.

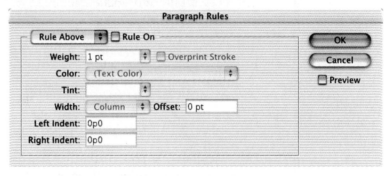

In a pop-up menu in the Paragraph Rules dialog box, you can choose whether a rule appears above or below the text.

Generally accepted composition rules require at least three letters to be left after the hyphen and two before. For example, "ac-tually" is acceptable, but "actual-ly" is not. It is also bad form to leave the ending of a broken word as the last line of a paragraph.

Instead of drawing lines under or over paragraphs with the Line tool, you can make them a part of the paragraph using InDesign's Paragraph Rules options. You can stipulate the rule's weight, the distance above or below the text, whether the stroke overprints colors below, the color, and the tint. You can also define whether the rule is to be the width of the column or of the text, its position relative to the baseline, and its indents or outdents.

Setting Tabs

Press Command/ Control-Shift-T to open the Tabs palette.

Tabs are a very common type element and you must learn how to use them correctly. Many users make the mistake of using the Spacebar to align columns of text, which results in wavy columns and looks unprofessional. The Tabs palette is accessed by selecting Type>Tabs; if you're working on a text frame at the time, the palette positions itself above the frame. In most cases, you can exactly position the Tabs palette at the top of a frame by selecting the frame, then clicking the magnet icon at the right edge of the palette. (This won't work, however, if your current page view is magnified to the point where the frame edges aren't visible.)

Tabs may be used for positioning text in a paragraph, but their primary function is to provide columnar alignment for rows of text.

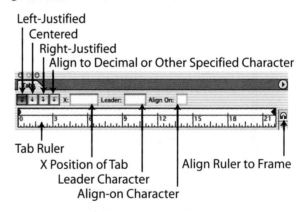

The Tabs palette.

Tabs may align left, center, right, or to a character (the decimal, or period, is the default). A *tab leader* is a series of characters that follow a typed tab and ends at another character, such as a page number preceded by a line of periods in a table of contents. The tab leader may be blank or a combination of multiple characters, including spaces. (Fixed spaces will not work.) It's preferable, however, to create layouts that don't require tab leaders to draw the reader's eyes to the information; for example, instead of setting a table of contents that's as wide as the page, use generous margins to reduce the amount of white space between the contents item and the page number.

The first step in creating tab settings is to determine the number of tabular columns that the table contains. Once you've determined the number of columns, you need to decide on their alignment. To create a tab, click the appropriate location on the Tab ruler. To move a tab, just select it on the Tab ruler and drag it to a new location. To delete a tab, you must select it and drag it above or below the ruler.

Precise tab settings aren't necessary when you first begin typing information — just set them at approximate positions. When the Tab key is pressed, the selected text moves to the positions defined in the Tab menu. After the text is typed, if tab settings are not positioned where you wish, select the affected text and reposition the tabs. InDesign interactively applies your tab settings, so you immediately see the effects of your changes.

In the next exercise, you will apply paragraph and tab formatting to create a professional-looking invoice form.

Format an Invoice Header

1. Open the document **invoice.indd** from your **RF_Intro_InDesign** folder.

2. Select Type>Show Hidden Characters. Take a moment to see how the document is put together. It looks like a mess, but you'll take care of that. The Character and Paragraph palettes should be available.

3. All of the text is set in ATC Mai Tai normal. Select the word "Invoice" in the first line and style it as 30 pt. with auto-leading.

4. Select "N° 536" and change the size to 8 pt. Note that text with a smaller point size in the same line always stays on the baseline.

5. Select the entire second line and change the size to 8 pt., auto-leading.

6. Select the first line, and set the Space After field to 9 pt.

Invoice · N°: 536¶

Please Retain this Document for your Records¶

7. Save the file as **invoice.indd** in your **Work_In_Progress** folder, and leave it open for the next exercise.

Create a Shaded Heading

1. Click the cursor in the second line. Select Paragraph Rules from the Paragraph palette Options menu. Check the "Preview" box if it's not already on.

Press Command-Option-I (Macintosh) or Control-Alt-I (Windows) to show or hide hidden characters.

2. With Rule Above selected, click the Rule On button. Make the weight 14 pt. and the color black. Because the text is also black, you can't see it anymore. Set the Tint field to 20% to make a gray rule. Make the Offset –4 pt. You can control the vertical position of a rule with the offset. Click OK.

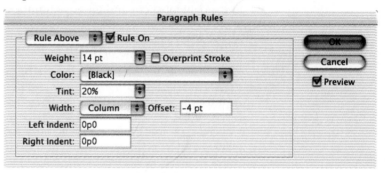

The second line now looks like this:

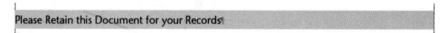

Please Retain this Document for your Records¶

3. Save, and leave the file open for the next exercise.

Apply Tabs

1. Select the next five lines (starting with "Sold To:" down to the line with the phone numbers).

2. Activate the Tab palette (Type>Tabs, or press Command/Control-Shift-T). Move the Tab palette above the selected text, or click the magnet icon at the right side of the Tab palette to precisely position the palette over the selected text.

3. Click the right-aligned tab icon, then move the cursor over the tick marks in the ruler area. Notice that the cursor turns into a hand, which lets you scroll the ruler. Move the cursor just above the ruler area; it changes to an arrow pointer. Click the mouse to set an initial tab, then drag the tab marker toward the right margin until the X value reads 27p0.

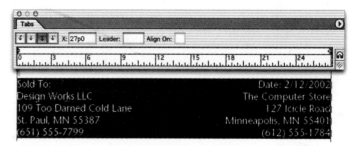

4. Select the next line starting with "Item N°" and apply the same shaded rule to it that you applied in Create a Shaded Heading.

5. Set the Space After field to 9 pt.

6. Select this line and the four lines following it (the list of items purchased).

7. Using the Tab palette, set a left tab at 3p6, and another left tab at 21p0. Notice the vertical black line that appears when you drag a tab marker along the tab ruler. This is a great visual aid for placing tabs.

8. Click the decimal tab icon and set a decimal tab at 18p0, and another at 25p0. Note how the prices align along the decimal point.

9. The shaded Items heading needs some refinement. Click anywhere in this line, then click the tab marker over the word "Price." Click the right-aligned tab marker to convert this left-aligned tab to a right tab, and move it to 19p0.

10. Click the tab marker over the word "Quantity" and change this left-aligned tab to a centered tab. Now change "Quantity" to the more space-efficient "Qty." Move the tab marker until "Qty." is centered over the values, approximately 21p0.

11. Right-align the tab for the word "Ext." visually using the black tab marker bar. It should be located near 26p2.

Item Nº	Description		Price	Qty.		Ext.
8528	» Power Macintosh G4 867MHz	»	$2495.00	» 1	»	$2495.00¶
8942	» Apple Studio Display 17″ LCD	»	$995.00	» 1	»	$995.00¶
7230	» Apple iPod MP3 player	»	$399.00	» 1	»	$399.00¶
2752	» Harmon-Kardon SoundSticks	»	$299.00	» 1	»	$299.00¶

12. Place the cursor in the "Subtotal:" line. Set the Space Before field to 9 pt., and apply a gray-shaded rule like the two you've already made.

13. Select the subtotal, tax, and total lines, and set a decimal tab at 25p0. There's no tab character present in the text, so type a tab before the dollar amounts on each line.

14. Place the cursor in the "Total:" line and apply shaded rule to it, with a tint value of 50%.

Subtotal:	$4188.00
MN State Sales Tax @ 6.5%:	$272.22
TOTAL DUE	$4460.22

15. Style the "Terms:" line as 8/auto, 9 pt. Space After, centered.

16. Style the last paragraph of legalese as 8/auto, justified.

The finished invoice should look like this:

Invoice Nº: 536

Please Retain this Document for your Records

Sold To:	Date: 2/12/2002
Design Works LLC	The Computer Store
109 Too Darned Cold Lane	127 Icicle Road
St. Paul, MN 55387	Minneapolis, MN 55401
(651) 555-7799	(612) 555-1784

Item Nº	Description	Price	Qty.	Ext.
8528	Power Macintosh G4 867MHz	$2495.00	1	$2495.00
8942	Apple Studio Display 17″ LCD	$995.00	1	$995.00
7230	Apple iPod MP3 player	$399.00	1	$399.00
2752	Harmon-Kardon SoundSticks	$299.00	1	$299.00

Subtotal:	$4188.00
MN State Sales Tax @ 6.5%:	$272.22
TOTAL DUE	$4460.22

Terms: 2/10, Net 30.

All invoices are due and payable upon receipt, unless other payment terms have been arranged in advance and are stipulated. In no event shall credit be extended for more than thirty (30) days. Delivery of product(s) is F.O.B. Minneapolis, MN.

17. Save the document to your **Work_In_Progress** folder, then close the document. You now have an invoice form that's easily modified for future use.

PRINT

Importing and Exporting Text Files

Often you will not type the bulk of your text into InDesign; it's more likely that you'll import it from a file created in a word-processing program such as Microsoft Word, or from a file containing raw, unformatted text.

InDesign has import filters for a variety of text formats:

- Microsoft Word and Excel 97, 2000, XP (Windows)
- Microsoft Word and Excel 98, 2001, X (Macintosh)
- WordPerfect 6.1–8.0
- RTF (Rich Text Format)
- Tagged Plain Text (ASCII)
- Plain Text (ASCII)

You can define the Import options when you import (or place) a text file. Options vary, depending upon which word-processing program was used to produce the text file.

You can place a file by choosing File>Place (Command/Control-D) to show the Place dialog box:

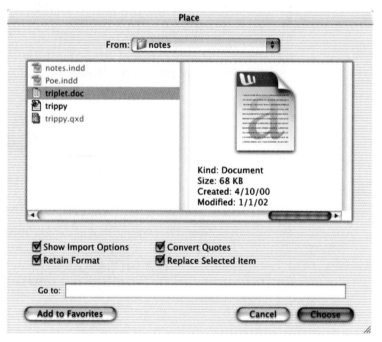

The Place dialog box (MacOS X).

After you select a file to place, the current cursor changes to a "loaded" icon, indicating there's something that needs to be placed.

If any text in your document is highlighted in pink, it was originally set in a font that's not installed on your computer.

If the loaded icon is clicked within the live area, but not over a text frame, the text flows the width of the live area (from left to right margin), starting from where you initially click the loaded icon to the bottom of the page.

If you click the loaded text icon over a frame on the page, the text flows into the frame. You can also create a new frame and place the text by clicking the loaded icon and dragging to create a frame.

InDesign presents a Missing Fonts dialog box if the file you are importing uses fonts that aren't available on your computer.

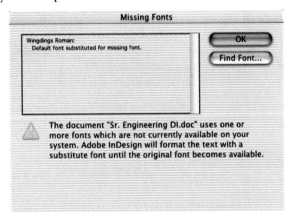

The Missing Fonts dialog box.

Clicking the Find Font button presents a list of all fonts in the document, missing or not, and gives you the ability to replaced missing fonts with any of the available fonts on your computer. Missing fonts are displayed with a yellow triangle next to the name. You can always replace missing fonts later by choosing Type>Find Font once the document is open.

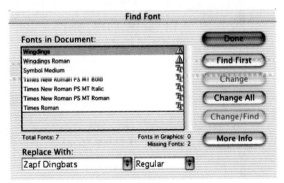

The Find Font dialog box.

You may also export text in a number of formats. To do this, you need to click the Type tool in the frame that contains the text you want to export, choose File>Export (Command/Control-E) to display the Export dialog box, and then select the export file format. The options are:

- Adobe InDesign Tagged Text
- Rich Text Format
- Text-only

Adobe InDesign Tagged Text is a text-only format that uses proprietary formatting tags and codes, similar in concept to an XML tagging schema, that InDesign can interpret when this text is imported. Rich Text Format is a similar concept, used primarily with Microsoft applications and with text documents in Mac OS X. Text-only is plain, unformatted, "raw" text that can be opened with nearly any application, pasted into an email, and so forth, but which lacks any formatting information.

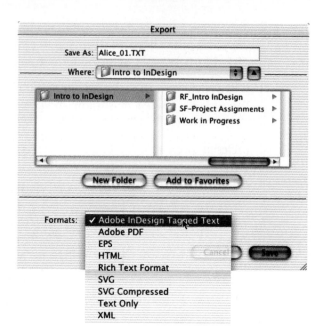

The Export dialog box, showing all available export file formats.

Even though there are more file formats displayed in the Export dialog box, only the three listed above export a file containing editable text in a format that most word processors can read. The other formats export the entire document or page. Here, we just want to export the text of the document, not the entire document.

Linked Text Files

Text placed into an InDesign document contains a link to the original file. The link is not automatically updated when the original file is altered, but it may be manually updated through the Links Manager. This can be especially useful when importing files containing dynamic data, such as price lists. If the updated text is altered much, however, the document may reflow and cause a big mess. You should update text links with caution.

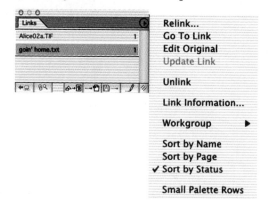

The Update Link option is grayed-out because the text file hasn't been altered. If it had, this option would be available.

Using the Unlink option on the Links palette effectively embeds the text within the InDesign document and breaks the link; InDesign does not notice any updates to the text file.

Threaded Text

As we mentioned earlier, sometimes text does not fit in a frame and becomes overset. In most cases, you are not able to simply resize the frame or the type, as we did earlier. When that is the case, the text must be linked to another frame. This is accomplished by clicking the Out port (the red "+" sign at the lower right) with the Selection tool. The cursor changes to a loaded text icon. You can then simply drag the icon to form another text frame, while holding the mouse button. When you release the button, the previously overset text fills the new frame. You can repeat this process as needed until the text is no longer overset. You can also thread text to an existing frame, as long as there isn't any text already in it; any text in a frame is replaced by the threaded text.

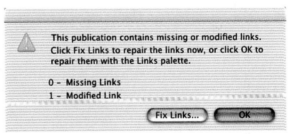

Text that is threaded flows from frame to frame. You can see this when you access View>Show Text Threads. This story still has overset text.

Place and Thread Text

1. Open the file **alice_01.indd** from your **RF_Intro_InDesign** folder. Click the Fix Links button if this warning dialog appears. (The linked items are present in the **RF_Intro_InDesign** folder, but the link can sometimes be broken when files are copied from the CD. Clicking Fix Links relinks the items.)

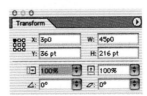

2. Select the Type tool, hold down the mouse button, and drag a text frame to the following dimensions:

   X: 3p0   Y: 36 pt   W: 45p0   H: 216 pt

   You can also draw a text frame anywhere, then switch to the Selection tool, click the frame, and adjust the dimensions in the Transform palette. Remember to reset the proxy reference point to the top left.

3. Choose File>Place and select **chapter_1.txt** from your **RF_Intro_InDesign** folder. The Show Import Options, Retain Format, and Convert Quotes boxes should all be checked. (If you elect to Show Preview (Mac OS 9 only; this option cannot be disabled in Mac OS X), you'll notice that the "text" contains a lot of code. This is because the file you're placing is an InDesign Tagged Text file.) Click Choose/Open.

4. The InDesign Tagged Text Import Options box appears. Select Tagged File Definition and ensure that the Show List of Problem Tags before Place box is checked. This is useful if any tags have been improperly entered. Click OK.

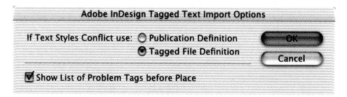

The placed text flows into the text frame.

CHAPTER I

Down the Rabbit-Hole

Alice was beginning to get very tired of sitting by her sister on the bank, and of having nothing to do: once or twice she had peeped into the book her sister was reading, but it had no pictures or conversations in it, 'and what is the use of a book,' thought Alice 'without pictures or conversation?'

So she was considering in her own mind (as well as she could, for the hot day made her feel very sleepy and stupid), whether the pleasure of making a daisy-chain would be worth the trouble of getting up and picking the daisies, when suddenly a White Rabbit with pink eyes ran close by her.

There was nothing so very remarkable in that; nor did Alice think it so very much out of the way to hear the Rabbit say to itself, 'Oh dear! Oh dear! I shall be late!' (when she thought it over afterwards, it occurred to her that she ought to have wondered at this, but at the time it all seemed quite natural); but when the Rabbit actually took a watch out of its waistcoat-pocket,

5. Notice that the Out port of the frame displays a red "+". This tells us there is more text to flow. Click the port with the Selection tool. The cursor changes to a loaded text icon.

6. Drag a text frame as follows:

   X: 3p0   Y: 264 pt   W: 20p0   H: 492 pt

   When you release the mouse button, the text fills the frame, and you can see there is still more text to place. (Adjust the size of the frame using the Transform palette, if necessary.)

7. Click the Out port and drag another text frame as follows:

   X: 24p0   Y: 264 pt   W: 24p0   H: 492 pt

   Release the button to fill the frame with text. Adjust the size of the frame in the Transform palette, if necessary. There may be more text to place.

8. Select the Type tool, place the cursor anywhere in the frame, and select all of the text in the story.

9. The word "hedge" might appear alone on the last line of the third paragraph, depending on your computer. Remember, Mac OS and Windows can exhibit slight differences in character metrics.

and looked at it, and then hurried on, Alice started to her feet, for it flashed across her mind that she had never before seen a rabbit with either a waistcoat-pocket, or a watch to take out of it, and burning with curiosity, she ran across the field after it, and fortunately was just in time to see it pop down a large rabbit-hole under the hedge.

This example is from Mac OS X.

InDesign can flow text slightly differently on Windows and Macintosh computers because of minor variations in how the fonts are built for each platform. Using OpenType fonts eliminates this effect, because the fonts are identical on both platforms.

You don't want single-word paragraph endings unless it's absolutely impossible to get rid of them. There are a few ways of doing this; because ATC fonts do not have kerning pairs, you can try Optical auto-kerning instead of Metrics. You could also try applying small amounts of positive or negative tracking to the paragraph, or adjusting the letter-spacing and glyph-scaling options in the Justification dialog box (located on the Options menu of the Paragraph palette), if changing the automatic kerning method didn't work. Apply the Optical kerning option to the text from the Character palette. Apply Optical kerning anyway even if the single-word line doesn't appear on your system.

> looked at it, and then hurried on, Alice started to her feet, for it flashed across her mind that she had never before seen a rabbit with either a waistcoat-pocket, or a watch to take out of it, and burning with curiosity, she ran across the field after it, and fortunately was just in time to see it pop down a large rabbit-hole under the hedge.
> In another moment down went Alice after it,

10. Save and close the document.

Summary

You have learned the properties of text frames, including columns, insets, and first baselines. You have learned to format text and paragraphs, how to find and insert special characters, and how to exploit the advanced typographic features of OpenType. You have seen how to manage text in frames by enlarging the frame, linking frames, and by working with the text itself to achieve a better fit. Now you're ready to go on to some more advanced text features that make working with text even easier.

Complete Project A: Central Market Ad

5 *Styles*

Chapter Objective:

InDesign offers a number of shortcuts you can use when you are working with text. You can save time by creating, applying, and editing styles; new styles can be based on existing styles or created independently. This chapter discusses how styles interact with each other and with other elements in InDesign documents. In Chapter 5, you will:

- Understand what style sheets are and how they can make production work extremely efficient.

- Learn how to define and use character styles to change attributes such as font, font size, leading, kerning, and color of selected text.

- Learn how to define and use paragraph styles to change attributes such as indents and spacing, drop caps, justification, tabs, hyphenation, rules, and keep options.

- Understand when to create a new style and when to base one style on another, as well as how to edit an existing style.

Projects to be Completed:

- Central Market Ad (A)

- Yellow Rose Menu (B)

- Travel Brochure (C)

- Good Choices Newsletter (D)

Styles

When you're building a document with more than a few paragraphs of copy, you will find yourself spending a great deal of time formatting the text. Styles allow you to format either characters or entire paragraphs with a single click or keystroke, eliminating the need to apply each attribute individually. You can also edit styles and apply the changes throughout the document quickly.

You can create character and paragraph styles by formatting a paragraph or text selection, then using that formatted text to create a named style in the Character Styles or Paragraph Styles palette. Later, you can apply the named styles to other paragraphs or text elements by selecting the desired style from the appropriate palette or by using keyboard shortcuts.

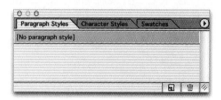

By default, Character Styles and Paragraph Styles palettes are included in the same panel as the Swatches palette, unless you've rearranged the palettes (expanded to show all three palette tabs).

Press "F11" to toggle Paragraph Styles and Shift-F11 to toggle Character Styles.

Styles can contain predefined settings for almost any available attribute. Character styles may include font, size, color, and other character attributes. Paragraph styles may include character attributes plus any information available from the Paragraph palette, including alignment, tabs, and rules. Character styles may be based on other character styles, and paragraph styles may be based on other paragraph styles.

Styles are used to their best advantage when working with long, text-intensive documents that have recurring editorial elements, such as headlines, subheads, captions, sidebars, and so forth. They are useful for documents on which several people work concurrently, such as books with different chapters composed by different individuals. They are also useful in documents with specific, recurring stylistic requirements, such as catalogs. In cases such as these, styles ensure consistency in text and paragraph formatting throughout a publication. This book — with its variety of headers, body copy, and sidebars — is an example of a document that benefits from the use of styles. Styles ensure that similar editorial elements are treated with design consistency throughout the document.

Another major advantage of using styles is the ease with which changes can be made to all text defined as a particular style. For example, with a few keystrokes in the character style definition dialog box, you can modify a headline style that appears many times in one publication to change the font size from 24 to 28 pts., or you can change a run-in head that appears a hundred or more times in a book from red to green. All text marked with the style that you modify changes instantly.

Character Styles vs. Paragraph Styles

Character styles only operate on selected text in a paragraph. Paragraph styles affect one or more paragraphs. If you click an insertion point in a paragraph, then change to a different style, the entire paragraph is changed to the specifications in the new style. This means you don't need to select any text in the paragraph to change its style.

character style is typically used as a subset of a paragraph style. For example, a paragraph style might be defined to set the paragraph in Adobe Garamond, 10/12, justified, with various Keep options, lock to baseline, and more. These are attributes that can only apply to paragraphs and not to characters. You could create a character style as a companion to the paragraph style that changes typographic attributes of selected text in a paragraph (for example, that sets text to Adobe Garamond Bold, or applies OpenType option such as fractions or contextual ligatures). You could also create a character style for run-in heads that affects color, size, or font without affecting the entire paragraph. Character styles override paragraph styles.

Character Styles

It may be helpful to consider a character style as the primary building block of all elements in a document. Let's take a look at how a character style is constructed. The Character Styles Options pop-up menu offers a number of choices; if you choose New Style, there is a series of options available in a list to the left of the New Character Style dialog: General, Basic Character Formats, Advanced Character Formats, Character Color, and OpenType Features.

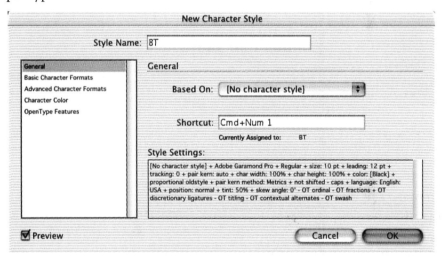

The New Character Style dialog box uses the options at the left to define styles interactively

The name assigned to the character style should be a descriptive one. In some cases, you might want to define a character style that is based on an existing paragraph style; the name of the character style should reflect that relationship. If, for example, you create a character style that is identical to the body-text paragraph style called "BT" with the exception of its color, then the character style could be called "BT_blue." You can also assign a keyboard shortcut in the General options pane of the New Character Style dialog, as long as the shortcut isn't already in use by an InDesign command.

With the Basic Character Formats option selected from the list, you can assign the primary character font, style, size, leading, kerning, tracking, case, and position attributes. You may also assign underline, strikethrough, ligature, oldstyle characters, and non-breaking options. These options and others in the New Style dialog box are blank when you first select New Style.

If an element of a character style is left blank, it picks up that characteristic from the style of the paragraph where it is applied. Where there are check box options, a "–" symbol

If you leave a character style attribute blank, that attribute is picked up from the paragraph in which the style is applied, even if that paragraph doesn't have a defined style applied to it.

A "–" symbol (Macintosh) indicates that the character picks up attributes from the underlying paragraph.

A gray checkmark (Windows) indicates that the character picks up attributes from the underlying paragraph.

A checkmark indicates that the attribute is added.

A blank box indicates that the attribute is not applied.

(Macintosh) or a gray "√" checkmark (Windows) indicates that the character style picks up the attribute from the underlying paragraph. A checkmark indicates that the attribute is defined, and a blank check box indicates that the attribute is not defined as part of the character style; you have to manually change these options if you want to apply them. Character styles are most useful when you need to make only a few changes (for example, formatting typed fractions as OpenType Fractions) but otherwise maintain existing the paragraph attributes.

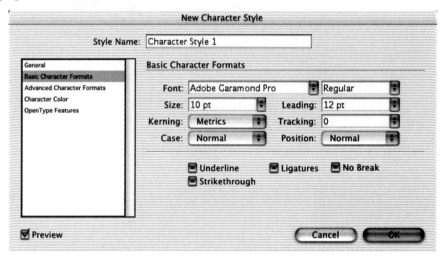

The Basic Character Formats options in the New Character Style dialog box.

The Advanced Character Formats options enable you to scale characters horizontally or vertically, apply a baseline shift, or skew characters (apply false italic). We don't recommend the scale or skew options. You may also select any of the active languages for spelling and hyphenation. A character style is a handy way of changing languages within a paragraph for spelling and hyphenation.

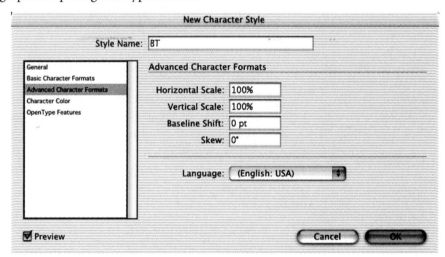

The Advanced Character Formats options in the New Character Style dialog box.

With the Character Color options, you can assign a color from the Swatches palette to the character style. In addition to assigning an overall color to the text, a stroke may be assigned as well. Stroke and fill may be forced to overprint. Generally, it's best not to assign a stroke to text, as it makes the text appear fat and distorted.

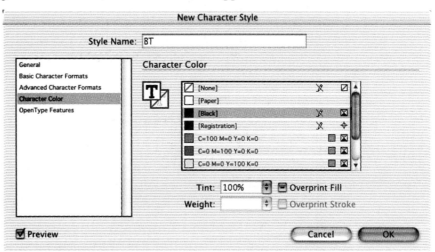

In the illustration above, the fill has been set to black and the stroke has been set with no color — None — applied.

In the OpenType Features panel, you can specify your preferred OpenType options from those available. As we just mentioned, the dash/gray checkmark means that the option derives from the base paragraph style.

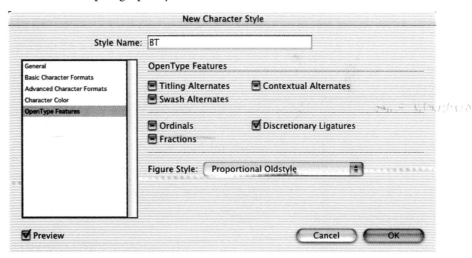

In this example, discretionary ligatures will be applied to selected text. All remaining attributes will be picked up from the underlying paragraph.

A bold, run-in headline in color differentiates the character style in this paragraph from the rest of the paragraph. It is handled through the Character Styles palette and can be applied with a keystroke (assigned by the user), such as Command/Control-1.

If you were to apply these style options manually, without using styles, you would find the process very time-consuming, particularly if you had a number of paragraphs with run-in headlines.

Note the last item in both the Character and Paragraph Options pop-up menu, "Small Palette Rows." This option is helpful when you have a lot of styles, but it makes it easier to click the wrong style because the style names are a lot smaller.

When you create your own styles, you begin to see the real power in publishing. There are two ways to create styles from scratch. The *designer method* involves applying formatting to the text until it looks good to the eye, then using the Type tool to select the text that has the desired characteristics, and creating a new character or paragraph style. All of the attributes thus defined are applied to the new style automatically. The *compositor method* requires creating the styles using the Character Styles and Paragraph Styles palettes. This is the preferred method when you are given typographic specifications. You will use the compositor method in constructing styles in the following series of exercises.

Build Character Styles

1. From the **RF_Intro_InDesign** folder, open the document **working_with _style.indd**. If the document does not open to the first page (the first line is "CHAPTER II"), double-click the Page 1 icon in the Pages palette to go there.

2. If it is not already open, open the Character Styles palette by selecting it from Type>Character Styles or by pressing Shift-F11.

3. Select New Style from the Character Styles Options pop-up menu.

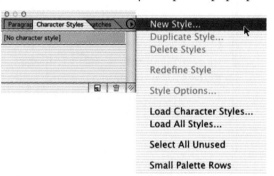

4. Type "Run-in Blue" in the Style Name field. Place the cursor in the Shortcut field and press Command/Control-1 (press the "1" key on your numeric keypad, not on the top row of your keyboard) to assign the shortcut.

Type the number "1" from the numeric keypad on the far right of your keyboard.

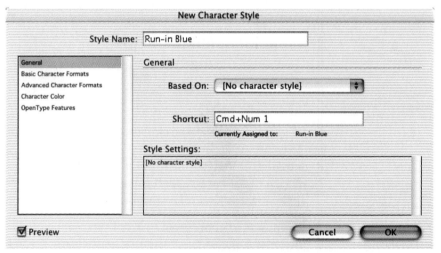

5. Click Basic Character Formats in the list, then define the format as ATC Mai Tai Bold, 12 pt. You can pick up the leading from the paragraph style.

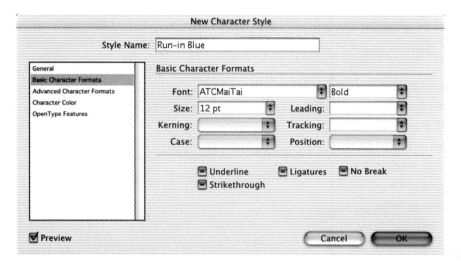

6. Click Character Color in the list. With the Fill icon active, click Pantone 286 CVC to assign this color. Return to the General pane. Note that the Style Setting box displays all of the options that you selected for this character style. Click OK to add the style to the Character Styles palette.

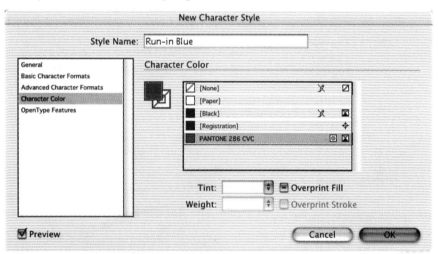

You will apply this style later in the chapter.

7. Save the document to your **Work_In_Progress** folder, and leave it open for the next exercise.

Paragraph Styles

All of the elements that may be applied to a paragraph (refer to Chapter 4, *Working with Text*) may be defined in a paragraph style. They may be entered directly (compositor mode), based on an existing paragraph style definition, or picked up from pre-formatted text (designer mode). We discussed the basics of paragraph formatting in the previous chapter, but it is with paragraph styles that we can harness the true power of the paragraph features.

This book is an example of a document built with styles. All of the headers, body text, lists, and hands-on exercises are formatted with paragraph styles, and with character styles as needed. There are many books in the Against The Clock series, and they all use identical styles, fonts, tab stops, formats, and indents.

As wonderful as the "Next Style" feature is when typing text directly into InDesign, it is of no value when importing text from a word processor. If you are working with imported text, don't waste your time working with the Next Style feature. Instead, use a similar feature on the word-processing software (if it has that capability).

General

Each paragraph style needs its own distinctive name. A paragraph style may have the same name as a character style, and this is often desirable for easy cross-reference. Like character styles, paragraph styles may be assigned keyboard equivalents. For convenience, or to maintain a relationship between styles, a paragraph style may also be based on another paragraph style that has similar character style, leading, or indents.

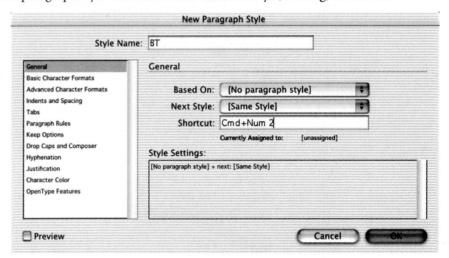

A new paragraph style named "BT" defined; Command-2 (using the "2" from the numeric keypad) was assigned as a shortcut.

A powerful feature of paragraph styles, if text is typed directly into InDesign, is the Next Style menu. For example, an H2 style (level-two headline), may be followed by a BT1 (similar to a BT but with no paragraph indent), followed by a BT. If the Next Style box is checked, the operator would simply select H2, type the headline, press Return/Enter to change to BT1, type the text, press Return/Enter and type in the BT style. The text might look something like this:

H2   **I. Down The Rabbit-hole**

BT1   ALICE was beginning to get very tired of sitting by her sister on the bank, and of having nothing to do: once or twice she had peeped into the book her sister was reading, but it had no pictures or conversations in it, "and what is the use of a book," thought Alice, "without pictures or conversation?" So she was considering in her own mind (as well as she could, for the hot day made her feel very sleepy and stupid) whether the pleasure of making a daisy-chain would be worth the trouble of getting up and picking the daisies, when suddenly a White Rabbit with pink eyes ran close by her.

BT   There was nothing so very remarkable in that; nor did Alice think it so very much out of the way to hear the Rabbit say to itself, "Oh dear! Oh dear! I shall be too late!" (When she thought it over afterwards, it occurred to her that she ought to have wondered at this, but at the time it all seemed quite natural); but when the Rabbit actually took a watch out of its waistcoat pocket, and looked at it, and then hurried on, Alice started to her feet, for it flashed across her mind that she had never before seen a rabbit with either a waistcoat pocket or a watch to take out of it, and burning with curiosity, she ran across the field after it, and fortunately was just in time to see it pop down a large rabbit-hole under the hedge.

Several paragraph features, such as leading and alignment, can be based on another paragraph style. It saves time to base new paragraph styles on existing ones. For example, you may create a document with four styles — Body Text, Body Text-First Paragraph, Bulleted Lists, and Numbered Lists. These may all share the same font and size, but may have different indents, tabs, and space above and below.

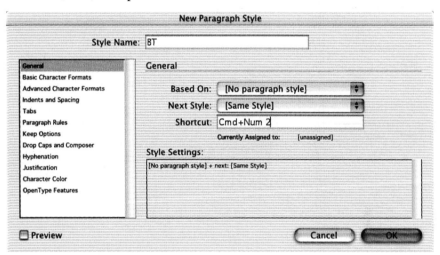

The General options in the New Paragraph Style dialog box.

Basic Character Formats

As in the Character Styles dialog box, the Basic Character Formats options of the Paragraph Styles dialog box enable you to set the character style that is applied to the entire paragraph. The Font, Style, Size, Leading, Kerning, Tracking, Case, and Position settings are all assigned in this pane. In addition, the Underline, Strikethrough, Ligatures, Oldstyle characters, and No Break options are accessed here. (No Break means that the entire paragraph is forced to fit on one line. You will rarely want to use this feature.)

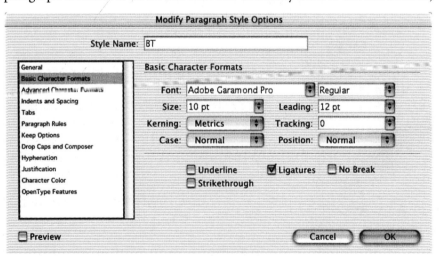

The Basic Character Formats settings in the Modify Paragraph Style Options dialog box.

Advanced Character Formats

Similar to the Advanced Character Formats in the Character Styles palette, these options allow you to specify horizontal and vertical scale, baseline shift, skew (false italics), and language for the entire paragraph. Remember that it's not a good idea to use the Scale and Skew options.

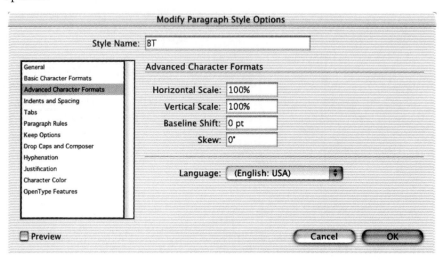

The Advanced Character Formats settings in the Modify Paragraph Style Options dialog box.

Indents and Spacing

Alignment, indents, and spacing are included in this pane. Many of the elements available here should be already familiar to you. Alignment may be Left, Center, Right, Justified (with the last line flushed left, right, or centered), or Full Justified (forcing the last line of the paragraph to both right and left margins). Left and right indentations affect the left and right margins of the paragraph in reference to its text frame. The First Line Indent setting affects the indentation of the first line of the paragraph; this distance is added to the Left Indent setting. The Space Before and Space After settings determine the space that appears in addition to the leading between paragraphs. You may also elect to align a paragraph to the baseline grid; most people leave the baseline grid at its default settings.

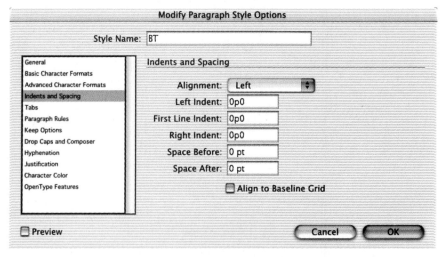

The Indents and Spacing settings in the Modify Paragraph Style Options dialog box.

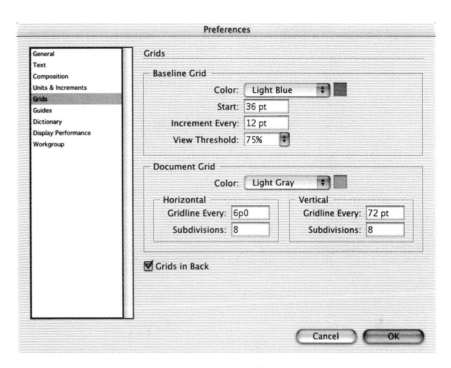

The default grid increment of 12 pt. should be set to half of the leading value of the text you plan to align to the baseline grid. You can only set one baseline grid increment.

Notice how the default baseline grid setting affects the placement of text on the page.

Headline 18/18¶	Headline 18/18¶
Body 10/12 +6pt space above Lor at alis nit at velis nibh esent in enis auguer iriusci sustrud molobor in hendreet autem vel dolore faccum doluptat prat, sendre molor incidui tisi.¶	**Body 10/12 +6pt space above** Lor at alis nit at velis nibh esent in enis auguer iriusci sustrud molobor in hendreet autem vel dolore faccum doluptat prat, sendre molor incidui tisi.¶
Duisi. Lortie commy nit augait prat, velit la feuipsummy nis et, sum zzrilisim diam quis nis dunt aut ver sit am, suscili uisit ad tet at, sequi eugiat. Ut utpate modit ulputat. Duisi tat utet alisl ut volorpe atumsan henim in utpate conse volenim quat luptat lobore molobor secte min velisi.¶	Duisi. Lortie commy nit augait prat, velit la feuipsummy nis et, sum zzrilisim diam quis nis dunt aut ver sit am, suscili uisit ad tet at, sequi eugiat. Ut utpate modit ulputat. Duisi tat utet alisl ut volorpe

The block of text on the left is set with the grid off, the block at the right with the grid on. With these settings, the grid interferes with the design specifications.

Headline 18/18¶	Headline 18/18¶
Body 10/12 +6pt space above Lor at alis nit at velis nibh esent in enis auguer iriusci sustrud molobor in hendreet autem vel dolore faccum doluptat prat, sendre molor incidui tisi.¶	**Body 10/12 +6pt space above** Lor at alis nit at velis nibh esent in enis auguer iriusci sustrud molobor in hendreet autem vel dolore faccum doluptat prat, sendre molor incidui tisi.¶
Duisi. Lortie commy nit augait prat, velit la feuipsummy nis et, sum zzrilisim diam quis nis dunt aut ver sit am, suscili uisit ad tet at, sequi eugiat. Ut utpate modit ulputat. Duisi tat utet alisl ut volorpe atumsan henim in utpate conse volenim quat luptat lobore molobor secte min velisi.¶	Duisi. Lortie commy nit augait prat, velit la feuipsummy nis et, sum zzrilisim diam quis nis dunt aut ver sit am, suscili uisit ad tet at, sequi eugiat. Ut utpate modit ulputat. Duisi tat utet alisl ut volorpe atumsan henim in utpate conse volenim quat luptat

In this example, with the same two text blocks, the baseline grid has been reset to a 6-pt. increment to better work with the body type leading and the 6-pt. space before.

Tabs

Tab settings may be included in a paragraph style. This is particularly useful when tabular data follows a consistent format, as in menus, tables of contents, and some financial tables. The tab location (horizontal position on the line), leader characters, and alignment within the tab area may be set here.

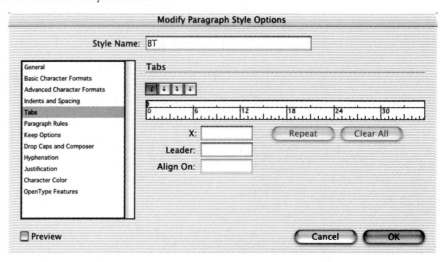

The Tabs settings in the Modify Paragraph Style Options dialog box.

Paragraph Rules

Rules (or lines) are frequently combined with tabs to create effective tables. You can also use rules to create more effective headlines, to better delineate financial elements, or to set off such items as callouts or pull quotes. You can apply rules quickly, easily, and consistently by defining them in a paragraph style.

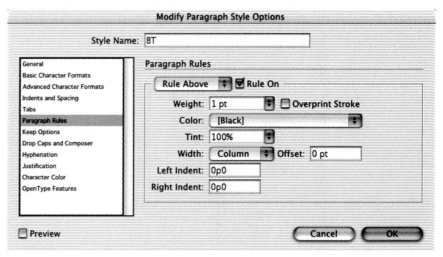

The Paragraph Rules settings in the Modify Paragraph Style Options dialog box.

Keep Options

The Keep options are sometimes thought of as widow and orphan control (see the previous chapter). At least two lines of a paragraph should remain together in running text. There are, however, some types of text (such as headlines, and bulleted or numbered lists) that should keep all lines in the paragraph together whenever practical. Some paragraphs, such as headlines, should also remain with the next paragraph. To ensure that the appropriate elements stay together, you can enter the number of lines in the following paragraph that should be kept with the headline in the Keep with Next ___ Lines field. Paragraphs may start anywhere, or they may be forced to begin on the next column or threaded frame. They may also be forced to the next page, the next odd page, or the next even page. Using the Keep options usually results in uneven columns, so it's often better to eliminate widows with tracking, editing, or adjustments to word spacing.

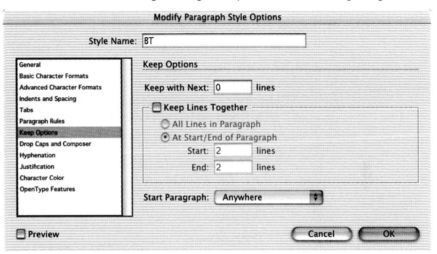

The Keep Options settings in the Modify Paragraph Style Options dialog box.

Drop Caps and Composer

This option allows automatic application of drop caps to a paragraph. You can specify the number of lines for the drop cap and the number of characters that are affected. This is particularly useful when used in conjunction with character styles. The Adobe Paragraph Composer or Adobe Single-line Composer may also be selected here.

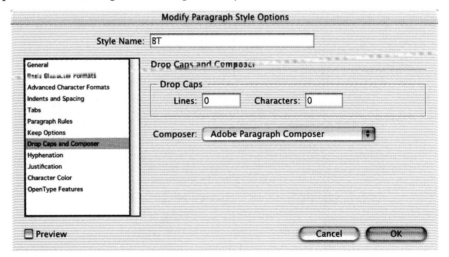

The Drop Caps and Composer settings in the Modify Paragraph Style Options dialog box.

Hyphenation

You can turn the Automatic Hyphenation option on or off, and specify the length (in number of characters) of the shortest word to be hyphenated. You can also stipulate the number of hyphens that can appear in sequence. Using too many hyphens creates an appearance called a "ladder" and is very distracting. Many publishing standards set this number at two or three. Advertising standards usually allow no more than one (and that with caution). The Hyphenation Zone determines how close to the end of a line the text must come before a hyphen is inserted. Hyphenation is inserted only if the previous word ends before the Hyphenation Zone begins and there is an acceptable hyphenation point within the word. The Hyphenation Zone only applies to text that is not justified to both margins and when the Adobe Single-Line Composer is used. A Hyphenation Zone value of "0" means there is no zone, and InDesign hyphenates according to all other hyphenation criteria, or wraps the entire word to the next line. The Hyphenation Zone should be considered carefully, taking into consideration the overall line length and type size. A zone of 3 picas (the default) may be appropriate for 12-pt. type on a 22-pica line, but entirely inappropriate for 9-pt. type on a 10-pica line.

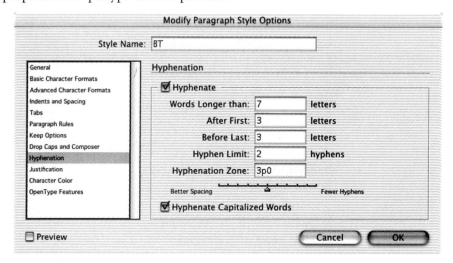

The Hyphenation settings in the Modify Paragraph Style Options dialog box.

Generally speaking, it is not proper to hyphenate capitalized words. If a document has very short lines and includes many long proper nouns, however, allowing them to break is often a good idea — the page looks a lot better. The Hyphenate Capitalized Words check box is at the bottom of this pane.

Justification

The Justification option controls InDesign's automatic features —the Word Spacing, Letter Spacing, and Glyph Scaling options — for making lines fit to avoid excessive hyphenation. This is also the pane where you can define the percentage for Auto Leading (by default, Auto Leading is set to 120% of the type size). Generally speaking, the Auto Leading option should not be used; if a character from another font or a graphic is inserted in a line, the automatic adjustments create uneven line spacing.

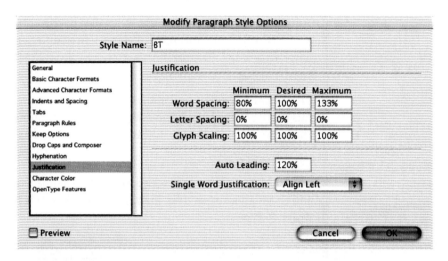

The Justification settings in the Modify Paragraph Style Options dialog box.

To properly justify a line or a paragraph of type, both word spacing and letter spacing, as well as the interplay between them, must be taken into consideration. The default word space allows InDesign to crunch word space to 80% of what the designer intended, and to stretch it to 133% when copy is justified.

You can define values for Minimum, Desired, and Maximum spacing. Word space percentages are expressed as a percentage of the word space designed into the font. Letter space percentages are based on the between-character space designed into the font; you should avoid adjusting letter spacing at all costs. InDesign always tries to give the desired spacing. If the Adobe Paragraph Composer is used, InDesign looks ahead several lines and apply the parameters defined here to make each line fit.

To the door of an inn in the provincial town of N. there drew up a smart britchka—a light spring-carriage of the sort affected by bachelors, retired lieutenant-colonels, staff-captains, land-owners possessed of about a hundred souls, and, in short, all persons who rank as gentlemen of the intermediate category. In the britchka was seated such a gentleman—a man who, though not handsome, was not ill-favoured, not over-fat, and not over-thin. Also, though not over-elderly, he was not over-young. His arrival produced no stir in the town, and was accompanied by no particular incident, beyond that a couple of peasants who happened to be standing at the door of a dramshop exchanged a few comments with reference to the equipage rather than to the individual who was seated in it. "Look at that carriage," one of them said to the other. "Think you it will be going as far as Moscow?" "I think it will," replied his companion. "But not as far as Kazan, eh?" "No, not as far as Kazan."

Fully justified text with Minimum, Desired, and Maximum Word Spacing settings of 50%, 100%, and 150%.

To the door of an inn in the provincial town of N. there drew up a smart britchka—a light spring-carriage of the sort affected by bachelors, retired lieutenant-colonels, staff-captains, land-owners possessed of about a hundred souls, and, in short, all persons who rank as gentlemen of the intermediate category. In the britchka was seated such a gentleman—a man who, though not handsome, was not ill-favoured, not over-fat, and not over-thin. Also, though not over-elderly, he was not over-young. His arrival produced no stir in the town, and was accompanied by no particular incident, beyond that a couple of peasants who happened to be standing at the door of a dramshop exchanged a few comments with reference to the equipage rather than to the individual who was seated in it. "Look at that carriage," one of them said to the other. "Think you it will be going as far as Moscow?" "I think it will," replied his companion. "But not as far as Ka-

Fully justified text with Minimum, Desired, and Maximum Word Spacing settings of 95%, 100%, and 105%.

Although character spacing can be managed using tracking, this should be approached with caution. Tracking in InDesign compresses letter space in addition to compressing word space; this is usually undesirable.

You can see from these two examples that justification settings can cause major differences in line breaks and word spacing. These differences are magnified when working in narrow columns. As columns narrow, you should expect to be more forgiving in your word-spacing specifications.

The Glyph Scaling option allows InDesign to compress or expand the actual letterform. If this feature is used at all, the scaling percentages should be minimal. In order of preference, you should adjust justification, tracking, and as a last resort, glyph scaling.

Character Color

The Character Color options enable you to define the color of the type in the paragraph, and to assign a stroke to it, if appropriate (although it's rarely appropriate to apply a stroke to type).

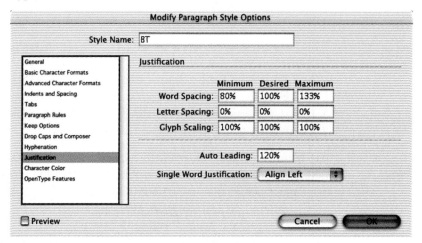

The Character Color settings in the Modify Paragraph Style Options dialog box.

OpenType Features

With the OpenType Features options, you can apply features present in OpenType fonts (see Chapter 4 for more information). You can also specify a default figure (numeral) style from the pop-up menu. For body text, Proportional Oldstyle is the preferred figure style; Tabular Lining is better for tabular material.

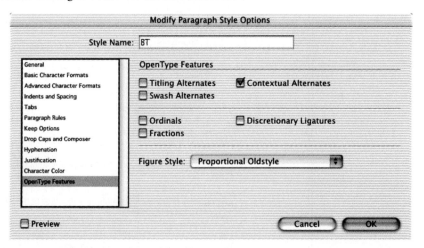

The OpenType Features settings in the Modify Paragraph Style Options dialog box.

Create the Body Text Paragraph Style

1. If it is not already open, open the **working_with_style.indd** file from your **Work_In_Progress** folder. Nothing should be selected in the document.

2. Click the Paragraph Styles tab.

3. Select New Style from the Options pop-up menu to access the General pane in the Modify Paragraph Style Options dialog box that appears.

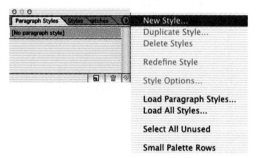

4. In the Style Name field, type "Body Text". Click once in the Shortcut field and press Command/Control-2 (use the "2" from the numeric keypad, not from the top row of the keyboard) to assign it as the shortcut.

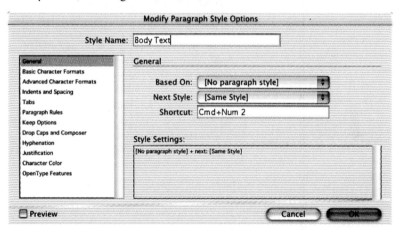

5. In the Basic Character Formats pane, select ATC Cabana Normal, 12 pt., with a Leading of 15 pt. (12/15), and Optical kerning.

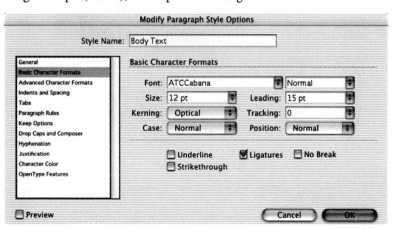

6. Do not apply any Advanced Character Formats. In the Indents and Spacing pane, set Alignment to Left Justify and First Line Indent to 1p6. Leave everything else at zero. Leave Align to Baseline Grid unchecked.

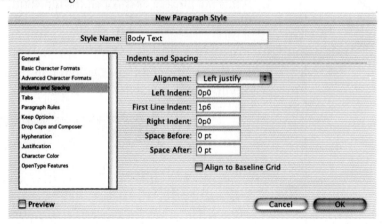

7. In the Keep Options pane, check the Keep Lines Together box, and enter "2" for both Start and End Lines.

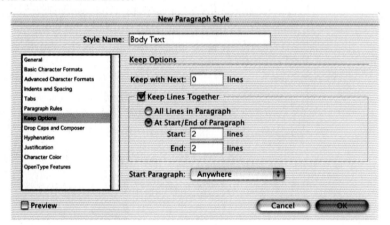

8. In the Hyphenation panel, uncheck Hyphenate Capitalized Words.

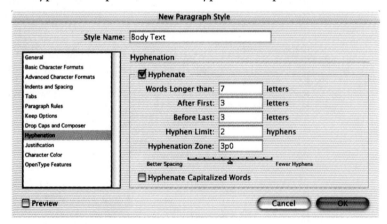

9. Set the Character Color to black.

10. Back in the General panel, note the information in the Style Settings field. Click OK.

11. Save, and leave the document open for the next exercise.

Create the Chapter Number Style

1. Select New Style from the Paragraph Styles Options pop-up menu. Be certain that you are using [No Paragraph Style] as the basis for your new style.

2. Name the style "Chapter Number". Do not assign it a shortcut.

3. Choose Basic Character Formats and assign ATC Mai Tai Bold, 12/15, Optical kerning.

If you aren't basing a new style on an existing style, it's best to select [No Paragraph Style] as the Based On option. Otherwise, you may include unwanted elements in your new style.

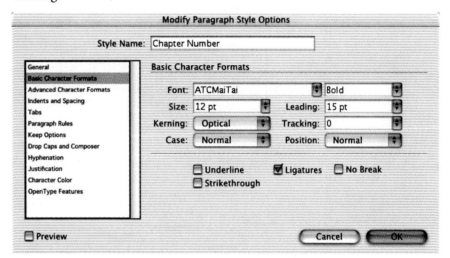

4. Select Indents and Spacing. Set the Alignment to Left (the default). All Indents and Space Before and After fields should be set to zero.

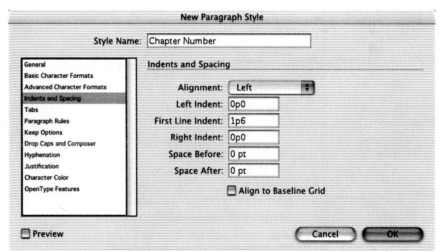

5. Click Paragraph Rules. Turn the Rule Above option on. Assign it a weight of 2 pt., a color of Pantone 286 CVC, and an offset of 12 pt.

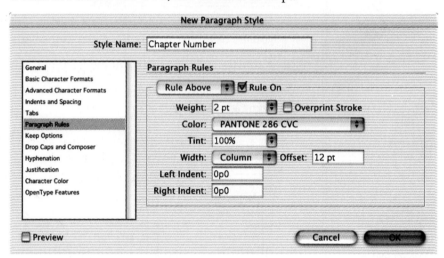

6. Click Keep Options, and set the Start Paragraph field to On Next Odd Page.

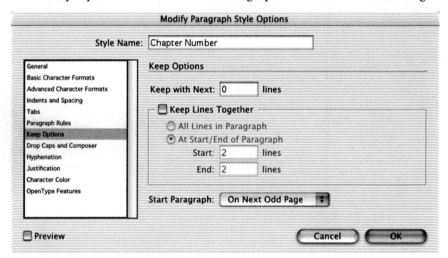

7. Select Hyphenation from the list and uncheck Hyphenate.

8. Set the Character Color to black. Click OK.

9. Save, and leave the file open for the next exercise.

Create the Chapter Name Style

1. Create another new paragraph style. Name this style "Chapter Name".

2. Select Basic Character Formats; assign ATC Cabana Heavy Italic, 18/30, and Optical kerning.

3. In the Indents and Spacing pane, set Alignment to Left and Space After to 30 pt. Indents and Space Before should be set to zero.

4. From the Paragraph Rules panel, be certain Rule Above is unchecked. Turn Rule Below on. Assign it a weight of 2 pt., a color of Pantone 286, and an offset of 6 pt.

5. In the Keep Options panel, keep all lines in the paragraph together. The paragraph may start anywhere.

6. In the Hyphenation panel, uncheck the Hyphenate box.

7. Assign black as the Character Color. Click OK.

8. Save the document and leave it open for the next exercise.

Create Styles Based on One Another

1. Continue in the open document. Click the Body Text style to highlight it, and create a new paragraph style. Name it "Body Text 1". Note that the style is automatically based on Body Text. Set the Shortcut to Command/Control-0 (zero, using the keypad "0").

When you base a new style on an existing style, InDesign picks up all of the attributes of the existing style, so make sure you turn off or adjust any attributes that you don't want in the new style.

InDesign styles can inherit attributes from "parent" styles; when shared attributes are changed in the parent style, they are also changed in the "child" style.

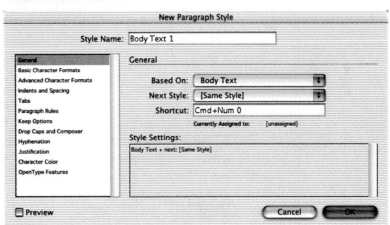

2. Select Indents and Spacing, and set the First Line Indent to 0p0. Click OK.

That's all it takes to set up a new style based on another. Now set up another style, based on Body Text 1.

3. Click Body Text 1 and select New Style.

4. Name the style "Poem".

5. Click Indents and Spacing. Set the Alignment to Left, Left Indent to 3p0, and Space Before to 6 pt.

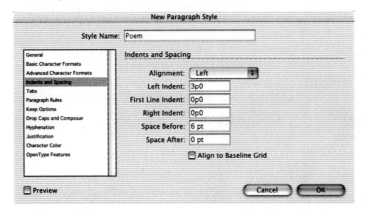

6. Click Keep Options. Click the All Lines in Paragraph button. Click OK.

7. Click the Poem style, and create a new style named "Poem Last".

8. Click Indents and Spacing and add Space After of 6 pt. to the current definition. Click OK.

   Your Paragraph Styles palette should look like this:

9. Save the document and leave it open for the next exercise.

Editing Existing Styles

You may discover that you made a mistake when you created a style, or (more likely) someone else may change the design parameters. Editing an existing style is easy — but you must be aware of the structure of the document's styles before making wholesale changes. Before you edit anything, you need to ensure that the style you're going to change doesn't have other styles dependent on it (unless you intend to similarly alter them as well). After you're confident that you won't hopelessly ruin the document, you can select the style to alter (by double-clicking its name) and make the necessary changes; clicking Save stores the changes.

Edit Styles

To remove local style overrides and revert back to the style specifications, you can select the text or paragraph, press Option/Alt, and then click the name of the desired style in the appropriate palette. This works for both character and paragraph styles.

1. Click the Poem style and select Style Options (or simply double-click the style name) to open it.

2. Navigate to Basic Character Formats. Change the font to ATC Coral Reef Regular. Click OK.

3. Open the Poem Last style and navigate to Basic Character Formats. You'll notice that it has already been changed to ATC Coral Reef Regular. This is because you based this style on the Poem style. This is an example of the parent-child relationship in styles derived from other styles. Click OK to close the style.

4. Save the document and leave it open for the next exercise.

Using the Styles Palettes to Apply Styles

There is a difference between the ways in which character styles and paragraph styles are applied. To apply a character style, all the characters to which the style is to be applied must be selected (highlighted). If you miss a letter, the style is not applied to it. After selecting the text, you need to click the name of the character style to be applied. To apply a paragraph style, you simply click anywhere in the paragraph and select the desired style. You may apply the style to multiple consecutive paragraphs. It doesn't matter whether character styles or paragraph styles are first applied — character styles always override paragraph styles.

You can tell if you or someone else has modified text that was previously assigned a style because the style displays a plus (+) sign next to it in the palette. For example, if you apply a character style that specifies Adobe Garamond, and then change the text to Adobe Minion with the Character palette (not the Character Styles palette), you have made a *local override*; the style name displays a plus sign.

The fastest way to apply a style is to use the keyboard equivalent that you previously assigned while creating your styles. For example, if you define the paragraph style Body Text to use Command/Control-2, you can simply click with the Type tool anywhere in a paragraph and type Command/Control-2 to automatically assign the Body Text style. To apply a character style, you just follow the same procedure, except you must first highlight the exact text to which the style is to be applied.

You may also apply styles from the styles palettes (Type>Character Styles or Shift-F11, or Type>Paragraph Styles or "F11"). Most people work with the styles palettes open.

Apply Styles

1. Continue in the open document. Choose Type>Paragraph Styles (or press "F11") if the palette is not already open. The styles palettes are used to apply styles to a paragraph, a range of paragraphs, or a range of characters.

2. Click the Type tool in the frame and choose Select All from the Edit menu (or press Command/Control-A) to select all of the text in the document, and assign the Body Text style by clicking it in the Paragraph Styles palette or by typing Command/Control-2 (again, use the "2" from the numeric keypad). That gets you started by applying the most common style all at once.

3. Click the first paragraph, "Chapter II," then click the Chapter Number paragraph style name to apply it.

4. Place the Type tool in the next line and assign it the Chapter Name style.

5. Assign the next paragraph the Body Text 1 style by placing the cursor in the paragraph and pressing Command/Control-0 (use zero from the keypad).

To strip out all overrides and remove the style from text, you can press Option/Alt and click [No Character Style] or [No Paragraph Style] in the appropriate palette.

CHAPTER II

The Pool of Tears

'Curiouser and curiouser!' cried Alice (she was so much surprised, that for the moment she quite forgot how to speak good English); 'now I'm opening out like the largest telescope that ever was! Good-bye, feet!' (for

I've kept her wait
was ready to ask I
came near her, sh
please, sir–' The
white kid gloves
the darkness as h
  Alice took up
was very hot, she
went on talking: '

---

6. In the lower-right section of the page are eight lines that are very badly spaced. These lines are ended with soft returns (Shift-Return/Enter). When soft returns are applied to justified text, as specified in the Body Text style, the lines are forced to spread to each edge of the frame.

> 'How   doth   the   little   crocodile
> Improve   his   shining   tail,
> And   pour   the   waters   of   the   Nile
> On every golden scale!
> 'How   cheerfully   he   seems   to   grin,
> How   neatly   spread   his   claws,
> And   welcome   little   fishes   in
> With gently smiling jaws!'

Place the Type tool in the first group of four lines and assign it the Poem style.

7. Assign the next group of four lines the Poem Last style.

> *'How doth the little crocodile*
> *Improve his shining tail,*
> *And pour the waters of the Nile*
> *On every golden scale!*
>
> *'How cheerfully he seems to grin,*
> *How neatly spread his claws,*
> *And welcome little fishes in*
> *With gently smiling jaws!'*

8. Remember the Run-in Blue character style you created? You will apply it now. Select the Character Styles tab from the styles palette container.

9. In the first paragraph of text, highlight the words " 'Curiouser and curiouser!' "

10. Press Command/Control-1 (from the keypad). Click anywhere in the document to view your work.

> **CHAPTER II**
>
> ## The Pool of Tears
>
> **'Curiouser and curiouser!'** cried Alice (she was so much surprised, that for the moment she quite forgot how to speak good English); 'now I'm opening out like

You probably noticed that the rule above "Chapter II" is above the text frame. You could adjust this with the offset in Paragraph Rules, but that option affects the distance of the rule from the baseline, and not from a frame edge.

11. Click the left text frame with the Selection tool.

12. Choose Object>Text Frame Options (or press Command/Control-B), then set the Top Inset Spacing to 6 pt. to bring the rule inside the text frame, and click OK. The page now looks much better.

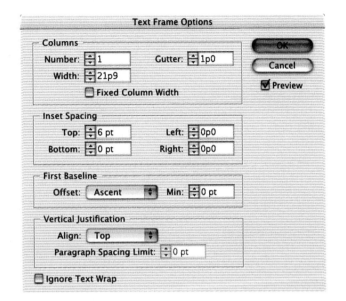

13. Save the document to your **Work_In_Progress** folder, then close it.

Summary

PRINT

In this chapter you have learned how to create and apply character styles and paragraph styles, how to edit styles, and how to base one style on another. You have learned how styles can interact with one another, and with other elements of InDesign, such as the underlying baseline grid and the Text Frame options.

Free-Form Project #1

Assignment

Assume you work for an ad agency. A marketing manager calls one day and asks for a new corporate identity for her employer, Tastevin Imports, Inc., a wine distributor. She wants a new logo along with letterhead, envelopes, and business cards that incorporate that logo, and she wants to see at least three different treatments. This is known as a "spec" (speculative) job, meaning your agency may or may not end up getting paid for it; it's a pretty common practice in the graphic design and advertising agency business.

Your assignment is to design one of the three identities. You have complete freedom in your design, which is unusual — clients generally impart some ideas of what they want, but this one trusts the talent at your agency to come up with something she likes. She did let slip that her company is looking for a modern, sophisticated, clean design; anything perceived as too conventional, cute, or sterile won't land the account. The entire job will be printed in just one color.

Apply Your Skills

To develop the identity package, you should apply the following processes, methods, and features:

- Create each item as a separate document at the actual size. Create an envelope, a sheet of letterhead, and a sample business card. Use "First Last" as the name and "Title" as the title for placeholders. These can later be replaced with real names if your design is successful.
- Use style sheets to test different fonts, heading styles, and paragraph formats.
- Combine text elements, special characters, OpenType features, and text composition techniques to create memorable, clean, and stylish typography. Use italics and/or boldfacing to add texture and interest. Don't use more than two different typefaces.
- Create graphic elements to emphasize text objects. Lightly tinted primitive shapes or type can greatly enhance a design when used sparingly.
- Experiment with different point sizes, leadings, and various styles of paragraph rules (such as dashed or dotted).
- Align objects properly.

Specifications

Letterhead:
> 8.5 in. × 11 in.

Envelope:
> #10 (9.5 in. × 4.125 in.)

Business card:
> 3.5 in. × 2 in.

Client info:
> Tastevin Imports, Inc.
> 111 Lyndale Avenue
> Minneapolis, MN 55401
> tel: 612-555-4956
> fax: 612-555-4959
> email: bacchus@tastevin.com

Publisher's Comments

Some of the most highly regarded work in the field of design and advertising is created with simple text and shape tools. Consider the corporate identities or logos for Volkswagen, IBM, Warner Brothers, United Airlines, General Motors, and many other companies. All of these are based on type — some heavily stylized, and some not — and are recognizable all over the world. You don't necessarily need graphics or drawings to create a memorable identity.

Review #1

Chapters 1 through 5

In Chapters 1 through 5, you learned the basic operations necessary to set up InDesign documents, and how to work with text and frames. You explored InDesign's setup preferences, font installation, and some of the differences between the Windows and Mac OS platforms. You learned about InDesign's principal tools, menus, and palettes; how to navigate within documents; how to create, open, and save documents; and how to set preferences to customize the InDesign work environment. You practiced working with text in text frames, and using and applying master pages and style sheets. After completing the discussions and exercises so far, we expect that you should:

- Understand the electronic document and the stages that a publication goes through from concept to delivery. You are aware of some printing industry terminology and customs concerning publishing.

- Be familiar with InDesign's tools, windows, menus, and palettes. You should be comfortable grouping and arranging palettes to configure your workspace efficiently. You're able to begin a new project and set the initial job definitions, and are familiar with customizing InDesign's preferences to suit your needs.

- Know about the structural elements of a page, and know how to work with multi-page documents, spreads, and master pages. You know the safe areas in which to work, how to set margins and gutters, and how to handle bleeds.

- Know how to work with text frames. You can create frames, import text, place and thread text between multiple frames, and work with the text within the frames. You're able to handle text overflow, work with tabular columns, insert special characters, and use basic OpenType composition options to produce attractive, legible type.

- Understand the power of character and paragraph styles, and how to create and apply them. You know how to base one style on another and how to edit existing styles for rapid global changes within a document.

6 Tables

Chapter Objective:

Tables in InDesign can be useful for organizing data for easy display. You can include both text (such as numbers) and graphics within tables. This chapter includes information about creating, importing, editing, and formatting tables for various purposes. In Chapter 6, you will:

- Understand what kinds of information are suitable for use in a table.

- Learn the differences between the types of data that make up columns and rows.

- Import a table from a Microsoft Excel file, and import tabular data from a text file.

- Learn how to convert tabular data to a table.

- Discover the ways you can select table elements, such as rows, columns, or the entire table.

- Recognize the distinction between table elements and the table itself.

- Learn how to apply formatting to table contents.

Projects to be Completed:

- Central Market Ad (A)

- Yellow Rose Menu (B)

- Travel Brochure (C)

- Good Choices Newsletter (D)

...king tables of numbers or text is new in InDesign 2.0.
... of *cells*, much as information is presented in a spread-
... Excel. A table cell acts like a miniature InDesign
...raphics, or even other tables. In many respects, tables
...n flow from one frame to another, and move in position
... important to be aware of this behavior when working
... can contain both tables and ordinary text. Once a table is
... a "super" character; in other words, it behaves like a giant
...r above it, it moves down; if you click the text cursor below
... is deleted. You can always set a table in its own frame if you
... with text reflow. Table controls are located on the Table
...ette.

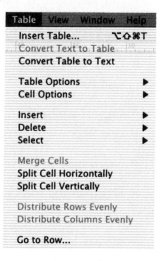

The Table menu.

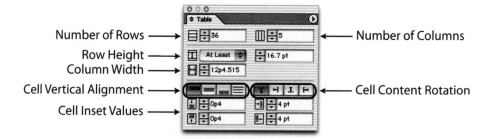

The Table palette becomes active when a table or a table cell is selected.

Of course, you can still create attractive tables by using the Tab features discussed in Chapter 4, *Working with Text*. If, however, you have tabular material that requires heavy formatting, inline graphics, or visual table cues such as shading and borders, then you'll probably want to use the Table function. You could do all of this with tabs and paragraph styles, but it would require a tremendous amount of work to recreate the design.

Here's an example of a drab Excel document that has been transformed into an upscale restaurant's daily wine list with InDesign's Table features:

Microsoft Excel data.

Liste quotidienne des vins — 1ᵉʳ avril 2002

Café Le Grande Snobbe

Beringer	Knight's Valley Cabernet	1997	€ 28	12
Beringer	Private Reserve Cabernet	1995	€ 125	4
Beringer	Private Reserve Chardonnay	1998	€ 45	8
Bollinger	Grande Année Rosé	1988	€ 250	3
Château Beaucastel	Châteauneuf-du-Pape	1990	€ 96	5
Château d'Yquem	Sauternes 325ml	1988	€ 299	6
Château d'Yquem	Sauternes 750ml	1988	€ 699	2
Château La Grange	St. Julien	1993	€ 65	4
Château Lynch-Bages	Pauillac	1990	€ 125	3

Excel data converted to an InDesign table.

Creating Tables

It's important to understand how tabular data is represented in most applications. Typically, the information is *delimited*, either by a spreadsheet column or a character such as a tab or comma, into *fields* of data. A field is the smallest part of a *record*, which in turn is part of a *database*. The example shows how each wine's record (the unit of information about the wine itself) is composed of fields that contain specific data about that wine. The entire Excel file is a small database of wine records. In Excel, a record is all of the information in a row of data, and the fields are the information recorded in the columns.

You can convert previously typed or imported text to a table in InDesign, but only if it has already been set up as tabular data — each field must be separated with a tab, and each record separated with a return. Each tab creates a new column, and each return creates a new row. You can also create an empty table and enter the data yourself.

InDesign tables are very flexible; you have a high degree of control over their appearance. You can easily resize rows and columns, and cells can grow to accommodate their contents (unless you create cells of a fixed size). You can also insert and delete rows and columns as necessary. Text in a table is formatted using the functions on the Character and Paragraph palettes. Cell contents can be vertically aligned (from the Table palette) to the top, bottom, or center of a cell, or justified to fill the cell. Horizontal alignment is done just as you would do with the Paragraph palette for a regular paragraph.

Create and Navigate a Simple Table

1. Make a new document with these specifications:

   Facing Pages: Off

   Master Text Frame: Off

   Page Size: Letter - Half

   Margins: Top and Bottom, 36 pt; Left and Right, 3p0

   Columns: 1

   Make sure that Frame Edges are visible.

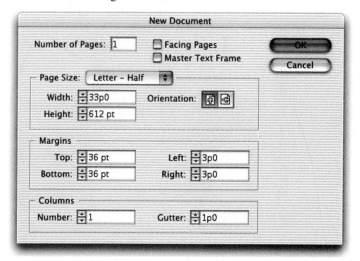

Don't confuse text columns with table columns on a page. Text columns are usually defined in a text frame, and text flows in a down-and-up fashion from one to another; table columns are part of a table and do not flow, except when the table itself flows to another text column or frame.

2. Using the Type tool, draw a text frame within the margins of the page.

3. Choose Table>Insert Table, and create a table with five rows and three columns.

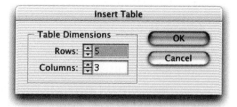

The new table fills the width of the frame. The height is determined by the number of rows that you specified. The actual height of the rows can vary, but is never less than the value specified in the row height field of the Table palette when set to At Least. The default row height accommodates 12-pt. text.

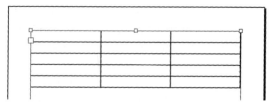

The new table becomes part of the text frame.

4. The text cursor should be active in the first cell. If not, click once in the cell. Type "Producer". Press Tab to go to the next cell to the right. Type "Wine", then press Tab once more to go to the upper-right cell. Type "Vintage" and press Tab.

5. When you get to the end of a row and press Tab, the cursor advances to the first cell in the next row. Press Shift-Tab to go back to the last cell, which selects the word "Vintage." Type "Color" to replace this word.

6. Press Shift-Tab twice to go to the first cell. Press the Down Arrow key once to move the cursor to the next row, which is empty. Press the Right Arrow key three times; notice that the cursor returns to the first cell in a row when you use the Left or Right Arrow keys and reach the other end. If there is any text in the cells, the cursor moves one letter at a time until it gets to the beginning or end of a word, then it jumps to the previous or next cell.

7. Use the Up and Down Arrow keys to move the cursor between rows. Notice that the cursor moves to the beginning or end of a word, depending on where you start and whether you press the Up or Down Arrow key.

8. Close the document without saving.

Formatting the text within a table is a little different than formatting normal text. Each cell can be formatted with different type specifications that do not carry over to the next cell when entering data. There are, however, techniques to select a full row, column, or even the entire table, so you can apply typographic specifications to the multiple cells' contents at one time. We will discuss these shortly.

InDesign treats table cells as independent items, and any text formatting you've applied to text set before or after a table is not applied to text in a table; instead, all typed text is styled with the default settings in the Character palette (Times or Times New Roman, 12 pt.). You have to select each cell, row, column, or the whole table, to change the character formatting. Tables imported from Excel files have the font and size applied that is set in the original Excel file, if the font is available on your system. If it's not, you receive an error message telling you that the font is missing.

Importing Tables

If you save an Excel, FileMaker, or other database file as a text-only file, you can create *delimiters*, which act to separate each field and record. A tab character is commonly used as a field delimiter, and a return character is used as a record delimiter. Exporting delimited text from a database is one way of getting tabular data into InDesign; you can also import Microsoft Excel or Word files that contain tables as InDesign tables.

If you are importing an Excel file, you can specify the number of rows and columns to place in the document. This is convenient if you just need a portion of the data in an Excel spreadsheet.

If you import a text-only file, it is not converted to a table. Instead, you have to place it as text, then convert it to a table with the Convert to Table function on the Table menu.

Import a Table

1. Create a new letter-size document using the defaults.

2. Using the Type tool, draw a text frame within the margins of the page.

3. Make sure the insertion point (text cursor) is active in the frame, then press Command/Control-D to show the Place dialog. Make sure the Show Import Options box is checked. Navigate to your **RF_Intro_InDesign** folder, select the **wine_inventory.xls** file, and click Choose/Open.

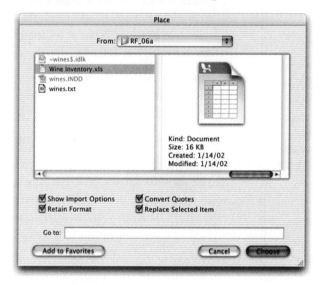

4. This file has more wine records in it than you really want. By checking the Show Import Options box, you can specify a range of Excel cells to import. First, choose the Wine Inventory sheet from the Sheet pop-up menu near the top, then type "a2:c16" in the Cell Range field. Verify that the Apply Default Spreadsheet Style box is checked, then click OK. (If you receive any warnings about missing fonts, ignore them; you will change fonts later).

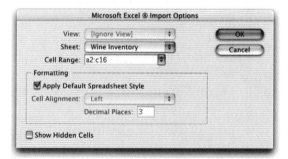

The selected cell range is placed as an InDesign table. The table is only as wide as necessary, which is different behavior than creating a new, blank table that fills the width of the text frame. InDesign uses the relative column width set in an Excel file to determine column widths when importing Excel files.

Notice that there's now a very tall blinking cursor to the left of the table. Remember that InDesign treats a table as a giant character, so this blinking cursor is the same height as the table.

5. To further demonstrate how InDesign treats tables as large characters, press the (forward) Delete key (the one under the "F13" and Help keys, not the Delete/Backspace key under the "F12" key). The table disappears. Press Command/Control-Z to undo the deletion. Press the Right Arrow key once, and the tall cursor jumps to the other side of the table. Press Return/Enter and notice how the cursor returns to its usual size underneath the table.

6. Press Return/Enter once more to make a blank line.

7. Save this file as **table_practice.indd** in your **Work_In_Progress** folder and leave it open for the next exercise.

Text to Table/Table to Text

With InDesign, you can either convert text to a table format, or convert an existing table to text. You need to convert text to a table when importing plain, delimited text files, because InDesign only converts Excel files and Word tables to InDesign tables. You can also use this function to convert tabular data information into a table. When converting text to a table, InDesign begins new rows at returns, and new columns at tabs. The text must be properly formatted with tabs separating each field and returns separating each record (line) before conversion.

Converting a table to text removes the gridlines, sets tabs at each column, and ends each row with a return.

Convert Text to a Table

1. Use the document (**table_practice.indd**) that you created in the previous exercise. The cursor should be one line down from the bottom of the table you imported.

2. Press Command/Control-D and navigate to your **RF_Intro_InDesign** folder. Uncheck the Show Import Options box, if it's checked. Select the **wines.txt** file, and click Choose/Open.

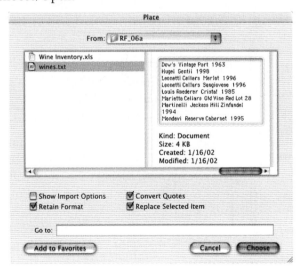

3. Using the Type tool, select all of the imported text, then choose Table>Convert Text to Table. Notice how this process fills the width of the text frame with three equal-width columns; this doesn't happen with imported tables. A plain text file contains no information about fonts or column widths, so the new table uses a default font and column width.

Beringer	Knight's Valley Cabernet	1997
Beringer	Private Reserve Cabernet	1995
Beringer	Private Reserve Chardonnay	1998
Beringer	Napa Valley Zinfandel	1998
Bollinger	Grande Année Rosé	1988
Château Beaucastel	Châteauneuf-du-Pape	1990
Château d'Yquem	Sauternes 325ml	1988
Château d'Yquem	Sauternes 750ml	1988
Château La Grange	St. Julien	1993
Château Lafite Rothschild	Pauillac	1982
Château Lynch-Bages	Pauillac	1990
Château Lynch-Bages	Pauillac	1992
Château Mouton Roth-schild	Pauillac	1982
Château Mouton Roth-schild	Pauillac "The War Vintage"	1945
Château Pétrus	Pomerol	1945

Dow's	Vintage Port	1963
Hugel	Gentil	1998
Leonetti Cellars	Merlot	1996
Leonetti Cellars	Sangiovese	1996
Louis Roederer	Cristal	1985
Marietta Cellars	Old Vine Red Lot 28	
Martinelli	Jackass Hill Zinfandel	1994
Mondavi	Reserve Cabernet	1995
Mondavi	To-Kalon Vineyard Sauvignon Blanc	1997

4. Save the file and leave the document open for the next exercise.

Selecting Table Contents

InDesign offers several methods for selecting cells, rows, columns, and entire tables. The Type tool must be active in the table for any of these selection methods to work.

The simplest way to select table elements is to click the text cursor in a cell, then drag through the cells you wish to select. You can drag vertically to select cells in the same column, horizontally to select cells in the same row, or diagonally to select a range of cells across rows and columns.

To quickly select a row with a single keystroke, you can click the cursor in any cell in that row and press Command/Control-3. To select a column, you can click in that column and add Option/Alt to the keystroke. Pressing Command/Control-/ selects the contents of a single cell. Pressing Command/Control-Option/Alt-A selects all of the cells in the table.

You can also make selections with the mouse. To select a column, move the cursor just above the top of the column; when the cursor changes to a downward-pointing arrow, you can click once to select the entire column. Row selection works similarly — move the cursor to the left end of the row (just outside the table) until it turns to a right-pointing arrow, and click once to select the row. To select all of the cells in the table, move the cursor to just outside the upper-left corner until the cursor changes to an arrow pointing down and to the right; a single click then selects all of the cells.

Use the Tab key to move the cursor to the next cell in the row (or to the first cell in the next row if you're at the end of a row). Add Shift to reverse the direction. Any text in a cell is selected when you move around a table with the Tab key.

Selecting columns (left), rows (center), and the entire table (right).

To select the entire table (not just its contents), you need to click the cursor outside of the table, but inside the frame that contains it. Now you can use the usual text-selection techniques to select the table. Remember that the table behaves as any other letter or word — you can delete it, copy and paste it somewhere else, or move it up or down by adding or removing text around it.

Basic Table Formatting

To understand table formatting, you need to differentiate the content of a table from the table itself. To format cell contents, you must use the Character and Paragraph palettes, the Character Styles and Paragraph Styles palettes, or the Type menu. To modify the table itself, you must use the Table palette, Table menu, or contextual Table menu (which appears if you Control/Right-click in the table when the Type tool is active, and replicates the functions of the standard Table menu). Many Table menu functions are also duplicated on Table palette Options pop-up menu.

A common table format change involves resizing rows and columns. You can do this interactively by moving the Type tool over a row or column boundary until it changes to a double-ended arrow. Clicking and dragging this arrow reduces or enlarges the row or column. The arrows point up and down for resizing rows, and left and right for columns.

The text cursor changes to a double-ended arrow when moved over a row (left) or column (right) boundary line.

If you expand a column in a table that fills the width of the text frame, it causes the table to extend past the edge of the frame.

1963		
1998		
1996		
1996		
1985		
1994		
1995		
1997		

Column expanded past frame edge.

You can resize the entire table interactively by first moving the text cursor over the lower-right corner of the table until you see a resize icon (double-ended diagonal arrow), then dragging this icon to resize the table. The cells become larger or smaller to accommodate the contents, but the contents themselves do not resize. Cell text can wrap within cells, making the row taller. If you hold the Shift key while dragging, InDesign maintains the proportions of the table.

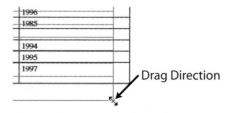

You can drag the lower-right corner of a table to resize it.

For better precision when resizing tables, rows, and columns, you can use the numeric controls located in the Table palette, Table menu, and contextual Table menu. In the Table palette, you can set the width of one or more columns, and the height of one or more rows. You can force row height to a fixed size by choosing Exact in the Row Height area of the Table palette, or you can allow the height to change as needed to accommodate cell contents. Forcing a fixed height can result in overset cell text. If you use the At Least setting of the Row Height area, then rows can expand as needed.

Adjusting Table Elements

1. Continuing in the open document from the last exercise, make sure the Type tool is active, and select the first (top) table on the page.

2. Open the Table palette by choosing Window>Table or pressing Shift-F9. Set the Row Height drop-down menu to Exactly, and type 18 in the field. Press Return/Enter to confirm your specs.

Note that the Column Width field is empty, because the table has varying column widths.

You can also use the inter-active tools to adjust the column width.

3. Repeat Step 2 with the second (lower) table. Click the text cursor in either table to deselect it.

Look at the rows in the first table starting with "Château Mouton Roth-". There's a small red dot in the lower-right corner of these cells. This dot indicates that the text in the cell is now overset. The same problem exists in the second table, in the last row. You need to fix this overset text condition.

Château Lynch-Bages	Pauillac	
Château Mouton Roth-	Pauillac	
Château Mouton Roth-	Pauillac "The War Vintage"	

Reserve Cabernet	1995
To-Kalon Vineyard Sauvignon	1997

4. Select the first column of the first table. Set the column width in the Table palette to 18p0.

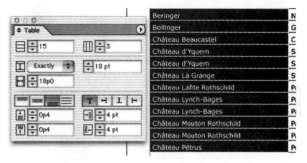

Set the width of the second column to 20p0, and of the third to 7p0. Now the table fills the width of the frame, and the instances of overset text have been eliminated.

5. Set the column widths of the second table to the same values used in Step 4.

6. Select the first table, and change the font to ATC Mai Tai Normal, 12 pt., auto leading. Do the same to the second table. Fix any cells that become overset after applying this font change by adjusting column widths.

7. Set the vertical alignment of both tables' cells to Center by selecting each table, then clicking the second Cell Vertical Alignment button.

Due to differences in the way Windows and Macintosh computers handle letter spacing of non-OpenType fonts, cells may become overset on one platform but not the other.

8. The last thing needed to make these tables identical in format is to reset the alignment of the third column in the first table. Remember, this table was imported from an Excel file, and Excel sets numbers as right-aligned by default. Select the column and set left alignment in the Paragraph palette. Now the two tables look the same.

Château Lynch-Bages	Pauillac	1992
Château Mouton Rothschild	Pauillac	1982
Château Mouton Rothschild	Pauillac "The War Vintage"	1945
Château Pétrus	Pomerol	1945
Dow's	Vintage Port	1963
Hugel	Gentil	1998
Leonetti Cellars	Merlot	1996

9. Save the file, then close it.

Summary

In this chapter you have learned how to create tables, how to import tables from other applications, and how to convert text to tables. You have also learned how to select table elements such as rows and columns, how to resize these elements, and how to format table contents.

Working with Graphic Elements

Chapter Objective:

InDesign contains many useful tools for drawing, manipulating, and painting vector graphics. Learning to use these can make you a more efficient user. This chapter describes the available drawing tools and the strategies you need to use them most effectively when creating InDesign documents. In Chapter 7, you will:

- Explore the uses of the Pen, Line, Ellipse, Rectangle, and Polygon tools for creating lines, paths, and basic shapes.

- Learn what Bézier curves are and practice drawing them.

- Learn how to draw and constrain lines and frames.

- Learn to use the Stroke palette to determine line thickness, corner type, dashed lines characteristics, and more.

- Become familiar with the painting tools and learn how to apply color and gradients.

- Learn the anatomy of frames, how to manipulate objects within frames, and how to alter the size of a frame and its content independently of one another.

- Become familiar with the Arrange menu for moving objects in front of and behind one another.

- Explore methods of rotating, scaling, and shearing objects manually and with the Transform palette.

- Learn the fine points of object scaling with the InDesign tools.

Projects to be Completed:

- Central Market Ad (A)

- Yellow Rose Menu (B)

- Travel Brochure (C)

- Good Choices Newsletter (D)

Working with Graphic Elements

The contents of any page include only two elements: text and graphics. You have already learned how to create and format type in earlier chapters. There are two categories of graphics in the context of InDesign: objects created with the InDesign tools, and objects that are imported from an outside source. In this chapter, we examine the objects that you can create with InDesign's drawing tools, and the operations you can perform with transformational tools.

Object Fundamentals

Objects created with InDesign tools consist of two basic parts: a path, and points. A *path* is any unbroken line or curve that describes a shape. An *open path* has a defined start and end point; a *closed path* (such as a circle) has no start and end points, but is still defined by points. A *point* is a position on a path that defines the direction, angle, and curve direction (if any) of the path that it intersects. These are also known as "anchor points," because they anchor the path's characteristics where they're set.

A *stroke* is a visible boundary of the path; a *fill* describes the contents of a path. Both fills and strokes can be colored with numerous options or set to None; fills can be solid colors, tints of colors, or graduated blends, vignettes, or gradients.

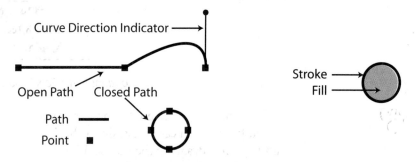

Basic terminology related to object creation.

Object Drawing Tools

There are six tools for drawing lines and objects: the Pen, Pencil, Frame, Rectangle, Line, and Scissors tools. Variations of these tools are located on pop-up menus, that appear when you click the base tool; for example, to choose the Polygon Frame tool, you must click and hold the Rectangle Frame tool icon.

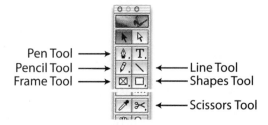

The object drawing tools in InDesign's toolbox.

Bézier curves are so named because they were first defined by the mathematician Pierre Bézier; he was the first to define a curve that could be drawn with only two points.

Holding the Shift key while clicking the Pen tool constrains it to a 45°-angle increments.

Holding the Option/Alt key while using the Pen tool activates the Convert Direction Point tool.

Each tool on the pop-up menu also lists its keyboard shortcut, if it has one. To use the tools that do not have keyboard shortcuts, you must select it from the toolbox.

Pen. The Pen tool is InDesign's most versatile drawing tool; it enables you to draw both straight and curved lines with a great deal of control. The curved lines are Bézier curves, and can be modified with the Direct Selection tool. Because of the Pen tool's flexibility, it can be one of the hardest tools to master. If you click and hold the Pen tool icon, a pop-up menu provides access to the Add Anchor Point, Delete Anchor Point, and Convert Direction Point tools.

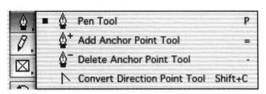

The options in the Pen tool pop-up menu.

Pencil. The Pencil tool is used to draw free-form lines as well as both open and closed paths. Its lines and paths become Bézier curves and may be edited with the Direct Selection tool. If you click and hold the Pencil tool icon, a pop-up menu reveals the Smooth tool and Erase tool. The Smooth tool is used to remove unwanted bumps from an existing path while retaining, as much as possible, the existing shape. The Erase tool is used to remove portions of a path.

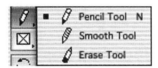

The options in the Pencil tool pop-up menu.

Frames. These tools are used to draw rectangular, elliptical, and polygonal (3–100 sides) content frames. You can constrain the horizontal and vertical dimensions by pressing the Shift key while dragging the mouse. When you hold the Option/Alt key, the point where you initially clicked is defined as the object's center; dragging draws the object outward from that point. As opposed to standard shapes (which are described below), content frames are preassigned as containers into which you can place text or images; they have no predefined stroke or fill. When you draw a text frame with the Type tool, you're actually creating a content frame with the preassigned content of text.

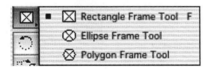

The frame options in the toolbox pop-up menu.

Shapes. These tools are used to draw rectangles, ellipses, and polygons (3–100 sides). You can constrain the horizontal and vertical dimensions by pressing the Shift key while dragging the mouse. When you hold the Option/Alt key, the point where you initially clicked is defined as the object's center; dragging draws the object outward from that point. Shapes are always drawn with the current stroke color and weight. You can convert shapes (or any other open or closed paths) to content frames later.

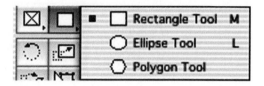

The shape options in the toolbox pop-up menu.

Line. The Line tool is used to draw a line from the point where the mouse is initially clicked to the point where the mouse button is released. Holding the Shift key constrains the lines to 45°-angle increments as it draws.

Scissors. This tool is used to split a path into two or more individual paths. It's useful for creating shapes that are part of a larger shape or object, when you don't really need the whole shape. For example, to make a semicircle, you can draw a circle with the Ellipse tool, use the Scissors to split it across the middle, and then delete the unwanted half.

The Bounding Box

Before we show you how to draw objects with the InDesign tools, we need to show you what you will see when the drawn objects are selected with the Selection tool. While the objects are being drawn by the various tools, you see only the object being created. If you select the object (even if it is in the midst of being created) with the Selection tool, a blue box with handles appears around the selected artwork. This blue box is known as the "bounding box." All objects, whether selected individually or as a group, have an imaginary box that marks the extreme perimeter.

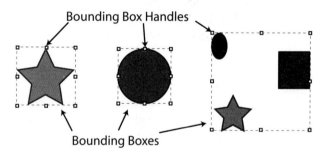

Bounding Box Handles

Bounding Boxes

The bounding boxes of objects and groups of various sizes and shapes.

The Ellipse, Rectangle, and Polygon tools automatically create closed paths. The Line tool can only create linear, open paths. Closed paths can be broken with the Scissors tool.

The symbols on the right of the Pen tool give insight into the status of the drawing process.

The **X** means the tool is not in progress and free to either start a new path, or continue an existing one.

The **O** appears when the tool touches an open path endpoint signifying that it will close the path if clicked.

The **I** appears when the tool touches an open path endpoint, signifying that it will continue drawing the path when clicked.

The ↖ appears when the tool touches an endpoint of an open path that is active.

No symbol means that the Pen tool is active and ready to continue the path in progress.

What Does this Box Do?

The bounding box not only shows the perimeter of the selected object(s), but also gives instant access to modify that object. There are four corner handles, four side handles, and a center point. Dragging any of the corner handles scales an object both horizontally and vertically; holding the Shift key while dragging a corner handle scales the object proportionally. You can drag the handles on the left and right sides to scale an object horizontally, or drag the top and bottom handles to enlarge or reduce an object vertically.

If the object is a frame with image content, scaling with the handles only resizes the frame; the size of the contents remains unchanged. You can force image contents to change size along with the frame by holding the Command/Control key as you drag a handle. Adding the Shift key constrains the proportions of the content. Text frames don't resize their contents unless you use the Transform palette to make the size adjustments; we don't recommend doing this. It's much better to use the text tools that you've already learned about to adjust text size.

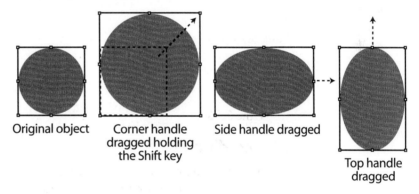

Original object | Corner handle dragged holding the Shift key | Side handle dragged | Top handle dragged

Dragging the handles is an easy way to resize objects.

Bézier Drawing Tools

The Pen and Pencil tools create paths comprised of Bézier curves. These are complex mathematical formulae that are entered by actually positioning the points with the Pen tool, or by drawing a free-form shape with the Pencil tool. Elliptical shapes created with the Ellipse tool are also made of Bézier curves that are generated when you draw the shape.

The Pen Tool

To use the Pen tool, you need to click the pen-tip cursor on the page; this defines a point that becomes the beginning of your line. When you click a second time, you define a second point; the distance between these two points is the path. As long as the Pen tool remains active, you can add any number of points to create an unending path. To deselect the path, choose the Selection tool, the Direct Selection tool, the Type tool, or any other drawing tool, and click an empty area of the page.

The anatomy of a path is fairly simple. Each click of the Pen tool creates a new anchor point. A single segment (or path), which can be straight or curved, connects each pair of adjacent anchor points. Paths are categorized as open or closed. You can easily identify open paths by their separate beginning and ending points; closed paths are continuous, and have no apparent beginning or end.

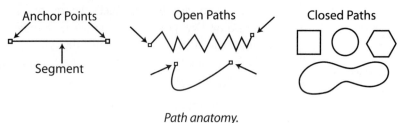

Path anatomy.

Curved lines are drawn with the Pen tool by dragging an anchor point to pull out a direction line that can be used to adjust the curve.

Corner Point

A *corner point* is an anchor point at which a path abruptly changes direction. It may connect two straight segments, two curved segments, or a straight and a curved segment.

In this example, the Pen tool was clicked at Point A, moved to Point B (with the Shift key held down to constrain the path to a straight line), then clicked again. To create a direction line, the Pen tool was then clicked again at Point B, dragged up and to the right, then released. While holding the Shift key, the cursor was then clicked at Point C, giving the curved segment an ending anchor point. Holding the Shift key while clicking the last point constrains its position to 0°, 45°, or 90° from the previous point. The corner point or the curving segment can be clicked with the Direct Selection tool to adjust the direction line.

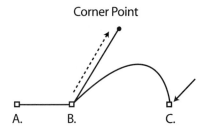

Smooth Point

The *smooth point* gets its name from the shape of the curved segments that surround it; the segments are smooth in their flow and continuity as they extend from the point. The clearest identifying aspect of the smooth point is that it has two direction lines that adjust both segments attached to the anchor point.

In the example that follows, the Pen tool was clicked on Point A; with the mouse button held down, an initial curve direction line was dragged up and to the right. The Pen tool was moved to the right, then clicked on Point B; again, with the mouse button held down, a direction line was dragged up and to the right from point B. The Pen tool was then moved to the right and clicked at Point C, and a direction line was dragged from this point, ending the drawing process. The result is a path possessing a smooth point. When its direction lines are moved, the segments before and after the smooth point are moved with it (D). Either segment, however, may be adjusted independently by dragging the appropriate direction line.

When using the Pen tool, be aware that there is an Automatic Add and Delete Points function that becomes active when touching an anchor point or segment of a selected path.

If the Pen tool touches the segment, the Pen takes on the Add Anchor Point symbol (+) in its lower-right corner. This works on any segment of a selected path.

If the Pen tool touches an anchor point of a selected path, the symbol becomes the minus sign (-) for the Delete Anchor Point tool. This works only for anchor points that occur on the segment, not on beginning or endpoints of a path.

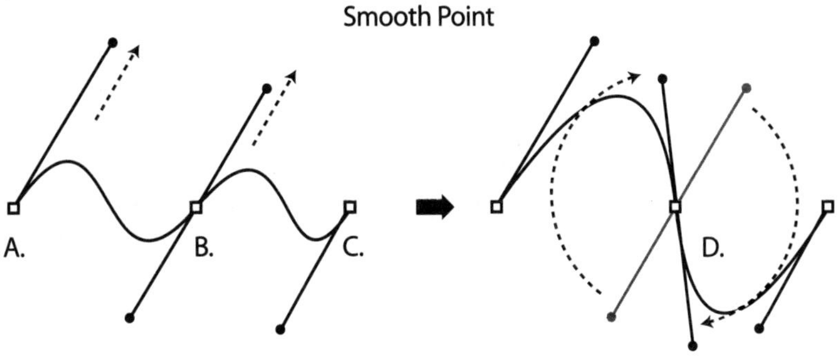

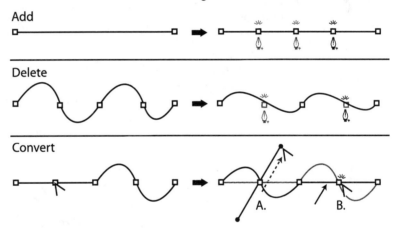

Smooth Point

Editing Paths

The tools in the Pen tool Options pop-up menu are used primarily for editing or modifying existing paths. Clicking a path with the Add Anchor Point tool adds a new point to that path segment. Clicking with the Delete Anchor Point tool removes an existing anchor point. Clicking or dragging an anchor point with the Convert Direction Point tool changes the type of point. Dragging a point converts it to a smooth point (A); clicking a smooth point removes the curves from the segments (B).

Add

Delete

Convert

Dragging a point with the Convert Direction Point tool converts it to a smooth point (A); clicking a smooth point removes the curves from the segments (B).

Draw with the Pen Tool

1. Before creating a new document, go to Preferences>Units and Increments, and make sure that the horizontal and vertical units are set to picas (you have used picas and points in previous exercises).

2. Choose File>New, and create a new document with one page, one column, and all-around margins of 3 picas.

3. In the toolbox, click the Default Fill and Stroke icon to set the stroke to a black line.

Default Fill/Stroke ⟶

The Default Fill and Stroke icon in the toolbox reverts any fill and stroke choices back to a black stroke and no fill. Press "D" to invoke the default Fill and Stroke.

4. From the vertical ruler on the left of the screen, drag a guide out to about the 12-pica mark of the horizontal ruler at the top. Make certain that Snap to Guides is checked in the View menu. Click the Pen tool icon in the toolbox. Single-click the tool on the guide to create a beginning point. This acts as a guide for keeping the alignment straight when the final clicks are applied to create this object. Move the cursor over to the right about 24 picas, press the Shift key to constrain, and click again. You have created a single segment or line. Do not deselect.

5. Move the Pen tool about an inch (72 pt.) below this point, hold the Shift key, and click again to continue the path. Do not deselect.

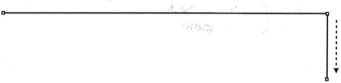

6. Move the Pen tool to the left and hold the Shift key as you click the guide again. The anchor point that you click snaps to the guide.

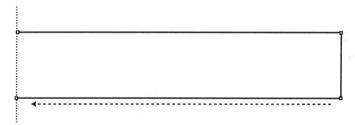

7. Holding the Shift key, move the Pen tool up and click the beginning point. The result is a rectangle drawn from scratch. Select this object with the Selection tool and delete it.

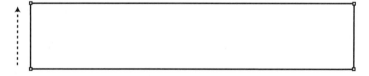

8. Select the Pen tool from the toolbox. Click near the center of the page to create a beginning point. Move the tool up and to the right, then click again.

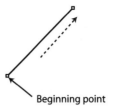

Beginning point

9. Move the Pen tool down and to the right, below the beginning point, and click again.

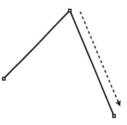

A single click with the Pen tool creates an anchor point. If you click one time to create a single anchor but then abort and deselect the path, the initial point remains, but it is invisible. This is a PostScript error waiting to happen. Get in the habit of cleaning up your work by selecting stray anchor points and deleting them.

10. Move the tool down and to the left, then click once more. Notice how the path grows with each click of the Pen tool.

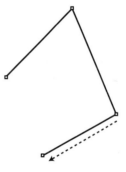

11. Move the Pen tool up to add a final click at the beginning point, closing the path. You have created a free-form object, without the constraint of the Shift key.

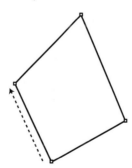

When using the Pen tool, Option/Alt toggles the Convert Direction tool.

The bounding box is also capable of reflecting the selected object. By dragging the selected handle toward and past the opposing handle, on the other side of the object, you change the horizontal or vertical appearance. This is also known as "mirroring" or "flipping" the object.

12. Click the Selection tool in the toolbox. This automatically selects the object you just drew. Notice the blue bounding box that surrounds it.

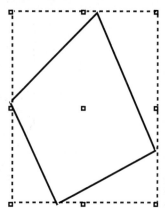

13. Drag the right-middle handle to the right.

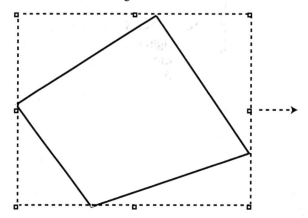

14. Drag the bottom handle upward. Notice that the bounding box has fast modifying features that eliminate the need to use the Scale tool (covered later in this chapter; note warnings there about using the handles for scaling) for fine-tuning purposes.

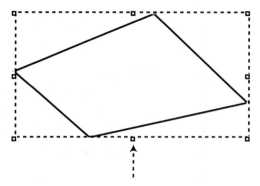

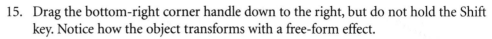

15. Drag the bottom-right corner handle down to the right, but do not hold the Shift key. Notice how the object transforms with a free-form effect.

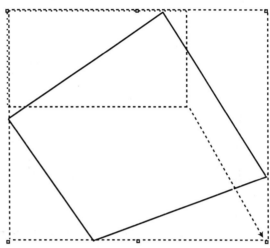

16. Release the mouse button and observe the object's alteration. Drag this bottom-right corner handle toward the upper-left corner of the bounding box again, this time holding the Shift key; notice that the object retains its proportions. Release the mouse button.

Shaping the object with the handles of the bounding box actually scales the object, which we discuss in greater detail in the Transformations section of this chapter.

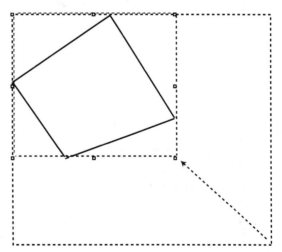

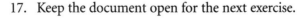

You have now learned how to draw objects containing straight line segments with the Pen tool; you have used the Shift key to constrain the angles of the drawing process, and used the bounding box to modify the object. You will now create curves with the Pen tool. Select the objects in the document and delete them.

17. Keep the document open for the next exercise.

Create Curved Segments

1. If the document from the previous exercise is not open, create a new document.

2. Select the Pen tool and click anywhere on the page. Move the cursor about 6 picas to the right. Holding the Shift key, click again to create a segment (A). Click the Pen tool on the endpoint and drag out a direction line for a curve. Release the mouse button. You have created a corner point (B).

A.   B.

When using the Pen to draw a path, it's best to set the fill to None (which is the default), so it doesn't interfere with drawing. You can apply a fill to an open path — the fill jumps from the starting point to the last clicked point as you draw.

3. Move the Pen cursor 6 picas further to the right, hold the Shift key, then *drag* on the page to create a smooth point with a double handle. (If you click without dragging, then this doesn't work.)

4. Move the Pen tool 6 picas further to the right while holding the Shift key. Single-click the Pen tool on the page to finalize the path.

5. With the Direct Selection tool, click the second point. You can see the direction line of the curved segment following the corner point. Drag the tip of the direction line to change the curve's shape.

6. Now click the third point. You can see its two direction lines. Drag either tip of this handle to alter the curve. The curving segments on either side of the anchor point change as you drag.

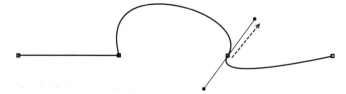

7. You have now used the Pen tool to draw the two types of curve points, and have adjusted them. Close the document without saving.

The Pencil Tool

The Pencil tool simulates freehand drawing with a mouse. To use it, click a starting point and draw the desired shape. InDesign automatically creates numerous Bézier points and curves as you draw. When you are using the Pencil tool and you release the mouse button, the path ends, unlike a path drawn with the Pen. Closed paths are created with the Pencil tool by pressing the Option/Alt key. If a gap remains between the beginning and ending points on the path, InDesign closes the gap.

Smoothing Paths

Beneath the Pencil tool is the Smooth tool. This tool is used to retain the general shape of the drawing, while getting rid of unwanted raggedness. Drag the Smooth tool along (not across) the part of a path that you want to smooth.

Erasing Sections of Paths

To erase portions of a path, you can use the Erase tool, which is also located beneath the Pencil tool. By simply dragging it along (not across) the part of a path you wish to erase, you remove the path (but not filled areas).

Create a Freehand Drawing

1. From your **RF_Intro_InDesign** folder, open the document **pencil_practice.indt**. We have created this file as a template (hence the ".indt" file extension) so you can practice using the Pencil and related tools. The owl image is on a locked layer (you'll learn about layers in *Advanced InDesign: Creating Electronic Documents*) beneath the layer you'll be working on, so don't worry about messing it up.

2. Select Window>Stroke, press "F10", or double-click the Line tool to activate the Stroke palette.

3. Set the stroke weight to 2 pt.

You can select the Stroke palette by double-clicking the Line tool in the toolbox.

4. Double-click the Pencil tool to access its Tolerance settings. Set the fidelity to 2 pixels and the smoothness to 0%. Click OK.

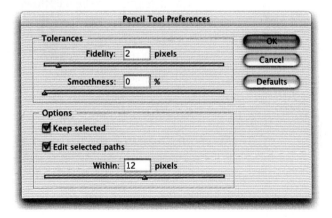

5. Select the Pencil tool and begin drawing the outline of the owl. Try to draw each logical segment in one smooth stroke.

Drawing with a mouse is about as precise as drawing with a bar of soap, so don't be too concerned about accurately reproducing the owl art. The important idea is that you learn how to use this tool.

6. Before drawing the claws, double-click the Pencil tool and set the fidelity to 0.5 pixels.

7. For the line across the owl's forehead and for the center line of the beak, switch to a 1-pt. stroke weight.

8. Before drawing the breast feathers, switch to a 4-pt. stroke weight and, in the Stroke palette, change to the round end cap. Choose Show Options from the Stroke palette's pop-up menu to access the end cap choices.

9. Before drawing the eyes, switch to a 0.5-pt. stroke weight. Set the fidelity to 0.5.

10. When drawing the eyes, press the Option/Alt key when you complete the path. A little circle appears to the right of the Pencil tool, indicating that the path will be closed. Release the mouse button to close the path.

11. With the path closed, select the Fill button and click Apply Color to fill the eye with black.

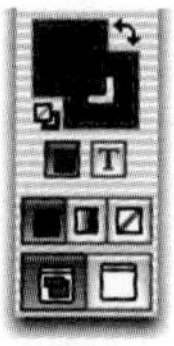

12. When you've finished the basic owl shape, use the Selection tool to select a line that is jagged. Select the Smooth tool and hold the Command/Control key down to temporarily change to the Direct Selection tool. Select a line you wish to smooth, then release the key. Use the Smooth tool to back over your work to smooth any jaggedness. Drag the smooth tool the length of the line — do not rub across the line. Repeat as necessary.

13. Close the file without saving — you won't be using it again.

By now you've probably realized that InDesign's Pencil tool is to quality drawing as a velvet Elvis painting is to fine art. It is much easier to create quality artwork with the Pen tool in the first place. But the Pencil has its place when you really do want a hand-drawn, rough appearance.

Shape Tools

The four tools that are used for creating basic shapes are the Ellipse, Rectangle, Line, and Polygon tools. To use these tools, you simply drag the tool cursor on the page. Holding the Shift key while drawing a line constrains it to 45°-angle increments. Holding the Shift key constrains the Ellipse tool to circles, the Rectangle tool to squares, and the Polygon tool to equilateral polygons. Holding the Option/Alt key (with or without the Shift key) starts the drawing of the shape from the center outward; otherwise drawing starts where you initially click the tool and continues in the direction you drag the mouse. By releasing the mouse button, you finish the shape.

The Line Tool

The Line tool draws a single line beginning where you first click the cursor; the line ends where you release the mouse button (A). If you hold the Shift key while dragging, the line is constrained to 45°-angle increments (B).

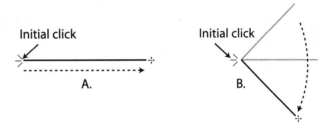

Initial click   Initial click

A.   B.

Holding Shift constrains line direction in 45°-angle increments (B).

Use the Line Tool

1. Select File>New to create a new document.

2. Click the Default Fill and Stroke icon in the toolbox, then select the Line tool.

3. Drag the Line tool on the page without holding any additional keys. The tool creates a line to wherever you move the cursor. Don't release the mouse button yet. Continue dragging the Line tool around near the initial anchor point while holding the mouse button. Add the Shift key as you move the Line tool. Observe how the dragging becomes jerky, snapping to 45° angles as you drag up and down.

4. Drag the Line tool 90° to the right, about 12 picas from the initial click, then release the mouse button. You have created a single line. Leave the line selected.

5. Double-click the Line tool icon in the toolbox. This brings up the Stroke palette on the screen. Use the palette Options pop-up menu to access Show Options, which brings up the full-size palette.

Press Command/Control to temporarily convert any tool to the Selection tool.

6. To the right of the Weight field is a drop-down menu of weights. Click this menu and select 3 pt. From the Type menu in the Stroke palette, select Dashed. The Dash/Gap section appears. Type "2" in the first Dash box, and "5" in the first Gap box. Press Tab or Enter to confirm your entries. The line is now a 3-pt. dashed line, with 2-pt. segments and 5-pt. gaps.

7. Click the middle Cap option to select rounded end caps.

The line that you drew becomes 3 pt. in thickness with rounded end caps.

8. From the End menu in the Stroke palette, select TriangleWide.

The right side of the line becomes a wide triangular arrowhead.

9. Delete the line and leave the document open for the next exercise.

Press "M" to change to the Rectangle tool, and "L" to change to the Ellipse tool.

The Ellipse Tool

The Ellipse tool creates ellipses or, if you hold down the Shift key, perfect circles. To use the Ellipse tool, you just select its icon from the toolbox then drag the cursor on the page.

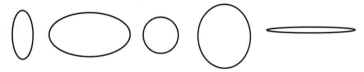

Ellipses.

The Rectangle Tool

With the Rectangle tool, you can create rectangles of any size. Holding the Shift key while dragging enables you to create a perfect square (which is defined as a rectangle with four equal sides).

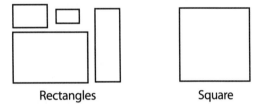

Rectangles   Square

The Polygon Tool

The Polygon tool allows you to create polygons and stars. If you hold the Shift key while dragging, you create an equilateral shape.

The difference between polygons (top row) and stars (bottom row) is that alternating corners are inset (or pointed inward) in stars.

Double-clicking the Polygon tool gives you access to the Polygon Settings dialog box.

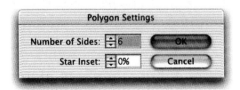

A Star Inset value other than zero moves alternating corners inward.

The Stroke Palette

An object's fill can consist of a solid color, tint, or gradient; a stroke, however, has more variables that determine its appearance. You can customize the settings of these variables in the Stroke palette.

The options in the Stroke palette.

- **Stroke Weight.** This option sets the thickness of the stroke. Stroke weights are always specified in points regardless of the measuring system you specified in the Units and Increments Preferences.

- **Miter Limit.** This option determines how rounded or angular the *joins* of a path are. A join is the corner where two segments meet at an anchor point.

- **Cap and Join.** *Caps* are the ends of open paths. Round and projecting end caps extend beyond the end of a stroke a distance equivalent to half the stroke width; butt end caps abruptly end at the path anchors or line endpoints.

Various end cap and miter styles.

- **Stroke Type.** The default stroke attribute is a single solid line, but you can choose a number of pre-built dashed line types from the Type menu on the Stroke palette, or you can create custom dashed lines by choosing Dashed from the Type menu.

The available Stroke Type options.

Dash, Gap. When you choose the Dashed stroke type, the Dash...Stroke palette appears. The increments typed in these boxes (meas...determine the length of both the dashes and the space between them...only the first two boxes (dash, gap) are used, the dashes and gaps remain...constant for the length of the stroke. By entering numbers in the other dash and gap boxes, you can make the appearance of the dashed line more creative, even alternating the size of the dashes and spaces. The Caps option that you choose also affects the appearance of dashes. If you specify rounded caps, each dash has a rounded end cap (remember that these extend beyond the measured endpoints of each dash). The Corners pop-up menu controls the appearance of dashes and gaps at the corners of the object; the default setting of Adjust Dashes and Gaps preserves an even appearance around corners, but there are other settings available.

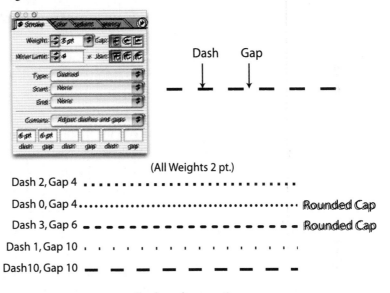

(All Weights 2 pt.)

Dash 2, Gap 4

Dash 0, Gap 4 .... Rounded Cap

Dash 3, Gap 6 ▬ ▬ ▬ ▬ ▬ ▬ ▬ ▬ ▬ ▬ ▬ Rounded Cap

Dash 1, Gap 10

Dash 10, Gap 10 ▬ ▬ ▬ ▬ ▬ ▬ ▬

Dash and gap options.

Start/End. The Start and End options in the Stroke palette determine whether any shape appears at the two ends of a path. The beginning point of a path is the Start, and the finishing point is the End.

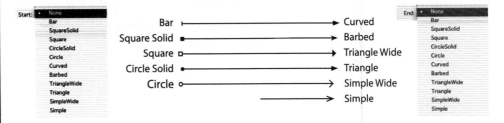

You can select from InDesign's built-in Start and End options to customize lines.

The Color Tools

Strokes can be invisible, colored, or (rarely) have an applied gradient. Fills can be empty, or made of colors, patterns, gradients, or imported graphics. You can apply a fill to either a closed or an open path. You should be careful when filling an open path that has no

...nnects between the two endpoints of an open path. You can easily tell if a ... closed, because closed paths (and frames) display their outlines in light ... paths don't (if View>Show Frame Edges is active).

... fill and stroke selection. Before you apply color to an object's fill or stroke, ... be certain that the correct icon for the desired attribute (fill or stroke) is active ... ther words, the icon for the attribute that you want to change should be in front of ... her icon. Clicking an icon brings it forward and makes it active.

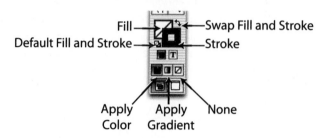

In this example, the Stroke icon is active; it is in front of the Fill icon.

- **Fill Icon.** When this icon is active, the selected object is filled with the applied color, gradient, or pattern.
- **Stroke Icon.** When the Stroke icon is active, the selected color or gradient applies to the stroke of the selected object.
- **Swap Fill and Stroke.** Clicking this icon reverses the current fill and stroke color attributes of the selected object. That is, the object's fill takes on the stroke color and the stroke assumes the fill color.
- **Default Fill and Stroke.** You can click this icon to reset an object with no fill and a black stroke. The stroke takes on the weight set in the Stroke palette.
- **Apply Color.** Double-clicking this box when an object is selected opens the Color palette, where you can create or modify colors. The resulting color is applied to the object as the colors are adjusted.

The Color palette.

Pressing "X ... between active ... Stroke icons, and pressin... Shift-X swaps the current fill and stroke colors. Pressing "D" resets the selected object to the default fill and stroke settings. You can press "," (comma) to apply the current color, press "." (period) to apply the current gradient, or press "/" (slash) to clear the current color or gradient and apply a value of None.

Remember that the correct Fill or Stroke icon must be selected in the toolbox before applying colors. If you want to fill an object with a color, the Fill icon must be active; to color a stroke, the Stroke icon must be active.

Applying a stroke to text makes it appear fat and artificially bold. This is an effect that should only be used with very large text sizes, where the addition of a stroke is less noticeable and can be used to provide a contrasting color around the type.

- **Apply Gradient.** The Gradient palette appears when you double-click the Apply Gradient box. A selected object receives a gradient fill if this button is clicked (gradients will be covered in Chapter 8, *Working with Color*).

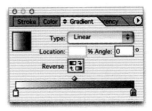

The Gradient palette.

- **None.** The None box removes colors or gradients applied to either the fill or stroke. When None is clicked, the active fill or stroke has no color applied.

Applying Colors

There are several ways to apply colors to an object's fill and stroke, or to fill selected text (you should rarely apply a stroke to text). Colors and gradients are covered in greater depth in the Chapter 8, *Working with Color*, but for now they can be summarized as follows:

- Clicking the color swatch in the Swatches palette when the object is selected.

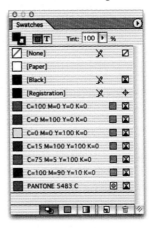

The Swatches palette.

- Clicking the Apply Color, Apply Gradient, or None icon in the toolbox when the object is selected.
- Selecting a named color swatch, then moving the color sliders in the Swatch Options dialog box (from the Swatches palette Options pop-up menu) and applying a global change — all objects that use the swatch color are changed to the new color.
- Adjusting the color sliders in the Color palette with the object selected.
- Dragging and dropping a different color swatch onto an object.

Draw and Color Shapes

1. With the document from the previous exercise open, select the Ellipse tool from the toolbox. Drag the tool cursor on the page and note how the object changes as the tool is moved. Hold the Shift key and notice how the shape is constrained to a circle. Draw a 6-pica circle on the page. With the Selection tool, move the circle to the upper-left corner of the page.

2. Click the Rectangle tool in the toolbox. Drag its tool cursor on the page and note how the rectangle can be made any size or shape. Hold the Shift key as you drag to constrain the rectangle to a square. Draw a 6-pica square and move it to the right of the circle. Deselect the square.

3. Double-click the Polygon tool in the toolbox. In the dialog box, set the Number of Sides field to 8. Leave the Star Inset field at 0%. Click OK.

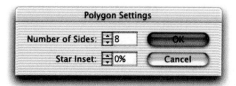

4. With the Polygon tool selected, drag the cursor on the page and note that the polygon grows disproportionately as you drag the cursor. Hold the Shift key and observe that the sides are constrained to the same size.

5. Draw a polygon 6 picas wide and high, and move it up to the right of the square. You should have three objects lined up — the circle, square, and polygon.

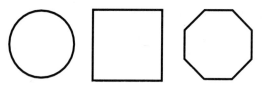

6. Now you can color these objects using the methods previously discussed. Select Window>Swatches to access the Swatches palette. The default colors appear; creating and editing colors is covered in Chapter 8, *Working with Color*, so you'll just use these default options for now.

7. With the Fill icon active (on top), click the circle with the Selection tool. In the Swatches palette, click the yellow swatch (C=0, M=0, Y=100, K=0). The circle is filled with yellow.

8. From the Window menu, select Stroke to display the Stroke palette, or double-click the Line tool. In the Weight pop-up menu, apply a 4-pt. stroke to the circle.

9. In the toolbox, click the Stroke icon to make it active. Now the stroke can receive a color. Click the green swatch in the Swatches palette (C=75, M=5, Y=100, K=0) to give the circle a green border.

10. Click the square with the Selection tool. In the toolbox, make the Fill active. In the Swatches palette, click the magenta swatch (C=0, M=100, Y=0, K=0) to fill the square with magenta. The Apply Color box takes on this color as well.

The first four default colors are None, Paper, Black, and Registration. Their names in the Swatches palette are enclosed with brackets, and these colors cannot be edited or deleted. The other colors are also created as defaults in a new document, but they can be edited and deleted.

Press "D" to apply the default settings of no fill and a black stroke.

11. In the Stroke palette, set the weight to 3 pt. Set the stroke type to dashed, giving the square a 2-pt. dash. Leave the gap box blank.

12. Activate the Stroke icon in the toolbox. Click the blue color swatch in the Swatches palette (C=100, M=90, Y=10, K=0). This gives the square a blue dashed stroke.

Notice in the enlargement below that half the stroke extends inside the object and half extends to the outside.

13. Activate the Fill icon in the toolbox.

14. Next, select the polygon you drew. This object currently has a fill of None, but the Apply Color box is still holding the magenta color that was applied to the square. Click the Apply Color box. The polygon fills with magenta. This is a shortcut for applying the last-used color to objects filled with None, rather than having to scroll through a Swatches palette that may be full of colors.

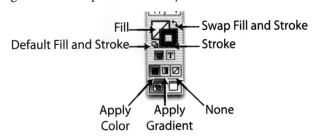

15. Click the Stroke icon in the toolbox to make it active. In the Stroke palette, set the Weight to 8 pt. In the Swatches palette, click the red swatch (C=15, M=100, Y=100, K=0) to apply an 8-pt. red border.

16. Just one more color adjustment — select all three objects, click the Fill box in the toolbox, and click the red swatch in the Swatches palette to fill them all with red.

17. Close the document without saving. *PRINT*

Frames

Frames are containers that can hold text, tables, pictures, graphic objects, and even other frames. A frame can contain either text or graphics, but not both. When you drag the Type tool on the page, you are actually creating a frame with a specific purpose — to hold imported or directly-entered text. When you create a frame with any of the Frame tools,

*There are two ways to get something into a selected frame: File>Place, or Edit>Paste Into. Placing and pasting images are covered in Chapter 9, **Working with Images**.*

InDesign automatically defines its content as graphic. You can change the content designation for any frame at any time by selecting the frame and choosing an option from Object>Content; if you do, however, InDesign deletes any existing frame content. The content type of an empty frame is determined as soon as you assign text or graphic content to it.

The Rectangle, Ellipse, and Polygon Frame tools are accessible from the toolbox. Pressing "F" selects the Rectangle Frame tool; you can click and hold the Rectangle Frame tool icon to show the other frame options. These frame tools work exactly as the shape tools, except that an empty frame has a big "X" through the middle and no default stroke or fill is applied.

InDesign includes Rectangle, Ellipse, and Polygon Frame tools.

You can easily identify a frame's content type. A graphic frame has an "X" through the middle; a text frame, when selected, displays In and Out ports, even if the frame doesn't contain any text.

In addition to the three standard frame shapes, you can designate any object drawn with InDesign's tools as a frame, even Bézier shapes drawn with the Pen. Shapes created with the Shape or Pen tools are fundamentally frames that have no content type assigned to them. You can convert a shape to a frame at any time by selecting it and choosing Object>Content>Graphic to make it a graphic frame, or Object>Content>Text to make it a text frame; you can also set a frame's content to Unassigned.

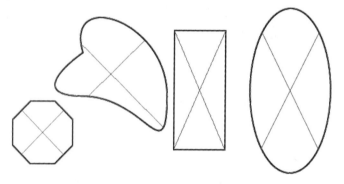

These polygon, rectangle, and ellipse graphic frames were created with the Frame tools. The blob-shaped frame was created with the Pen tool, then converted to a frame with Object>Content>Graphic.

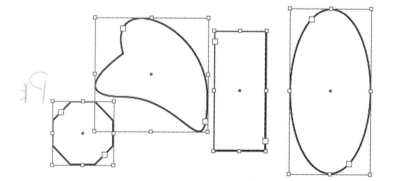

The same frames as above, converted to Text frames. Notice the In and Out ports.

Anatomy of Frames

When a frame is selected, a box with handles surrounding the frame appears. This is the frame's bounding box; you can use the handles to resize or reshape the frame. The handles normally act on the frame itself, not on its contents.

The bounding box of a rectangle frame is not easy to see because the shape of the frame defines the bounding box. The bounding box is more apparent for ellipse and polygon frames.

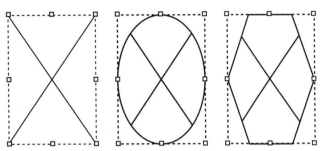

The three standard frame shapes, with the bounding boxes rendered as dashed lines. The frames are selected to show their bounding boxes and handles.

Moving the box handles resizes a frame accordingly. If you hold the Shift key while moving any of the handles, the frame enlarges or reduces proportionally on both the vertical and horizontal axes. Using the Command/Control key, with or without Shift, resizes frame content along with the frame. This only affects graphic content; text does not scale when a text frame is resized interactively like this. Text *does* scale if you resize the frame with the Transform palette, which generally produces undesirable results.

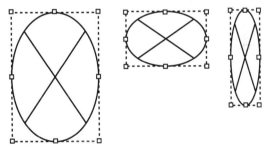

A frame can be resized and reshaped.

Frames are not just containers. Like anything else made with the drawing tools, you can modify a frame's fill and stroke characteristics.

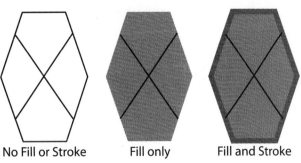

No Fill or Stroke   Fill only   Fill and Stroke

If you press Command/Control while resizing a frame or otherwise manipulating its handles, the content (graphic only) is also resized or reshaped. Holding Shift constrains the frame to its current proportions; pressing both Shift and Command/Control constrains both the frame and its contents.

An interesting design effect is to fill a frame with a color, then place a graphic inside of it. The object floats on top of the color. This is an easy way to give an object a colored background if you want one.

This frame was filled with yellow with a black stroke, and then the cat graphic was placed.

All frames have a center point, which isn't a handle. To move the frame with either of the Selection tools, you simply drag the center point. It's easy to inadvertently alter a frame's shape when using the Direct Selection tool, but using this point makes that less likely.

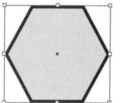 

The same frame activated by the Selection tool (left) and the Direct Selection tool (right). Both types of selections display the center point, which is either solid (Selection tool) or open (Direct Selection tool). Both tools let you drag the center point to move the frame without altering it.

Manipulating Objects and Frames

Whether it is placed in the frame with File>Place, or pasted inside the frame with the Edit>Paste Into command, an object defaults to the upper-left corner of the frame's bounding box. Once an object is placed inside a frame, the first consideration is how to move either the frame or the object so the object has a more practical location. There are four ways to organize the frame and object's shape and position:

- Adjusting the frame's control handles
- Clicking a graphic with the Direct Selection tool and repositioning it within the frame
- Clicking the frame with the Selection tool and repositioning it
- Using the Object>Fitting menu selections

*If you use Paste Into to paste a frame inside another frame, the frame that is pasted becomes a **nested** frame.*

The Selection tool moves both the frame and its contents.

When handles are moved with the Selection tool, the frame is resized.

Using Command/Control and the Selection tool resizes the frame's content along with the frame itself; adding the Shift key constrains both the frame and content proportions.

The Direct Selection tool moves either the frame or the contents independent of each other.

Press the "A" key to choose the Direct Selection tool.

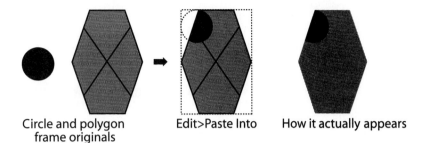

Circle and polygon frame originals   Edit>Paste Into   How it actually appears

To create this example, we first drew the circle with the Ellipse tool, then selected and cut it. We then drew and selected the Polygon frame. We used the Edit>Paste Into command to put the circle inside the frame; the circle went into the upper-left area of the polygon frame's bounding box. We show this with dashed lines, though it actually looks as if the circle is cut off at the frame's edges.

Adjusting the Frame Handles

To fine-tune the fit of a frame around an object, you can drag the frame's handles to resize the frame. This makes it easy to manipulate frames for correct object placement.

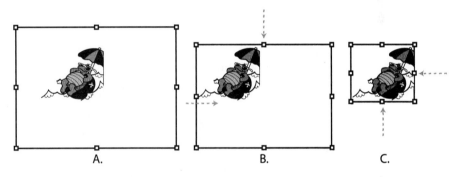

A.   B.   C.

We pasted this turtle artwork into a frame (A), then moved the box handles of the frame inward (B, C) to better fit the art.

Using the Direct Selection Tool

The fastest way to move the frame or the object is to drag either the frame or the object with the Direct Selection tool. Remember, when moving objects, the Shift key constrains the movement to 45° angles.

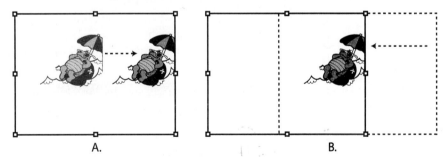

A.   B.

We selected the turtle image with the Direct Selection tool and dragged it to the right (A). A different way to produce the same effect is to select the frame with the Direct Selection tool and drag it to the left (B).

Frames can only hold one object at a time. If a frame already has content, and you paste something else into it, the old content is replaced with the new.

Frames that already contain objects or text cannot be converted to other frame types unless you first remove the content.

Frames assume the frame type of their contents. If you click the Type tool in an empty graphic frame, it becomes a text frame.

Fitting Objects by Menu

There are four options in Object>Fitting to automatically fit objects and frames. These options are Fit Content to Frame, Fit Frame to Content, Center Content, and Fit Content Proportionally.

Fit Content to Frame scales the object to the frame's largest dimension. The horizontal and vertical proportions may not be retained.

Fit Frame to Content fits the frame to the contours of the object that it holds, as well as the frame's structure allows. This option does not change content proportions.

Center Content centers content within the frame, without changing the content proportions.

Fit Content Proportionally enlarges or reduces the object to fit the frame, while maintaining the object's horizontal and vertical proportions. This option places the content at the upper left of the bounding box and scales it up or down until it "fits" within the frame's smallest dimension. You can then use the Center Content option to center the object within the frame.

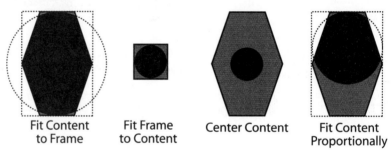

Fit Content to Frame   Fit Frame to Content   Center Content   Fit Content Proportionally

Here, the frame is the polygon (gray) and the content is a circle (black).

Converting Paths and Frames

You are not restricted to the three predefined (rectangle, ellipse, and polygon) frame shapes. If you draw a path with the Pen tool, or alter an existing path, you can convert it to a frame with the Content options of the Object menu.

You can define any drawn object as a frame with the Object>Content options.

There are three frame states: graphic, text, and unassigned. The Graphic option converts a path to a graphic frame. Empty text frames can be converted to graphic frames, and vice versa. Both graphic and text frames can be converted to the Unassigned option, which is a generic path. Whatever the frame type, it is indicated in this menu. If a frame already has

content, the other choices are grayed out, because you can't change the type without losing the content. A path drawn with the Pen, or a shape drawn with the Shape tools, is designated by the Unassigned option until you choose to give it a content type.

Work with Frames

1. Select File>New to create a new document.

2. In the toolbox, select the Ellipse tool and draw a circle 6 picas wide and high on the page. Color the circle with a red fill and a yellow stroke.

3. With the Rectangle tool, draw a 12-pica × 6-pica rectangle and color it with a blue fill and a green stroke.

4. With the Polygon tool, draw a 6-sided polygon 6 picas high, with its width constrained to height. (Note that even though the polygon is symmetrical, the width is actually greater than the height, according to the Transform palette.) Color it with a yellow fill and a red stroke.

   You now have three objects to work with and place inside the upcoming frames. Select all three objects and use the Stroke palette to set their stroke weights to 2 pt.

5. Click and hold the Frame tool icon to access its pop-up menu, then select the Ellipse Frame tool. Drag its cursor on the page to draw an oval frame 12 picas × 288 points. 24picas

6. Draw equal-size frames with both the Rectangle Frame and Polygon Frame tools.

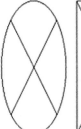  

```
 72
 72
144
144
288
```

7. Select the circle object created earlier and cut it. (Edit>Cut or Command/Control-X). Click the oval frame and paste the circle inside the frame (Edit>Paste Into or Command-Option-V/Control-Alt-V).

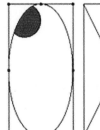  

```
 72
 72
 72
 72
288
```

*A frame can act as a mask for any graphical content it contains. A **mask** is used to hide parts of an image, and show others. Anything outside of the mask doesn't show.*

8. Using the Direct Selection tool, click the circle and move it around inside the oval. Move it so part of the circle is outside of the oval boundary. The frame masks out part of the circle. Leave the circle where it is.

9. Select the ellipse frame with the Selection tool. Choose Object>Fitting>Center Content. The circle moves to the exact center of the frame.

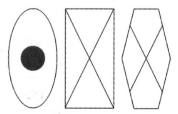

10. Click the control handles of the frame and reduce the size of the oval frame until it tightly surrounds the circle. In the toolbox, click the Fill box to make it active. In the Swatches palette, click the cyan (light blue) swatch to color the oval frame. Notice that the color of the frame appears behind the circle.

11. Select the polygon object and use Edit>Cut to cut it. Select the rectangle frame and choose Edit>Paste Into to place the object inside the frame. Click the frame with the Direct Selection tool and move the frame to center the object.

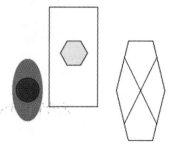

12. Select the rectangular frame with the Selection tool. From the Object menu, choose Fitting>Fit Frame to Content. The frame shrinks to conform to the edges of the polygon. Click the control handles of the frame to drag them outward, enlarging the frame to see more of its interior.

13. The Fill box should still be selected, so click the cyan swatch to color the frame. Click the Stroke box in the toolbox to make it active. Click the green swatch. Access the Stroke palette from the Window menu and change its weight to 4 pt.

14. Click the polygon with the Direct Selection tool and move it around within the rectangle frame. Reselect the rectangular frame. From the Object menu, select Fitting>Fit Content Proportionally. The polygon enlarges to fill the frame's narrowest dimension, while retaining it proportions.

You can also use a contextual menu to access the Fitting options. Control/Right-click a selected frame to show the contextual menu, and choose Fitting from there.

Command/Control-Option/Alt-V is the shortcut for the Paste Into command.

15. Select the rectangle object with the Selection tool and cut it. Select the polygon frame and choose Edit>Paste Into to paste the object inside the frame.

16. Press the "A" key to switch to the Direct Selection tool.

17. Click the center point of the polygon frame to move it around and better center the rectangle inside it. (If you click inside the frame, you move the rectangle instead.)

18. From the Object menu, choose Fitting>Fit Content to Frame to enlarge the rectangle. Notice that the entire polygon is filled. The rectangle has not just filled the polygon shape — it has filled the entire bounding box area.

19. Color the frame with a red fill and a yellow stroke. Change the weight to 3 pt. in the Stroke palette. You can't see the fill because the rectangle is covering it.

20. Click the oval frame that you first created. Cut this frame (Edit>Cut) then, with the Direct Selection tool, click the rectangle within the polygon frame and select Edit>Paste Into. You have now "nested" one frame inside another.

21. Use the Direct Selection tool to click any of the objects or frames and observe how the elements can be moved around individually. Experiment with the center point using both of the Selection tools.

22. Close the document without saving. *PRINT*

Arranging Objects

When drawing multiple objects or frames, one object may obscure another by being in front of it. Layers provide one way to stack objects in front of or behind one another. There is another way, however, to arrange objects and their relationship to each other. The arrangement of objects from front to back on a single layer is known as the "stacking order." This order has two basic rules:

- Newly created objects (graphics and text frames) are automatically placed in front of all other objects in the document.

- Any object that is pasted into the document goes in front of all other objects in the document.

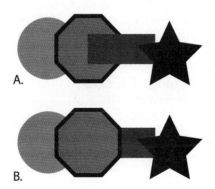

In this example, we drew the circle first, then added the other objects in the order you see, left to right (A). We then selected, cut, and pasted the polygon; when pasted, the polygon was positioned in front of all other objects (B), because InDesign treats it as the most recently inserted item.

These are the keyboard shortcuts for the Arrange options:

Bring to Front:
Command/Control-Shift-]

Bring Forward:
Command/Control-]

Send Backward:
Command/Control-[

Send to Back:
Command/Control-Shift-[

The Arrange Menu Options

The Arrange feature in the Object menu allows you to rearrange the hierarchy (or stacking order) of the objects on a page. These four Arrange menu options save valuable time in moving objects forward and backward, as desired.

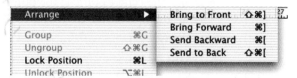

There are four options in the Object>Arrange menu.

- **Bring To Front** moves all selected objects to the immediate front of all other objects (while retaining their stacking order relative to one another).
- **Bring Forward** moves the selected object up one level in the stacking order.
- **Send Backward** moves the selected object back one level in the stacking order.
- **Send To Back** moves all selected objects to the immediate back of all other objects (while retaining their stacking order relative to one another).

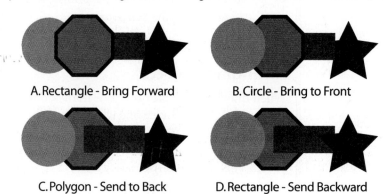

A. Rectangle - Bring Forward   B. Circle - Bring to Front

C. Polygon - Send to Back   D. Rectangle - Send Backward

In this example, we copied and pasted the polygon, which made it the front object. Next, we selected the rectangle and applied the Bring Forward command; this moved it in front of the star, but kept it in back of the polygon (A). We then selected the circle and applied the Bring To Front command; this made it the front most object (B). We then selected the polygon and chose Send To Back; this put it behind all other objects (C). To arrange the rectangle behind the star, but in front of the polygon, we selected it then applied Send Backward.

Arrange Objects

1. From the File menu, navigate to the **RF_Intro_InDesign** folder and open the document **arrange.indd**. It looks like there's just a picture of some asparagus on the page, but if you open the Links palette, you'll see that there are actually three placed images in the document. This can all be fixed by using the Arrange options to get everything in order.

Document window at 50% view.

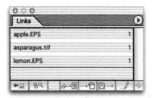

Other images are present in the document, but where are they?

2. With the Selection tool, click the picture of the asparagus, and choose Object>Arrange>Send To Back to put it at the back of the stack of images. Now you can see the apple and the lemon slice in the document.

3. Drag the lemon slice over the apple. Because this image was placed before the apple was, it is behind the apple in the stacking order, and seems to disappear behind the apple. Use Object>Arrange>Bring to Front to move the lemon slice in front of the apple.

4. With the lemon slice still selected, press Command/Control-[(Send Backward) once, then once again, and watch the position of the lemon's stacking order change.

If you scale objects with the Selection tool, InDesign does not remember anything about this type of transformation. You should get into the habit of using the Direct Selection tool, Transform palette, or the transformation tools to modify objects, because you can always revert back to the original setting. For example, if you proportionally scale a frame that contains a graphic by pressing Command/Control-Shift and dragging a handle with the Selection tool, the X and Y scale percentages in the Transform palette do not change; they still read 100% when you finish. If you use the Direct Selection tool and click the frame content, the percentage of scaling is shown in the Transform palette, and you can change it back to 100% or any other value later on.

5. Press Command/Control-] (Bring Forward) twice, slowly, and watch the lemon pop back to the top of the stack. It might help to visualize the elements as a stack of dishes; Bring Forward or Send Backward moves the selected dish up or down in the stack, and Send to Back or Bring to Front puts the dish at the bottom or top of the stack.

6. Close the file without saving.

Transforming Objects

Objects often need further enhancements, such as altering their size to fit a layout, rotating them, or shearing them to give a simulated perspective view. All of these modifications are considered to be *transformations*. To transform an object is to alter its original state. In InDesign, there are options for rotating, scaling, shearing, and free transformation.

There are two ways to transform objects:

- **Transform Palette.** In the Transform palette, you can type specific numeric transformations into a variety of fields. This is the method to use when numbers or angles must be exact, such as a 45° rotation. InDesign "remembers" object transformations when they are done with the Transform palette (except for scaling of text frames).

- **Manually.** In this process, you can drag a selected object with one of the dedicated transformation tools (such as the Rotate tool). This method relies on the appearance of the selected object. You can, however, observe the precise percentages and angles in the Transform palette as you manipulate the object. InDesign also remembers manual transformations done to graphic frames or graphic objects with the transformation tools.

If you want to resize a text frame, you should use the Selection tool to do so. InDesign remembers rotation and shear transformations applied to text frames. InDesign does *not* remember scaling of text frames no matter how you do it; in addition, scaling text frames with the Transform palette or Scale tool *always* scales the text. It is much better to use the Selection tool to resize text frames.

InDesign does remember text frame transformations as they apply to the text in the frame. For example, if you scale a text frame using the Transform palette to 150% in the X axis and 200% in the Y axis, the Transform palette reads 100% for both afterward; however, if you select the text with the Type tool and look at the Character palette, the settings for Horizontal and Vertical scale reflect the transformation. If you scale a text frame in the Transform palette with equal percentages of vertical and horizontal scaling, the Character palette displays the new point size of the type. We discourage the use of frame scaling for altering type sizes and shapes. Instead, use the Character palette, Character and Paragraph styles, and other tools you've learned for these purposes.

The Transform Palette

The Transform palette has eight fields in which you can type numbers to create various transforming effects. After you type a number into one of these fields, you can either press the Return/Enter or Tab key, or just click in another field to apply this information to the selected object.

An easy way to apply numbers typed in a Transformation palette field to a selected object is to click the cursor into another field. If you type "45" in the Rotate field and then click any other field in the palette, the selected object rotates 45 degrees.

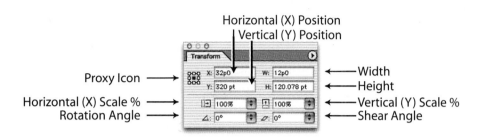

The InDesign Transform palette.

The Proxy Icon

At the left of the Transform palette is a pattern of squares, with one square blacked out when an object is selected. All nine points, taken together, are a *proxy* of the bounding box of the object selected. This black square represents the *reference point*. This is the point, or axis, on which the transformation performs its operation. The default reference point is the center point.

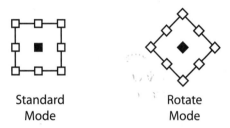

Standard Mode   Rotate Mode

InDesign's default settings define all nine reference points perpendicular to one another; if, however, you rotate an object 22.5° or more, the proxy symbol changes to represent a more angular appearance.

The proxy reference point in the Transform palette is the point that the object uses as the anchor for the transformation. It is set in the proxy, or it can be moved manually when a transformation tool is active.

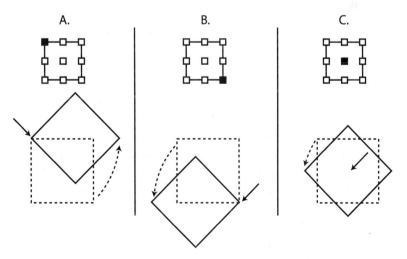

The original position of the square is represented by the dashed line. We typed "45" into the Rotate field of the Transform palette, and rotated the square using three different proxy reference points: the upper-left corner (A), the lower-right corner (B), and the exact center (C). In the third example, the proxy is shown prior to rotating.

The Transformation Tools

InDesign has four tools used for transforming objects:

- **Rotate.** The Rotate tool spins the selected object around the reference point.
- **Scale.** The Scale tool reduces or enlarges an object, either uniformly (proportionately) or disproportionately.
- **Shear.** The Shear tool skews a selected object to make it appear as if it were being viewed from an angle.
- **Free Transform.** The Free Transform tool allows you to move, rotate, scale, shear, and reflect objects without changing tools.

Positive numbers rotate objects toward the left, or counterclockwise. To rotate an object clockwise, a negative sign must be placed in front of the number (for example, –45).

Rotating Objects

With the Rotate tool, you can revolve a selected object around the reference point, which you set either with the proxy in the Transform palette, or by manually dragging the point to a new location. The rotation is performed either by typing the angle into the Rotate field of the Transform palette, or clicking the Rotate tool in the toolbox and dragging the object. To use the Transform palette to rotate does not require clicking on the Rotate tool in the toolbox. When rotating by manual dragging, you should leave the Transform palette on the screen so you can monitor the exact angle of the rotation as the object moves.

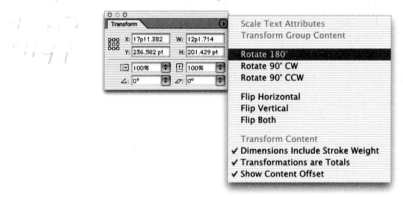

The Transform palette has a pop-up menu that offers three other rotating options: Rotate 180°, Rotate 90° CW (Clockwise), and Rotate 90° CCW (Counterclockwise).

Reflecting an Object

Objects often need to be reflected, mirrored, or flipped. InDesign doesn't have a Reflect tool, so you need to use the Transform palette's Options pop-up menu to select Flip Horizontal, Flip Vertical, or Flip Both to meet the need.

Scaling Objects

You can scale objects either by using the Transform palette or by manually dragging. The Transform palette can be set to maintain uniform (proportional) scaling. When dragging the object with the Scale tool, you need to hold the Shift key to constrain the object to uniform proportions.

Scaling with the Transform Palette

When you scale a selected object with the Transform palette, the object's new size is based on the units that you type into the X and Y Scale Percentage fields. The X Scale Percentage represents the width (horizontal) of the object; the Y Scale Percentage is the height (vertical).

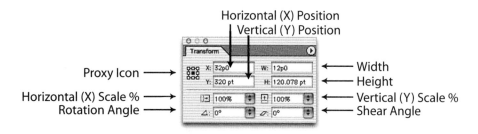

The Transform palette.

To keep the scaling proportional, the two percentage fields must be identical in number. 100% is the object's original size. Percentages higher than 100 increase the size; values lower than 100 reduce it.

If the scaled object needs to be returned to its original size, you can simply type "100" into both the X and Y Scale Percentage fields (or choose 100% in both pop-up menus).

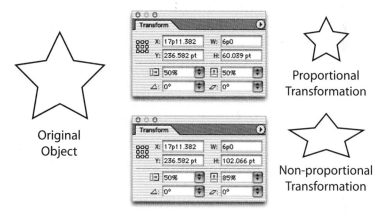

In this example, the star was scaled with both proportional and non-proportional values.

Sometimes a scaling value is too big to accommodate the object; InDesign warns you if you try to make something too large to fit your current work area. If the size causes the object to crash into the limits of the pasteboard, you'll get an error message:

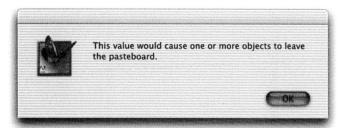

You cannot scale an object so large that it extends completely beyond the pasteboard limits.

If you see this error message, you need to either reposition the object being transformed so it doesn't hit the limits of the pasteboard, or choose a smaller scaling value. This message can also appear when rotating objects around a distant reference point. InDesign doesn't

The reference point is not visible on the selected object until a transformation tool is selected from the toolbox.

To apply the same (proportional) scaling value to both X and Y dimensions, you can type the value into either field and then press Command/Control-Return/Enter. This copies the value from one field to the other, and applies both to the object.

let you move things completely off the pasteboard, but you can move things nearly off the pasteboard (so only a small portion of the object remains on the pasteboard).

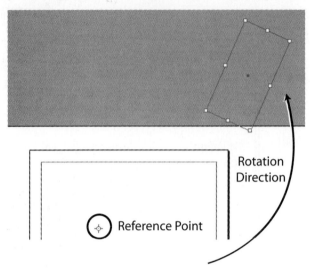

*Here, an object with a distant reference point is rotated as far as possible;
InDesign doesn't allow it to be completely rotated off the pasteboard.*

If the center of the object is designated as the reference point, the object remains centered on its current position when it is scaled.

Scaling with the Scale Dialog Box

With the Scale dialog box, you can resize wither the selected frame (with or without its contents) or an exact copy of that frame. Double-clicking the Scale tool in the toolbox provides access to this dialog box.

You may select Uniform to scale both horizontal and vertical dimensions to the same percentage, or you may select Non-uniform to scale disproportionately. You can also choose whether to scale the content of graphic frames.

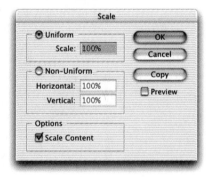

The Scale tool dialog box.

Direct Scaling

To directly scale an object, you must first click the Scale tool. The cursor appears as crosshairs, and changes to an arrowhead when you select the object and begin the transformation. Dragging sizes the object in relation to its reference point. The arrowhead cursor is used to drag the object. If you hold the Shift key while dragging, the object scales uniformly (constrained both horizontally and vertically).

You can copy any object by holding the Option/Alt key while dragging. If you press the Shift key after you start dragging, the movement of the copy is constrained to 45° increments.

If you want an object duplicated exactly on top of itself, you can choose Edit>Step and Repeat, then set the Repeat Count field to "1" and the Horizontal and Vertical Offset fields to "0" (zero).

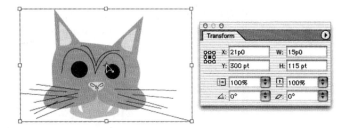

Here, the reference point is active (arrow cursor) and can be moved, but we used the default center reference point as shown in the proxy.

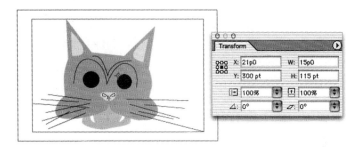

Here, the scaling move has started — note the arrowhead cursor being dragged down. The outline of the bounding box is visible as you scale.

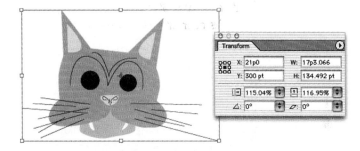

After releasing the mouse button, the new scale percentages, as well as the adjusted width and height values, are displayed in the Transform palette.

The Shear Tool

The Shear tool distorts or skews objects. This might be used to create the impression that an object is being viewed from a different perspective. Another use of the Shear tool is to transform a duplicate of an image to look like the object's cast shadow.

Original

Sheared samples

Direct Shearing

Shearing is best performed directly. The Transform palette can seem restrictive when used to shear an object because exact units must be typed into the Shear field. This can be tedious when you are experimenting with effects. By manually shearing an object, you see the effect as you drag the object.

The location of the reference point is important when shearing manually. The best choices for the reference point are the four corners of the object's bounding box; the worst location for the reference point is the center of the object. If the object's center is designated as the shearing axis, erratic skewing is almost impossible to control. You should set the Reference Point in the Transform palette, and then relocate it manually.

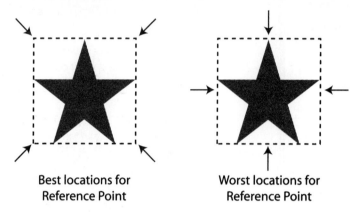

Best locations for
Reference Point

Worst locations for
Reference Point

Even more important than the reference point are: the point where you initially click with the Shear tool, and the direction in which you drag. You typically get the best results by dragging the tool cursor away from the corner directly opposite the reference point.

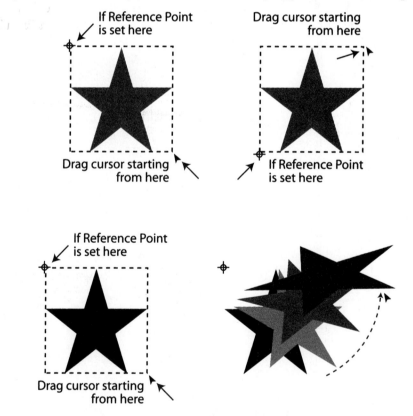

In this example, we first selected the star object, then the Shear tool. We set the reference point to the upper-left corner, then placed the tool on the lower-right corner and dragged upward. The star sheared as the tool was dragged.

Transform Objects

1. Create a new document from the File menu.

2. Use the Ellipse, Rectangle, and Polygon tools to draw three objects 6 picas wide by 72 points high: a circle, a square, and a 6-sided polygon.

3. Fill the circle with red. Give it a 3-pt. stroke of yellow. Fill the rectangle with green, and apply a 2-pt. stroke of yellow. Fill the polygon with cyan, and apply a 1-pt. blue stroke.

4. Click the square with the Selection tool. If the Transform palette is not visible, choose Window>Transform. Make sure the reference point is set for the middle point. In the Rotate field, type "45". Press Enter/Return to apply the rotation. The square rotates 45°.

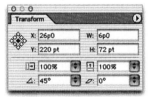

5. Select the polygon, then click the center-right proxy reference point in the Transform palette. Click the Rotate tool in the toolbox and drag it down on the left side of the polygon. The object rotates on the axis set by the reference point.

  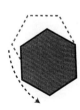

6. Holding the Shift key, select all three objects. Click the Rotate tool in the toolbox to see the reference point crosshair. Drag it to the right to relocate it manually.

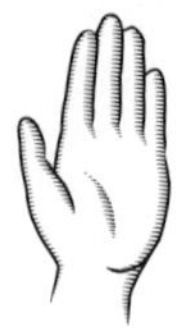

The location and angles of your objects may not exactly match those shown here.

7. Click the Rotate cursor to the left of the circle and drag downward. All three selected objects rotate as you drag.

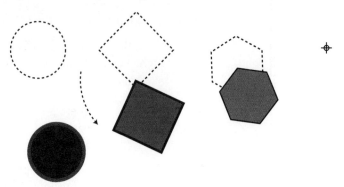

8. With all objects still selected, click the Scale tool in the toolbox. Drag the crosshair to the upper left of the area surrounding the three objects.

9. Drag the Scale cursor toward the crosshair, holding the Shift key to constrain the scaling to uniform proportions. Stop at approximately 50%. You'll have to release the mouse button to check the scaling percentage, because the values don't change while you use the tool.

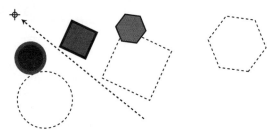

10. In the Transform palette, set the reference point as the center of the objects. In the scale fields, type "200" for both the X and Y percentages. Press the Enter/Return key to apply this. The objects scale to approximately their original sizes.

11. From the Transform palette Options pop-up menu, select Flip Vertical. The three objects flip across a vertical axis in their combined center.

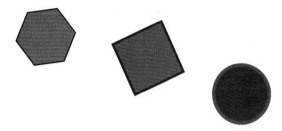

12. From the same pop-up menu, select Flip Horizontal. The objects flip again, this time over a horizontal axis.

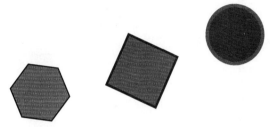

13. Click the Rotate tool in the toolbox. The proxy reference point is still set for the center of the objects. Click the cursor on the circle and drag down to rotate the objects.

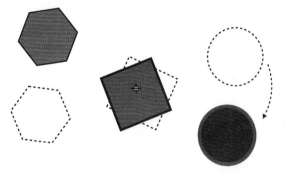

14. Select the Shear tool. Drag the reference point crosshair to the upper-left corner of the area surrounding the polygon. Click with the Shear tool cursor near the bottom right of the circle, and drag up and to the left to shear all three objects.

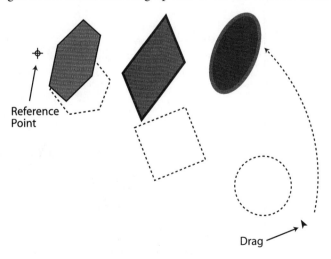

15. In the Transform palette, click the center proxy reference point. Drag the cursor to the right of the circle, moving it up and to the left, shearing the objects even more.

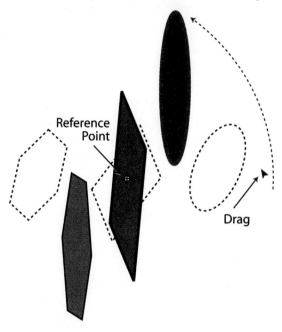

16. Click the Rotate tool in the toolbox and set the proxy reference point to the left center of the selected objects. Drag the cursor from the circle, pulling down. While you are dragging, press Option/Alt to duplicate the rotated objects.

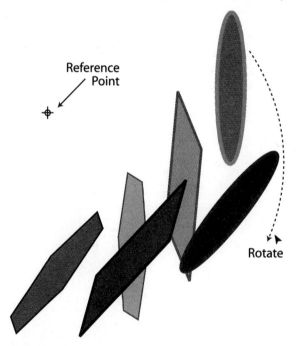

17. Close the document without saving.

The Duplicate, Step & Repeat, and Paste in Place Commands
You'll often encounter situations in which one or more objects must be duplicated and arranged precisely on a page; this typically occurs for production purposes, but also has

Press Command-Option-Shift-D (Macintosh) or Control-Alt-Shift-D (Windows) to duplicate one or more selected objects.

Press Command/Control-Shift-V to access the Step and Repeat dialog box.

Press Command-Option-Shift-V (Macintosh) or Control-Alt-Shift-V (Windows) to invoke the Paste in Place function.

Press Command/Control-G to group selected objects. Add Shift to ungroup a selected group of objects.

various artistic purposes. The Duplicate function basically replaces a Cut or Copy and Paste sequence with a single command; it places a copy of the selected object(s) offset a few points away from the original.

The Step and Repeat function derives its name from a technique used in the printing industry to image multiple copies of a page onto a printing plate by using a special exposure device called, unsurprisingly, a "step and repeat machine" (generically known as a "Misomex" after the now-defunct company that manufactured them) that exposed a portion of the plate, then "stepped" over to the next area and "repeated" the image. A step-and-repeat layout is required for generally small, repetitive pages or other types of art such as business cards and forms, stamps, small folding cartons such as cigarette packs and cosmetics packaging, and other products that are printed on a large sheet or roll of material, then cut into individual products.

InDesign's Step and Repeat feature enables you to specify how many copies to make of one or more objects, and how the copies should be distributed across the page.

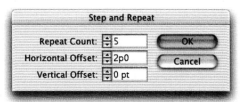

This Step and Repeat setup produces five copies of the selected object, spaced two picas apart horizontally with no vertical offset.

If you want to make a copy of a selected object directly on top of the original, you can use the Paste in Place function to effectively "clone" an object. Some designers prefer doing this, and then moving the copy with the Selection tool while constraining the move with the Shift key; it is the same as a Step and Repeat of one with no offsets. It's solely a matter of personal preference.

Group/Ungroup

The Group feature allows you to take multiple objects of any kind and combine them into a single larger object. This is a handy feature when working with art that requires multiple parts with precise positioning requirements, or when you need to copy, move, or transform a number of objects simultaneously.

When you group objects, the resulting object is a frame with the group as its content. It has a single bounding box that encloses the dimensions of the group.

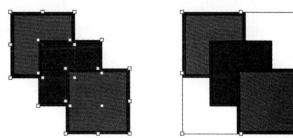

Three selected objects before (left) and after (right) the Group command was applied. Notice the group's bounding box outlines all of the objects.

You can select grouped items individually with the Direct Selection tool, and you can apply the usual transformations and edits to them as to any other object. You can also place content into any grouped frame by selecting it with the Direct Selection tool, and placing or pasting text or graphics into it.

Use the Group and Step and Repeat Functions

1. Create a new document with the following specifications: letter-size, no facing pages, vertical orientation, 36-pt. top and bottom margins, 3p0 left and right margins, 1 column.

2. Draw a rectangular frame 9p0 wide and 180 pt. tall with X and Y coordinates of 3p0 and 36 pt. at the upper-left corner of the frame (remember to reset the proxy from the center reference point to the upper-left reference point). Give the frame a black 1-pt. stroke, and no fill. Make sure the frame is selected for the next step.

3. Choose File>Place (or press Command/Control-D) and navigate to your **RF_Intro_InDesign** folder, then place the file **lemon.eps** into this frame. It's a little too big to fit, so choose Object>Fitting>Fit Content Proportionally to wedge the lemon slice into the frame. Try Control/Right-click to use the contextual menu instead of the main Object menu; these contextual menus are designed to reduce mouse movements.

4. Select the Type tool and draw a text frame 9p0 × 90 pt. It doesn't really matter where you draw it as long as you use those dimensions. You'll move it later.

5. Type the following:

   U Pickem Fruit Farm

   17 County Road #2

   Snoutville, MN 55021

   <Return/Enter>

   Clem Odegaard, Prop.

   Center this text, and apply the following type specs: Caflisch Script Pro, Regular, 14 pt., auto leading.

6. Switch to the Selection tool, set the proxy reference point to the bottom-left corner, and move the text frame to the following coordinates (check the Transform palette values as you drag, or enter the values directly into the Transform palette):

X = 3p0, Y = 216 pt.

7. Select both frames by Shift-clicking the lemon's frame, or by dragging a selection box around both frames.

8. Press Command/Control-G to group the two frames.

9. Notice that this grouped object looks suspiciously like a business card, although its dimensions differ from those of a standard U.S. 3 × 2 in. business card. The inner margin dimensions of the defined page are 45 picas × 720 points, which just happens to be perfectly divisible by 9 and 180 into five across and four down. These cards can be printed 20 per sheet, or "20-up," and cut into individual cards after printing.

To create the print layout, select the card group, and then choose Edit>Step and Repeat. You want five cards across, so enter these values and click OK:

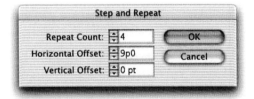

You already have one card in place, so you only need four more copies across.

10. Zoom out to view the page at 50%. The cards should look like this:

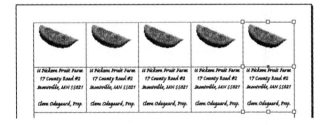

11. Press Command/Control-A to select a ll of the objects on the page, then choose Edit>Step and Repeat again. Set the Repeat Count to 3, the Horizontal Offset to 0p0, and the Vertical Offset to 180 pt., and click OK:

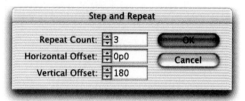

The finished page should look like this.

If it doesn't, double-check your Step and Repeat settings, your X and Y coordinates, and your frame dimensions, and try again.

12. Save the document, if you wish, as **lemoncards.indd** to your **Work_In_Progress** folder.

It's easy to see how the Step and Repeat function, especially in conjunction with the Group feature, can save a significant amount of time in the process of building certain types of documents.

Direct Transformations

Manually transforming a selected object involves manipulating the object with one of the transformation tools to change its appearance. You need to select the object, select a transformation tool (Rotate, Scale, or Shear) from the toolbox, then drag the tool's cursor near the object, transforming its appearance.

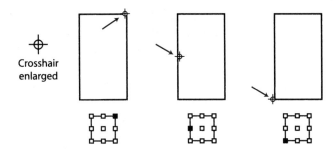

When you select a transformation tool from the toolbox, the reference point crosshair becomes visible on the selected object. You can change the reference point by clicking any of the other squares in the proxy.

In addition to designating a reference point with the proxy, you can also manually drag it to a custom location. For example, let's say that you want to rotate the object around a distant point, but the Transform palette's proxy reference points make no provision for this. After you select the object and click the Rotate tool in the toolbox, you can drag the crosshair to any location on the pasteboard.

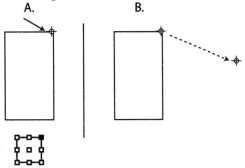

After the reference point crosshair appears (A), you can drag it to any location of your choice (B).

When you manually relocate the reference point, the transformed object uses the new location as its axis.

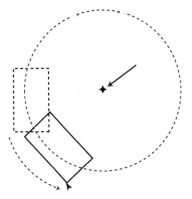

After the reference point was moved (with the Rotate tool activated), we dragged the rectangle to revolve it around the relocated reference point.

Duplicating While Transforming

Sometimes it's necessary to transform a duplicate of an object. It can be tedious to first duplicate the path, then select this copy to make transformations. Instead, you can duplicate the original object before making the transformation by selecting the object and double-clicking the tool's icon in the toolbox, which shows a dialog box for that tool. In the dialog box, there's a Copy button that makes a copy of the selected object and applies any specified transformations after you click OK in the tool's dialog.

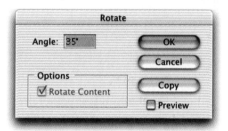

Dialog box for the Rotate tool.

To use this dialog, you need to first specify your transformation (such as rotation angle or scale percentage) and then click the Copy button to apply the transformation to a copy of the object. Checking the Preview box allows you to see what's happening as you make your choices.

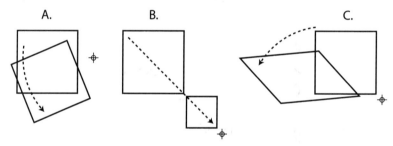

In this example, we duplicated the square while rotating it (A), scaling it (B), and shearing it (C) by using the dialog box associated with the tool.

Summary

You have learned to use InDesign's graphic object creation tools and frame tools. You have learned to draw Bézier paths and objects with the Pen tool, and to create basic shapes with the Rectangle, Ellipse, and Polygon tools. You learned how to apply strokes and fills to objects, and how to manipulate those objects using the transformation tools and change their stacking order. You've also learned the intricacies of InDesign's scaling features.

Working with Color

Chapter Objective:

Using color correctly can seem complicated at first, but it is important for bringing your documents to life. Color can add emotional and visual appeal to both printed and electronic documents. This chapter introduces the various color models used in the graphics industry, and describes how you can use them effectively as you create files with InDesign. In Chapter 8, you will:

- Understand the different color models, and why it's important to use the proper color model for a particular job.

- Become familiar with standard terms for discussing color.

- Learn how to use InDesign's Swatches palette to create new CMYK and RGB colors, and to edit colors.

- Understand how to choose spot colors from the available spot color libraries, and how to make tints.

- Become familiar with gradients and how to create successful blends.

- Understand how to import color from other InDesign documents, and from placed files.

- Learn to apply color to elements such as InDesign objects, frames, images, and text.

- Learn about InDesign's new transparency, drop shadows, and feathering features.

Projects to be Completed:

- Central Market Ad (A)

- **Yellow Rose Menu (B)**

- Travel Brochure (C)

- Good Choices Newsletter (D)

Working with Color

We can communicate perfectly well using black and white (and even tints of black), but color gives life to photographic images and other graphic elements, allows us to highlight elements, and lends variety to documents. Color production costs have decreased markedly in the past decade, which is why most newspapers now have a full-color front page. The term "color" covers a lot of territory, which we explore in this chapter. It's important to understand why you should always create or specify colors with the end product in mind.

It's also important to understand how colors interact: how they combine visually, how they work together in the design and layout programs that we use, and how they appear when ink finally hits paper. Documents printed on an ink jet printer, on a printing press, or published on the Web all have different color requirements.

Think about a time when you have tried to capture a spectacular scenic view with your camera. The reds may have turned out a little orange, or the blues a trifle green, on the prints or slides that you received from the developer. Then you may have scanned the picture with a desktop scanner; it seemed to lose still more of the original character when you viewed it on your monitor. When you finally printed the scanned photo, even in a high-resolution printed piece, all of the original luster may have seemed absent.

To deal effectively with color, you must become familiar with its components so you can clearly communicate your specifications to clients, colleagues, and vendors. You also need to understand why the same color image can look different on different monitors, in various color proofs, and in the final printed piece.

Understanding Color

In its purest form, color is light. So, while we may speak of the color of one's shirt being red, what we really mean is that the shirt reflects red rays of light to our eyes and absorbs green and blue light; green grass reflects green light, but absorbs blue and red. Because we see color as a result of reflection, objects that have smooth surfaces usually appear more brilliant than those with textured surfaces. When light strikes a surface, both the density of the surface and the pigments bend the light rays to allow us to see them as colors.

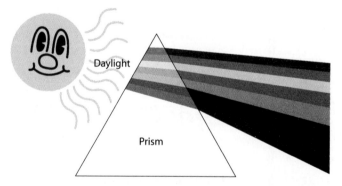

When light passes through an object, it is bent or refracted. Daylight is made of a number of wavelengths, each refracting differently, that produce the visible spectrum. These colors progress from the shortest wavelength, violet, to the longest one, red. The colors are violet, indigo, blue, green, yellow, orange, and red. Many of us learned them from longest to shortest, creating the memory hook "Roy G. Biv." Wavelengths beyond the visible spectrum, such as infrared, ultraviolet, radio, x-ray, and microwave, are either longer or shorter in wavelength than visible colors.

This phenomenon is particularly noticeable with different types of paper. Glossy paper, such as that used in most popular magazines, is coated with clay, and is *calendared* (shined up) with heavy rollers, so the ink tends to remain on the shiny surface. Uncoated and matte papers have more irregular surfaces and more of the ink is absorbed into the paper fibers; the same color of ink looks darker and duller on uncoated papers than on coated papers. If you compare the same color photograph printed on very glossy paper and printed in a newspaper, you can see that the newspaper reproduction is far less saturated because the paper is rough, has a yellowish cast, and cannot hold very much ink.

Color looks brightest on computer screens and television sets, because the light that forms the image is emitted by glowing phosphors or liquid crystal elements, rather than reflected from a surface. Emissive color is always much brighter than reflective color, which depends not only on the reflective surface but also on a good light source.

The Interaction Between Color and Chemistry

The apparent color of an object is visualized by the light reflected back to your eyes from an object's surface. Nearly every object on earth contains pigments and/or dyes, substances with chemical properties that cause them to absorb some part of the visible spectrum of light, and reflect another part.

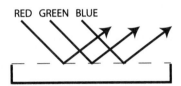

A white object reflects nearly all light that falls on it.

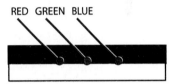

A black object absorbs nearly all light that falls on it.

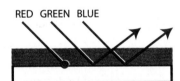

A cyan object absorbs red light, and reflects blue and green light.

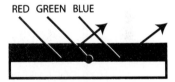

A magenta object absorbs green light, and reflects red and blue light.

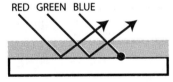

A yellow object absorbs blue light, and reflects red and green light.

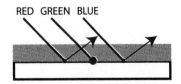

A purple (violet) object absorbs green light, and reflects most of the red and blue light but also absorbs some of each.

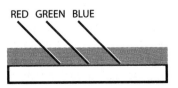

What does a green object reflect or absorb?

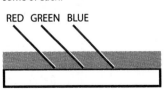

What does a brown object reflect or absorb?

Can you guess what light wavelengths green and brown objects reflect? Turn the page upside down to read the answers.

A green object reflects colors and reflects green light, and absorbs red and blue. A brown object absorbs some of all colors and reflects a portion of the red and green, and sometimes blue, light.

To view colors in the best possible light, you should purchase fluorescent 5,000 K lighting ("K" is a temperature unit referring to the Kelvin scale). This is the measurement of "daylight" and it is the standard illumination used in the graphic arts when comparing color reproductions to originals.

To further complicate matters, color looks different when viewed in different lighting conditions. Incandescent lights create a yellowish hue, and fluorescent lighting often gives a bluish appearance. Furthermore, few people see color exactly the same. Once you factor in all of these variables, you can appreciate the difficulties of reproducing colors that closely match those of an original image.

The Color Models

There are four color models that concern us in the printing industry. *CIE L*a*b** defines color by its luminance (lightness) and chromatic components across three axes — the L* axis ranges from 0–100, or black to white; the a* axis ranges from green to magenta; and the b* axis ranges from blue to yellow. In the *RGB* color model, the colors of light — red, green, and blue (also known as the "additive primaries") — combine to produce white. In the *CMYK* color model, the *subtractive primaries* (or *additive secondaries*), combine the pigments cyan, magenta, yellow, and black to reproduce a subset of the possible RGB colors; these four pigments produce black when added together. *Spot color*, which includes the Pantone color matching system, is used to achieve exact color matches, or when a limited budget does not allow for CMYK printing.

◪ L*a*b*

CIE L*a*b* was introduced as a color-measurement standard by the *Commission Internationale de l'Eclairage* (CIE), an international standards-making body. Their idea was that two colors that appear the same should be described in the same manner. For example, "pure red" might be defined as R:255, G:0, B:0 in the RGB color space; as C:0, M:100, Y:100, K:0 using CMYK space; or simply as "bright red" in vernacular English.

Because different programs and monitors describe colors differently, and different types of printing devices create them differently, there are widely divergent definitions for the same color. This is particularly true if we describe a color in one space (RGB) but need to recreate it in another (CMYK).

In 1931, the CIE developed the first widely used independent color model, known as CIE XYZ, named for the three axes used to describe the location of the colors. The values in this color model are expressed as a percentage of luminance, together with 256 levels (ranging from –128 to +128) across two axes. In 1976, CIE XYZ was redefined, simplified, and renamed CIE L*a*b*. InDesign simplifies the spelling and calls the color model "LAB."

Hue is the property we refer to when we call a color by its name — for example, red, purple, or teal. Hue changes as we travel in a circle around the axis of the color wheel. As you see, hue is defined as beginning at red (0°) and traveling counterclockwise around the wheel.

In grade school, many of us learned that the "primary" colors were red, yellow, and blue. What we were working with then were paints, which exhibit subtractive color behavior — just like inks, they absorb some colors of light and reflect others. The true primary colors **of light** are the additive red, green, and blue, because those are the base colors that the receptors in our eyes can interpret. All visible colors are actually mixtures of varying levels of red, green, and blue light.

The **color space** of a particular color model refers to the range of colors that can be reproduced within that model; this space can then be plotted within the three-dimensional LAB coordinate system. The LAB system is actually a color space that contains definitions for all possible colors in the visible spectrum.

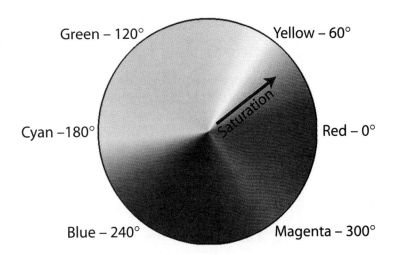

A slice of LAB color space, with all hues represented.

Saturation, also called "chroma," refers to a color's intensity. Color is dulled when elements opposite it in the color wheel are introduced. Red, for example, is neutralized by the addition of cyan, or of blue and green. When the center of the wheel is approached, the color becomes a neutral gray.

Luminance, or *value*, refers to the amount of white or black added to a pure color. A luminance of 50 means there is no addition of white or black. Luminance of 100 is pure white; luminance of 0 is pure black.

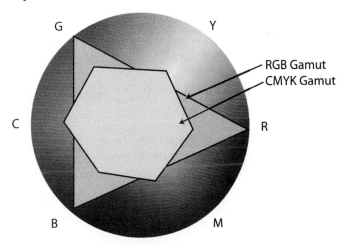

The color gamuts used in color reproduction take up only a portion of the visible spectrum. RGB and CMYK color spaces cannot reproduce every color. Above are the ranges of colors available in the RGB and CMYK color gamuts. You can see that some colors in one space cannot be reproduced in the other.

■ RGB

With the exception of the LAB model (which is abstract and theoretical, and limited in its practical use), RGB color is capable of displaying the largest area of the color spectrum. Red, green, and blue are the additive primary colors. When they are all added in equal quantity, the result is white; when they are all absent, the result is black. Where they

There are RGB monitors, and CMYK presses, but there's no such thing as a LAB device. The LAB model is necessary for InDesign's internal translation between RGB and CMYK spaces, but is essentially valueless for the purposes of color reproduction. Any color specified as LAB must be converted to either RGB or CMYK before it can be imaged and seen. A LAB color created in InDesign is converted internally to RGB for monitor display, because that's the only color space a monitor can display. Few printers know how to set up a proper LAB-CMYK conversion. This means that colors created with the LAB model in InDesign documents generally do not reproduce properly for either print or the Web.

overlap, they create the additive secondary colors (cyan, magenta, and yellow). RGB is the color model used by monitors, television sets, scanners, and digital cameras.

You can use the RGB color model for documents that you intend to print on most inkjet and laser printers, or for documents that will be distributed electronically and viewed on monitors (such as CD distribution or publication on the Internet). Although most color inkjet and laser printers use CMYK inks and toners to reproduce color, these typically expect image data in the RGB color space and perform an internal conversion to CMYK.

Indexed color is a subset of RGB that is used to create GIF files, which are generally images with areas of flat color, as opposed to photographs. The greatest number of colors that may be contained in an indexed-color image is 256. This reduced color model is unsuitable for print work, but it is very useful for images intended for monitor displays.

⊠ CMYK

The CMYK model is based on the absorption and reflection of light, as opposed to the emission and transmission of light used by the RGB model. A portion of the color spectrum is absorbed when white light strikes ink-coated paper (or any pigment-coated material). The color that is not absorbed is reflected.

Theoretically, a mixture of equal parts of pure cyan, magenta, and yellow should produce black. Pigments are generally not pure, however, so the result of mixing these colors is usually a muddy brown. To obtain good, strong blacks, and to be able to clearly print solid black elements such as text, black ink is used along with the three subtractive inks. CMYK is also called "process color."

Process color is used to print documents that contain multiple distinct colors or color photographs. A pattern of dots in varying sizes (called a "rosette") fools the eye into thinking that it is seeing continuous tones instead of tiny cyan, yellow, magenta, and black dots. The resolution of these dots, when used in the printing process, is described in lines per inch. If there are 150 lines per inch, there can be as many as 22,500 distinct dots in a one-inch square area. The resolution of the printer itself is usually about 2,400 spots per inch, giving it the capability to place 5,760,000 miniscule spots in that one-inch square.

Color separation is the process of converting RGB or LAB colors in a document to varying amounts of the four process CMYK colors. Any colors defined in the RGB and LAB color spaces must be separated to CMYK components before they can be printed.

◉ Spot

Spot color is used in one-, two-, and three-color documents, and can be added to process color documents when a special color, such as an official corporate logo color, must be reproduced. There are many specifications for spot color, but the most popular in the United States is the Pantone Matching System, also known as "PMS." Other systems include Toyo, DICColor, Focoltone, TruMatch, and HKS.

In the InDesign color system, "spot" refers to any color that must be printed and separated as a special ink color. There are thousands of defined spot ink colors, and few of them can be accurately reproduced with process inks. For example, printing standard yellow ink over standard magenta ink creates a typical process red. But a specific ink color such as the exact red used in the Eastman Kodak logo requires a custom ink mixture; the exact shade is not reproducible by overprinting process colors; it must be defined as a "spot" color.

Printing with CMYK inks is the basis for most color printing; the CMYK color space is also known as "four color," "process color," and "four-color process." As these names imply, a CMYK print job requires four applications of ink — either four runs through a single-color press, or a single run through a four-color press that can print all four inks in one pass.

There are conflicting opinions about why "K" represents black in the CMYK model. One theory is that "K" instead of "B" differentiates it from blue (which is how printers commonly refer to cyan); another is that it stands for "Key," and another is that "K" is the last letter in the word "black." Regardless of the reason, though, black is always referenced as "K" in four-color process printing.

At any time when you are creating an InDesign document, you can convert a spot color to process, or a solid process color to spot. Converting a spot color to its process equivalent, however, may involve some compromise because there may not be an exact CMYK match for every custom ink color.

The Pantone system defines colors by names and numbers that are printed in Pantone color swatch books. When you hear designers making comments such as, "Oh, that's about 327," they're actually referring to a teal color from the PMS color system. After you use it for a while, you too will probably start referring to colors using their PMS numbers.

InDesign's Swatches Palette

The set of colors used in an InDesign document resides in the Swatches palette. Colors in the Swatches palette are referred to as "named" colors. You can also mix new colors in one of the basic color modes (LAB, CMYK, or RGB) and apply them directly to objects. Colors applied directly (without being placed in the Swatches palette) are referred to as "unnamed" colors. The advantage of named colors is that you can reproduce them elsewhere in the same document, import them into other documents, and easily make global changes that apply throughout a document.

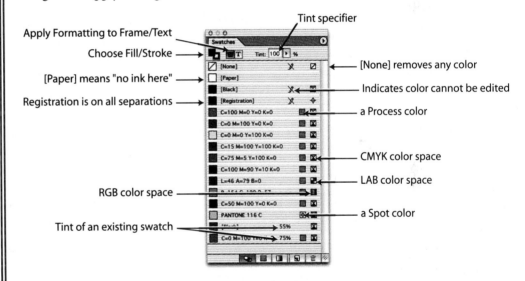

InDesign's Swatches palette.

When you create a new document, the Swatches palette contains four swatches that you cannot delete.

- **None** has no color associated with it; it removes any existing color from fills or strokes to which it is applied.
- **Paper** is used to represent the non-printing areas of a document. The Paper swatch appears white by default, but you can edit it to approximate the color of a non-white substrate on which you are printing. Doing so has no effect on the final document. To get white text on a black background, for example, you would set the frame's fill to black, and the text fill to Paper.
- **Black** always appears in the Swatches palette and cannot be edited.

Always check with your service provider before specifying an ink matching system for spot colors. If you specify a Toyo ink and your vendor uses Pantone, you have a problem. In general, printers in the United States and Canada are very familiar with the Pantone system, so it's usually pretty safe to stick with Pantone spot colors if you're working in these countries. Toyo and DICColor (Dainippon Ink and Chemicals) are common in Asia; Focoltone, TruMatch, and HKS colors are frequently used in Europe.

Spot inks are mixed from about 15 base colors, similar to the way paints are mixed for you at a paint shop.

• **Registration** should be used only to create crop, registration, and other printer's marks on a sheet. Some printer's marks are used in the binding processes to guide trims and folds; others are used in multicolor printing presses to align the printing units. Registration marks print on every color separation. This swatch cannot be edited.

In addition to these four colors, the Swatches palette also contains default swatches for cyan, magenta, yellow, and CMYK swatches for red (magenta + yellow), green (cyan + yellow), and a dark blue (cyan + magenta). You can edit or delete any of these colors.

The Swatches palette Options pop-up menu.

When you choose New Color Swatch from the Swatches palette Options pop-up menu, you are prompted to set the Color Type field to either Process or Spot, and to set the Color Mode field to LAB, CMYK, or RGB.

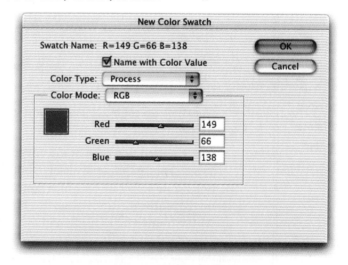

The New Color Swatch dialog box.

Each spot color in a document requires its own separation, because each requires a custom ink.

The default color-naming scheme assigns new colors names that reflect the percentages of the relevant color components. In the example above, the color name is composed of its RGB values. You can set your own name for the color by deactivating the Name with Color Value check box.

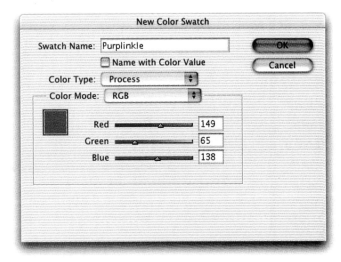

Purplinkle is a color between purple and periwinkle.

Create a Custom Color

1. Create a new document.

2. Select Window>Swatches to display the Swatches palette.

3. From the Options pop-up menu, select New Color Swatch.

4. To create a soft blue, similar to that used for Wedgwood china, first uncheck the Name with Color Value box and type "Wedgwood Blue" in the Swatch Name field.

5. Leave the Color Type field as Process and the Color Mode as CMYK.

When creating a new named color swatch, you should create it in the color space that's appropriate for the final form of the document. If the document will be printed on a printing press, use CMYK; if it is for electronic distribution or digital printing (inkjet or laser), use RGB. It's always best to ask the final producer of the job what they prefer for color definitions. Most printers want you to provide final job files in CMYK color space. Digital printers convert RGB colors to CMYK colors that are appropriate for that device.

Be careful when specifying Pantone colors. The names of Pantone Coated colors end with "C," Pantone Uncoated colors end in "U," and Pantone Matte colors end in "M." If you specify coated, uncoated, and matte versions of the same color, separate printing plates are generated. Printers hate that. You should pick only one set of colors to use for each project.

6. Set the sliders (or type the numbers) as follows: C:25, M:10, Y:0, K:10. Click OK.

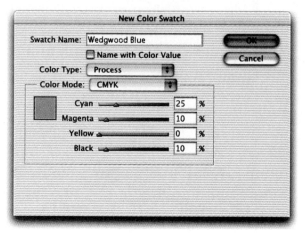

The color is added to the palette and becomes the active fill color, if the Fill icon is active in the toolbox.

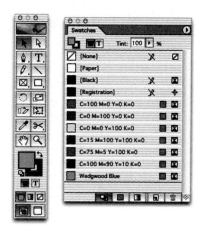

7. In the Swatches palette, double-click the Wedgwood Blue swatch to bring up the Swatch Options menu.

8. In the Swatch Options menu, change the Color Type to Spot. Click OK.

9. Note that the Color Type icon changes to indicate that the color is spot, not process, and the CMYK icon indicates that it was created in CMYK mode.

Printers typically use a shorthand for CMYK color builds; for example, a color build of 25% Cyan, 10% Magenta, 0% Yellow, and 10% Black is written C:25, M:10, Y:0, B:10.

This Swatches palette has two definitions for Pantone 116, which is a bad idea. There's no significant difference between the Pantone Coated, Matte, and Uncoated colors, so we recommend you choose from the Coated color library.

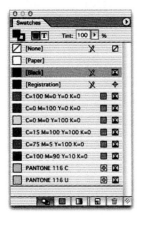

10. Now you need to create another color compatible with the color scheme. Select New Color Swatch.

11. Name this swatch "Medium Blue". The Color Type should be Process and the Color Mode CMYK.

12. Use the sliders, or type the following percentages into the fields: C:50, M:30, Y:0, K:20. Click OK.

13. Save the document to your **Work_In_Progress** folder as "color_work.indd". Leave the document open.

What you have just done is the best way to create a process color that is not part of an existing swatch library. If you want to "steal" a color from an existing InDesign document to ensure consistency, you can simply drag the color from the Swatches palette of the old document into the new document.

Add Colors from Other Documents

1. With color_work.indd still open, open the document **color_swiper.indd** from your **RF_Intro_InDesign** folder.

2. Select Window>Tile to reduce the window so you can see both documents.

3. Click the color Wedgwood Green in the Swatches palette and drag it into the color_work.indd document. InDesign automatically switches to the document into which you dragged the color.

4. From the Window menu, select color_swiper.indd.

5. Drag the Medium Green swatch into color_work.indd.

6. Save color_work.indd and leave it open. Close color_swiper.indd without saving.

If you are working with spot colors in North America, it's usually best to use the Pantone Matching System (PMS).

*If you need to reproduce Pantone spot colors with process inks, you can purchase the **Pantone Solid to Process Guide**, which lists the closest CMYK builds that approximate a Pantone spot ink, along with printed samples of the spot ink and the CMYK simulation. Many spot inks cannot be accurately reproduced with process inks, so be aware of this limitation when specifying CMYK builds to replace spot inks.*

To access any colors in a matching system, you must use the appropriate color library. These are accessed from the Color Mode menu in the New Color Swatch dialog box.

You can access InDesign's built-in spot libraries from the Color Mode drop-down menu in the New Color Swatch dialog box.

InDesign has a number of swatch libraries built into it. These can be broken down into three types — spot, process, and RGB. Spot libraries include Pantone Coated, Pantone Uncoated, Toyo Color Finder, DICColor, and the four HKS libraries. Process libraries are Pantone Process Coated, TruMatch, and Focoltone. Process libraries are similar to spot libraries, except they contain pre-built formulas for specific colors that can be printed in CMYK rather than specific ink numbers and mixing proportions. The RGB libraries are the Macintosh and Windows System colors, and the optimized Web palette.

Pantone is the most popular color matching system in North America. The Pantone Process library uses a different numbering system than the Coated, Matte, and Uncoated libraries do, and the process color numbers do not correspond to the spot color numbers. TruMatch and Focoltone are rarely used in North America, and are more common in Europe. HKS is a complex system used primarily in Germany. Toyo and DICColor (Dainippon Ink and Chemicals) are used primarily in Japan and other Asian countries.

Create Spot Colors

1. With the document color_work.indd still open, select New Color Swatch, and choose Pantone Solid Coated from the Color Mode menu.

2. Type "185" in the Pantone field, then click OK.

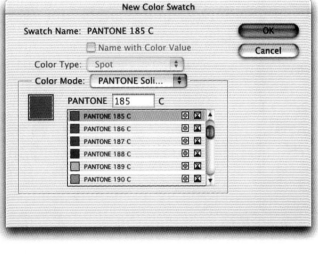

Pantone colors, although they are technically spot colors, contain built-in CMYK definitions. Both Spot and CMYK icons display when you designate Pantone colors. InDesign converts the CMYK values to RGB for display on your monitor, and uses these values if you decide to convert the spot colors to process.

3. Repeat the process, and choose Pantone 286.

4. Make a third spot-color swatch with Pantone 320.

5. Save the document and leave it open.

Tints of Colors

A tint is a lightened derivative of a solid ink color that is produced on paper by creating a halftone screen of the color at the chosen percentage. Tints are created using the Swatches palette. Tints may be created from process-color builds, but the results are somewhat unpredictable. You should create tints only from spot colors and the four solid process colors.

Create a Tint

1. With the document color_work.indd open, select PMS 185C from the Swatches palette.

2. Choose New Tint Swatch from the Swatches palette Options pop-up menu.

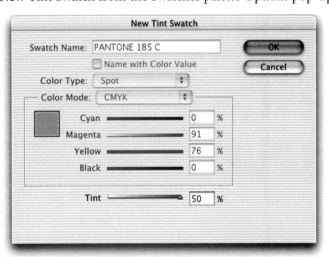

Although black is technically one of the four process colors, in most respects you can treat it as a spot color. You can also treat the other three process colors as spot colors, but yellow does not show well when tinted. It's pretty common for the decision about a spot color to be made at the last minute, so many designers simply use cyan or magenta in a spot-color job and instruct the printer to substitute the chosen Pantone ink for the process ink. This isn't a very predicable method and it can lead to some finger pointing if someone forgets to make the switch.

3. Move the slider so the Tint percent reads 50% (or type "50" in the Tint field), then click OK. The tint is added to your Swatches palette.

4. Colors are added to the palette in the order they are created. For better palette organization, click the tint with the Selection tool, and drag it up so it is just below the PMS 185C swatch. This has nothing to do with the way InDesign handles colors — it's simply easier to find things that are grouped in a logical order.

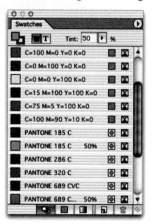

5. Save the document and leave it open for the next exercise.

Gradients

A *gradient* is a fill or blend consisting of two or more colors or tints that blend into one another. A gradient can be linear or radial. A gradient creates a smooth blend of colors from one to the other; it employs the mathematics of PostScript to work.

When there are too few steps for the length of the gradient at a specific resolution, the result is the banding effect you see here.

You may have seen gradients that have distinct bands between tones. There are only 100 possible steps in a printed gradient, from 0% to 100%; if any step is wider than about 0.05", it is usually visible to the eye. Gradients prepared for display on monitors can use up to 255 steps. Visible banding in a gradient can occur for two reasons: either the gradient is too large for the available resolution or line screen of the device that imaged it, or the gradient doesn't have enough levels. A 30-pica gradient from 0% to 100% black, for example, might not band, but a 30-pica gradient from 0–50% or 50–100% does, because there aren't enough levels to make the steps invisible to the eye.

You can't create a smooth-looking gradient that extends from the top to the bottom of a letter-size page with versions of PostScript earlier than Level 3. Many newer laser printers and graphic arts imaging devices use PostScript Level 3, so banding problems have become less common than they were in the past. Because many print providers still use PostScript Level 2 equipment, though, you should be aware of the potential for gradient banding.

Create Gradients with Named Colors

1. With the document color_work.indd still open, choose Black from the Swatches palette and select New Gradient Swatch from the Swatches palette Options pop-up menu.

Spot and process colors displayed on a monitor usually don't match the printed results on paper unless you've carefully calibrated and profiled your monitor. Be sure to use a current swatch book so you are not disappointed with the final color. Colors printed in swatch books can fade and discolor over time, so for critical color jobs, use newer swatch books.

2. Name the swatch "Black to White".

3. Click the first (leftmost) stop icon in the Gradient Ramp.

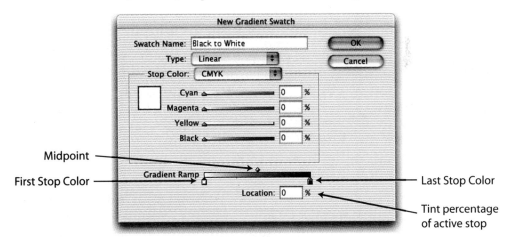

Midpoint

First Stop Color — Gradient Ramp

Last Stop Color

Tint percentage of active stop

4. Leave the Type field as Linear and choose Named Color in the Stop Color drop-down menu.

5. Click Black as the named color.

6. Click the last stop icon in the Gradient Ramp, and choose CMYK from the Stop Color menu. If the default color isn't already C:0, M:0, Y:0, K:0, then set these values in the Stop Color fields.

7. Click the diamond icon above the bar and move it to the left and right. Note how it affects the midpoint of the gradient. If the diamond is moved to 70%, how does this affect the maximum length of the gradient? The 20% difference makes the

In prior versions of InDesign, users could choose Paper as a named color for any stop. In Version 2.0, Adobe decided to remove this feature, so to create a white stop color you need to specify a zero-percent CMYK build.

If you mix color spaces in gradients, InDesign converts all of the colors to CMYK. Be sure to use the same color spaces when creating gradients (all spot, all CMYK, or all RGB).

If you make a gradient that uses black and one of the other three process colors, for example, cyan to black, make a new CMYK swatch built of 100% black and 50–75% cyan. The resulting gradient prints with a much richer tone than with pure black alone.

maximum length of the gradient 40% shorter, because it increases the length of the 0–50% area of the black. It's easy to see why so many banding problems occur because of this. When you are finished, reposition the diamond at 50% and click OK.

8. Next, you need to create another blend using three colors. If the gradient swatch does not appear, check Show All Swatches or Show Gradient Swatches in the Color palette.

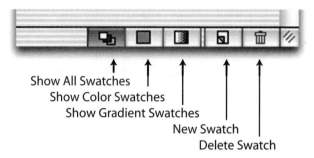

Show All Swatches
Show Color Swatches
Show Gradient Swatches
New Swatch
Delete Swatch

Select New Gradient Swatch from the Swatches palette Options pop-up menu.

9. Name it "Red, White & Blue."

10. Click the leftmost stop icon in the Gradient Ramp.

11. Leave the Type as Linear and set the Stop Color to Named Color.

12. Click PMS 185C as the named color.

13. Click the right stop and set it to PMS 286C.

14. Click just below the Gradient Ramp bar, beneath the diamond at 50%. This inserts a new stop. Apply C:0, M:0, Y:0, K:0 (white) to this stop. Click OK. Click any blank area within the Swatches palette to deselect the Red, White & Blue gradient.

15. Save the document and leave it open for the next exercise.

Create CMYK Gradients

1. With the document still open, select New Gradient Swatch.

Changes made to gradients with the Gradient palette aren't reflected in the Swatches palette. You need to drag the altered swatch to the Swatches palette to save the changes.

2. Name this gradient "Blue to Yellow". Leave its Type set to Linear.

3. Click the leftmost stop. The Stop Color field should remain CMYK; if not, change it. Assign the color as follows: C:0, M:20, Y:100, K:0.

4. Click the rightmost stop. Change the Stop Color field to CMYK. Assign the color as follows: C:100, M:80, Y:0, K:0. Check that the midpoint (diamond icon) is at 50%; if not, move it to the 50% point. Click OK to save the new swatch. You've created unnamed colors, but you've used them in a named gradient, so you can always change them later.

5. You should reverse this gradient so the name makes sense. With the Blue to Yellow gradient still selected, choose Window>Gradient (the Gradient palette appears), then select Show Options from the palette's Options menu.

6. Click the Reverse button to flip the stop colors, and drag the reversed swatch from the Gradient palette to the Swatches palette. Delete the original Blue to Yellow swatch by selecting it and clicking the Delete Swatch button. Rename the copied swatch Blue to Yellow.

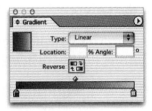

7. Save the file. Leave it open for the next exercise.

Importing Color

There is still another way to add colors to your Swatches palette. When you import an EPS graphic, any colors in the image that are not already included in your palette are added. If an imported color shares the same name but is defined differently than a color already in the palette, InDesign asks you which definition you wish to use.

Import Color Files

1. With the document color_work.indd still open, place the graphic **dragon.eps** from your **RF_Intro_InDesign** folder. Choose File>Place, or press Command/Control-D to place the file.

   Notice that five spot colors have been added to the palette. You can't edit imported colors, and you can't delete them unless you first delete the imported graphic that carried them in. The only change you can make is to define imported spot colors as process. This keeps you from having to rework the graphic in the original application if process colors are required.

You can drag color and gradient swatches from or to the Swatches palette, the Gradient palette, a selected object, the Fill and Stroke icons in the toolbox, and the Apply Color box in the toolbox. Dragging a swatch to an object applies that swatch's color or gradient to the active fill or stroke of the object.

2. Next, you'll learn how to use another method to create colors from an imported graphic. Place the file **your_vacation.tif** from your **RF_Intro_InDesign** folder.

3. Be sure the Fill icon is active (on top). Select the Eyedropper tool from the toolbox.

4. Position the eyedropper over one of the blue areas of the man's shirt, and click the mouse button. The icon changes from 🖋 to 🖋, indicating that the eyedropper is filled. It also makes the color you selected the active fill color.

5. Drag the new color from the fill block in the toolbox into the Swatches palette. Notice that it is named by its CMYK composition and that it is a CMYK color.

Applying Color

Now you're ready to apply the colors in the document to a variety of created and imported elements. In the next exercise, you will apply color to an InDesign object, to a frame, to images, and to text. You'll see how applying color is straightforward and consistent across the variety of color applications.

Use the Colors

1. With the document color_work.indd open, place the graphic **atwv_logo.tif** from your **RF_Intro_InDesign** folder.

2. Be sure the Fill icon is in front in the toolbox.

3. With the Direct Selection tool active, click the logo (not the frame). You'll know if you selected the logo, because the fill color turns black.

4. Click PMS 320C to recolor this bitmap graphic.

5. Deselect by clicking anywhere on the page and switch to the Selection tool.

6. Select the frame and, from the Transform palette Options pop-up menu, deselect Transform Content. Resize the frame to a width of 12p and a height of 144 pt. with the Width and Height fields in the Transform palette.

7. Choose Object>Fitting>Center Content to center the logo in the new frame.

8. With the Selection tool still active, choose PMS 286C to fill the frame with blue.

9. Press the "X" key to make the Stroke box active, and press "F10" to activate the Stroke palette.

10. Assign the stroke a weight of 4 pt.

You can apply color to bilevel (bitmap) images such as the vacation logo, and to grayscale images such as the Charge It photo, but not to color images.

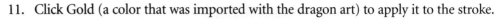

11. Click Gold (a color that was imported with the dragon art) to apply it to the stroke.

12. Click anywhere on the page to deselect this art.

13. Place the grayscale image **charge_it.tif** from your **RF_Intro_InDesign** folder.

14. Click the image, and return the Fill icon to the top (press the "X" key).

15. Click the swatch for the color named Medium Green to colorize the artwork.

16. With the charge_it.tif image still selected, click the color Medium Green, and select Duplicate Swatch from the pop-up menu on the Swatches palette.

17. Double-click the color named "Medium Green copy" and Shift-drag the Cyan slider to 30%. Rename the swatch "Light Green", then click OK.

18. Create a Text frame and type your name in 48-pt. ATC Cozumel. Press Return/Enter, and type "Gradient Type" on the next line. Adjust the frame width if necessary to accommodate your name.

19. Make sure the Fill icon is in front. Highlight your name, and select PMS 185C from the Swatches palette. Note how the Fill icon changes to a Text Fill icon in both the toolbox and the Swatches palette.

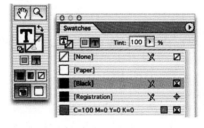

20. Highlight the words "Gradient Type" with the Type tool and assign a black stroke.

21. Switch to the Fill icon, and click the Blue to Yellow gradient swatch.

22. Save and close the document.

Shift-dragging a color slider in the Swatch Options panel effectively lightens or darkens the color by reducing or adding percentages of all the component colors. Use this option carefully.

Transparency, Drop Shadows, and Feathering

Transparency is a new feature in InDesign, based on technology developed for Illustrator 9 and PhotoShop 6. It is a fairly simple concept: an object's opacity defaults to 100% (completely solid), but you can adjust this value down to 0% (completely transparent). Any objects underneath a transparent object are visible to a greater or lesser extent. This impressive new feature enables you to do things in InDesign 2.0 with transparency, drop shadows, and feathering that you couldn't do before without a long session in Photoshop.

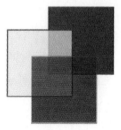

This example of transparency uses three rectangles: the uppermost rectangle is solid, or 100%; it is positioned at the back of the stacking order. The other two rectangles have transparency of 75%. Anything underneath an object with a transparency value less than 100% shows through to some degree.

Any object in an InDesign document can have transparency, including text, objects drawn in InDesign (such as the rectangles above), and imported graphics such as this lemon slice.

Transparency can be applied to one or more selected objects (or to grouped objects) from the Transparency palette. To display this palette, simply choose Window>Transparency, or press Shift-F10.

To change the transparency level of a selection, you can either click and hold the small black triangle and move the slider that appears, or type a value into the Opacity field and press Return/Enter.

Transparency affects grouped objects differently than if the objects were ungrouped but selected. Transparency is applied to multiple, selected, ungrouped objects relative to each object's stacking order; overlapped areas amplify the transparency effect. A group of objects that has transparency applied is treated as a single object, and transparency is not applied to any overlapping areas in the group.

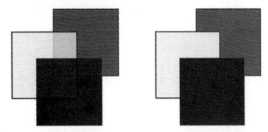

The rectangles on the left aren't grouped, but they were all selected when 75% transparency was applied. The rectangles on the right were grouped before 75% transparency was applied. You can easily see the different transparency behaviors of grouped and non-grouped objects.

The Knockout Group option in the Transparency palette gives you the choice of having a group of transparent objects imitate the behavior of a transparent group. In other words, let's say you select three objects and apply 75% transparency, and group them *after* applying the transparency.

If you wanted the group to look like the example below on the right, check the Knockout Group box; otherwise, don't. Essentially, the Knockout Group function changes the transparency of multiple objects to that of a single object, and it has no effect on groups that had transparency applied after the group was created.

It might help by showing you an example that has objects below a transparent group:

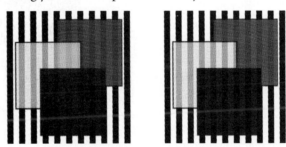

The same group with Knockout Group off (left) and on (right).

You can see from the example that this produces results that are different from what you'd get if you grouped the objects and *then* applied 75% transparency.

The technology that enables transparency can also be used to generate drop shadows and feathering effects. A drop shadow simulates a shadow cast by an object that is illuminated from a direction you can specify. Feathering softens hard edges of objects by increasing the transparency of the edge from 0% to 100% over a distance you specify.

Drop shadows, like transparency, can be added to imported graphics, text, and objects drawn in InDesign.

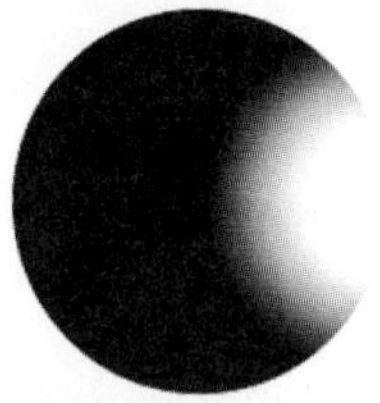

An example of feathering. A white circle overlapping a black one was given a generous feather edge, resulting in a gradient starting at 0% and increasing to 100% over a distance of 4 picas.

To apply a drop shadow to one or more selected objects, you can either choose Object>Drop Shadow or press Option/Alt-Shift-M to display the Drop Shadow dialog box.

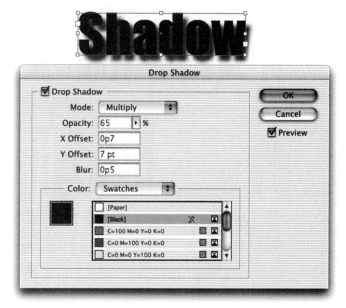

The Drop Shadow dialog box.

The default shadow color is black, but you can choose any color that's present in the Swatches palette. Opacity defaults to 75%, and the default offsets are shown above. The X and Y Offset values specify how far the shadow is moved from the casting object; the Blur value sets the size of the shadow. Small Blur values make smaller, denser shadows; larger Blur values make longer, more diffuse shadows.

To feather one or more selected objects, choose Object>Feather (there's no keyboard shortcut) to access the Feather dialog box.

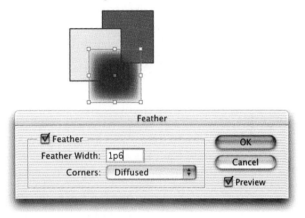

The Feather dialog box.

The Feather Width value determines the length of the feathering effect. The default value (in picas) is 0p9. In the Corners drop-down menu, you can define how feathering applies to objects with sharp corners, such as the rectangles in the example above. The default Corners setting, Diffused, insets the feather at corners, making them appear approximately even with the edges. The Rounded setting applies a denser feather, and rounds off the corners; Sharp extends the solid area out at the corners, giving them a pointed appearance.

Rounded (left) and Sharp corners (right).

InDesign, like Illustrator, uses a technique called "flattening" to replace transparent objects with individual objects that replicate the appearance of the originals. Flattening is required when printing a document that contains transparency, drop shadows, or feathering.

The rectangles shown above, after flattening, are broken into multiple separate objects that simulate the effects of transparency. We've removed the strokes and spread these apart a bit for clarity.

Flattened art may be required if your output device or service provider cannot image files with applied transparency. Flattening occurs only while printing or exporting to PDF, so your original art always remains intact. In the example above, you can see that areas of transparency are converted into separate objects. Drop shadows and feathering applications can result in the generation of hundreds of separate objects to reproduce the effect; it's possible that some printers and other output devices cannot image such complex artwork.

Colors can be used in transparency, drop shadows, and feathering, but if multiple colors are used, these should all use the same color space. It is best to use RGB colors for drop shadows applied to RGB images, for example, and CMYK colors for drop shadows applied to CMYK images. You can set a "blend space" that forces mixed-space colors to one that you choose from Edit>Transparency Blend Space.

You should use Document CMYK when a document is intended for print production; you should use Document RGB when a document is intended for on-screen display or for use in an RGB print workflow.

Summary

You've learned the basics of color, which types of documents require RGB color and which require CMYK, and when to use spot colors. You've also learned how to create custom colors and gradients in both spot- and process- color models, and how to import color from other InDesign documents and from EPS and TIF graphics. You have added color to bitmap and grayscale images, to the fill and stroke of frames, and to type. Lastly, you have learned the basics of transparency, and how to apply drop shadows and feathering to artwork.

Complete Project B: Yellow Rose Menu

⑨ Working with Images

Chapter Objective:

InDesign allows you to incorporate images created in other applications into its page layouts. This chapter includes important information about distinguishing between vector and raster graphics. It also discusses the types of images that you can import into InDesign, as well as how to place and transform them. In Chapter 9, you will:

- Understand the types of images that InDesign can import, as well as the purposes, advantages, and disadvantages of each.

- Learn to distinguish vector and raster graphics, understand their typical applications, and discover the consequences of scaling both types.

- Understand image resolution and know how to determine the appropriate resolution for particular uses.

- Learn how to place, transform, resize, and reposition images within frames.

- Understand the pros and cons of image embedding, and learn how to work with linked images, including re-establishing broken links through the Links palette.

- Learn the different methods for placing images.

- Explore different techniques for scaling and cropping images.

Projects to be Completed:

- Central Market Ad (A)
- Yellow Rose Menu (B)
- Travel Brochure (C)
- Good Choices Newsletter (D)

Working with Images

As we have already stated, documents usually combine text and graphic images to communicate some idea. Although you can create lines, basic shapes, and Bézier curves in InDesign, you should generate complex artwork and detailed illustrations in software designed for that purpose. Likewise, you should prepare photographic images scanned from photo prints or slides, or captured with a digital camera, with an application designed for manipulation of such images. Once complete, you can import these images into InDesign, and position, crop, scale, and frame them on the page along with text and graphic elements created with the InDesign tools.

Placing images or graphics into an InDesign layout is a fairly simple process. Deciding *what* to place, however, is a far more complex matter. Graphics and images have more confusing terminology than perhaps any other aspect of desktop publishing. Because so much of the confusion and error in the industry relates to this kind of file, we first need to define some important terms.

Types of Images

You should understand the three primary types of pictures that you will work with in desktop publishing — vector graphics, raster images, and line art. Each type of image has specific advantages and drawbacks, depending on your intended outcome.

Vector Graphics

Most of the drawing elements on a desktop-layout page, including those you create with InDesign's drawing tools, can be described as a series of *vectors* or mathematical descriptors. This type of graphic is *resolution independent*; it can be freely scaled and adopts its resolution at the time of printing from the resolution of the output device. Vector-art files can be saved in a file format associated with the application used to create the file (for example, Adobe Illustrator or Macromedia FreeHand format) or in a common interchange format called Encapsulated PostScript (EPS).

Fonts used to produce text on monitors and in print are also vectors; each character is composed of points and curves, just like the ones you can create with the InDesign Pen tool. Many applications, including InDesign, enable you to convert selected text to its component vector elements for further editing. This is a good way to create special text effects, but it's really only useful with very large text. Once you convert text to vectors, InDesign no longer recognizes it as text, so you can't edit the words. Instead, InDesign treats it like any other vector graphic, which means you can apply fills, strokes, or design elements; you can even treat the converted vectors as frames to contain other material.

The term "graphic" in the context of page creation and computer publishing generally means anything that isn't text. "Image" refers more specifically to raster graphics, and "drawing" to vector graphics.

Vector-based programs can incorporate raster images into illustrations; for example, many of the screen captures in this book were annotated with arrows and text after importing the raster screen-capture file into Adobe Illustrator, where the raster image became just another element in the drawing. With raster-based programs such as Photoshop, you use vector tools to manipulate a raster image. For example, with the Pen tool in Photoshop you can create Bézier curves just as you can with the Pen tools in InDesign and Illustrator; in Photoshop, however, these curves are used only to create masks, selections, or to otherwise isolate portions of an image. The final output is always a raster image composed of pixels.

An example of a vector drawing.

Raster Images

While vector-art files are composed of mathematical descriptions of a series of lines and geometric shapes, raster files are made up of a grid of individual rasters (bits, pixels, or picture elements) composed in rows and columns (called a "bitmap"). The word "pixel" is a contraction of "picture element" (also known as a "pel" in some industries). Merriam-Webster defines "raster" as "a scan pattern (as of the electron beam in a cathode-ray tube) in which an area is scanned from side to side in lines from top to bottom; *also*: a pattern of closely spaced rows of dots that form the image on a cathode-ray tube (as of a television or computer display)."

Each pixel is a tiny square of color, and thousands of pixels next to each other in different colors and shades create the illusion of smooth, continuous-tone shading. In contrast to vector files, which are resolution independent, raster files are *resolution dependent* — they receive their resolution at the time of input (scanning or capture with a digital camera). A raster file specifies the number of pixels within it. A 3 × 5-in. one-color file created at 72 ppi (pixels per inch) contains 77,760 pixels. If a raster graphic is created at 72 ppi and then resized to twice its geometric size, the pixels enlarge to fill the extra space, reducing the resolution to 36 ppi and making the image appear much coarser or *pixelated*. Raster files for print are generally saved in TIFF or EPS formats; for the Web, raster files are generally saved in JPEG or sometimes GIF formats.

An example of a photographic, continuous-tone raster image.

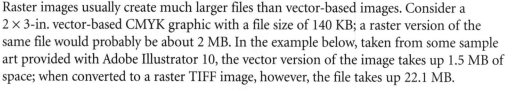

Raster images usually create much larger files than vector-based images. Consider a 2 × 3-in. vector-based CMYK graphic with a file size of 140 KB; a raster version of the same file would probably be about 2 MB. In the example below, taken from some sample art provided with Adobe Illustrator 10, the vector version of the image takes up 1.5 MB of space; when converted to a raster TIFF image, however, the file takes up 22.1 MB.

Images that aren't simply black and white, such as scanned color and grayscale photographs, are known as "contone" (continuous tone) raster images.

Line Art

Line art is a special kind of raster image made up entirely of 100% solid areas. The pixels in a line art image have only two options: they can be all black or all white. Line-art images are sometimes called "bitmap," "bi-level," or "one-bit" images. Examples of line art are UPC bar codes, pen drawings (without shading), signatures, or printed text.

Example of hand lettering scanned as line art.

The rule for line art reproduction is to scan the image at the same resolution as the output device. Think about it like this: a 600 dpi (dots per inch) printer can create a maximum of 600 × 600 (360,000) dots in one square inch. With line art we want to give the printer the most information available, which in this case would be 600 pixels per inch. If the art were created and printed at only 300 ppi then the printer would have to skip to every other possible space to put a dot. The result is known as "stair-stepping" or "bitmapping."

Line art refers to high-contrast, monochrome illustrations or artwork. In desktop prepress jargon, the term "line art" is sometimes used to describe vector-based illustrations such as those created by Illustrator or FreeHand. Be aware of this distinction. By its traditional definition, a line-art file might be rendered as a vector-based image or a bitmap (raster) image.

Most laser printers today image at 600 to 1,200 dpi, but film on an imagesetter is typically produced at a much higher resolution, usually at least 1,200 dpi and often greater than that. Fortunately, the human eye is not sensitive enough to discern bitmapping beyond 1,200 dpi, so the best rule for scanning line art is always to use 1,200 ppi, unless you know that the image will be printed on a device with lower resolution such as a laser or inkjet printer. It's appropriate to scan line art at a device's maximum resolution, up to 1,200 dpi. Above 1,200 dpi, there's no increase in apparent quality; the increase in file size and processing time produces little benefit.

Resolution

Image resolution refers to how many pixels or dots per square inch (ppi for input devices or dpi for imaging devices) are contained in the raster graphic. Every pixel is one block of one color. When each block or pixel is very small, it blends with the pixels surrounding it to smoothly form the shapes, coloring, and shading in the picture. It's important to understand when and how to adjust resolution when preparing graphics for import into InDesign.

Each graphic below is a tiny diamond shape filled with a gradient. The pixels have been outlined and enlarged to demonstrate the effect of resolution. The graphic on the left is a higher resolution, showing more tonal variations and a cleaner edge. The graphic on the right appears as large chunks and has a noticeable stair step edge. If the left graphic were enlarged, it would appear much like the right graphic, thus raster images are resolution-dependent. Their appearance depends on their resolution.

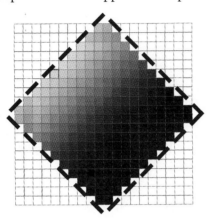 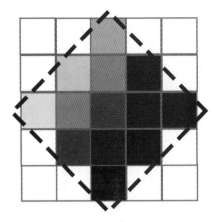

The left image has higher resolution than the right image.

In general, a greater resolution results in a cleaner, smoother appearance, but higher resolution is not always better. The most important consideration is to match image resolution to the requirements of the output device. Every digital device has a unique capacity for displaying resolution. Monitors, for example, are limited by the number of light-emitting units in their grids, so they can display images only at relatively low resolution — Macintosh monitors typically display 72 ppi and Windows monitors, 96 ppi. Thus, if you are preparing a graphic for output on a screen for a Web page, you should set its resolution at 72 ppi. The graphic will contain one pixel for each pixel displayed on the monitor (1:1) at 100% size.

In comparison, desktop printers reproduce images by applying tiny amounts of ink or toner onto paper; typical resolution for inkjet or laser printers is 300–800 dpi. High-end imagesetters, on the other hand, are capable of printing at exceptionally high resolution, from 1,600–4,000 dpi or more.

The human eye cannot really distinguish improvements in resolution beyond 1,200 dpi.

One of the advantages of vector art is its feature of unlimited scaling. Vector graphics adopt the highest possible resolution of the intended output device, so you can freely scale, resize, rotate, or otherwise manipulate them without worrying about degrading the illustration quality.

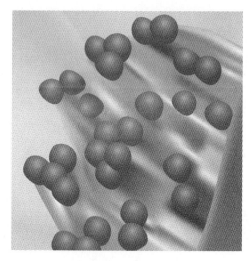

Vector image
at 100% view

Enlarged view of the same
vector image at 800%

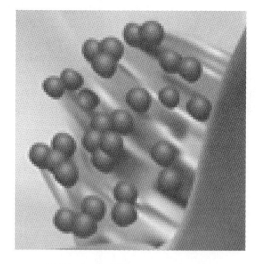

A rasterized version of the image
at 100% view

800% view of the rasterized image.
Notice the pixelization effects.

Raster images are exactly the opposite — the image size depends directly upon the resolution. When we discuss resolution we speak in terms of "pixels per inch" ("ppi"), "dots per inch" ("dpi"), "lines per inch" ("lpi"), and sometimes "spots per inch" ("spi").

- **Pixels per inch (ppi).** This measure is the number of pixels in one horizontal or vertical inch of a digital raster file.

- **Lines per inch (lpi).** This measure is the number of halftone dots produced in a horizontal or vertical linear inch by a high-resolution imagesetter to simulate the appearance of continuous-tone color.

- **Dots per inch (dpi) or spots per inch (spi).** This measure is the number of dots produced by an output device in a single line of output. This term is sometimes incorrectly used interchangeably with "pixels per inch."

When reproducing a photograph on a printing press, the image must be converted into different-sized dots that fool the eye into believing that it sees continuous tones. The result of this conversion process is a *halftone image*; the dots that are used to simulate continuous tone are called "halftone dots." Light tones in a photograph are represented as small halftone dots; dark tones become large halftone dots. Prior to image-editing software, photos were converted to halftones with a large graphic-arts camera and screens. A picture was photographed through a screen to create halftone dots; different screens produced different numbers of dots in an inch (hence the term "dots per inch"). Halftone dots are easily visible in most black-and-white newspaper photos.

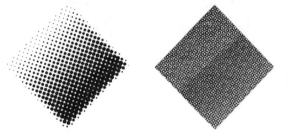

Enlargement of halftone dots and the rosette halftone pattern of process color.

Screen Ruling

The screens used with old graphic-arts cameras had a finite number of available dots in a horizontal or vertical inch. That number was the *screen ruling*, or lines per inch (lpi) of the halftone. A screen ruling of 133 lpi means that in a square inch there are 133×133 (17,689) possible locations for a halftone dot. If the screen ruling is decreased, there are fewer total halftone dots and a grainier image; if the screen ruling is increased there are more halftone dots and a clearer image.

Line screen is a finite number based on a combination of the intended output device and paper. You can't just randomly select a line screen. Ask your service provider or printer what line screen will be used before you begin creating your images. If you can't find out ahead of time, or are unsure, follow these general guidelines:

- Newspaper or newsprint: 85–100 lpi

- Magazine or general commercial printing: 133–150 lpi

- Premium quality paper jobs (such as art books or annual reports): 150–175 lpi (although some specialty jobs may use screen rulings of 200 lpi or higher)

Image Resolution

When a printer creates halftone dots, it calculates the average value of a group of pixels and generates a spot of appropriate size. An image's resolution controls the quantity of pixel data that a printer can read. Regardless of their source — camera, desktop scanner, or purchased stock images — images must have sufficient resolution to enable the output device to generate enough halftone dots to create the appearance of continuous tone. Ideally, the printer has four pixels for each halftone dot created. The relationship between pixels and halftone dots defines the rule of resolution for all raster-based images — the resolution of an image should always be 1.5 to 2 times the screen ruling that is used for printing.

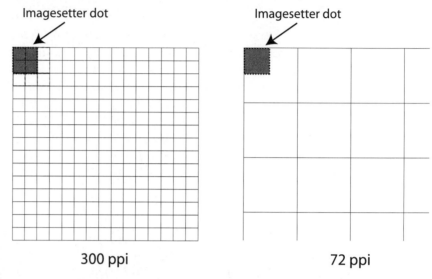

Imagesetter dot   Imagesetter dot

300 ppi   72 ppi

Each white square symbolizes a pixel in a digital image. The colored area shows the pixel information that is used to generate a single halftone dot or spot. If an image has only 72 pixels per inch, the output device has to generate four halftone dots per pixel, resulting in poor printed image quality.

To be certain about the final resolution of your images, you can use the following formula:

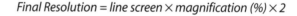

$$Final\ Resolution = line\ screen \times magnification\ (\%) \times 2$$

The same raster image is reproduced here at 300 ppi (left) and 72 ppi (right). Notice the obvious degradation in quality when the resolution is set to only 72 ppi.

If an image's resolution is too high for the imaging requirements, the extra information does not help the printer render a better image. It does, however, consume file space and processing time. If the resolution is too low or the image is further enlarged in InDesign, the printed picture will be blocky and will contain insufficient detail and color definition to accurately reproduce the image.

The resolution of an image should always be 1.5 to 2 times the screen ruling that is used for printing. The resolution:screen ruling "quality factor" of 1.5 is a common industry average. If an image contains fine detail or patterns, increase the factor to as much as 2. If special screening processes are to be applied, an even higher factor is required. Images with soft, diffuse detail may print well using a quality factor of 1, but using 1.5–2 ensures successful results.

An example of a raster TIFF image that has been enlarged too much and exhibits a blocky, rough appearance in the areas of detail.

All of this can be confusing to a beginner. If you are preparing a document to be professionally printed, remember these general rules:

- Scan or create all pictures, raster and vector alike, as close to the final size as possible.
- Most raster images should be about twice the pixel resolution as the line screen that is output.
- Line art or bitmaps should be the same pixel resolution as the output device.

If you are preparing a document for the Internet, the rules are very easy: prepare all raster images at 72 ppi (pixels per inch).

Effects of Scaling on Resolution

Vector files describe an image and its components mathematically. When a vector graphic is scaled, the enlargement or reduction percentage is merely applied to the equations that represent the position, size, and shape of each path or object. After the computer has calculated how the image will look at the new size, it applies the resolution of the output device to render it. Vector graphics render smooth output at any size (as long as it doesn't contain any raster data). The image, however, looks somewhat rough in your InDesign document because it displays a low-resolution preview of the image. Although it can look a little ragged on the screen, the graphic will be nice and sharp when it prints to a

PostScript printer. You can use InDesign's High Quality Display setting if you prefer to see high-resolution previews, but this slows things down if you have placed complex EPS files in your document.

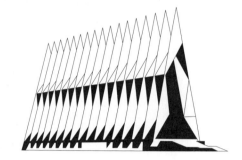

An EPS image imported to InDesign and scaled to 25% and 200%.

Because resolution-dependent raster files are assigned a resolution upon creation, scaling them requires them to be *resampled*. Resampling an image involves changing its resolution in the native graphics program to accommodate the final output size or resolution. Images can be *downsampled* (brought to a lower resolution) without loss of quality. *Upsampling* images (increasing their resolution) beyond a certain point forces the program to create new pixels without sufficient information about the appropriate colors; this results in unacceptable reproduction quality. Upsampling is very uncommon, but downsampling is very common. You should acquire each image only once, at the highest reasonable resolution; this prevents the need to acquire the same image multiple times for different uses.

Because its physical size is a factor in a raster image's resolution, you may be able to salvage a low-resolution image depending on your final goal. Imaging software can modify pixel information from existing data. Many digital cameras take all pictures at low resolution; they "control" resolution by allowing the user to set a higher capture size. In other words, all images may be captured at 72 ppi, but some may be only 4 in. wide and others as much as 22 in. wide.

If you scale a large, low-resolution image to a small enough size, you increase its *effective resolution*; you can then print this image to a high-quality output device. The effective resolution is determined as a factor of the image's resolution and its scaling when placed into the final layout. A physically low-resolution image may have enough effective resolution to output if it has been reduced to a sufficiently small size in the layout document.

Graphics File Formats

Although sophisticated programs have blended the use of vector and raster technologies, the visual appearances and the editing methods for each type of graphic remain distinct. Image file formats are also divided by these two categories, though many allow a combination of raster and vector data. Each format has special characteristics and capabilities that make it suitable for specific uses and final output. The following chart lists the graphics formats that you can import into an InDesign document, along with a description of each type and notes about the suitability of each to a particular purpose.

Most vector file formats can contain raster data. EPS, in particular, is a common file format written by Photoshop that contains nothing but raster data in a PostScript "wrapper" that includes a low-resolution preview image. You cannot enlarge such EPS files much without encountering the same problems as you would with a TIFF or other raster file.

If the document is exported to HTML for the Web, InDesign converts all graphics to JPEG or GIF files. Except for the SVG (Scalable Vector Graphic) format, all Web graphics are rasters.

Lossy and *lossless* are two types of raster compression schemes.

The word "lossy" alludes to the fact that data is thrown away, or lost, in the compression process. JPEG (still images) and MPEG (video) files use lossy compression techniques that discard image data deemed unnecessary to a "good enough" reproduction. DVD video is an example of MPEG compression; the blocky artifacts you sometimes see in a DVD movie are the result of too-aggressive compression, as are the noisy halos you sometimes see in JPEG images on the Web. The areas with discarded data must be regenerated for display, and the artifacts you sometimes see are the result of fill-in of missing data. But gentle levels of lossy compression can result in both high-quality displays and a big reduction in file sizes. You can control the level of compression applied when saving images as JPEG files from Photoshop and other applications. Lower-quality settings produce smaller files; higher-quality settings produce larger files. Even at the highest quality setting, a JPEG version of a TIFF image, for example, is significantly smaller than the original, uncompressed TIFF image. JPEG images saved using low-compression, high-quality settings are suitable for print production.

Lossless compression encodes redundant data, and discards only that which can be reproduced mathematically from the encoded data upon decompression for display. The LZW (Lempel-Ziv-Welch) scheme is a common lossless compression method. Lossless compression schemes can't achieve the degree of compression that lossy schemes can, but they present no risk of image degradation.

Format	Type	Notes
Illustrator (.ai)	A	**Illustrator file (5.5 and later)** Transparency preserved in v9.0 and later files. Art can be copied and pasted from Illustrator into InDesign as editable objects, but importing/placing is preferable.
Photoshop (.psd)	B	**Photoshop file (4.0 and later)** Photoshop layers and masks are flattened on output; original file isn't altered.
BMP (.bmp)	Raster	**Windows bitmap file** Windows-only raster format. Not recommended.
CT (.ct)	Raster	**Scitex CT (Contone)** Once common in high-end prepress workflows, this CMYK-only format largely exists in legacy files.
DCS (.dcs)	C	**Desktop Color Separations** A subtype of EPS that contains preseparated CMYK and spot-color vector and raster data. Useful for CMYK+spot artwork.
EPS (.eps)	C	**Encapsulated PostScript** Exchange format for PostScript art, can contain raster and vector data, uses low-resolution TIFF, PICT, or JPEG raster preview for display. Can be exported by most vector, raster, and page-layout applications.
GIF (.gif)	Raster	**Graphics Interchange Format** Very limited color support. Patent claims may restrict use. Not suitable for print.
JPEG (.jpg)	B	**Joint Photographic Experts Group** Raster format that uses a "lossy" type of compression that can degrade image quality if applied too aggressively. Supports grayscale, RGB, and CMYK color spaces, and clipping paths from Photoshop.
PCX (.pcx)	Raster	**Picture Exchange** Windows-only raster format. Limited color support. Not recommended.
PDF (.pdf)	D	**Portable Document File** Self-contained format that includes all raster and vector data and, optionally, fonts used in the original document. Native format of Adobe Acrobat; generally originates as PostScript and is "distilled" or "normalized" to a simplified, portable form. Can contain audio, video, forms, metadata, and other information.
PICT (.pct)	A	**Macintosh Picture** Macintosh-only legacy format. Not recommended.
PNG (.png)	Raster	**Portable Network Graphic** Lossless compression format intended for Web use. Supports RGB only. No patent issues; alternative to GIF.
TIFF (.tif, .tiff)	B	**Tagged Image File Format** The *de facto* raster format for print use; supports LAB, RGB, grayscale, and CMYK color spaces in 8- or 16-bit modes.
WMF (.wmf)	A	**Windows MetaFile** Windows-only legacy format. Not recommended.

Type Legend

A A primarily vector format that can also contain raster data.

B A raster format that can contain masking data in vector format.

C Can contain vector and raster data.

D Can contain vector, raster, text, font, video, audio, and other data types.

A number of these graphic formats are unsuitable for use in projects that are destined for print or, in some cases, Web use. Primarily, you want to use EPS, PDF, TIFF, and possibly JPEG files if the final output of your project is printed. You can easily repurpose a print job as a Web job — InDesign converts all graphics to low-resolution JPEG or GIF images suitable for use in a Web document if you export the document as HTML — but you can't go the other way. You can also save any InDesign document as PDF, which can be used for Web, print, and many other purposes depending on the PDF Export settings.

There will undoubtedly be occasions when you receive a graphic file that's in one of the "not recommended" formats. You can usually open these in an application such as Photoshop, Illustrator, FreeHand, or CorelDraw, then save them in one of the preferred formats.

Place and Position Images

Press Command/Control-D to invoke the Place function.

1. Open a new document. Choose File>New. In the New Document dialog box, set the following options:
   Number of pages: 1
   Facing Pages: No
   Page Size: Letter
   All margins: 3p0/36 pt. (Remember, you can enter pica values even if you defined vertical units in points in the Preferences.)
   Columns: 1
   Click OK.

2. Choose File>Place. Navigate to the **RF_Intro_InDesign** folder. Click the Show Preview button (Mac OS 9 only) to view a thumbnail of each file. Select **academy.eps** and click the Choose/Open button.

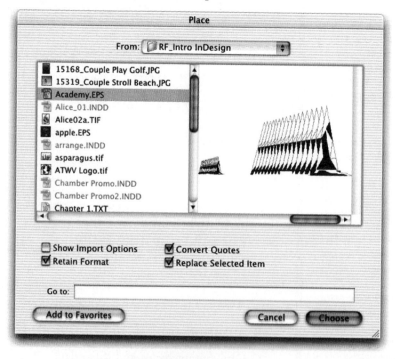

Mac OS X Place dialog box.

3. The cursor changes to a loaded graphics icon, marking where the upper-left corner of the graphic is placed. Click this icon near the top-left margin. Because this is an EPS file, a low-resolution proxy (preview) image of the graphic appears at 100%.

Loaded graphics icon.

4. With the Selection tool, click the image and drag it to the upper-left corner of the page until it "snaps" to the margin guides. The Selection tool moves the bounding frame and the image it contains.

5. Select the Zoom tool and drag a marquee around the placed graphic to enlarge the view.

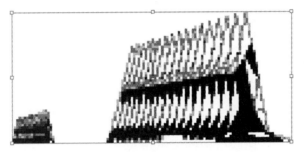

This is a vector graphic, but it looks terrible. Why? The graphic is vector, but the image showing on the screen is a low-resolution raster thumbnail. Using proxy images on the page for imported EPS files saves memory and allows faster screen draw while the page is being composed. The graphic can be sized, positioned, and cropped to suit the layout. When the page is printed, the image looks crisp because the actual PostScript vector data is sent to the printer with all the adjustments made to the proxy image in InDesign.

6. Control/Right-click the graphic, and choose High Quality Display from the Display Performance submenu. This instructs InDesign to render a high-resolution preview from the PostScript data in the file, which significantly improves the preview quality.

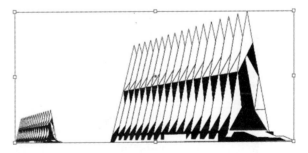

Using this display mode can significantly slow things down if you have many placed EPS files; you can either turn this on or off with the Display Performance submenu, or you can set the display quality in InDesign's Preferences.

You can change the resolution of the proxy or preview image when you place the graphic if you check Show Import Options in the Place dialog box. The recommended resolution for proxy images is 72 dpi.

You can control how placed graphics are displayed in Preferences>Display Performance. Optimize shows a gray box and no image, which is very fast but obviously of limited value if you need to see the image. Typical shows a low-resolution proxy preview. High Quality renders the contents of EPS files for a very sharp display, and also shows placed raster images at a higher resolution; this quality comes at the expense of overall speed. Generally, the Typical setting is fine for most needs, but you can always change a single image's display quality with Control/Right-click>Display Performance.

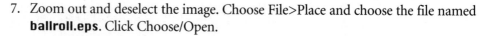

Always deselect any selected items when placing. If a frame is selected when you place anything, the new content replaces the existing content of the frame.

7. Zoom out and deselect the image. Choose File>Place and choose the file named **ballroll.eps**. Click Choose/Open.

8. When the loaded graphics icon appears, click the top margin at the center of the page and drag a frame across to the right margin and down to 216 pt. on the vertical ruler.

9. Save the document as "picture_practice.indd" in your **Work_In_Progress** folder and leave it open for the next exercise.

Placing an image and letting InDesign create a frame for it is one technique of composition; another is to draw a frame with the loaded pointer then release the mouse to drop the content into the frame. Images can also be placed into specific frames that were built before the graphic was imported.

Place Graphics within Frames

1. Continue in the open document. Make sure the Transform palette is visible.

2. Select the Rectangle Frame tool, then drag the tool to create a frame on the page under the **academy.eps** image. Adjust the Transform palette coordinates to:
   X: 3p0   W: 24p0
   Y: 216 pt   H: 198 pt

3. Leave the frame selected, choose File>Place, and select the file **farmer.tif** to import.

4. The image is smaller than the frame, so you can resize either the frame or the picture. Resize the frame this time. With the Selection tool, drag the bottom-right corner point up and left to the edge of the image, and deselect.

If an image is not suitable, or you picked the wrong one, press Command/Control-Z to undo the placement, then click the Selection tool icon in the toolbox to clear the loaded status of the place pointer. Now you can try placing again.

Any closed path or shape created in InDesign can be designated as a frame for any type of content.

5. The frame tools, designated by the "X" in their toolbox icons, are intended to draw frames that hold imported or pasted graphics or text. (You can also use any of the regular shape tools and later convert the shapes drawn to either text or graphic frames.) Select the Rectangle tool and drag to the right of the farmer to create a frame that is 9p0 wide and 234 pt. high.

6. At this point, the rectangle is a graphic element (remember, these get a 1-pt. black stroke by default, and the stroke prints), but it may be used as a frame. You can place content inside of a graphic element in one of two ways. The first method places content into a selected graphic element, just as if it were a frame. Select the rectangle, then choose File>Place and import **flowers2.tif** from the **RF_Intro_InDesign** folder. The image appears in the rectangle automatically, and the rectangle is now a frame. Note that this new frame retains the black stroke; graphic elements that are converted to frames retain their original fill and stroke attributes.

7. Now try the second method. Press Command/Control-Z to undo the placement of the flowers. Now you see the loaded pointer, and the rectangle is still selected. Press Command/Control to temporarily switch to the Selection tool, click a blank area to deselect the rectangle, and then release the Command/Control key to switch back to the loaded pointer. Now, move the pointer over the rectangle and watch it change.

A loaded pointer poised over a potential container.

If frame edges aren't visible, choose View>Show Frame Edges, or press Command/Control-H.

If you use Mac OS X, you may have found InDesign has hijacked the system-wide Command-H (Hide Foreground Application command) keystroke. You can Option-click a visible part of the desktop or choose InDesign>Hide InDesign to hide the program.

To center a graphic in the frame, select both the frame and image using the Selection tool, then choose Object>Fitting>Center Content, or use the Contextual menu.

InDesign detects when you've moved a loaded pointer over any potential container, regardless of whether it was created as a frame. The new pointer appears enclosed in parentheses, indicating that you've moved it over a container of some type. Click once to drop the flowers into the rectangle and to convert it to a frame.

8. The frame container is smaller than the imported image. You can solve this problem in two ways:

   a) Use the Selection tool to drag the lower-right handle out until the frame is approximately 16p6 wide and 252 pt. high. (Make sure you click the handle only, not inside the frame — if you click the image, it moves the frame and image rather than resizing the frame.)
   b) Control/Right-click the image, and choose Fit Frame to Content from the Fitting submenu. You could also choose Center Content if you require a fixed frame size, but this crops image areas that extend past the frame's perimeter.

9. Save this file to your **Work_In_Progress** folder. Leave it open for the next exercise.

Linking vs. Embedding

It's important to understand how InDesign deals with placed image files, because managing imported graphics ensures correct output. Placing a graphic *imports* the image onto the InDesign page, but it does not copy the graphic into the InDesign file unless the file size is smaller than 48 K (kilobytes). For anything larger than that, InDesign utilizes a technique known as "linking" to store and display a preview of the image on the page and to store the *location* of the original graphic. Linking does not store a copy of the graphic file in the InDesign document file. When the file is printed, InDesign locates the original graphic, applies the positioning, cropping, and scaling that you applied to the preview, and sends the adjusted file to the output device in place of the preview.

Linking allows page designers to position, crop, and scale graphics alongside page elements without significantly increasing the document's file size. InDesign stores all previews within the document file, so documents with many placed graphics can become quite large. Keeping files small minimizes memory requirements and maintains efficient processing speeds while you are composing or printing a document.

Linking also offers a convenient mechanism for modifying the original graphic; making changes a single time in the original file updates every instance of that graphic in your InDesign document. This occurs because InDesign records the relative path to a graphic file when it is imported. If you move, rename, or delete a linked graphic file, then you will see a warning message the next time you open or print your InDesign document. You may also see this message if graphic files from a CD or network server are not available (removed from the drive or not connected) when the document needs them.

InDesign also alerts you of graphics that have been changed since you first placed them; all files have a date/time creation "stamp" associated with them, as well as an additional stamp that indicates if and when the file was edited and saved. These stamps allow InDesign to detect anything that has been modified after it was placed.

Press Command/Control-Shift-D to show or hide the Links palette.

Items created on the desktop (Mac OS and Windows) are rooted to the startup drive, so items copied to a folder created on the desktop from another drive are copied, not moved.

Hold the Shift key while repositioning a graphic inside a frame with the Direct Selection tool to constrain its movement horizontally or vertically.

Manage and Update Image Links

1. Continue in the open document. Choose Window>Links to view the Links palette. You can see the name of each graphic file, along with the page number on which that graphic is placed (at the right). If no symbol appears between the name and page number, the graphic is linked and ready for output.

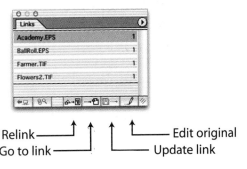

Relink ——— ——— Edit original
Go to link ——— ——— Update link

2. For the purpose of demonstration, you're going to break the links. Save and close the **picture_practice.indd** file that you've been working on.

3. Create a new folder on your desktop named "Temp". Locate the **RF_Intro_InDesign** folder and move (do not copy) the following files to the **Temp** folder: **academy.eps**, **ballroll.eps**, **farmer.tif**, and **flowers2.tif**. If the files remain in the **RF_Intro_InDesign** folder, that means you had them on a second drive originally, so delete them. If you have been working from the Resource CD, copy the files from **RF_Intro_InDesign** to the new **Temp** folder.

4. Change the name of the **flowers2.tif** file in the Temp folder to "flowers2new.tif".

5. If you have been working from the Resource CD, eject it so the links are no longer accessible.

6. Reopen the file. You receive the following warning:

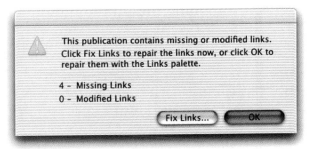

Click OK to dismiss the warning. The Links palette should look like this:

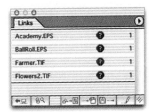

Another type of broken link occurs when the original graphic has been modified and resaved in the original program. The link must be updated to display and print the latest version of the graphic. The exclamation point symbol indicates that a graphic has been edited. You can update modified links easily by clicking the Update Link button on the palette (second from right, with the disk icon).

Locating and relinking moved graphics can be time-consuming. Be careful not to rename or move graphics after you link them to an InDesign file. Do not delete placed graphic files, because the InDesign document won't print correctly. Always send copies of the graphic files with the document for output.

The red question mark symbol indicates that InDesign can't find the files for these placed graphics. They must be relinked.

7. Select academy.eps in the Links list and click the Relink button (furthest left at the bottom of the palette). Navigate to the **Temp** folder you made on the desktop, select the **academy.eps** file, and then click Choose/Open.

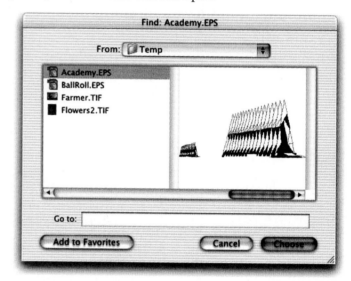

8. After you locate the first graphic in a set of unlinked files, you can easily relink all other graphics that now reside in this location without browsing to their location. Select the next graphic in the list, ballroll.eps, and click the Relink button, then select farmer.tif and click the Relink button.

9. Select flowers2.tif and click the Relink button. Click Browse. Navigate to the desktop and select the file that you renamed **flowers2new.tif**, and click OK. A dialog box like the one below appears. Click Yes. All of the broken links are now resolved.

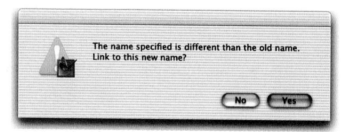

10. To simulate updating modified graphics, move the files back to the **RF_Intro_InDesign** folder.

    Note: if you are working from the Resource CD, delete the files you moved, and reinsert the CD.

11. Return to InDesign, then select each file and click the Relink button to use the graphic files from the **RF_Intro_InDesign** folder. You need to navigate to and locate the first file, and then you can just click the Relink button to do the rest.

12. Save the document and keep it open for the next exercise. Delete the **Temp** folder you made at the beginning of this exercise.

Embedded Graphics and File Size

Instead of linking graphic files to InDesign documents, you can choose to *embed* them. Embedding a graphic saves a copy of the entire graphic file within the InDesign file, which makes the file larger. Because every embedded image is packaged inside the document, embedding makes documents more easily portable, and eliminates linking problems when a file is output or transported to another computer system. Graphics smaller than 48 K are always embedded into InDesign documents. Every time a graphic is copied to an additional location in the document, the copy is also stored in the file, adding to the file size.

Generally, we do not recommend embedding images larger than about 100 K. Doing so can cause the document file to become unmanageably large, and most print shops and other service providers strongly prefer that any images in a submitted job are included *with* the document file (linked), not *in* it (embedded). You can extract embedded graphics and save them to disk for further editing; you can also relink an embedded graphic to the original file, or to a different file. Embedded graphics are listed in the Links palette, but InDesign does not track the status of the original file after the graphic is embedded.

Embed Placed Graphics

1. Continue in the open document to embed a graphic manually. Select flowers2new.tif in the Links palette. From the Links palette Options pop-up menu choose Embed File.

   The graphic file is copied into the InDesign document and is no longer a linked file, but the graphic name remains in the Links palette with a small symbol showing that it is now embedded.

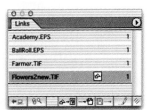

2. If you alter the original file and need to incorporate the change, you must either delete and re-embed the image, or select the image in the document, choose Unembed from the Links palette Options menu, and direct InDesign to relink to the new file.

3. Save and close this file.

Alternatives to Placing

Importing graphic files using the Place command offers the most control and highest quality for using images in an InDesign document, but there are additional methods that may be suitable in certain circumstances. InDesign does not support Windows' Object Linking and Embedding (OLE), or the Mac OS Publish and Subscribe feature, but it does

If you have a placed a file in a document, and the program that created it is installed on your computer, you can select the file name in the Links palette and click the Edit Original button at the bottom to edit the file in its original program. After you save the file, the new version is automatically updated in the InDesign document.

File formats such as WMF, PICT, and BMP usually cause printing problems. As a rule of thumb, you should use standard TIFF, PDF, and EPS files when preparing files for print.

In Illustrator 9 and 10, you can turn off the "Copy as: PDF" option in the Files & Clipboard Preferences if you selected Prefer PDF in InDesign's General Preferences. Otherwise, Illustrator objects won't paste as editable InDesign objects. You can leave Copy as: PDF enabled in Illustrator if you disable Prefer PDF in InDesign's General Preferences as long as you have Copy as: AICB enabled in Illustrator's preferences.

permit graphics to be copied to the system clipboard and pasted into a document. It also supports drag-and-drop placement of importable graphic files from open file windows on the desktop into the InDesign page.

If you can save, export, or otherwise convert outside material to PDF, then you can place (not paste) it in an InDesign document with high-quality results. Mac OS X users can "print" any document to a PDF file, and users of other operating systems can purchase Adobe Acrobat, which offers a simple means of creating PDFs from all applications.

- **Copying and pasting to InDesign from other applications.** It's difficult to predict how data (text or graphics) will behave when it is copied from one program and pasted into an InDesign document. Text is usually pretty safe (although formatting may be lost), but graphics are another story. In general, you shouldn't copy and paste graphics unless there's no other way of getting the artwork into InDesign. The system clipboard isn't compatible with vector data, so unless the originating application can convert data to an encapsulated format that can survive a trip through the clipboard, copying and pasting graphics is a risky move. Illustrator, for example, converts copied art to a format that InDesign can understand; in most cases, graphics copied from Illustrator are fully editable after pasting to InDesign. If you copy a chart from Microsoft Excel, however, it is simply passed to the clipboard "as is"; the only other programs that can easily read it are Microsoft Word and PowerPoint. An Excel chart pasted into an InDesign document shows up as a low-resolution raster graphic that doesn't look very good. Any graphic pasted into InDesign from another application is not listed in the Links palette, but is otherwise treated as an embedded graphic.

- **Copying and pasting within a single InDesign documnet.** If you copy a graphic from one InDesign page to another, the graphic acts and prints just as if you had placed it directly onto the page, including its linking information. Embedded graphics also transfer smoothly within an InDesign document.

- **Dragging and dropping graphics between InDesign documents.** If two InDesign documents are open, you can drag a graphic (or anything else) from one document into the other document. All linking information is preserved.

- **Dragging and dropping from an open folder window.** If there are any folder windows open when you reduce an InDesign document window, you can drag and drop the files from those folders directly into the document (assuming they're in a format that InDesign can import). Graphics placed using this method are listed in the Links palette.

- **Copying and pasting or dragging and dropping art from Illustrator.** You can drag (or copy) selected art from an Adobe Illustrator document window and drop (or paste) it into an InDesign document. Any text within the pasted art is converted to a non-editable graphic. Copied elements from Illustrator documents can be transformed and manipulated like any other imported graphic. Artwork from Illustrator 9 and later can be copied or dragged, but InDesign treats the resulting graphic as a single, non-editable object unless you choose "Copy as: AICB" in Illustrator's Files & Clipboard Preferences settings. We do not recommend copying and pasting or dragging and dropping Illustrator art; you'll get better and more reliable results if you import the Illustrator, EPS, or PDF file containing the artwork.

- **Importing other Adobe File Formats.** You can place native Illustrator (.ai) and Photoshop (.psd) files without first saving them in a standard interchange format such as EPS or TIFF. Imported Photoshop graphics with layers are flattened for purposes of placement, and alpha-channel transparency effects are not recognized, but the original files are untouched and remain fully editable in Photoshop.

- **Editing Imported Graphics.** To edit a graphic in its native program, you can select its name in the Links palette and click the Edit Original button on the palette's far right (the pencil icon). The graphic opens in its originating program (if possible, and only if the originating program is installed on your computer) for alterations. When you return to the InDesign program, the graphic in InDesign is updated automatically.

Scaling and Cropping Placed Graphics

Scaling, shearing, and rotating graphic images is easy to do in InDesign but, especially with raster graphics, such transformations can cause very long print times. Don't overdo it.

Placed images are imported at the full size created in their native application. During page composition, however, that size may not fit the page layout. InDesign provides several ways to reduce or enlarge imported graphics to suit the needs of any design. Remember that vector graphics may be scaled to any percentage larger or smaller without concern for resolution and print quality, but resolution-dependent raster images must contain a sufficient number of pixels per inch to print at the resolution and scaling percentage chosen in the document. For each raster image, you should check the resolution against the scaling percentage assigned in InDesign to ensure it is still within acceptable parameters. If not, you must either *resample* the raster image (to change its resolution), or rescan it in the original application and update it in InDesign before outputting the document.

Another way to control the appearance of placed images on the page is to crop them. Cropping essentially draws a frame beyond which image areas are masked so they don't display or print. Cropping can occur automatically if an image is placed into a small or irregularly shaped frame. You can also crop images by reducing the frame size after placing an image. You can combine scaling and cropping to manipulate imported images and blend them with other InDesign elements.

Create a Newspaper Ad

1. Start a new document. Choose File>New. In the New Document dialog box, make the following changes:
   Number of pages: 1
   Facing Pages: No
   Page Size: Custom
   Width: 25p
   Height: 360 pt.
   All margins: 0p
   Columns: 1
   Click OK.

2. If the Transform palette is not already visible, choose Window>Transform.

3. Choose File>Place, be certain Show Import Options is unchecked, and place **travellogo.eps** from your **RF_Intro_InDesign** folder.

4. Position the loaded graphics icon in roughly the middle of the page and click (don't drag) once to place the image.

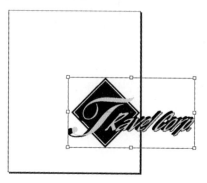

5. This file is an EPS graphic, so scaling it does not adversely affect the output. With the image still selected, go to the Transform palette and enter 40% for width. Press Command/Control-Return/Enter to apply the same scaling to the height.

6. Position this graphic in the lower-right corner, but not at the edge of the page. Deselect the image.

Select a proxy reference point in the Transform palette to scale from a specific position. Choose the center anchor point to scale the image or frame evenly on all sides from the center.

7. Place the image named **border.eps** from your **RF_Intro_InDesign** folder. Click the loaded graphics icon near the upper-left corner of the page.

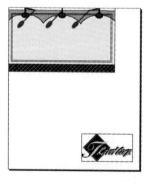

Scaled frame content shows "100%" in the Transform palette regardless of how much the frame and its contents are scaled, but if you select the contents with the Direct Selection tool, the true scaling percentage is shown in the Transform palette.

Transforming (especially rotating) placed raster images may affect print quality and slow output to some devices. Significant transformations should be completed in the original drawing program before placing the image. The vector graphics used in this exercise can be transformed extensively without affecting print quality, although the alterations can impact output speed.

8. This is also a vector graphic. You need to scale it unequally to fill the ad area. With the Selection tool, while holding down the Command/Control key, drag the lower-right corner of the image frame to the right edge of the page, about 36 pts. below the bottom edge of the page.

Select the graphic with the Direct Selection tool and look at the Transform palette. It should indicate that the image was scaled approximately 125% vertically and 280% horizontally. Make sure that the image is enlarged enough that the cross-hatched pattern at the bottom is below the bottom margin of the page.

9. You want to crop the bottom of this image to hide the crosshatch pattern. With the Selection tool, click the bottom-center handle of the frame. Drag the frame edge up until the crosshatch pattern disappears. Leave the solid black line showing. Choose Object>Arrange>Send to Back, then deselect the image.

10. Save the document as **ad.indd** in your **Work_In_Progress** folder, and leave it open for the next exercise.

When interactively scaling a frame, click-hold the Selection tool on the frame handle, and wait until the pointer changes to a single arrow then back to a two-headed arrow before beginning the move. The portions of the image outside of the frame's bounding box appear to be "ghosted," so you can see the relationship between the content and the frame bounds while resizing the frame.

Pressing the Command/Control key while resizing with the Selection tool resizes both frame and contents simultaneously. If scaling uniformly, add the Shift key.

Add and Manipulate Images

1. Continue in the open ad.indd document. Place the image named **cruiseship.eps** from your **RF_Intro_InDesign** folder. Click the loaded graphics icon on the inside of the left border and under the shadow of the overhead lights.

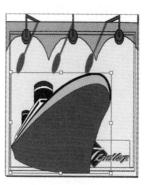

2. The ship needs to fit on the left side of the ad and nestle into the top of the border, so you need to shape the frame to the space and then fit the image. With the Selection tool, click the lower-right control handle of the frame and drag it left and up until the frame is about 10p6 wide (check the Transform palette) and the bottom clears the lower border.

3. With the graphic still selected, choose Object>Fitting>Fit Content to Frame. While holding the Command/Control key, use the Selection tool to drag the frame's top-center control handle up to meet the shadow cast by the lamps, if necessary. Deselect the frame.

4. Place the image named **ace.eps** from your **RF_Intro_InDesign** folder. Click the loaded graphics icon at the bottom of the ship's hull. Leave the card image selected.

Click and hold the tool for a moment when using the Rotate, Scale, or Skew tool to view a live preview of the transformation. If you move the tool right away, you'll just see the outline instead of the content.

5. Select the Scale tool and click-hold the lower-right control handle of the card image frame. Drag the handle up and to the left to make the image smaller. Hold the Shift key to constrain the image's proportions. Watch the Transform palette, and drag until the image is approximately 3 picas wide.

6. Select the Rotate tool. Click-hold the tool cursor outside the bottom-right corner, dragging counterclockwise until the Transform palette indicates approximately 20° rotation. Choose the Selection tool, reposition the card image if necessary, and then deselect it.

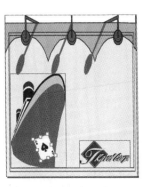

7. Place the image named **10hearts.ai** from your **RF_Intro_InDesign** folder. Click the loaded graphics icon near the ace card.

8. Deselect the graphic and choose the Direct Selection tool. Click the Ten of Hearts image inside the frame. In the Transform palette, enter 50% in both the Horizontal and Vertical Scale fields. Press Return/Enter.

9. With the Selection tool, select the Ten of Hearts frame. Choose Object>Fitting>Fit Frame to Content. Position the card on top of the ace card, and deselect.

10. Place the image named **ad_text.ai** from your **RF_Intro_InDesign** folder. Click the loaded graphics icon at the bow tip of the ship. With the Selection tool drag the image into place as shown, so the dollar sign is just touching the ship's bow. Adjust the position of the ad copy so the phone number at the bottom clears the border. The copy overlaps the logo a little; that's OK for now.

11. Move the logo up and position it so it clears the "call now" text and the phone number. Surprise! You can't select the logo because it is below the placed ad copy in the stacking order. To select elements underneath others, Command/Control-click the stack until the element you want is selected. Here, just click once; if you click twice, the background graphic is selected. Move the selected logo so it clears

Command/Control-click stacked objects to select objects behind the ones in front. Continue until the correct object is selected.

the ad copy. The finished ad should look like this (with Display Performance set to High Quality):

12. Save this file as **travelcorp.indd** in your **Work_In_Progress** folder and close this document.

Adding Borders to Imported Images

Depending on the layout, some images require borders. With InDesign, the frame container itself, or another frame behind the image, can provide the border. Borders may be added to rectangular, circular, or irregularly shaped graphic containers using the Stroke and Swatches palettes.

Create Borders for Imported Graphics

1. Open **picture_practice.indd** from your **Work_In_Progress** folder.

2. Adjust the view so the academy.eps image is visible. Select the frame's handles with the Selection tool and resize it to be slightly larger than the image itself. Choose Object>Fitting>Center Content.

3. With the image frame still selected, click the Stroke box in the toolbox, and then click the Default Fill and Stroke icon (small icon at the immediate left of the Stroke box) to assign a black stroke to the frame border.

4. Choose Window>Stroke to display the Stroke palette. From the palette Options menu, choose Options to display the entire palette. Select 5 pt. from the Weight menu. Choose Solid from the Type menu.

5. Select the ballroll.eps graphic with the Selection tool. Make certain Stroke is selected, then click black in the Swatches palette. In the Stroke palette, change the weight of this frame to 2 pt.

6. Choose Object>Corner Effects from the menu. First check Preview, and then change the Effect to Fancy in the pop-up menu. The frame does not appear to change until the size is increased. Type "3p" into the Size field for this frame and click OK. Deselect the image.

7. Select the farmer.tif image with the Selection tool. Choose black for the stroke color of this frame and assign it a 10-pt. weight in the Stroke palette. Choose Window>Color to open the Color palette and enter "50" in the percentage (%) field. Press Return/Enter to create a 50% black tint border to this graphic.

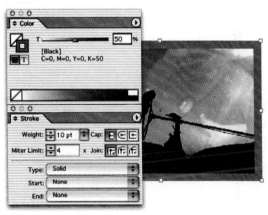

The Weight Changes Bounding Box option, located in the Stroke palette Options pop-up menu, allows a frame to enlarge to accommodate a thicker stroke.
If unchecked, the frame does not change size, but the stroke moves inwards and possibly covers the edges of the frame content.

8. Choose Object>Corner Effects and check its Preview option to view your selection. For the effect displayed, choose Rounded and enter 1p6 in the Size field. Click OK and deselect.

9. Borders can also be made separately using an empty frame. Below the farmer image, create a rectangular frame 25p6 × 360 pt. in the empty space on this page. Move or scale the flowers2new.tif image if you need more room.

10. For the next type of frame, you need to import the newspaper ad created in the last section. You could cut and paste or drag and drop the ad from the other file, but we have provided a completed ad in another file format that InDesign can both export and import. With the frame active, choose File>Place and select

PDF (Portable Document Format) is becoming a common file exchange standard. InDesign can place any PDF file (version 3.0 or higher), including those created by Acrobat Distiller or the PDF printer extension; it can also export PDF in a number of ways.

The Dimensions Include Stroke Weight option changes a setting in the Transform palette to display the item's dimensions around the outside of the graphic including the border. When it is unselected, thick borders may add to the size of the bounding box.

ad.pdf from the **RF_Intro_InDesign** folder. The ad is placed in the frame that you just drew.

11. Check that Dimensions Include Stroke Weight is checked on the Transform palette's Options menu. Open the Stroke palette Options menu and make certain that the Weight Changes Bounding Box option is not checked. These two options combined ensure that the graphic and border does not grow beyond your dimension settings in the Transform palette.

12. Select the frame with the Selection tool. Check the toolbox to ensure that its fill is None, and then change its stroke to black. Select 4-pt. weight for this frame in the Stroke palette.

13. Choose Dashed from the Type menu, and define the following customized dashed border (pressing Tab to move between fields):
Dash: 10 pt., Gap: 3 pt., Dash: 6 pt., Gap: 8 pt.
Press Tab again after entering the last Gap value.

14. Save this file and close it.

Image Display Mode

You can specify a default preview setting for new documents in the Display Performance Preferences dialog box, but you can also choose to override any image-specific display settings and force a setting for all graphics in a document. We described the Optimize, Typical, and High Quality options earlier in this chapter.

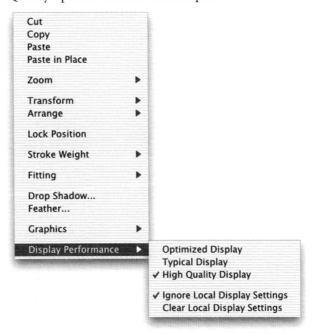

InDesign's Display Performance options.

There are two additional options that allow you to override any document-wide settings defined in the Preferences dialog box. The Ignore Local Display Settings option overrides the display performance settings from InDesign's Preferences; instead, a user-selected setting is applied to one or more images in the document. Choosing the Clear Local Display Settings option resets every image's display settings to those specified in the Preferences.

Summary

In this chapter you have learned about the types of graphics that can be imported into InDesign, the differences between vector and raster images, and how to determine the necessary resolution for resolution-dependent images. You have placed and transformed a variety of images, and you have learned how to manage images using the Links palette. You have learned how to effectively use the Selection and Direct Selection tools when working with graphics, and how to modify content and content frames.

10 Text Utilities

Chapter Objective:

InDesign includes several tools that simplify the editing process by allowing you to find and change defined text elements, use and update built-in and custom dictionaries, and automatically check spelling. In Chapter 10, you will:

- Explore the uses of InDesign's Find/Change feature.

- Learn how to locate or alter individual instances or every instance of a character, word, or phrase.

- Explore methods for finding and changing a specific style or a style attribute in all styled and unstyled text.

- Learn how to search for special characters, and how to reveal and search for hidden characters.

- Become familiar with the uses and weaknesses of InDesign's Check Spelling feature.

- Discover how to select, use, and edit dictionaries.

Projects to be Completed:

- Central Market Ad (A)

- Yellow Rose Menu (B)

- **Travel Brochure (C)**

- Good Choices Newsletter (D)

Text Utilities

Working with large amounts of text can be cumbersome when clients make changes, or when you must proofread text for accurate spelling. Hunting for mistakes by reading the text word-for-word takes considerable time. When deadlines are looming, there usually is very little time for this degree of scrutiny.

InDesign offers several text utilities that make it easy to find and replace words or phrases, and to check spelling. You can edit the User dictionary to include words that are not found in most dictionaries, such as proper nouns or trademarks. The following text utility features are found on the Edit menu:

- Find/Change
- Find Next
- Check Spelling
- Edit Dictionary

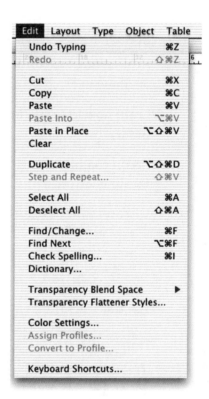

InDesign's Edit menu.

If no text or text frames are selected, the Search menu of the Find/Change dialog box defaults to Document, which searches all of the text frames in the document.

*A **search term** is the letter, word, or phrase that you're searching for. A **replacement term** is what you want to replace the search term with.*

The Find Next option in the Edit menu is not a separate function as are the Find/Change and Check Spelling options. Instead, it is one of the Find/Change dialog box features. If you select Edit>Find Next, InDesign locates the word or phrase that still occurs in the Find What field. The Find/Change dialog box does not have to be open for this to work.

Find/Change

With the Find/Change feature, you can search for specified text or special characters, and determine whether to apply a change. The Find/Change dialog box offers several options for making text changes. This dialog behaves a little differently than most you've seen; it's a *non-modal* dialog, which means you can leave it open while you work with the document. (Most other dialogs are *modal*, which means you can't do anything until you explicitly dismiss them by clicking an OK or Cancel button.) One advantage of this feature is that you can perform searches and edit text without closing the Find/Change dialog box; it doesn't disappear until you click the Done button.

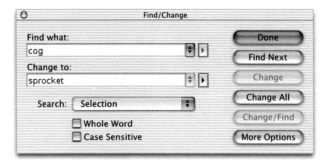

InDesign's Find/Change dialog box.

- **Find What.** In this field, you enter a search term, which can be a single letter, a word, or a phrase. If the search term is a phrase, InDesign finds instances of the entire phrase, but doesn't single out individual words within the phrase.

- **Change To.** In this field, you can specify the text that InDesign uses to replace the Find What text; again, the Change To text can be a letter, word, or phrase.

  You can also leave the Find What and Change To fields blank, and base your search and replace on formatting, styles, fonts, and other non-text attributes.

- **Find Next.** When InDesign locates the search term, it can either replace it or, if you click the Find Next button, ignore it and search for the next occurrence of the search term.

- **Change.** Clicking this button prompts InDesign to replace the found search text with the replacement term typed into the Change To field.

- **Change All.** Clicking this button changes all occurrences of the search term throughout the selection, story, document, or all open InDesign documents. You have no option to pick and choose which instances are affected, so be careful that the search term doesn't appear in a different context. For example, if you define a search term of "air" and a replacement term of "gas", the replacement could mangle words such as "stair" and "airport" unless you click the Whole Word check box.

- **Change/Find.** Clicking this button directs InDesign to change the highlighted search term, then to find next occurrence of that term. It's a shortcut for repeatedly clicking the Find Next and Change buttons.

- **More Options.** If you click the More Options button, the Find/Change dialog box expands to show the Format buttons. You can define search and replacement

If you want to find and change fonts, use Type>Find Font, or change the appropriate style.

terms based on their character and paragraph formatting. We will describe the use of these fields in more detail later in this chapter.

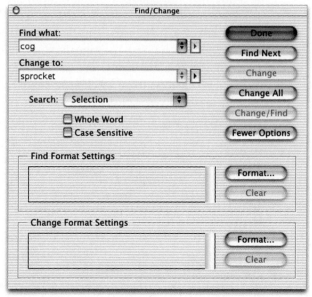

The expanded view of the Find/Change dialog box. Notice that the More Options button now reads Fewer Options.

• **Search.** Documents often contain multiple text frames. This pop-up menu allows you to specify where InDesign should search for the Find What text. If you select the Document option, InDesign searches all of the text frames in the active document. The All Documents options searches every open InDesign document. The Story option searches the entire active story, beginning at the cursor's current location to the end of the story, then from the beginning of the story back to the cursor location. The To End of Story option searches from the cursor's location to the end of the active story, then stops. The Selection option searches only the highlighted words.

The options in the Search drop-down menu.

*A continuous flow of text, whether it occupies one frame or multiple threaded frames, is considered a **story**.*

• **Whole Word.** The words defined as the Find What text sometimes occur as sections of other larger words, such as "cat" within "catastrophe." If your search term is "cat," then InDesign highlights those three letters within words such as "catastrophe" and "scatter." To restrict the search to only those instances where the Find What text appears on its own, you can click the Whole Word option; the search term is then ignored within words.

• **Case Sensitive.** When the Case Sensitive option is on, the case of all the letters in the search term must match exactly. This lets you differentiate between, for example, "sprocket" and "Sprocket" when performing a search.

Find and Replace Text

1. Open the document **dead_souls_ch_1.indd** from the **RF_Intro_InDesign** folder. This is the first chapter of *Dead Souls*, by the 19th-century Russian novelist Nikolai Gogol, and you're going to take a few liberties with this masterpiece of dry wit. If you receive any missing font warnings, ignore them (although you shouldn't get any if you've already installed Adobe Garamond Pro).

2. Choose Type>Show Hidden Characters, and look at the first page. You can see spaces and not much else — but zoom in on the beginning of the second paragraph. There are two dashes with dots under them, which indicate that en spaces (half of an em space) were used to set the indent, rather than a tab. As you learned in the steakhouse menu project, en spaces are useful for setting spacing that's proportional to the type size, in contrast to tabs, which are always of a fixed stop size. In a book like this, however, the type size isn't likely to change.

3. Select the Type tool and click in the first paragraph of the text frame on Page 1. Choose Edit>Find/Change, or press Command/Control-F.

4. You want to replace the two en spaces with a tab, but how do you type an en space into the Find What field? You can't type it directly; instead, you have to use a *meta-character*, which is one or more characters that define another. Most word-processing and page-layout applications use meta-characters to represent characters that can't be typed on the keyboard — for example, the meta-character for a tab is "^t" (the "^" character is Shift-6), and for a paragraph return it is "^p".

If you don't know the meta-character for an en space (or any other common special character that you can search for), click the triangle to the right of the Find What field; a pop-up menu lists some of the special characters and symbols that InDesign can search for.

Some special characters have unique search codes. For a paragraph break, type: "^p" (Shift-6, then "p").

If you choose Story from the Search pop-up menu, InDesign checks all linked text frames — even those that precede the present cursor position. When you select To End of Story, InDesign only searches the text between the cursor position and the end of the story. This can be a small time-saver when dealing with long stories such as book chapters.

InDesign can only search for what you tell it to. Always check whether the Whole Word or Case Sensitive check boxes are activated.

Choose En Space from the Find What menu. InDesign inserts the meta-character for an en space, which is "^>" (Shift-6, then Shift-[period]), into the Find What field. Because you're looking for occurrences of two en spaces together, you need to specify that as the search term. Type "^>" into the Find What field, just after the meta-character inserted by choosing En Space from the menu.

5. Click the Change To field, or just press Tab. Note that, although you want to define the Change To text as a tab, pressing the Tab key simply moves the cursor from one field to another. You need a meta-character here too. Choose Tab Character from the Change To pop-up menu, or type "^t".

6. Click the Find Next button to highlight the first occurrence of two en spaces in the text. If InDesign could not find the search term, it would display a message to that effect:

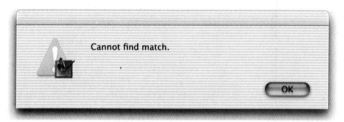

7. Click Change/Find to replace the two en spaces with a tab, then find the next occurrence. Click Change All to replace all instances of two en spaces with a tab. A message appears stating that the search is complete, and that nine changes were made. Click OK to dismiss this modal dialog box.

8. Next, you need to replace the British spelling of the word "rouble" with the North American "ruble". Type "rouble" into the Find What field, and "ruble" in the Change To field. Make sure that Whole Word is not checked, because you want to change all occurrences of "rouble" including plurals. Click Find Next to highlight the first occurrence of the search term (within "roubles"). Click Change/Find; because the search term only occurs once in the document, you see a dialog stating that the search is complete. Close this dialog by clicking OK.

9. Lastly, your picky editor wants to change all occurrences of the protagonist's surname, Chichikov, to the more accurate transliteration of Tchichikov. Enter these terms, and then click Change All. Dismiss the completion dialog, then click Done.

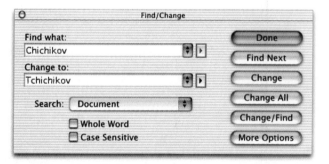

10. Save the document to your **Work_In_Progress** folder, and close it.

More Options

If you click the More Options button in the Find/Change dialog box, you have the opportunity to define search terms based on character or paragraph formatting. (The Fewer Options button hides these extra settings.) You can use these options to change overall style settings, or to limit a search to words in a particular typeface or that match a specific character or paragraph style. You can search for any character or paragraph attribute that can be defined in a style; for example, you can replace one style with another, change all 10-pt. text to 12 pt., or change text from one color to another. These are powerful functions that can save a lot of tedious manual work.

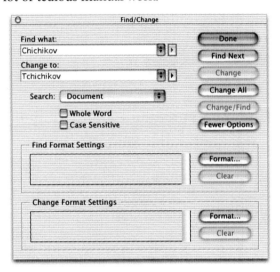

Clicking the More Options button reveals the Format buttons.

Format Settings

You can define specific formats for search or replacement terms by clicking the Format button of either the Find Format Settings or the Change Format Settings. The dialog box that appears is similar to the one used when creating or editing styles, except that all of the options are blank. This lets you choose exactly which formatting options you want to use as search criteria.

- **Style Options.** In the Style Options pane of the Find/Replace Format Settings dialog box, you can define a character or paragraph style as the search or replacement term.

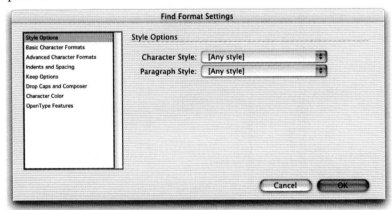

Typists in the past used two spaces after a period to help the reader better distinguish the end of a sentence in a typewriter's monospaced font. This practice has become obsolete, but many writers still use two spaces after a period. This drives typesetters crazy. You can easily fix the problem by searching for double spaces and replacing them with single spaces.

- **Basic Character Formats.** With the Basic Character Formats settings, you can search text by font, size, leading, case (as long as the case was defined in InDesign), and many other character attributes. For example, you might want to change all text formatted as 14/18 Adobe Garamond Pro, no tracking, to 12/auto with –5 em units of tracking.

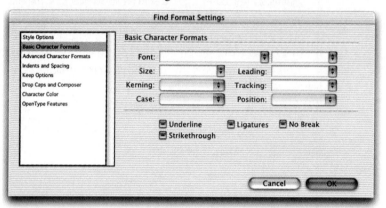

- **Advanced Character Formats.** You can search for text has been modified with scaling, baseline shift, or skewing; you can also use language as a search/replacement term to modify spelling or quotation mark style. For example, you can change English: US to English: UK.

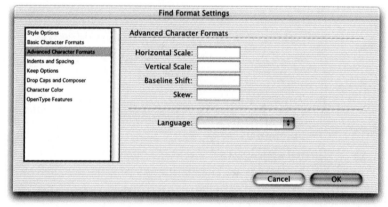

- **Indents and Spacing.** These settings allow you to search based on paragraph attributes, including alignment, indentations, and space before and after.

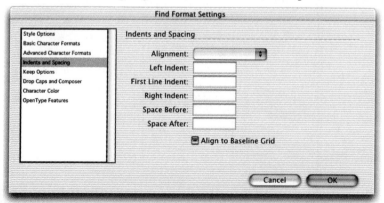

- **Keep Options.** You can use a paragraph's Keep options as search/replacement terms. For example, you could search for all paragraphs defined to keep All Lines in Paragraph if you wanted to correct bad pagination.

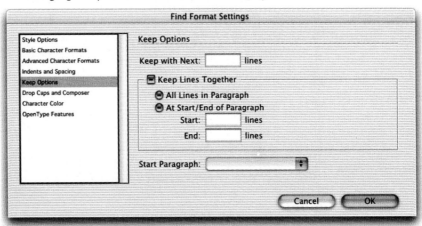

- **Drop Caps and Composer.** In this pane of the dialog box, you can define the number of lines and characters affected by drop caps as search or replacement terms. You can also use the composition option as a search criterion (for example, you could find all text composed with the Adobe Paragraph Composer).

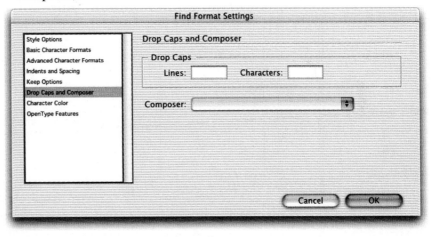

Be very careful when using these Format Settings to find and make changes to text. The format settings are retained and are applied to the next search unless they are cleared. When you finish a Find/Change using Format Setting search terms, you should click the Clear button before moving on to other tasks.

- **Character Color.** You can search for text that has a specific stroke or fill applied to it.

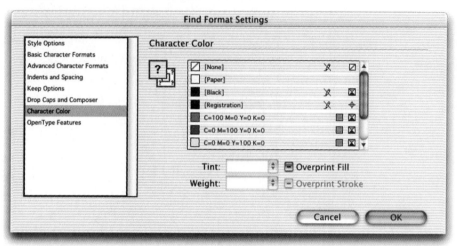

- **OpenType Features.** You can use any OpenType feature as a search or replacement term. For example, you could replace text set as super or subscript with the OpenType superior or inferior glyphs (as long as the OpenType font you're using supports these glyphs).

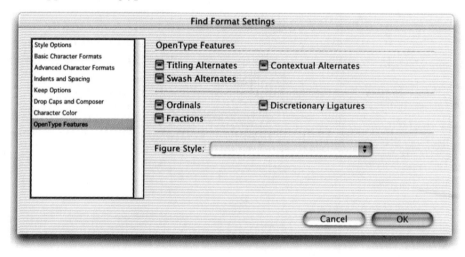

Don't confuse the End of Paragraph marker (an invisible character accessed by typing "^p") with the visible Paragraph symbol, or pilcrow (¶, which is represented by the meta-character "^7").

Similarly, don't confuse a Section marker (an invisible character defining an InDesign section, and accessed by typing "^x") with the visible Section symbol (§, which is represented by the meta-character "^6").

Searching on Format

After you define any format settings in any of the Find or Replace Format Settings panes and click OK, your choices are listed at the bottom of the Find/Change dialog box. Clicking the Clear buttons deletes all of the settings. If only the style settings are to be changed, you can leave the Find What and Change To fields empty; InDesign then finds all text that has the defined formatting applied and makes changes as usual.

The yellow caution symbols above the Find What and Change To fields alert you that a search term is based solely on style parameters.

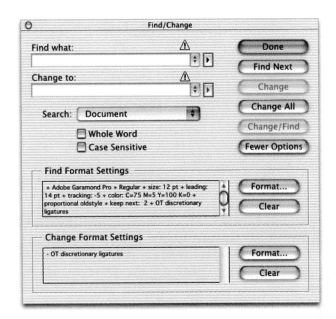

This example has a very stringently defined search term, but the replacement term only turns off discretionary ligatures in any text that meets the criteria of the search term. You can be as specific or general as you please when creating search terms.

More about Meta-characters

Not all searches must look for words. You can look for other attributes of a text block, such as the End of Paragraph marker ("^p"). By selecting from a variety of special text characters and attributes in the Find What and Change To pop-up menus, you can easily include these characters in search or replacement terms. The *wildcard characters* are "^?" (any character), "^9" (any digit), and "^$" (any letter). These can be useful in situations where, for example, you want to find all occurrences of four-letter words ending in "ng." If you define your search term as "^$^$ng", InDesign finds all words such as sing, rang, and long. You can't use wildcards within replacement terms; they are only useful for finding words, or for changing the formatting of found words. If you type a wildcard into the Change To field, InDesign treats those symbols as text and performs a literal replacement.

Remember, you can always use the pop-up menus next to the Find What and Change To fields to enter meta-characters.

Change Text Styles

1. Open the document **formatted_text.indd** from the **RF_Intro_InDesign** folder. This document contains several recipes that must fit on a single page. The text was not formatted correctly, so you must make changes to fit the text.

2. There are a number of unnecessary empty paragraphs (two hard returns) entered to increase the space between paragraphs in the document. You need to get rid of those first. Click with the Type tool before the word "Recipes" so the cursor is at the beginning of the story. Choose Edit>Find/Change. Remove any terms remaining in the Find/Change dialog box from the last exercise. Type "^p" into the Find What field. You're looking for instances of two End of Paragraph marks, so type "^p" again.

Never use extra returns to add vertical space. Use the Space Before/After feature to add any desired vertical spacing between paragraphs.

When InDesign performs a Find/Change, it looks for the entire group as typed, then looks for the next match. So, when looking for ¶¶, there may be three returns in a row. InDesign finds the pair of returns it is looking for...

¶

¶

¶

...and deletes one.

¶

¶

It then looks for the next pair of returns. If the search is run again, it sees the two remaining returns and deletes one of them.

3. Click the cursor in the Change To field and type "^p" again. You're going to replace double returns with a single return. Make sure the Search option is set to Story. Click Change All, and then dismiss the completion notice.

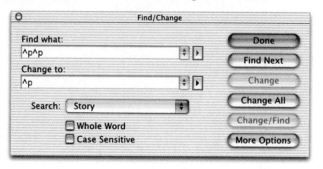

4. If there are any occurrences of triple returns, these are changed to double returns. To make sure that all returns are changed, click Change All again, and dismiss the completion notice. Click Change All a third time to make sure that you've caught all of the multiple returns, which can be verified when the completion notice tells you that no more changes were made.

5. Choose Type>Show Hidden Characters. You can see that even the listings of ingredients end with End of Paragraph markers (*hard returns*). You want to change these to *soft returns*, also known as "line breaks." These effectively break a line without signaling an end of paragraph.

6. Select the first four lines of the ingredients for Orange-glazed Bananas Foster. Be sure your selection includes the ¶ markers. You only want the first four lines, because the fifth line really is the end of the paragraph and you need to retain that marker.

7. In Find/Change, set Find What as "^p" and Change To as "^n" (the symbol for the Forced Line Break). Set the Search field to Selection. Click Change All. Click OK at the Completion notice. Note that text selected prior to a search doesn't remain selected after the search is finished.

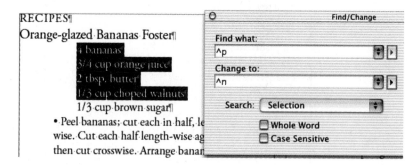

8. Repeat Steps 6 and 7 for the ingredients of Key Lime Pie, Chocolate-Orange Pudding, Florida Orange Bread, and Orange Sunshine Cookies. Remember, don't select the last line of the ingredients because you need those End of Paragraph markers. Check the Search pop-up menu every time, because it reverts back to Story instead of retaining Selection.

You must reset the Search pop-up menu every time you do a search, because it defaults back to Story.

9. Delete the second page, because all of the text now fits on one page. Save the file to your **Work_In_Progress** folder.

10. Now you need to modify the text. The recipe titles are set in 14-pt. type; they are the only elements using that type size. You need to tag all of these titles with the Recipe Title style. Select Edit>Find/Change and click the More Options button.

11. Delete any leftover terms in the Find What and Change To dialog boxes.

12. Click the Format button in the Find Format Settings section, and select Basic Character Formats. Set the Size at 14 pt. and click OK.

13. Click the Format button in the Change Format Settings section, and select Recipe Title from the Paragraph Style menu (the Style Options pane appears by default). Click OK.

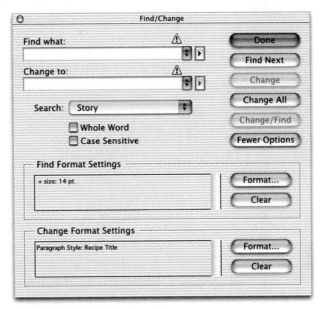

14. Position the Type tool at the beginning of the document and click Change All. Click OK at the search completion notice. Go to Page 1 to see the changes.

15. Next, you want to search the ingredients list. This was set with an indent of 5p0, a searchable parameter. In the Find/Change dialog box, click the Clear buttons for both Find Format Settings and Change Format Settings to delete the information you entered in your last search.

16. Click the Format button in the Find Format Settings section, and select Indents and Spacing. Type "5p0" in the Left Indent field to search for text with that indent. Click OK.

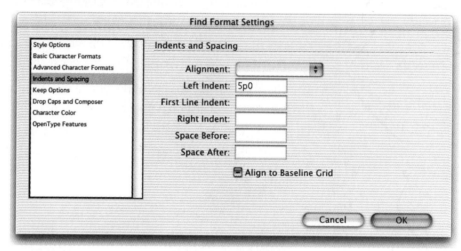

17. Click the Format button in the Change Format Settings section. In the Change Format Settings window, select Ingredients from the Paragraph Style menu. Click OK.

18. In the Find/Change box, click Change All, and then dismiss the completion notice.

19. The body text could be set to fill the margins. Click the Clear buttons for both the Find and Change Format Settings sections.

20. Click the Format button in the Find Format Settings section. Select Basic Character Formats. Because body text is the only text still set in 12 pt., this is a good search parameter. In the Size field, choose 12 pt. from the menu. Click OK.

21. Click the Format button in the Change Format Settings section. From the Paragraph Style menu, select Body Text. Click OK.

22. Position the Type tool at the beginning of the document, and click Change All. Click OK when the search is completed. Save the file.

23. With the Type tool, highlight the word "Recipes" at the top of the page. Change the font to 24-pt. ATC Margarita Bold in the Character palette. In the Paragraph palette, center the text, remove all space before the paragraph, and set the Space After to 16 pt.

24. Save the document to your **Work_In_Progress** folder and leave it open for the next exercise.

Fine-tune the Document

1. Continue in the open document. The Chocolate-Orange Pudding recipe should remain together as a unit. First modify the style sheets to make this happen automatically. Change to the Selection tool.

2. Click the Ingredients paragraph style and select Style Options from the Options pop-up menu.

3. Select Keep Options from the list. Keep all lines in the paragraph together. Click OK.

4. Select the Recipe Title style and change its Keep Options. Type "1" in the Keep with Next field, then click OK.

5. Now you have some extra space to fill in. Click the picture of a pie in the upper left of the pasteboard and cut it.

6. Click the Type tool at the end of the "Keylime Pie" heading. Press Return/Enter. In the Character menu, change the leading of the empty paragraph to 75 pt.

7. Paste the picture into the text frame. The text flows to make room for the pie.

8. Turn off Show Hidden Characters in the Type menu. In the View menu, select Hide Guides and Hide Frame Edges. The page is now correctly formatted with the help of Find/Change's Style windows.

RECIPES

ORANGE-GLAZED BANANAS FOSTER

4 bananas
3/4 cup orange juice
2 tbsp. butter
1/3 cup chopped walnuts
1/3 cup brown sugar

• Peel bananas; cut each in half, lengthwise. Cut each half length-wise again, and then cut crosswise. Arrange bananas in an 8-inch square baking dish.
• Brush orange juice over bananas. Dot with butter.
• Bake at 400° for 10 minutes, basting occasionally with orange juice.
• Combine walnuts and brown sugar; sprinkle over bananas and bake 5 additional minutes. Serve immediately over vanilla ice cream.
Yield: 8 servings.

KEY LIME PIE

4 large eggs, separated
1 (14 oz.) can sweetened condensed milk
1 /3 cup keylime juice
1/2 tsp. cream of tarter
1/3 cup sugar
1 baked 9-inch pastry shell

• Combine egg yolks, condensed milk, and lime juice in a heavy non-aluminum saucepan. Cook, stirring constantly, over low heat until mixture reaches 160° (about 10 minutes).
• Beat egg whites and cream of tarter at high speed with an electric mixer just until foamy. Gradually add sugar, 1 tablespoon at a time, beating until stiff peaks form and sugar dissolves (2 to 4 minutes).
• Pour hot filling into shell. Immediately spread meringue over lime filling, sealing to pie crust edges with a spatula.
• Bake at 325° for 25 to 28 minutes.
Yield: 1 (9-in) pie.

CHOCOLATE-ORANGE PUDDING

1 6 oz. package semi-sweet chocolate bits
3 eggs, separated
2/3 cup heavy cream, whipped
4 to 6 tbsp. orange juice

• Melt chocolate over very low heat. Place in mixing bowl. Add egg yolks slowly, beating well as you mix. Mixture will be quite thick.
• Fold in orange juice and whipped cream.
• Fold in stiffly beaten egg whites. Chill an hour or more.
Yield: 6 small portions.

FLORIDA ORANGE BREAD

Peeling of 4 small oranges
1 cup sugar
1/2 cup water
1 egg
1 cup milk
2 1/2 cups flour
2/3 cups sugar
3 tsp. baking powder
1/2 tsp. salt
1 cup orange peel

• Parboil peeling of 4 oranges. Cook in syrup of 1 cup sugar and water until dry. Add beaten egg to milk; add orange mixture, sifted dry ingredients, and 1 cup orange peel cut fine.
• Put into well greased loaf pan. Let rise 1 hour. Bake 1 hour at 300°.
Yield: 1 loaf

ORANGE SUNSHINE COOKIES

1/2 cup butter
1 cup sugar
Rind of 2 oranges, grated
1 egg
1/2 cup orange juice
3 cups sifted flour
1/2 tsp. cinnamon
4 tsp. baking powder

• Cream together butter, sugar, and orange rind. Gradually add lightly beaten egg, orange juice, flour, cinnamin and baking powder.
• When dough is thoroughly mixed, drop from a teaspoon onto an ungreased cookie sheet. Bake in 325° oven 10 to 12 minutes until light brown.
Yield: approximately 6 dozen cookies.

9. Save the document to your **Work_In_Progress** folder, and keep it open for the next exercise.

Check Spelling

We all make mistakes, and giving text that is going to press a last-minute spell check can save a lot of embarrassment. The InDesign Check Spelling dialog box has features that can give you much control over finding and changing words, as well as the ability to add your own words to the dictionary.

InDesign's Check Spelling dialog box.

- **Not in Dictionary.** This field shows the word that the spell checker does not recognize.

- **Change To.** When a word is selected in the Suggested Corrections box, it appears as the preferred choice for replacing the highlighted word; alternatively, you can type a custom correction in this field and click the Change button to apply it.

- **Suggested Corrections.** These are words from the dictionary that the program suggests as possible replacements for the suspect word. You can select the appropriate replacement for the suspect word by clicking it.

- **Ignore.** When you click the Ignore button, the spell checker makes no change and moves on to the next word it questions.

- **Change.** When you click the Change button, InDesign replaces the questionable word with the Change To word.

- **Ignore All.** Clicking this button tells the spell checker to ignore all future instances of the highlighted word within this particular document.

- **Change All.** Clicking this button prompts the spell checker to change all instances of the highlighted word to the replacement word in the Change To field.

- **Search.** In this pop-up menu, you can choose the range of text to be spell checked. These are the same options that appear in the Search field of the Find/Change dialog box, with the exception of the Selection option.

The options in the Search menu of the Check Spelling dialog box.

- **Add.** Clicking this button adds the word in the Not in Dictionary field to the dictionary.

Edit Dictionary

Most dictionaries contain basic words in the chosen language, but many words are specific to a particular profession or discipline, even including slang or jargon. If the spell checker continuously flags words the writer uses frequently, it may be best to add these words to the dictionary by clicking the Add button in the Check Spelling dialog box.

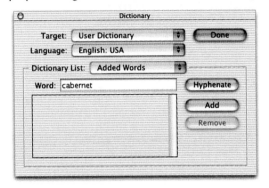

InDesign's Dictionary dialog box.

- **Target.** You can add a word to either the User dictionary or the document's dictionary. The User dictionary is available to all documents, and a document dictionary stays with the document. Generally it's best to use the User dictionary.

- **Language.** This option selects the target language for the added word. For example, if you use a lot of French words in mostly English copy, and are tired of having them marked as incorrect, you can add them to the English: US dictionary, instead of marking each one as French using the Language pop-up menu in the Character palette. You can add words to any installed dictionary.

- **Dictionary List.** This menu allows you to view words that have been added or removed from the selected dictionary.

- **Word.** The word that appears or is typed here is added to the dictionary.

- **Hyphenate.** When you click the Hyphenate option, the word currently in the Word field is separated to show where hyphens would appear if required.

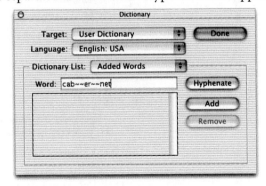

Clicking the Hyphenate button shows how the word "cabernet" would be hyphenated if it appeared within the hyphenation zone at the end of a line.

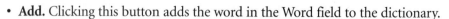

- **Add.** Clicking this button adds the word in the Word field to the dictionary.
- **Remove.** If you click a word (or words) in the dictionary list below the Word field, then click the Remove button, those words are deleted from the User dictionary.

Check the Spelling

1. Continue in the open document. Deselect all text or text frames that may be selected. Choose Edit>Check Spelling.

2. Click the Start button to begin. If, by some chance, the button says Ignore, click it. Either button starts the Check Spelling search.

3. The first word to be questioned is "tbsp", the abbreviation for tablespoon. Recipes use this quite frequently, so there are probably more in the document. Click Ignore All to keep the checker from questioning this again.

4. The next word questioned is "butter." The checker offers a capitalized replacement. If you look at the top of the dialog box, you see the words "Capitalization Error." The checker sees that the abbreviated word prior to "butter" ends with a period, and interprets this as the end of a sentence. It recommends that "butter," as the start of a new sentence, should begin with a capital letter. Click Ignore.

5. The next word is "choped." This is a misspelled word. The suggested replacement "chopped" appears in the dictionary list. Click this word, then click Change.

6. The checker moves on and finds "8-inch". Click Ignore.

7. "KEYLIME" is the next word to question. The replacement in the dictionary list separates this into two words, "KEY LIME". Select this and click Change. The lowercase version of the same word is questioned next. Replace with "key lime".

8. Next, the word "tsp" is questioned. This is the abbreviation for teaspoon and is used in recipes. Click Ignore All, in case there are further examples of this.

9. The next word to appear is "cream." The checker thinks this should be capitalized because it follows a period. It does not need a capital letter, so click Ignore. It also questions "9-inch". Ignore this as well.

10. Next up is the "9-in", which is almost correct. In the Change To input field, add "ch" to spell out the word "inch," then click Change. Even though this is correct, the checker still questions it as "9-inch". Click Ignore to move on.

11. The next word to appear is "orange." The checker thinks this should be capitalized because it follows a period. Click Ignore.

12. Now the checker has caught something you might have skimmed over were you proofing by sight. Have you ever noticed how similar a lowercase letter "l" and the number "1" appear? In the Change To field, change the letter "l" to the number "1". Click Change.

13. The next words are questioned for Capitalization Error — baking, salt, cinnamon, and baking (again). Click Ignore for these.

14. The next questioned word, "cinnaminn", is a misspelled word. There is a correct version in the dictionary list. Select "cinnamon" in this list and click Change.

15. The word "ungreased" is correct, even though the checker does not find it in its dictionary. If further recipes were to be spell checked, this would be a constant word that the checker would question, so add it to the dictionary. Click Add in the dialog box. It changes to the Dictionary dialog box. Click Hyphenate in case the word needs to be hyphenated at any time. Click Add, then Done.

16. You are back at the Check Spelling dialog box. Click Ignore to move on.

17. You find yourself back at the beginning of the text. The Check Spelling session is finished. Click Done to close the dialog box.

18. Now here's proof that a human proofreader is also required. The third ingredient in the Key Lime Pie recipe is "1 /3", which has an extra space. It should be "1/3". Remove the extra space.

19. In the fourth ingredient and the second bulleted item of the Key Lime Pie recipe, the word "tarter" appears. Although that is a word (so the spell checker didn't flag it), you want to use cream of "tartar". Make this change to "tartar."

20. Florida Orange Bread's first item is listed as "smell oranges." You'd probably prefer to use "small" oranges. Make this change also.

21. Save the changes and close the document. *PRINT*

Summary

In this chapter you used InDesign's powerful text tools to automate the editing process. You learned to find and change text elements based on a variety of criteria. You became acquainted with the dictionaries and with the power of InDesign's spell checker. You also became aware of some of the general deficiencies of spell-checking programs, which can only check spelling, not context or grammar.

Complete Project C: Travel Brochure

11 Printing and Packaging

Chapter Objective:

It is very important to prepare documents properly before you submit them to an external service provider. You need to collect all required elements and use printer's marks correctly. This chapter describes the procedures for printing color documents on color or black-and-white desktop printers, and printing oversized documents for proofing purposes. In Chapter 11, you will:

- Understand how to set up the proper driver and print settings for your printer.

- Learn how to proof a color document for printing on either a color or black-and-white printer, and to send the correct type of printout to the service provider.

- Understand how to work with oversized documents by tiling and scaling.

- Become familiar with the purpose of different printer's marks and know how to set them in InDesign.

- Explore the many options available through the Print dialog box, and learn how to set them appropriately for the document and use desired.

- Learn how to package documents for service providers.

Projects to be Completed:

- Central Market Ad (A)

- Yellow Rose Menu (B)

- Travel Brochure (C)

- **Good Choices Newsletter (D)**

Printing and Packaging

As you build a document, you typically need to print and review numerous drafts; after you finalize the content and layout, you either print the document or prepare it for a service provider for professional imaging to film or printing plates. Even documents designed for Web viewing usually need to be printed so they can be proofed, reviewed, or referenced.

If your document is larger than the paper size your printer can use, or if you want to proof specifications for commercial printing (such as bleed, trim, and color), you can adjust some of the print settings to get the output you need. When you're ready to pass the file on to a service provider, you can use InDesign's "Package" feature to simplify the process and ensure the service provider gets all the necessary components to image your InDesign file successfully.

Setting Up to Print

You need to do a little document and system preparation before printing to a desktop printer connected to your computer. InDesign creates PostScript files suitable for high-end commercial printing, so you must have a PostScript printer driver installed on your computer. Although some non-PostScript printers will output InDesign pages, these types of printers aren't suitable for high-quality reproduction; some printing features and document elements, such as EPS files, do not print at all. Many inkjet printers can be equipped with a PostScript RIP or "front-end processor" that effectively turns them into PostScript devices.

If you don't have a suitable printer, you can create portable PostScript files, and then move them to another computer that is connected to a suitable printer. Alternatively, you can export one or more pages of an InDesign document to Acrobat PDF files and print those elsewhere. We discuss these functions in *Advanced InDesign: Creating Electronic Documents*.

Adobe provides its own PostScript drivers on the InDesign installation CD. Most operating systems include their own PostScript drivers, but to obtain the greatest functionality from InDesign, we recommend that you install and use the Adobe PostScript driver appropriate for your computer's operating system.

Adobe does not currently have a native PostScript driver for Mac OS X. Instead, Mac OS X users should use the LaserWriter driver installed with OS X for printing to PostScript devices. Adobe offers a "universal" PostScript driver installation utility for Windows computers on its Web site that automatically determines the best driver for your version of Windows.

Along with the PostScript printer driver, InDesign also requires that the appropriate PostScript Printer Description (PPD) file be available. The appropriate PPD file is the one that matches the printer you're using. Windows users can add a printer through the Add Printer wizard, or by running the AdobePS PostScript driver installation utility. Macintosh users choose the PPD when setting up a new printer in the Chooser (Mac OS 9) or Print Center (Mac OS X). PPDs are generally located as follows, but can be stored anywhere:

  • **Mac OS 9.x.** System Folder>Extensions>Printer Descriptions

The latest versions of the Adobe PostScript drivers are always available for free from Adobe's Web site (www.adobe.com). Enter http://www.adobe.com/support/downloads/main.html in your Web browser's URL field, and then navigate to the printer drivers section that's appropriate for your operating system:

- *Adobe PS 8.7.x driver for Mac OS 9.0 or greater (but not Mac OS X)*

- *Adobe PS 4.x driver for Windows 98 and Windows ME*

- *Adobe PS 5.x driver for Windows NT 4, 2000, and XP*

- **Mac OS X.** Library>Printers>PPDs>Contents>Resources>en.lproj
- **Windows.** PPD locations vary greatly between different versions of Windows. They may be loose in the \Windows or \WinNT directory, or may be located in \WinNT\System32. You can search your hard drive for "*.ppd" to locate your computer's main PPD directory.

Once the PostScript driver and the PPD file are correctly installed, you're ready to prepare the specific document. See your operating system's documentation for printer driver installation instructions.

In version 2.0, the InDesign print functions have been standardized across all supported platforms, so printing now works the same on both Windows and Macintosh computers. (Differences can arise, however, if you use the built-in PostScript drivers included with the operating system instead of the Adobe drivers.) The examples shown here were created in Mac OS X, but aside from appearances there is no difference, even though Mac OS X uses Apple's LaserWriter driver and not Adobe's.

The initial Print dialog has some features you need to know about:

Adobe offers a range of PPD files for many brands of printers and imaging devices on its Web site, but the selection is not very up to date. You can usually find the latest PPD files for your printer on the manufacturer's Web site.

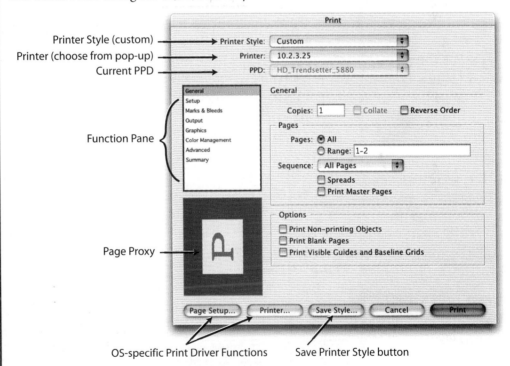

The initial Mac OS X Print dialog box.

The Printer Style pop-up menu lists available printer styles; you can save your choice by clicking the Save Style button at the bottom of the dialog box. Printer styles are handy when there is a specific output format that you use frequently, or if you use different formats with different output devices.

The Printer pop-up menu shows all currently available printers installed on your computer. If you prefer to create a PostScript file instead of actually printing the job, you can choose "PostScript File" from this menu.

The PPD pop-up menu is only active if you choose PostScript File from the Printer pop-up menu; if you select an actual printer, the PPD pop-up is grayed-out and unavailable. You need to reinstall the printer (Windows), or select a new PPD in the Chooser (Mac OS 9) or Print Center (Mac OS X) to change the PPD.

The Function pane is a list of all available output options. A different pane of options appears in the dialog box depending on the function you select.

The page proxy shows a miniature representation of a page of the current document that reflects the orientation and sizing of the page relative to the selected paper size and orientation of the output device.

The OS-specific buttons (Mac OS: Page Setup and Printer; Windows: Setup) should not be used to set printer parameters. The settings in the dialog boxes accessed by these buttons are generally overridden by the settings you make in the InDesign print dialog.

Prepare a File for Printing (All Operating Systems)

You should always ensure that graphic links are updated before selecting Print. Open the Links palette by selecting File>Links. Scroll through the palette. There should not be any symbols indicating broken or modified links.

1. Open the ~~atwu_brochure.indd~~ Project C B file that you created in Project C from your **Work_In_Progress** folder. This is a process-color (CMYK) brochure to be printed front and back, trimmed to 8.5 × 11″, and folded into a three-panel brochure. You will send a composite of this file to your desktop printer to proof copy, placement, and the general design of the piece.

2. Choose File>Print (or press Command/Control-P) to show the General pane of the Print dialog box.

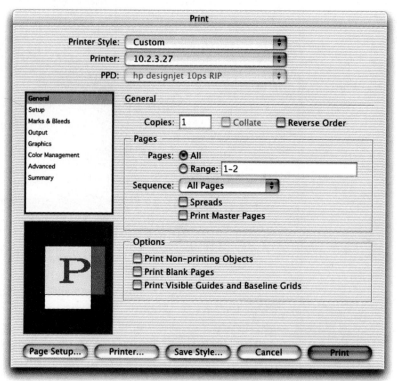

Here, you specify which pages you want to print, and the printing sequence. You can also choose to print spreads on one sheet of paper, but you would probably

*Most printers and service providers prefer to receive final printouts of the document along with the job, printed at 100% without printer's marks. In some cases they might ask you to supply **color breaks** in a spot-color job, along with a composite printout. Color breaks are separations done on a desktop printer that show the service provider how page elements are colored with spot inks; they serve to prevent any misunderstandings about which elements get printed with each specific ink.*

need to scale the output to fit a spread on the sheet (unless you have a printer that can print on sheets larger than US Letter or A4 paper). You can also print any blank pages and guidelines. It can be helpful to print guides when you're still in the composition stage of document design.

Note that the page proxy shows a sideways orientation. That's because the document was created as a *landscape* or wide page, and most printers need such pages rotated so they fit on the sheet. The default orientation is usually *portrait* or tall, and the page proxy may show a disparity between the InDesign document page and the printed sheet.

3. You establish the page size and orientation of your design when you first create the document. Click Setup in the function pane to apply the document's size and orientation to the print job. The Setup pane allows you to position the page on the available sheet. Choose Letter from Paper Size (this size might appear as "US Letter" depending on the PPD for your printer). Click the Landscape icon of the Orientation options. The page proxy shows how the document appears on the chosen paper size. The Scale factor should be 100%.

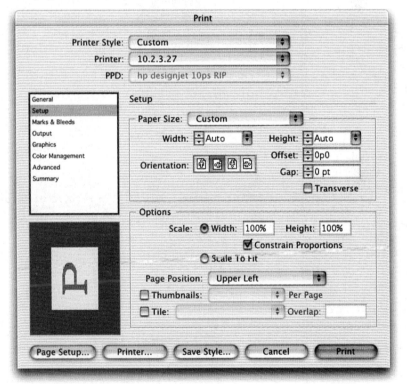

This document requires a bleed area and printer's marks, so you need to choose a paper size that provides enough room to print these marks. If you can, change the Paper Size choice to LetterExtra, Tabloid, A3, or 11 × 17. If your printer doesn't support these larger paper sizes, leave the paper size set to Letter, and click the Scale to Fit button (or choose Custom from the Paper Size menu, and set the width and height fields to Auto).

Never use print scaling when printing the final version of your document. It's acceptable to use print scaling for making comps or proofs, but this should never be used for the final output to a service provider. Make sure scaling is off before making your final prints. It's an easy option to forget.

Choose Center in the Page Position pop-up menu.

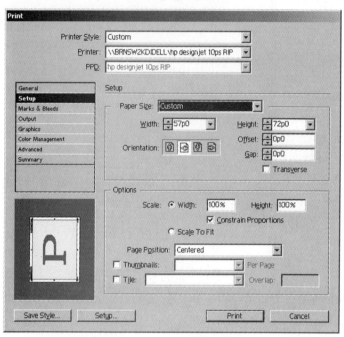

4. Click Marks & Bleeds in the function pane. You need printer's marks on this job, so click the All Printer's Marks check box. If you chose a Custom paper size and used the Auto width and height function, the size changes to accommodate the marks.

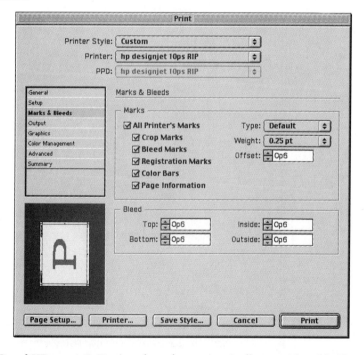

Like QuarkXPress 4, InDesign doesn't automatically provide a bleed area. You need to specify this in the Bleed section of the Print dialog box. Give the document a 6-pt. bleed on all four sides. (Remember that half a pica is six points.)

Separations produce an individual page or plate for each ink color, whether process or spot. Separations are discussed in more depth in **Advanced InDesign: Creating Electronic Documents**.

The Text as Black check box next to the Color pop-up menu can be activated to print all text in the document as black; this is helpful for printing proofs of colored text to a black-and-white printer.

Color laser printers used with Windows computers sometimes have one driver installed for PostScript and another driver installed for a different page description language, so be sure to choose the PostScript version from the Printer pop-up menu.

5. Click Output in the function pane.

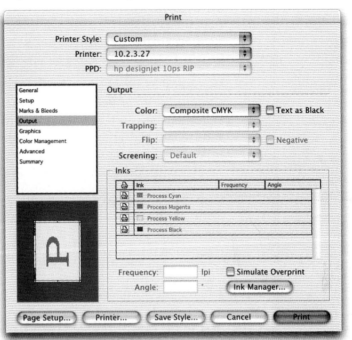

Your selection from the Color pop-up menu depends on the type of printer you're using. If it's a black-and-white laser printer, choose Composite Gray. If it's a non-PostScript inkjet printer, choose Composite RGB. If it's a PostScript inkjet or a color laser printer, choose Composite CMYK.

6. Click Graphics in the function pane.

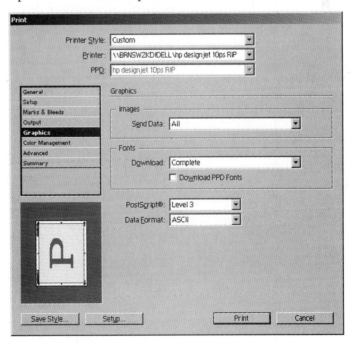

You shouldn't need to change any of these settings.

Depending on your printer and how it's connected to your computer or network, the value in the PostScript menu is either Level 2 or Level 3. This value is derived from the PPD. The Data Format value is either Binary or ASCII. If your printer supports binary data, then binary is the default; otherwise, ASCII is the default. You can't change this setting because it is also derived from the PPD.

7. We cover the Color Management and Advanced functions in *Advanced InDesign: Creating Electronic Documents*; skip them for this exercise. Click the Print button. Watch the message box as InDesign processes this file. It displays names of fonts and graphics files as they are sent to the printer. These files are not included in the InDesign file and must be supplied by the computer. In a few minutes, two pages should come out of your printer.

8. Examine the output. Note the printer's marks, which include the trim (cutting) marks, the bleed area marks, and some document information. There are also color bars, which are used when the job is on press for quality control, and registration marks, which are used on press to ensure that all of the separations are in alignment.

9. Save the document and leave it open for the next exercise.

Printing Oversized Documents

If you have a printer that prints 11 × 17 in. (or A3) paper, you can print letter-size documents that have bleeds and trim them back to the edge of the 8.5 × 11 in. (or A4) size, retaining the true bleed. At some point, however, you might need to proof an oversized document to a printer that cannot handle larger paper sizes. There are two options to help you, depending on what qualities you need to proof: tiling and scaling.

Tiling

Tiling prints an oversized document by cropping blocks of the document page and printing the sections onto several sheets of paper. Once printed, you have a full-size proof that you can cut out of the different sheets, assemble, and tape together.

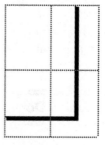

Documents too large to fit on one page are tiled — split into overlapping sections that can be cut out and taped together to represent the actual size of the final document.

Scaling

Scaling offers a different approach, when proofing at exact size is not a critical factor. The Scaling option of the Print dialog box reduces the document, allowing more of the image to print on the sheet. Elements in the document are proportionally sized, but are not true to the finished size. For basic proofing purposes, this is sufficient, but you should always print final proofs at 100%.

Printer's Marks

Printer's marks, which we have mentioned several times throughout this book, can be one of the keys to successful proofing. Printer's marks include trim, bleed, and registration marks, as well as file information (to identify what was printed on the page, and when) and color information. All of these are printed outside of the page margin. InDesign can automatically print five kinds of printer's marks to ensure that the commercial printer has the proper instructions to reproduce your document.

- **Crop Marks.** These short lines outside the image area indicate where to trim or cut the sheet to its final size.

- **Bleed Marks.** These short perpendicular lines indicate the edge of the image area including ink that prints beyond the final size trim or crop.

- **Registration Marks.** These marks are small concentric circles intersected by a cross hair. These fine lines are used to align color separations precisely, ensuring that elements printed in different inks fit and appear as you designed them. These marks can also be used to overlay different versions on the same base design (e.g., different names printed in the exact same position alongside the art and address of a preprinted, generic business card).

- **Color Bars.** This row of small squares reproduces different tints and tint combinations of ink colors. The value and consistency of these color patches is measured during a press run with an instrument called a "densitometer" to establish and maintain consistent print reproduction.

- **Page Information.** This information is printed outside the image area at the bottom of the page. InDesign automatically prints the file name, the date and time the page was printed, and the page number of the image. If you are printing separations, InDesign also prints the name of the ink intended for each separation (for example, Cyan, Magenta, or Pantone 231).

Print a Scaled Document with Printer's Marks

1. Open the file **atwu_brochure.indd** from your **Work_In_Progress** folder, if it isn't already open. The settings established in the previous exercise remain unless you have changed them or canceled the Print dialog for some reason. Choose File>Print.

2. In the Pages area of the General pane, select Range instead of All, and type "2" into the field, because only Page 2 contains the bleed you need to proof.

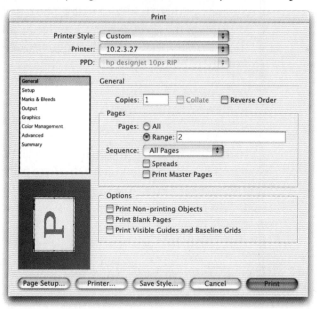

3. You already set marks and bleeds in the previous exercise. Click Setup in the function pane and choose Letter from the Paper Size menu. In the Options area, click the button next to Scale to Fit. The scaling percentage is shown next to this option, and the page proxy reflects the change.

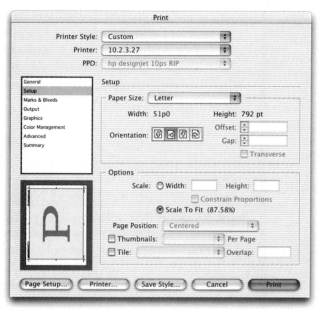

4. Click Print. You can see a few file names flash quickly on the screen, but then your computer is released. As the document is processed in the computer's RAM (in the background), you are free to work on other files or programs. When the page comes out of the printer, proof the bleed and trim marks, checking that they do, in fact, leave sufficient image area outside the page to produce a consistent bleed.

5. Save and close the document.

Print

Print an Oversized Document by Tiling

1. Open the file **poster.indd** from the **RF_Intro_InDesign** folder.

2. Choose File>Print. In the General dialog, you can see the page proxy showing that the document is far too large to print on the default paper size of your current printer.

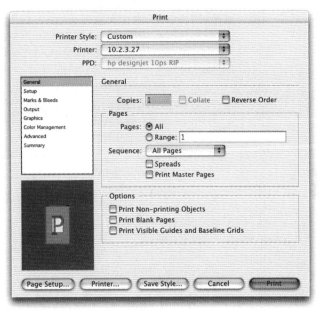

3. Click Setup in the function pane and choose Letter from the Paper Size menu. If your printer can print on larger paper, choose the largest sheet size you have available.

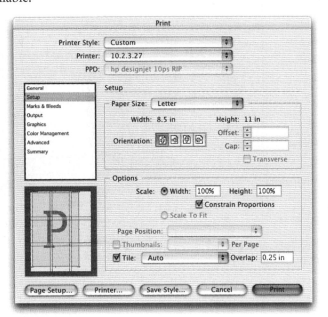

The Auto tiling option centers the page image amongst the tiled sheets, automatically adjusts the sheet overlap, and prints as many sheets as are necessary to accommodate the document's actual size. The Manual option lets you print just a portion of a large page; you simply have to drag the zero-point crosshair from the rulers to the upper-left corner of the area you want to print. In the Scale and Fit options of the Print dialog box, you then select Manual and designate the overlap distance.

If you select the Optimized Subsampling option, InDesign evaluates the installed PPD and resamples high-resolution image data to a lower resolution more appropriate for your printer. The resulting low-resolution output is not so low that obvious pixelization appears, as it does if you select the Proxy option. Optimized Subsampling is useful when proofing high-resolution images to desktop printers, not high-resolution devices.

In the Options section, click the Tile checkmark, and then choose Auto from the Tile menu. Use the default overlap of 0.25 in. The overlap determines how much of the image intersects on adjoining sheets as the page is broken into tiles. If the document contained a lot of space with large gaps between type or images, the overlap would need to be greater to match the pieces more accurately. Note how the page proxy shows the tiles and overlap; if you chose a paper size larger than US Letter, you would see fewer tiles in the proxy.

4. Some desktop printers can choke on an image of this size. Because the purpose of this output is to proof the type, positioning, bleed, and trim, you can print a lower-resolution proxy image instead of trying to force the high-resolution image through a printer with limited memory. Choose Graphics from the function pane, and choose Optimized Subsampling from the Send Data pop-up menu. This speeds printing and might avoid a printer error. If you get a print error with Optimized Subsampling, choose Proxy from the Send Data menu to send a low-resolution version of the image. If you still get a printer error with the Proxy option, then there's probably a communication or driver problem with your printer that needs to be solved.

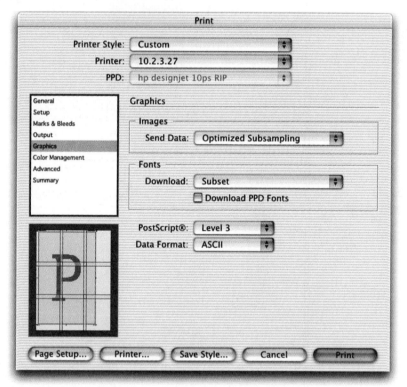

5. Click Print. When the pages come out of the printer, note how the large image was divided up. Use a pair of scissors to cut out the image pieces and, like a jigsaw puzzle, tape them together to accurately reproduce the image of the page.

6. Close the document without saving.

Packaging Documents for a Service Provider

When everyone has approved the proof of your document, you probably need to send the files to another company for final output. This can involve creation of high-resolution film or plates for a press run, or using your document files to print the job digitally on a high-speed printer or a digital color press. The service providers use their own equipment, computers, and networks to produce this output — they do not have access to the files that you used to create the job unless you supply them. In addition to the InDesign file itself, they need all external files used to create the document, including the fonts used in the page-layout document and in imported EPS files, the EPS files themselves, and all other imported graphic files not embedded in the document. Ensuring that all necessary components are given to the service provider is called "packaging the document."

Package a Brochure for Output

1. Open the file **travel_brochure.indd** (this is an older version of the brochure you created in Project C) from your **RF_Intro_InDesign** folder, then choose File>Package. This function performs a "preflight" check automatically; on a fast computer you might not even see the progress indicator of the preflight operation. If there's anything amiss, such as a lost image link, the file is not ready to package and a warning appears.

Example of a preflight warning. You should not receive any warnings in this exercise.

Always click View Info to find out what issues are present if the warning appears.

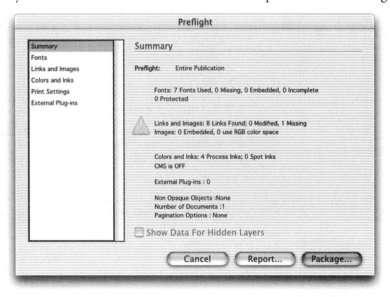

The Preflight summary indicates where the problem lies.

The term "preflight" comes from the procedures that aircraft pilots perform before every flight, where critical systems and functions are checked and tested. It's become a standard term in the graphic arts industry.

Preflight is discussed in depth in Advanced InDesign: Creating Electronic Documents. This file should not display any warnings if you open it from the **RF_Intro_InDesign** folder, because all of the linked images are located there as well.

2. Click Package, and a message appears asking to save the document. It is saving a final version of the document prior to packaging. This ensures that the packaged file has all the modifications you have made. Click OK.

3. The next dialog box that appears asks you to complete a form that contains your contact information and any instructions you want to pass on to the service provider. This file name identifies the Printing Instructions text file that accompanies the packaged document. Enter your name and contact information, as well as the following instructions: "Qty 5000, 4/4, 80 lb. Foldi Matte Cover, bleed 6 pts, trim size 8.5 × 11 letter fold, self mailer outside back."

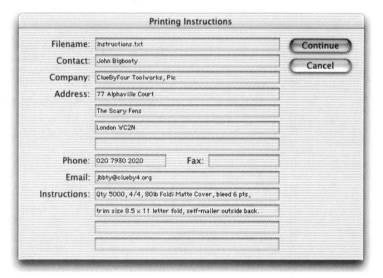

4/4 is printer's parlance for "print this job with the four process colors on both sides." 4/4 is spoken "four over four." A job with a single color on both sides of the page is 1/1, a job with four colors on the front and one color on the back is 4/1 ("four over one"), and so forth.

4. Click Continue. The Create Package Folder/Package Publication dialog box asks you for a place to copy the folder that contains all of the packaged contents. For this exercise, you can store the folder on the hard drive. You can also save this folder to any type of removable media, such as a Zip disk. Make a new folder, name it "To_Printers", and then open this new folder. The folder containing the packaged files will be inside this new folder; by default, it has the same name as the document, but you can rename it.

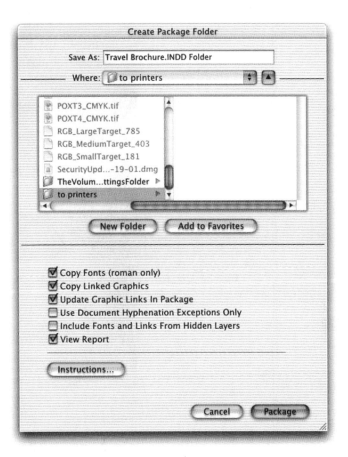

5. The options below the file window let you select exactly what you want to package. Check the Copy Fonts and Copy Linked Graphics boxes. Also check Update Graphic Links in Package. This reestablishes the link path of linked images to the new location of the packaged document. Otherwise, the links would still point to the original location on your computer's hard disk drive, and would produce link errors at the destination. Check View Report, then click the Package button. Clicking the Instructions button sends you back to the instructions to make changes.

6. A Font Alert message displays. Read it and click OK. Font vendors' licensing agreements vary widely with regard to copying fonts for imaging at another location. Some vendors prohibit it absolutely, and some allow a one-time use.

7. A progress bar and file names display across the screen while files are copied and packaged with the document and instructions. The instructions file opens in your system's default text editor (for example, TextEdit, Simpletext, or Notepad). Review the instructions and information.

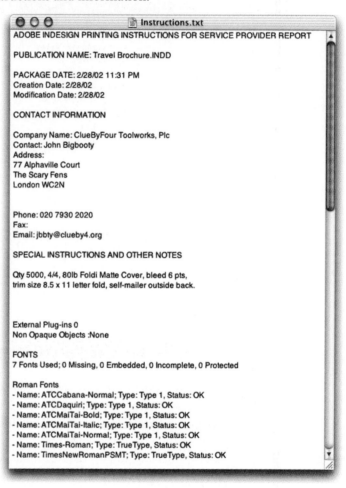

It's a good idea to include a printed copy of the report when sending a job to a service provider. It allows them to quickly determine if they have all of the linked files and fonts necessary to produce the job.

The report contains the information you entered in the Printing Instructions dialog box. It also lists all fonts and colors used in the document and in imported EPS files, along with link information, the print settings last used for the document (including specifications for line screen and angle), the status of InDesign's color management system, the presence of any applied transparency, and the files packaged in the folder.

8. Once you've reviewed the report, print a copy of it then quit the text editor. Go to the location where you saved the package and look at the contents of the folder you made. The folder should contain two documents (the InDesign file travel_brochure.indd and the instructions.txt file) and two folders (Fonts and Links). Inside the Fonts folder are the required printer and screen fonts used in the document. Entire font families are not copied; only the actual fonts used in the job are packaged. The Links folder should contain an EPS file, the logo, and several TIFF files. This folder is ready to deliver to a service provider that supports the imaging of InDesign documents. The folder can be copied to a Zip disk, burned to a CD, or compressed and delivered electronically via the Internet FTP protocol.

InDesign does not package Asian fonts. These must be copied manually, and they are often subject to strict licensing terms and software copyright protection.

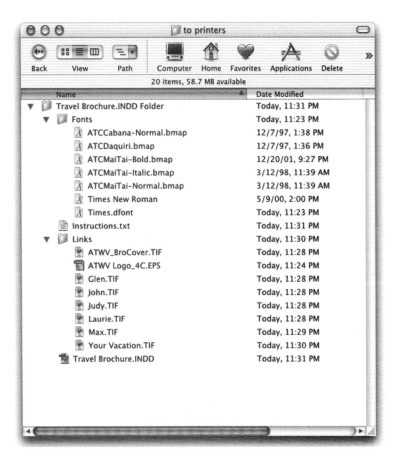

The actual font file names used in your package may differ from these.

9. Return to InDesign and close the travel brochure without saving it.

Summary

In this chapter, you have learned to print your files to a desktop printer and to collect the elements of your document prior to submitting a job to a service provider. You have set up and printed a document with printer's marks, and understand how these marks are used. You have also prepared and printed an oversized document by tiling it, sand packaged a job for delivery to an external service provider.

Complete Project D: Good Choices Newsletter

Free-Form Project #2

Assignment

A public relations and marketing firm representing a new airline is looking for the right ad agency to help them create the initial buzz to coincide with the airline's launch. Your agency is one of three finalists for the airline's print ads (more spec work), and you've been asked to create two different ad designs for the campaign. The PR people have asked that each of your two design submissions include two ads — one for a double-page spread in a magazine, and one for a newspaper. (You'll need to create four separate documents.)

This new airline, cleverly called Snowbird Express, specializes in low-cost, no-nonsense flights from dank, cold, landlocked places to nice, sunny, warm, coastal ones where the people are pretty, the fish are always biting, and the drinks all have little paper umbrellas in them. The ads should convey a sense of relief, anticipation, and a "forget your cares" attitude.

Apply Your Skills

To develop the set of ads, you should apply the following processes, methods, and features:

- Establish a color theme. The ads will run as four-color process (CMYK) in both the magazine and newspaper. Use the Swatches palette to create CMYK colors; you can also create CMYK gradients.
- Use style sheets to test different fonts, heading styles, and paragraph formats.
- Combine text elements, special characters, OpenType features, and text composition techniques.
- Experiment with tables to produce a list of fares. As with all such airfare tables, there will need to be a block of very fine print below it. Use the Insert Placeholder Text function to create "dummy" text that will fit cleanly under the table. Try a condensed font such as ATC Flamingo, Light, for this material; don't forget to create a style from it for future use.
- Use transparency, feathering, or interesting groupings to draw attention to placed photos or artwork. Use transparency with type to create interesting effects, but don't overdo it; the type must be legible to someone flipping through a magazine.
- Use the Pen tool to draw fun little shapes that can add a touch of whimsy or character to the ads.
- Don't forget the transformational tools, and the power of the Step and Repeat function.
- Print proofs to a laser or inkjet printer; use tiling if necessary to produce full-size output. Don't forget to set printer's marks, so you can see exactly where your bleed and trim marks fall. Choose Composite RGB for output to a color printer, or Composite Gray for output to a black-and-white laser printer.
- When you're satisfied with all four ads, preflight and package them for the magazine and newspaper.

Specifications

- **Magazine ad.** Each page is 7 in. × 10 in., so the ad's live area is 14 in. × 10 in. If your design uses any bleeds, a bleed of 0.125 in. is required according to the magazine's specifications card. Magazines are generally printed on enormous, high-speed presses and there needs to be some allowance in the bleed to accommodate typical production variances in the folding and trimming process.
- **Newspaper ad.** The final size of the ad is 35 × 54 picas. There is no bleed.

Ad Components

We've supplied images on the Resource CD that you can use for this project. You can collect images and write your own ad copy. In a small agency, you may need to act as designer, copywriter, and even photographer.

Publisher's Comments

Not all advertising work is glamorous logo design, corporate identities, or high-concept art. Projects such as these are the lifeblood of the advertising industry. You may find yourself absolutely hating one of your designs as you work on it (this happens more often than you might think), but don't be discouraged if this happens. Even what you consider the "worst" projects can often be used to create something great.

Review #2

Chapters 6 through 11:

In Chapters 6 through 11, you learned how to work with images and with color to expand the possibilities of a document. You learned about tables and their uses, and then delved into the subjects of graphic elements, and applying colors, gradients, and transformations to document objects. You explored the utilities that InDesign offers to make it easy to review and change text. You learned how to print proofs and oversized documents, and how to prepare your files for delivery to service providers. After completing the second part of this course, you should:

- Know how to create tables from a spreadsheet file and from plain imported text, apply basic table and cell formatting, and understand differences in behavior between tables and ordinary text.

- Know how to create basic shapes and frames with the appropriate tools, and how to draw smooth, interesting art with the Pen tool. You've explored the Line tool, the Stroke options, created dashed lines, and experimented with various shapes you can append to the ends of lines.

- Understand the intricacies of the Fill and Stroke tools in the toolbox, be able to apply different fills and strokes to objects, and change these attributes. You understand the important distinction between objects, frames, and frame contents, know the appropriate tools for each context, and are able to manipulate and edit them.

- Be familiar with the different color models — RGB, CMYK, Lab, and spot color. You should know how to mix and adjust colors, work with placed spot colors, and create tints and gradients. You should know how to import color from other documents and how to apply color to objects, frames, images, and text.

- Understand the types of images with which InDesign works, and distinguish between vector and raster images. You should understand the basic concepts of image resolution and how to determine the necessary resolution for a particular use. You should also know how to import, place, and link images, as well as how to reconnect broken links.

- Be comfortable using InDesign's text utilities. You should know how to use the Find/Change feature to affect individual words or the entire document, to locate and change special characters, and to edit specific styles or overall style attributes. You should know how to use and update the dictionaries and the spell checker as well as the limitations of each.

- Understand how to properly configure your computer for printing, the purpose of printer drivers and PPD files, and how to print a proof of your document. You should know how to print oversized documents for proofing purposes on a regular desktop printer, and how to set up marks, bleeds, and tiling. You should be familiar with the process of packaging documents for service providers, including collecting the required elements and providing appropriate instructions.

Project A: Central Market Ad

Many design projects are simple, one-page layouts that appear in a magazine or newspaper. This ad uses images already placed on the page, as you might find if you were working from comps created with placeholder text. This project focuses on text placement and formatting, using InDesign's built-in tools to complete the ad.

Our project ad has had some initial copy already typed into it, but it's not formatted. The two required images are already placed exactly where the ad manager has specified, and their positions cannot be changed without approval. The original ad designer has also set up some guides for specifying the position of text elements.

Place the Text

Copy writers often submit all of the text for a job in the same document. As a rule of thumb, it is a good idea to use as few text blocks as possible for a job to avoid problems with text repositioning. In other words, if the body copy changes but the sub-headline is placed into a different text block, the sub-headline may not appear in the proper position within the story.

Ignore any references to missing fonts. You will change all type to Adobe Garamond Pro, so make sure this typeface is already installed and ready to use.

1. Open the file **cheese_ad.indd** from the **RF_Intro_InDesign>Project_A** folder.

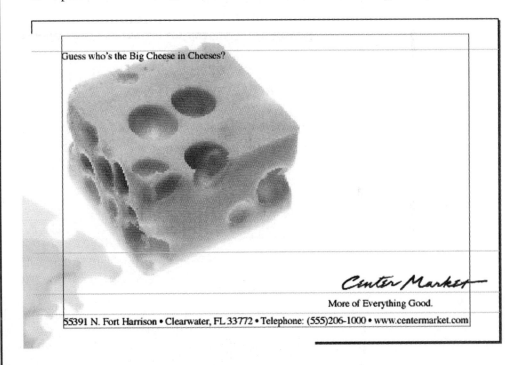

Guess who's the Big Cheese in Cheeses?

Center Market

More of Everything Good.

55391 N. Fort Harrison • Clearwater, FL 33772 • Telephone: (555)206-1000 • www.centermarket.com

Notice the guides for text frame position.

2. Choose File>Place. Locate the file **cheese_ad_copy.txt** in the **RF_Intro_InDesign>Project_A** folder and click Choose/OK. This is a plain text file and requires no import options, but make sure Convert Quotes is checked. The cursor becomes a loaded text icon, indicating that the text is ready to place.

3. Click the loaded cursor at the intersection of the left margin guide and the second horizontal guideline, 272 pt. from the top edge of the page; notice that the new

text frame fills the width between the margin guides, and the red plus sign indicates an overset text condition. That's OK, because you still need to apply text specifications to the copy.

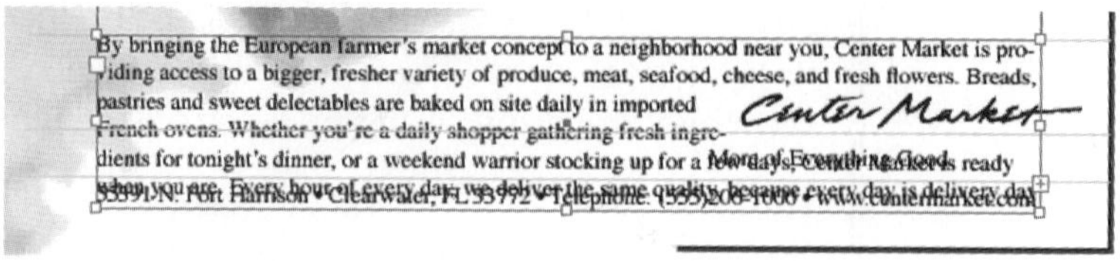

Notice that the text wraps around the Center Market logo,
because the designer already applied a text wrap to the logo.

4. Save the file as "cheese_ad.indd" in your **Work_In_Progress** folder.

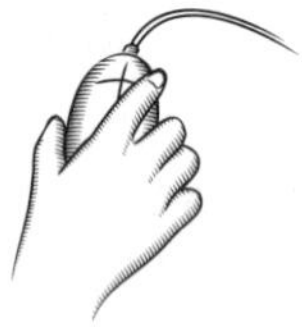

Format Ad Copy

1. Using the Type tool, select all of the text in the ad copy frame (the one you just placed). In the Character palette, change the font to Adobe Garamond Pro. Apply Justify, Last Line Left from the Paragraph palette, and uncheck the Hyphenate option.

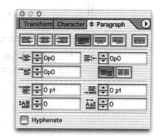

2. The copy still doesn't fit, but you're getting closer. The art director has specified Adobe Garamond Pro for the ad's body copy, and has a strict minimum type size limit of 9 pt, and a maximum of 11 pt. Obviously you need to make this type smaller to comply with the maximum limit, and to make it fit attractively within the constraints of the other objects in the ad. With all of the type still selected, decrease the font size one point at a time, until there's no overset text indicator and all of the copy clears the logo and the line below this frame. You'll find that 9 pt. is the best setting.

The actual text wrap throughout this project may appear different on Windows computers from that shown here.

3. Change the leading of this text from Auto (10.8 pt.) to 11 pt. Such a small change isn't very noticeable, but it's often easier to work with whole units instead of decimals.

4. Switch to the Selection tool, and drag the lower-center handle up to raise the bottom of the frame until it just clears the text. This gives you easy access to the single-line text frame at the bottom of the ad.

5. Zoom in a bit if necessary and examine the word spacing of the body copy. It may or may not look like there's a little too much white space between words and letters. This is a purely subjective evaluation. Switch to the Type tool and select all of the text, then experiment with the Tracking values and the Optical/Metrics Kerning options. Try tracking values of ±5 units and ±10 units, and both Kerning options, until you achieve a visually pleasing look. Pay attention to the line breaks.

Typographically, it doesn't matter if a word followed by a comma or period wraps to the next line, but assume the art director wants the phrase "Every hour of every day" to remain all on one line. Adjust the tracking until these words are all on one line. Ultimately, you will probably find that Metrics kerning with –5 em of tracking produces the desired result.

6. Save the file, and continue with the next section.

Format the Headline

1. For the headline, the art director's specs indicate a headline typeface of Adobe Garamond Pro, Regular, with a maximum point size of 84 pt. and a minimum of 60 pt., to accommodate headlines of varying lengths. The headlines are to be set flush right against the right margin, and shouldn't obscure the product shot.

Switch to the Selection tool and drag the headline frame's lower edge down about two-thirds of the way, down the page.

2. With the Type tool, select all of the text in the headline and set it flush right, Adobe Garamond Pro, Regular.

3. Press Command/Control-Shift-> to enlarge the selected text. Keep pressing these keys until the headline wraps to three lines. Watch the Character palette while you do this; the text should wrap to three lines when it is at about 66 pt. You may need to move the bottom edge of the frame down a bit more if the text oversets, but don't drag it past the top of the frame that contains the ad copy you just set. Keep pressing Command/Control-Shift-> until the last line disappears and becomes overset. Press Command/Control-Shift-< once or twice until the last line reappears. This should happen at 74–76 pt.

4. Set the type to 70 pt., because the lower line is a little too close to the ad copy frame and looks crowded.

5. The leading value of the headline is too high, so you can experiment with solid or even negative leading. *Solid leading* means that the leading value is the same as the point size of the type. *Negative leading* occurs when you set the leading value to be

smaller than the type size. This might seem strange, but it can result in more attractive type at large sizes. Set the leading initially to solid, or 70 pt.

6. The art director hates the headline and wants the leading set tighter. Select all of the headline text and pretend that the art director is looking over your shoulder (because in reality, they do that a lot). Reduce the leading value 5 pt. at a time, and evaluate the appearance. You now know that the art director likes tight leading on headlines, so a leading value of 55 pt. will probably make her happy. Set it to 55 pt. The ad should now look like this:

Guess who's the Big Cheese in Cheeses?

By bringing the European farmer's market concept to a neighborhood near you, Center Market is providing access to a bigger, fresher variety of produce, meat, seafood, cheese, and fresh flowers. Breads, pastries and sweet delectables are baked on site daily in imported French ovens. Whether you're a daily shopper gathering fresh ingredients for tonight's dinner, or a weekend warrior stocking up for a few days, Center Market is ready when you are. Every hour of every day, *Center Market* we deliver the same quality, because every day is delivery day at Center Market. Shopping for food is no longer a chore, it's a treat for the soul.

More of Everything Good.

55391 N. Fort Harrison • Clearwater, FL 33772 • Telephone: (555)206-1000 • www.centermarket.com

7. Save the file and keep it open.

Finishing the Ad

1. All you need to do now is set the info line and the line under the Center Market logo. Start with the info line. Select it with the Selection tool, set the proxy reference point to the upper left, and verify that the X and Y positions are 3p0 and 344 pt. If it's not at these coordinates, move it with the Selection tool until it is in the right place.

2. Change to the Type tool and select all of the text in this line. According to the art director's specs, this line should be set in Adobe Garamond Pro, 10 pt., Italic, centered, and tracked to fill the width of the margins. Start by setting the specified typeface and type size in the Character palette, and center the text in the Paragraph palette.

3. The text should still be selected. You need to spread the text out to fill the frame's width. First, click the Force Justify icon in the Paragraph palette (the last upper icon on the right edge of the Paragraph palette). This forces the text to fit the width, but it leaves ugly gaps between the words.

55391   N.   Fort   Harrison   •   Clearwater,   FL   33772   •   Telephone: (555)206-1000   •   www.centermarket.com

*Pressing Tab applies the new tracking setting; you don't really want to go to the next field, but that's one way of applying settings that you type into palette fields. You could also press Return/Enter, but this changes the **focus** to the selected text; in other words, if you then typed a Tab to change to another field in the palette, you'd accidentally wipe out the selected text and replace it with a Tab character.*

4. Set the text back to Centered. Change to the Character palette and in the Tracking field of the palette, type "25", then press Tab to advance to the next field.

5. Tracking 25 em units is a step in the right direction, but you need more spread in the text to get it to fill the frame width. Press Shift-Tab to highlight the value of 25 in the Tracking field, and type "50". Press Tab to apply your change. Still not enough! Try 100 em units. Now you're getting close. Add tracking in 5-em increments until the text becomes overset, then reduce the tracking value by 5 units. This should fill the frame width without causing the text to overset. The final tracking value should be approximately 110 units.

6. That pesky art director forgot to tell you that she wants all of the numbers in the information line to be Oldstyle. No problem, because you're using an OpenType font. From the Options pop-up menu on the Character palette, choose OpenType>Proportional Oldstyle.

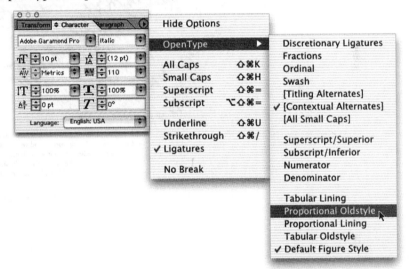

7. Now the tracking is all messed up, because the Oldstyle numbers take up less space than the tabular numbers (Adobe Garamond Pro's default figure style). To help balance the spacing of these characters, choose Optical from the Kerning pop-up menu on the Character palette. The Metrics kerning method for automatic kerning really isn't that effective when text is tracked out this far, and the Optical method considers the shapes and point size of the letters, and any applied tracking, and determines the best kerning. Now the text is spaced out a little better, but it still doesn't meet the ad director's specs.

8. Adjust tracking until the text fits. Remember, if you overset the text, don't worry; just change the tracking back to the last value you used. You'll probably find that a tracking value of 125 units provides a good fit when used with Optical automatic kerning.

9. The last item to set is the line underneath the Center Market logo. The Type tool should still be active from the last step. Try to select the text in this line. You can't, because the ad copy frame is positioned over the frame containing this line. Hold Command/Control to temporarily switch to the Selection tool, and try to select the line's frame. You still can't do it. To select an object that's underneath another

one, choose the Selection tool from the toolbox, then hold Command/Control while clicking over the object. The first click selects the topmost object, and each subsequent click selects the next object in the stacking order. To select the information line frame, choose the Selection tool, press Command/Control, and click once on the logo text frame. This selects the ad copy frame. While still holding the Command/Control key, click once more on the logo text frame. This selects the information line. Now, to edit the text in the frame, press "T" to change to the Type tool, then click in the active frame. Press Command/Control-A to select all of the text.

10. Set this text as Adobe Garamond Pro, regular, 10 pt., auto-leading, centered. Experiment with the Optical/Metrics Kerning options. Zoom in to 400% to get a good look at this type. Optical kerning sets a slightly looser line in small sizes; this is a good look for this copy, so leave the kerning set to Optical. Press Command/Control-0 (zero) to fit the entire ad within the document window and look at the finished ad.

11. The headline text needs a little work — some of the kerning could be better, and the type looks a little loose. Large type looks better with tighter letter spacing, and small type looks better with more generous letter spacing. This is why the Optical kerning method loosens small type and tightens large type. Select all of the type in the headline and apply Optical kerning. Not surprisingly, the type tightens up a bit. The Optical kerning engine is simply following basic typography rules.

12. Look carefully for any visually uneven spacing between the letters of the headline. Zoom in as necessary. We suggest you look at the "G-u" combination in the word "Guess," at "B-i" in "Big," and the "o-'-s" sequence in "who's." Place the text cursor between the "G" and the "u," and look at the automatic kerning value, which should be –30. This value is enclosed in parentheses to let you know that the kerning engine automatically determined it.

13. Change the kerning of the "G-u" pair to –40. It's a slight change, but it makes the spacing more visually consistent with that of the other letters. Change the kerning of the "B-i" pair to –42 for the same reason. These adjustments tighten the serifs of the lowercase letters against the open areas of the uppercase ones, giving both pairs a more balanced look.

14. The apostrophe is a special case. Usually, automatic kerning routines don't tighten enough around both sides of this character. Put the text cursor between the "o" and the apostrophe and look at the automatic kerning value, which should be about –48. Move the cursor between the apostrophe and the "s" and check the automatic kerning value there. It's much more aggressive, around –95. Visually, it looks like there's more space before the apostrophe than after, which is in fact the

case. To tighten up the spacing between the "o" and the apostrophe, change the kerning value to –72. This provides a much better balance of the "o-'-s" characters. If you applied –95 units between the "o" and the apostrophe it would look unbalanced, even though the same amount of kerning is applied to the other side of the apostrophe. Try it and see for yourself, then set the kerning back to –72. Zoom out and take a final look at the ad, especially the headline. Choose View>Hide Guides to get an unencumbered view of the entire ad.

Guess who's the Big Cheese in Cheeses?

By bringing the European farmer's market concept to a neighborhood near you, Center Market is providing access to a bigger, fresher variety of produce, meat, seafood, cheese, and fresh flowers. Breads, pastries and sweet delectables are baked on site daily in imported French ovens. Whether you're a daily shopper gathering fresh ingredients for tonight's dinner, or a weekend warrior stocking up for a few days, Center Market is ready when you are. Every hour of every day, we deliver the same quality, because every day is delivery day at Center Market. Shopping for food is no longer a chore, it's a treat for the soul.

Center Market
More of Everything Good.

55391 N. Fort Harrison • Clearwater, FL 33772 • Telephone: (555)206-1000 • www.centermarket.com

The final ad.

15. Save and close the file.

Your experience with creating this ad should tell you that there's a lot more to composing a layout than simply dropping text into a frame. Good composition is a result of paying attention to details such as manual kerning of large type when necessary, and experimenting with the tracking and automatic kerning options of complete lines and paragraphs. But don't overdo kerning; as we said in the text, too much kerning is worse than none at all. Even with all the fine-tuning you've done, this ad-creation process should have been a relatively quick exercise.

Project B: Yellow Rose Menu

This project focuses on text formatting, styles, tables, and color, using InDesign's built-in tools. There are no images in this project, and all graphic elements will be created with InDesign's various drawing and shape tools.

Let's assume that the restaurant's manager gave you the following items: a Microsoft Word file containing all of the menu copy and an old, stained, printed menu. Your job is to recreate the look of the old menu (which, for unknown reasons, doesn't exist in digital form anymore), without the stains of course, and incorporate the new menu text.

The original menu is two-sided, folded in half, and is a square 72-pica sheet printed on a slightly yellow, uncoated stock. The ink colors used are three Pantone spot inks: PMS 194 (deep brick red), PMS 116 (warm yellow) and PMS 5757 (dark olive green), plus the standard black. The closest fonts you have to those used on the original menu are all ATC fonts: ATC Mai Tai, ATC Cabana, and ATC Monsoon. Make sure these fonts are active before starting.

Create the Document

1. Start InDesign and set your Units preferences to Picas for the horizontal and vertical measurements.

2. Create a new, 2-page document that's 72p0 square, with two columns having a gutter of 6p0, and all margins set to 3p0.

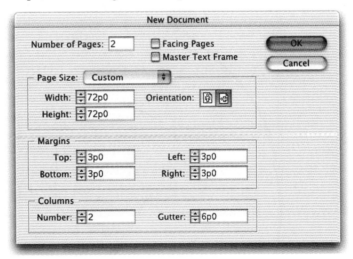

3. Delete all of the unused default swatches by choosing Select All Unused from the Swatches palette Options menu, then clicking the little trash can icon on the lower border of the palette.

Click OK when the following warning appears:

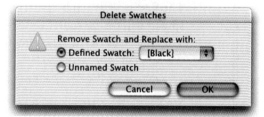

4. Create the new colors by choosing New Color Swatch from the Swatch palette Options menu. Choose PANTONE Solid Coated from the Color Mode pop-up menu, then type "116" in the PANTONE color number field.

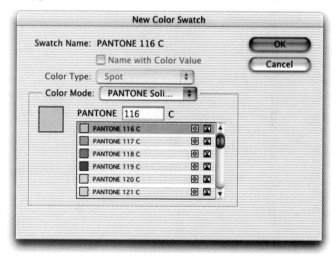

Click OK, then repeat for PANTONE 194 and 5757. You should have the following in your Swatches palette:

The last color you create will be selected as the Fill color in the toolbox. Click the Default Fill and Stroke button or press "D" to clear this selection.

Design the Cover

1. The first spread will be the front and back covers of the menu, and the second spread will be the center of the open menu. Picture the menu opened and laid flat. The right half of the first spread will appear to be the front cover to the diner, and the left half will be the back cover; the second spread will include Pages 2 and 3 (the center of the menu).

   Start with the first page, or cover. First, drag a vertical ruler guide out from the left ruler to the 36-pica mark, to show the middle of the spread. Create a large rectangular frame 37p0 × 74p0, positioned at X = 36p0, Y = –1p0. The resulting frame will have a 1-pica bleed around the edge of the cover, which is required to print to the very edge of the paper. Note the position of the proxy reference point; it must be set to the upper left for these measurements to be accurate.

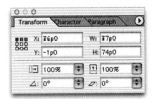

   Set the Fill to Pantone 194, and the Stroke to None.

2. Select the Type tool, and drag anywhere to draw a text frame. Type "Yellow", press Return/Enter, then type "Rose". Change to the Rotate tool and rotate the frame 90° counter-clockwise. Change to the Selection tool, and position the frame so its lower-left corner is at the intersection of the lower-left margin and column guides, at X = 39p0 and Y = 69p0 with the proxy reference set to the lower left.

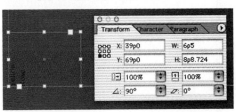

3. Resize the frame until it fills the column and margin guides. Watch the Transform palette while you do this; notice that the Width and Height fields appear to be backwards. This is because we rotated the frame, and InDesign always references the original orientation in terms of width and height. The frame should be 66p0 × 30p0.

4. Select the two words and set them to ATC Monsoon, 144/144 (solid leading), and apply Optical kerning.

5. Make sure the Type Fill icon is active in the toolbox, and not the Stroke icon. (The standard Fill icon changes to the Type Fill icon when any text is selected.) Click the Pantone 116 swatch to color the words with the swatch color. Now change to the Stroke icon, and assign a 0.5-pt. stroke of Pantone 194. Choose Window>Attributes, and click the checkmark next to Overprint Stroke.

The Text Fill and Stroke icons after you've applied the yellow fill and thin red stroke.

This step produces a *trap*, which will help the printer compensate for any misalignment of the paper as it goes through the press. The stroke is small enough not to be noticeable.

6. Switch to the Selection tool and make sure nothing is selected. Place the file **yrtlogo.eps** from your **RF_Intro_InDesign>Project_B** folder on the cover, above the word "Rose." A warning dialog will ask about replacing one of the Pantone colors you created earlier.

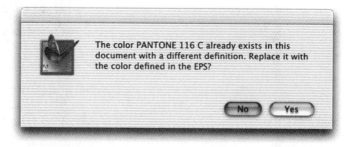

This happened because the same colors defined in your InDesign document were also defined in the logo graphic, which was created in Adobe Illustrator. It's OK to replace the color, so click Yes. You'll be asked again for each Pantone (spot) color in the document that matches one already in the graphic. Click Yes for the second color, then click the loaded cursor a few picas above the "e" in "Rose" to place the logo on the cover.

*We introduce trapping in **Advanced InDesign: Creating Electronic Documents**, but this is a very simple trap that will help you become familiar with the concept. You should always check with your service providers to see if you should apply any traps, or if they prefer to do this themselves.*

Windows users may see a white background in the Rose logo. Change your Display Performance to High Quality to eliminate the white background.

7. Visually center the logo over the vertical word "Rose." Press Command/Control-Shift, and drag a corner handle to proportionally resize the logo until it's about 12p0 wide. Then reposition it if necessary to better center it over the "e."

This is a vector graphic, so you can resize it as much as you want without destroying its appearance.

8. Resize the Yellow Rose text frame to H = 22p0. Remember, this appears to change the width of the frame, even though you're altering the height value. Change to the Type tool and draw another text frame anywhere on the page about 37p0 wide and 4p2 high, because you're going to rotate this one too. Type "Steakhouse", select the entire word, set it to 24-pt. ATC Monsoon, and fill it with Pantone 116C. Give it a 0.5-pt. overprinting stroke of Pantone 194C.

9. Rotate the Steakhouse frame 90° and place the bottom edge against the lower margin, at about X = 62p0 with the proxy reference point set to the lower left.

10. Select the contents of the Steakhouse frame, and adjust the tracking until the entire word is about as tall as the word "Rose". This will require a lot of tracking. Start at 500; you may find that you'll need to apply 1150–1200 units of tracking to get the ends of both words to visually align.

11. Zoom out, or press Command/Control-0 to fit the page to the window size. Your cover should look like this:

We've hidden the frame edges for a clearer view.

Press Command/Control-H to show and hide frame edges.

12. Save the file as "yr_menu.indd" in your **Work_In_Progress** folder, and leave it open.

Flow the Menu Text

1. Go to the second page of the document by pressing Page Down. Choose View>Fit Spread in Window to see the entire spread.

2. Place the **yellowrosemenu.doc** file from your **RF_Intro_Indesign>Project_B** folder.

3. Position the loaded cursor at 3p0, and click once to flow the text into the first column. You defined the two columns when you created the document. The new frame should show a red plus sign in the Out port, indicating that text is overset.

4. Switch to the Rectangle Frame tool, and draw a new text frame in the right column that fills the area in the margin and column guides. With the proxy reference point at the upper left, the frame should be positioned at X = 39p0, Y = 3p0; the size should be W = 30p0, H = 66p0.

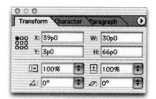

5. Press Page Up to return to the first spread. Create another rectangular frame on the left side of the spread with the same width and height. The X and Y positions should both be 3p0 with an upper-left proxy reference point. Zoom out or fit the spread to the window if necessary.

6. Press Page Down to go to the second spread. Switch to the Selection tool and click the red plus sign in the Out port of the left frame. Move the now-loaded cursor over the empty right frame (notice how the cursor changes shape and looks like it has parentheses around it — this indicates that you're over a usable frame). Click once to flow the text into this frame.

7. Now the right frame indicates overset text. Select the frame, then click once on the red plus sign, and press Page Up. Move the loaded cursor over the empty frame you made on the left side of the spread, and click once to flow the text. This frame indicates overset text, but that's OK because you'll make all of the text fit within the three frames.

8. Choose View>Show Text Threads to see how the text is flowing. Zoom out to see all of the spreads.

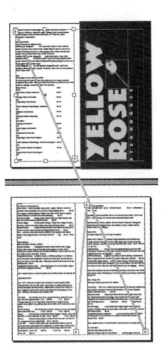

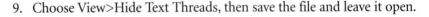

9. Choose View>Hide Text Threads, then save the file and leave it open.

Modify and Create Styles — 1

There are several paragraph styles imported along with the text: Heading 1, Heading 2, Heading 3, and Normal. You can keep these names or change them, but the important thing is that someone has already marked up the text with some structuring information. Naturally you won't keep the plain formatting specified by these styles; instead, you will modify them.

The text is structured as a heading (Heading 1) with a subheading (Heading 2), then the menu item text (Normal). Some sections use a third style, Heading 3, at the end of the section. Each menu item has a lead-in that's set in a sans-serif typeface, and the rest of the item is set in a serif typeface. Using a character style is the easiest way to create a different lead-in. All of the prices on the menu need to be set in italics, so there's another application of a character style. There may be some instances of copy that isn't well-tagged; you'll have to deal with these as they arise. In some cases, a unique instance of formatting doesn't merit the time it takes to create a style.

1. Go to the second spread. Zoom in to get a better view; scroll if necessary to view the left column.

2. Choose Type>Show Hidden Characters.

3. Bring the Paragraph Styles palette to the front if it's not already. Choose the Type tool and click in different areas to see what styles are assigned to different paragraphs.

4. Select the first line on the left spread. Be sure to include the return character at the end. Triple-click the line quickly to select all of it. The Heading 1 style will be active in the Paragraph Styles palette.

5. You're going to use the designer method to modify the Heading 1 style, because you're trying to reproduce the look of a printed piece without the benefit of any specifications. Set the selected line to 24-pt. ATC Monsoon with the Character palette. Center the line using the Paragraph palette.

STARTERS¶

6. Choose Redefine Style from the Paragraph Styles palette Options menu. Now every text element that was tagged with the Heading 1 style will change to the new specifications you just made.

7. Select the entire second line, which is tagged with the Heading 2 style. This is going to be a bit more complicated, because this style uses rules (lines) above and below it. Choose Style Options from the Paragraph palette Options menu.

8. Check the Preview box at the lower left of the Modify Paragraph Style Options box. You might need to move the dialog box around a little to see the changes occur. Click Basic Character Formats. The type is set to ATC Mai Tai, Normal, but you want it bold, so choose Bold from the menu to the right of the font name. The type also needs to be all caps, so choose All Caps from the Case pop-up menu. Choose Optical kerning, because ATC fonts do not have kerning pairs.

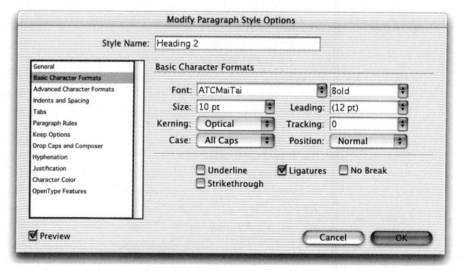

9. Click Indents and Spacing, and choose Center from the Alignment pop-up menu. Apply 0p3 of Space Before and 0p2 of Space After.

10. Click Paragraph Rules. You want the entire line to have a green (Pantone 5757) background, but it would be a lot of work to manually draw filled rectangles behind each Heading 2 line. You can, however, define a single, fat rule that performs the same function, and which will remain in the correct position if the text reflows.

    Click the Rule On check box next to Rule Above. Watch the text as you go, so you can see how each parameter affects the appearance of the rule as you build it. The text is 10 pt., so apply a rule thick enough to show above and below the text. Type "12" in the Weight field. The new, thick rule appears slightly above the text, which

On a Windows computer, an offset value of –0p1 may be better suited for the rule.

means you need to adjust the offset. First, though, choose PANTONE 5757 C from the Color pop-up menu, because if you leave it black you won't see the text as you work. (Besides, this is what the old menu used.) Change the Width to Text.

To determine the Offset, think about where you want the rule to go. It needs to move down, so we need to apply a negative value in the Offset field. Type "–0p1" and press Tab to apply this setting. It helps, but it's not enough. Press Shift-Tab to return to the Offset field, type "–0p2", and press Tab again. This offset centers the rule against the text.

Lastly, the rule needs to extend out one pica on each side. You can do this by applying an indent value for the left and right sides. Type "1p0" in the Left Indent field and press Tab, then type "1p0" in the Right Indent field and press Tab again to apply it. If you've positioned the Options box so you can see text tagged with the Heading 2 style, you'll see that the rule actually gets shorter, because these indent values are measured from the frame edge inwards. You need to set negative values for both indents, so change the values in both Indent fields to "–1p0", then click OK. All of the Heading 2 text should display the new settings.

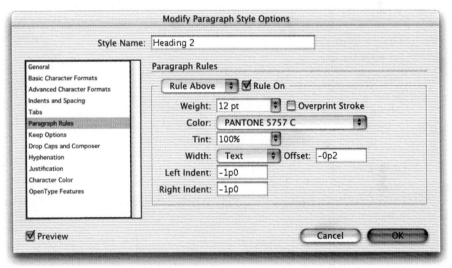

11. Click OK to apply your changes. The new Heading 2 style should look like this:

FRESH CHICKEN
WHO YOU CALLIN' CHICKEN, MISTER?

12. Save the file and leave it open.

Modify and Create Styles — 2

1. The Show Hidden Characters option should still be on. If not, turn it back on. Zoom in if necessary and look at the body (menu item) text. Instead of tabs, the copywriter used em spaces, which we discussed in Chapter 4, *Working with Text*. Em spaces are always the same size in width as the current point size of the text.

They allow enough visual spacing to set off the copy, and reflow with the text, unlike tabs.

Texas Onion — Jumbo Spanish onion petals, lightly battered, fried and sprinkled with seasoning. Served with a tangy dipping sauce. — $5.99

When Show Hidden Characters is turned on, em spaces appear as raised em dashes with the space "dot" indicator underneath.

2. Click anywhere in the third paragraph in the left column of the second spread, which is the first menu item under "Starters." Zoom in if necessary to get a good look at the paragraph. The type is defined by the Normal style, which is selected in the Paragraph Styles palette. You're not going to modify this paragraph style, but you need to create two character styles to achieve the same look as the original menu. Select the first two words, "Texas Onion," and change the typeface to ATC Mai Tai Bold. Now the style name Normal shows a plus sign after it, which means you've applied an override to the style's typeface definition.

3. Activate the Character Styles palette, then choose New Style from the pop-up menu. Name the style "Lead In" and click Character Color. Select PANTONE 194 C as the color, then click OK.

4. Because the character styles don't exist in the original Microsoft Word file, nothing happens to any of the text. You have to select every instance of the lead-in words and apply the Lead In style, including the two words on which the style is based, which are still tagged as Normal+. Click Lead In from the Character Styles palette to assign that style to the selected words.

5. The process of tagging all of the lead-ins can become tedious, so you can apply a shortcut to the style. Choose Style Options from the Character Styles palette Options menu, and click in the Shortcut field. Press Command/Control and the number "2" on the numeric keypad to assign this shortcut to the style, then click OK.

6. Select the next lead-in words, "Fried Peppers." Remember the text selection shortcuts you learned in Chapter 4. Place the cursor in front of the word "Fried", then press Command/Control-Shift-Right Arrow to select the word to the right of the text cursor, then repeat once. All the lead-in words should be selected. Now apply the shortcut you just created (Command/Control-2).

7. Press Command/Control-Down Arrow twice to position the cursor at the beginning of the next paragraph. Select the item's lead-in, and apply the Lead In style with the shortcut. Be careful not to select any text past the lead-in. Repeat for the entire menu. Using the shortcuts makes this task go pretty quickly. Of course, skip past any text tagged as a Heading. When you get to the Wines section, tag the text "White Wines" and "Red Wines" with the Lead In style. Stop when you reach the overset text. You'll format that text later.

8. Return to the left column of the second spread, to the third ("Texas Onion") paragraph. You need to italicize all of the prices. Select the price, set it in ATC Cabana Italic, and create a new character style named "Price". Apply the Price style to all of the prices in the menu, except those in paragraphs tagged as Heading 3. As before, use the selection and navigation shortcuts you learned in Chapter 4 to speed up this process.

The following are a few text selection shortcuts, discussed in Chapter 4, Working with Text.

Press Command/Control-Shift-Left Arrow or -Right Arrow to select one word to the left or right.

Press Shift-Up Arrow or -Down Arrow to select a line up or down.

Press Shift-Home or -End to select the start or end of a line.

9. The last style change is to the Heading 3 paragraph style. Make sure nothing is selected, then double-click the style's name in the Paragraph Styles palette and apply these specifications in the Modify Paragraph Style Options dialog box: (Basic Character Formats) ATC Mai Tai, 10/auto, italic, optical kerning; (Indents and Spacing) centered, 1p0 left and right indents, 0p2 space before. Click OK.

Tidy Up the Front Spread

1. Look at the second spread. The copy describing the steak add-ons is broken across the two columns. You need this copy to start on the second column. Click the text cursor at the beginning of the line reading "Great Steak Additions" and press the Enter key on the far right of the keyboard. This forces any text following it to the next column.

2. Now you have a little room to play. You're going to highlight a paragraph with one of the colors by using a very large paragraph rule. Select the paragraph under "Legendary Steaks" and apply these settings in the Paragraph palette: left and right indents 1p0, justified last line left, space before and after 0p6.

3. Choose Paragraph Rules from the Options menu and check the Preview box to watch the progress of your work. Start by activating the Rule Above and Rule On check boxes, then choose PANTONE 116 C as the color. You want to highlight this entire paragraph in yellow, with about 1p0 of yellow extending around it. You know the indents of this paragraph are 1p0, so leave the Width set to Column. Now you just need to watch the top and bottom. Apply what you think is a reasonable weight to cover the paragraph; vertically, the paragraph is about 6 picas tall; 6 × 12 = 72 pt., so enter "72" in the Weight field. Now you need to fix the offset, because the default offset starts the rule on the baseline of the first line. You want the rule to start on the baseline of the last (fifth) line of the paragraph so set an offset of –5p0.

4. This is close, but you need to make the rule a little taller to extend past the top and bottom of the paragraph. Change the Weight to 8p0, which will add 4 pt. to the top and bottom. You'll now need to adjust the Offset to compensate for the increased rule width, so enter –5p8 in the Offset field. Now the rule is a little too low. These measurements don't account for the ascender height of the first line, so take away two points (–5p6). This will visually center the rule behind the paragraph. Click OK to apply the rule.

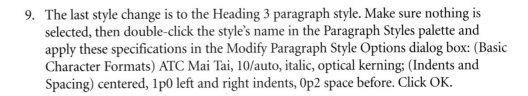

LEGENDARY STEAKS¶

Since 1971, it's been a Yellow Rose tradition to serve quality steaks, cooked just the way you like them. Our steaks are always fresh (never frozen) and hand-cut from USDA, Midwestern corn-fed beef. We go to great lengths to ensure your steak is absolutely the best quality we can serve. We hope you enjoy every delicious bite.¶

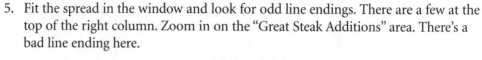

5. Fit the spread in the window and look for odd line endings. There are a few at the top of the right column. Zoom in on the "Great Steak Additions" area. There's a bad line ending here.

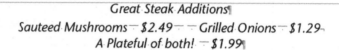

Great Steak Additions¶
Sauteed Mushrooms ⎯ $2.49⎯ ⎯Grilled Onions ⎯ $1.29⎯ ⎯ ⎯A Plateful of both! ⎯ $1.99¶

Put the text cursor to the left of the "A" in "A Plateful." Delete the em spaces, then press Shift-Return/Enter to break the line here. The result is a line without the awkward break.

Great Steak Additions¶
Sauteed Mushrooms ⎯ $2.49⎯ ⎯ Grilled Onions ⎯ $1.29⌐
A Plateful of both! ⎯ $1.99¶

6. Add line breaks to the choices of salad dressings, before "Thousand Island" and "Honey Mustard."

Great Steak Additions¶
Sauteed Mushrooms ⎯ $2.49⎯ ⎯ Grilled Onions ⎯ $1.29⌐
A Plateful of both! ⎯ $1.99¶
Legendary Steaks and Prime Rib are served with your choice of one side item, a Mixed Green or Caesar Salad and hearth baked bread.¶
Salad Dressings: House, Ranch, Fat Free Ranch, Balsamic Vinaigrette, ⌐
Thousand Island, Tangy Ranch, Bleu Cheese, Caesar, Italian, ⌐
Honey Mustard and Oil & Vinegar¶

7. At the bottom of the right column, click the text cursor in front of "Specialty Drinks" and press Enter (on the far right of the keyboard) to force this line to jump to the next column (the left column on the first spread).

   Your view will also jump to this location. Press Page Down to return to the second spread, fit the spread in the window, and check your work for any other bad breaks. Fix any you see.

8. Save the file, and leave it open.

Set the Table

The wine list is formatted with tabs and the prices are all over the page. This is causing an overset text condition. You could reformat the tabs to clean up the mess, but for this project you'll use a table instead.

1. Go to the first spread and select the wines, starting with the line "White Wines" and ending with the $23 Cabernet.

On a Windows computer, your "Specialty Drinks" line may already have jumped to the next column on its own. This is more evidence of the differences that can arise between working on the Macintosh and Windows platforms.

White Wines — Glass
Bottle
Sutter Home White Zinfandel $3.99
$14
Beringer White Zinfandel $4.49
$16
Copperridge Chardonnay $3.79
Robert Mondavi Woodbridge Chardonnay $4.29
$15
Meridian Chardonnay $5.49
$19
Kendall-Jackson Chardonnay $6.79
$24
Red Wines
Turning Leaf Merlot $4.49
$16
Fetzer Eagle Peak Merlot $5.49
$19
Columbia Crest Merlot $6.29
$23
Copperridge Cabernet Sauvignon $3.79
Robert Mondavi Woodbridge Cabernet Sauvignon $4.29
$15
BV Coastal Cabernet Sauvignon $5.49
$19
Geyser Peak Cabernet Sauvignon
$23

2. Choose Table>Convert Text to Table.

White Wines	Glass	Bottle
Sutter Home White Zinfandel	$3.99	$14
Beringer White Zinfandel	$4.49	$16
Copperridge Chardonnay	$3.79	-
Robert Mondavi Woodbridge Chardonnay	$4.29	$15
Meridian Chardonnay	$5.49	$19
Kendall-Jackson Chardonnay	$6.79	$24
Red Wines		
Turning Leaf Merlot	$4.49	$16
Fetzer Eagle Peak Merlot	$5.49	$19
Columbia Crest Merlot	$6.29	$23
Copperridge Cabernet Sauvignon	$3.79	-
Robert Mondavi Woodbridge Cabernet Sauvignon	$4.29	$15
BV Coastal Cabernet Sauvignon	$5.49	$19
Geyser Peak Cabernet Sauvignon	-	$23

Be sure that the first column's contents do not break to two lines.

3. Click the right edge of the first column, and drag it to the right until each wine name is on one line only. The rest of the columns will move beyond the edge of the frame, but that's OK for now.

Kendall-Jackson Chardonnay	$6.79	$24
Red Wines		
Turning Leaf Merlot	$4.49	$16

Another difference between the Mac OS and Windows is how each interprets line break characters. On a Windows computer, you may not have an empty last row.

4. Resize the right two columns by moving their right edges back to the left. Start with the middle column, and finish with the right column. Drag the right column's edge back to the frame edge/column guide. Adjust the width of the price columns until they appear the same.

Kendall-Jackson Chardonnay	$6.79	$24
Red Wines		
Turning Leaf Merlot	$4.49	$16
Fetzer Eagle Peak Merlot	$5.49	$19

5. The last row of the column may be empty. If so, click the cursor in any cell of this row, then choose Table>Delete>Row.

If the word "Dessert" is no longer centered, it may have lost its Heading 1 formatting. If this happens, simply reapply the Heading 1 style to the heading.

6. The table looks OK now, but the gridlines are distracting. Select the entire table by clicking once at the upper-left corner (the cursor will change to a diagonal arrow).

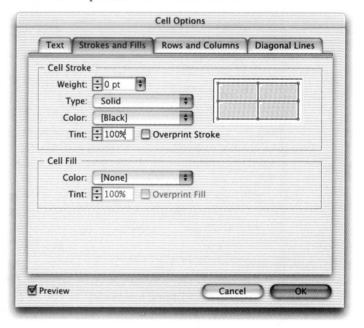

7. Choose Table>Cell Options>Strokes and Fills.

In the Cell Stroke area, set the Weight to zero, then click OK. The bothersome gridlines are gone. Zoom out and take a look at the table. Using the Table functions really speeds up the process of setting tabular data, instead of using tabs. You would probably want to use tabs instead of the table feature when setting data that requires precise formatting, such as financial data where the decimals must all align. But here, a table is a fine alternative to setting tab stops.

8. After formatting the wine list, you'll see that the hidden part of the Desserts section and the entire last section, Beverages, is no longer overset. You should not have any overset text at this stage on a Macintosh, but you may still have overset text on a Windows computer; if this occurs, manually reduce the leading value of the menu items in the column until all of the text fits. If the red plus sign is still present, make sure that you've correctly set the line breaks and column breaks on the second spread. Apply the required styles to this now-visible text.

9. Save the file and leave it open. You're almost done!

Finishing the Menu

The restaurant manager likes the menu, but wants a barbed-wire motif on the top and bottom of the menu spreads (except the cover). You can draw a simple piece of art that you can step and repeat along the top and bottom.

1. Navigate to the top of the first spread and fit the left column into view. Set the stroke color to black, or press "D" to select the default stroke and fill colors. Select the Pen tool, and make your first click about 1p0 to the left of the page edge. Click to the right, in the page area and up a bit, and drag a bit to make a curve point. Move to the right a few picas and down a bit, then drag to make another curve point. Click without dragging a few more picas to the right, and up a bit.

2. Command/Control-click to deselect the path, then draw another path that roughly mirrors the first one. You should end up with two paths overlapping each other that look more or less like this:

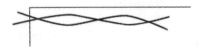

3. Now you need to make some barbs. Choose the Polygon tool, then double-click its icon to show the Polygon Settings dialog. Set it to create a five-pointed star with a 75% inset and click OK. Hold Option/Alt to draw from the center, and draw a star about 0p6–0p8 tall and wide where the "wires" intersect on the left. Fill the star with black, and apply a stroke of None.

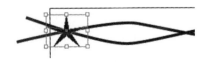

4. You'll need to zoom way in for this part, probably to 600–800%. Choose the Direct Selection tool and click the star once. You want to adjust the tips of the star's rays

so it doesn't look so perfect. Click and move each of the five tips, and adjust a few of the inset points to make some rays thinner than others.

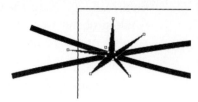

While you're at it, change the end caps of the wires to Rounded. Remember, you need to choose Show Options from the Stroke palette Options menu to see the Caps choices.

5. Change to the Selection tool, and copy and paste the star. Move it to the third intersection of the wires, then use the Rotate tool to randomly rotate it so it doesn't obviously look like you copied and pasted it (old designer trick!).

6. Zoom out a little and examine the result. Your barbed wire should look something (but not exactly) like this:

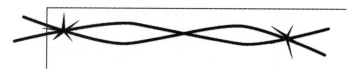

Here, we chose Hide Frame Edges to show the stars more clearly.
Press Command/Control-H to show or hide frame edges.

7. Fit the page in the window. Using the Selection tool, drag a marquee around the wires and barbs/stars to select all of them, then press Command/Control-G to group them. Visually center the group between the top of the page and the top margin.

8. Choose Edit>Step and Repeat. The manager wants the barbed-wire theme across the top and bottom of the menu pages, but not the cover. Look at the Transform palette to determine the width of the group. Here, it's about 10p2. Set a repeat count of 3, a Horizontal offset of the width reported in the Transform palette, and a Vertical offset of 0, then click OK.

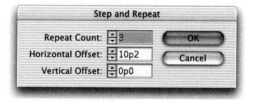

9. The repeated elements step across the top of the page. The last element remains selected and overlaps the cover, so choose Object>Arrange>Send to Back to hide the portion that overlaps the cover.

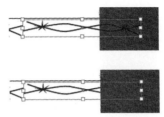

10. Select all of the barbed-wire objects, choose Edit>Copy, then choose Edit>Paste in Place. Click and hold the selected copies, which appear exactly over the originals, then drag them down to the bottom of the page, between the bottom margin and the bottom of the page. Move them to the left a little so they don't exactly mirror the ones at the top, and send them to the back so the last one doesn't overlap the cover.

11. The objects are still on the clipboard. Press Page Down to go to the second spread, and fit the entire spread in the window.

12. Choose Edit>Paste, and the copied objects will appear in the middle of the spread. Drag them to the top of the left side to about the same position they are on the first spread. Paste another copy in place. Hold Shift to constrain up and down motion, and drag the copies to the right side of the spread. Move them so they appear to repeat the pattern.

13. Use the Selection tool to draw a marquee around all of the barbed-wire objects at the top of the page. Copy them, then paste them in place. Hold Shift and drag the copies to the bottom of the spread. Move these to the left a little to avoid repetition.

14. Save and close the document.

Project C: Travel Brochure

A travel agency may feature many vacation packages, but more important than those packages is the necessity of convincing customers to use the agency rather than booking vacations for themselves. This project requires you to use most of the skills you have learned in creating a standard marketing piece, the six-panel brochure. All object coordinates given in this exercise assume that the upper-left proxy reference point is selected in the Transform palette; be sure to check frequently because the proxy reference point will default to the center.

Set Up the Brochure Format

1. Create a new document. Set the Number of Pages field to 2, and uncheck the Facing Pages and Master Text Frame boxes. Set the page size to Letter and the orientation to Landscape. Set the Top and Bottom margins to 18 pt., and the Left and Right margins to 1p6. Set the number of columns to 1. Click OK.

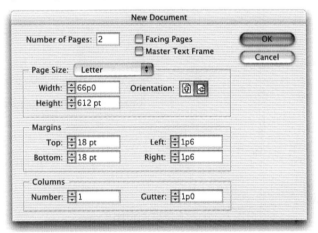

It might seem easier to simply create three equal columns, but this doesn't work with the folding machines used to fold printed sheets. The "tuck in" panel must be about 1/16 in. shorter than the other pages.

2. Press Command/Control-K to show the InDesign preferences. In the Units & Increments pane, set the Horizontal Ruler Units to Picas, and the Vertical Ruler Units to Points, if you have not previously set these as your default.

3. Next you need to adjust the guides for the fold marks. These can be tricky, and require exact specifications. Creating three equal columns will not work, because automatic folding machines require that the inward-folding panel be slightly shorter than the two outside panels.

   On the first page, place two vertical guides at 22p1 and 44p2 by dragging them out from the left page ruler. This will be the inside sheet.

Items in dialog boxes not mentioned in the instructions should be left at the default settings.

4. Double-click Page 2 in the Pages palette. Place vertical guides at 21p9 and at 43p10. This will be the outside sheet, including the front and back cover.

5. From the left ruler, drag the guides for your live copy areas 1p6 to either side of the fold marks. They should be positioned as follows — Page 1: 20p7, 23p7, 42p7, 45p7; Page 2: 20p3, 23p3, 42p4, 45p4. You can see the position of guides in the Transform palette as you drag them.

6. Save your file as "atwv_brochure.indd" in your **Work_In_Progress** folder.

Establish the Color Scheme

Your brochure will use process color and will be printed 4/4 (four process colors on both sides). All colors you specify will have a color type of Process and a color mode of CMYK.

1. From the Swatches palette, select New Color Swatch.

2. Uncheck the Name with Color Value box and type the name "Dark Green" in the Swatch Name field. Set the CMYK specifications to C:100, M:0, Y:75, K:50.

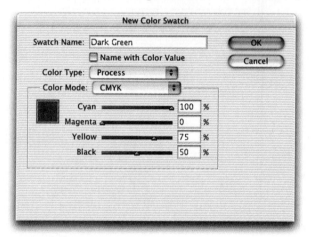

3. Click OK to save this color.

4. Create a new color named "Dark Blue", defined as C:100, M:75, Y:0, K:25.

5. Create another new color named "Light Blue", defined as C:85, M:5, Y:0, K:0.

6. Save the document.

Set Up Styles

1. Choose New Style from the Paragraph Styles palette menu. Name it "BT".

2. Click Basic Character Formats. Set the font to Adobe Garamond Pro, Regular, 12/15.

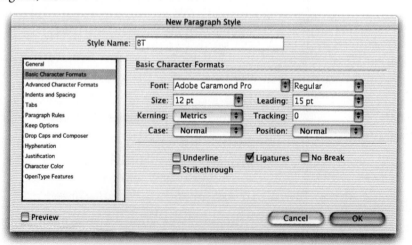

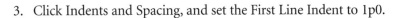

3. Click Indents and Spacing, and set the First Line Indent to 1p0.

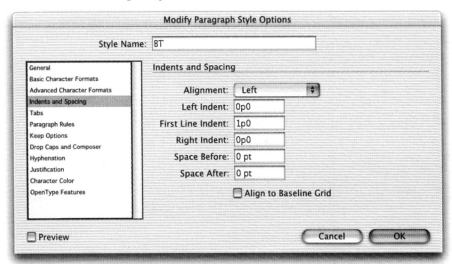

4. Click OK to save the style.

5. You need another style without a first-line indent. Make sure the BT style is selected in the Paragraph Styles palette, and then choose Duplicate Style from the palette menu. Rename "BT copy" as "BT1". Click Indents and Spacing, and set the First Line Indent to 0p0. Click OK to save the new style.

It's common to set the first paragraph of a chapter or section with no indent, and all following paragraphs with an indent.

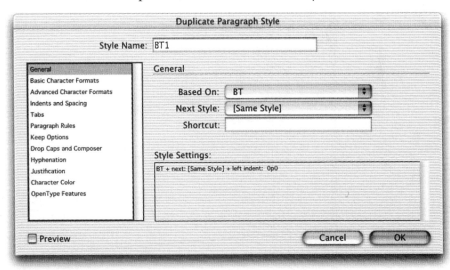

6. Next, you need a subhead style. Choose New Style from the palette menu and name it "SH". Choose No Paragraph Style from the Based On pop-up menu. Note how new styles pick up the attributes of the last one created, so be careful.

7. Set the Basic Character Formats of the style SH as:

   Font: ATC Mai Tai, Bold, 12/15

   Left justification, no indents

   Space Before: 10 pt.

Keep Options: Keep with Next 1 Lines, Keep Lines Together, All Lines in Paragraph

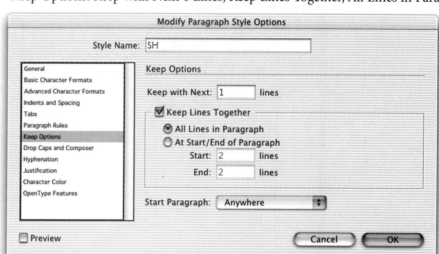

Hyphenation: Off

Character Color: fill of Dark Green, no stroke color.

8. Click OK to save the style.

9. Make a duplicate of the BT1 style and name it "LB"; this will be a bulleted list. In the Indents and Spacing dialog, set the Left Indent to 3p0 and the First Line Indent to –0p9, and then click OK.

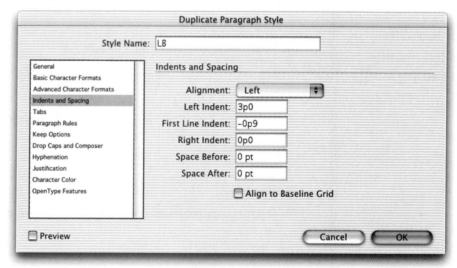

10. Make a duplicate of the LB style called "LB1", and set the Space Before to 7.5 pt. This will be the first item in a bulleted list. Make another duplicate of LB called "LB2", and set the Space After to 7.5 pt. for use as the last item in a bulleted list.

11. Make a duplicate of BT1 called "Bio"; in its Indents and Spacing dialog, set Space After to 7.5 pt.

12. Save the document.

All positional coordinates in this project are measured from the upper-left corner of the object. Be sure to reset the proxy reference point in the Transform palette to the upper-left corner.

Apply Styles

1. Be sure you are on the first spread. Create three rectangular text frames with the following specifications (this should be easy because the guides you set up previously will help you draw these frames exactly):

   X: 1p6   W: 19p1

   Y: 18 pt   H: 576 pt

   X: 23p7   W: 19p1

   Y: 18 pt   H: 576 pt

   X: 45p7   W: 18p11

   Y: 18 pt   H: 576 pt

2. Click in the far-left text frame with the Type tool.

3. From File>Place (Command/Control-D), place the file **atwu_text.rtf** from your **RF_Intro_InDesign>Project_C** folder.

4. With the Selection tool, click the red overflow icon at the lower right of the text frame. With the loaded text icon, click the second text frame to flow text into that frame.

5. Place the Type tool in the first paragraph and select BT1 from the Paragraph Styles palette.

6. Select the second paragraph and define its style as BT.

7. Choose the third paragraph — "Meet Our Travel Specialists" — and select the style SH.

8. Select the next paragraphs — down to the subhead "How Can We Serve You?" — and select the style Bio.

9. Choose the next paragraph — "How Can We Serve You?" — and select the style SH.

10. Select the style BT1 for the next paragraph.

11. The text overflow symbol now shows. Choose the Selection tool, click the red plus sign, and flow the text into the third text frame on the page.

12. The next paragraph begins a bulleted list. Click with the Type tool at the beginning of the "Guided Tours" line, insert a bullet by typing Option/Alt-8, and then insert a tab.

How Can We Serve You?
By now, you have a pretty good idea of what we can do for you. We specialize in vacation travel (but, of course, we'll be happy to book your travel for whatever reason).

• Guided Tours

Type a bullet and a tab in front of the remaining lines of bulleted text.

13. Place the cursor back in the Guided Tours line. Define its style as LB1.

14. Select the text "The British Isles" through "Cruises" and define these paragraphs as LB.

15. Select "Theatre and On the Town" and define it as LB2.

16. Select the last paragraph and define it as BT1.

17. Return to the first paragraph and select it; you're going to add a drop cap. From the Paragraph palette, assign the number of lines as 4 and the number of characters as 1.

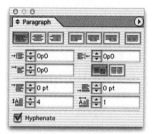

18. Place the cursor between the "W" and the "h" of the first word, and force a line break (Shift-Return/Enter).

19. Highlight the "W" and apply a fill of Dark Blue.

Whether your next vacation is designed to take you around the world in eighty days (more or less), or you're constrained to a long weekend closer to home, we're the people who can make

20. Save the file and leave it open for the next exercise.

Place Images in Frames

1. Under the subhead "Meet Our Travel Specialists" is a paragraph about each person. You're going to place the faces beside the names, so clients can identify the people who are booking their travel arrangements.

2. Using the Rectangle Frame tool, create the first picture frame with the following specifications:

   X: 1p6   W: 6p0

   Y: 290 pt   H: 102 pt

3. Select Window>Text Wrap. Choose the second button, Wrap Around Bounding Box. Set the Bottom Offset to 9 pt. and the Right Offset to 0p9. You will use these margin settings for all the pictures in the biography section.

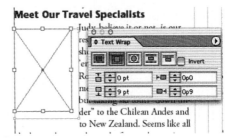

In Windows, you may need to set the Y value of the picture frame to 300–302 pt. to get the proper placement.

4. Switch to the Selection tool. Choose File>Place (Command/Control-D) and place **judy.tif** from your **RF_Intro_InDesign>Project_C** folder.

Meet Our Travel Specialists

Judy, believe it or not, is our resident ski bum. Last winter she was the guide for six (count 'em) trips to the American Rockies and Sierras. This summer where else would she be but taking ski tours "down under" to the Chilean Andes and to New Zealand. Seems like all she knows how to do is take fun to the max!

5. Click Judy's image frame, copy it, and choose Edit>Paste in Place to put a duplicate exactly on top of the original. Hold Shift, and drag the copy of Judy down to the paragraph about Max. Visually align the top of the frame with the top of the paragraph about Max.

6. Place **max.tif** from your **RF_Intro_InDesign>Project_C** folder into the copy of the frame.

7. Choose Object>Fitting>Fit Frame to Content.

8. The lower offset is too large; it creates an ugly white area under Max's picture.

Reduce the bottom offset in the Text Wrap palette to zero, which causes the line starting with "been here" not to wrap. Note how the Adobe Paragraph Composer takes these things into account when composing text, and how the entire paragraph is recomposed.

Max's picture is still a bit off — too much white space remains under her image. Press Shift-Command/Control and enlarge the frame by dragging the lower-right handle until the bottom of the image aligns with the baseline of the seventh line.

9. Copy and paste Judy's frame in place, and move it to the second column next to Laurie's bio paragraph. (You don't want to use Max's frame because you scaled it.) Place **laurie.tif** into the frame, and choose Object>Fitting>Fit Frame to Content.

10. You have a similar problem with Laurie as you did with Max — too much white space under her image. Reducing the bottom text wrap offset to zero still doesn't eliminate the white space. Look at Laurie's picture: would you be better off

reducing or enlarging it slightly to eliminate the white space? Try both; you'll probably find that reducing her image slightly provides a better appearance.

What can we tell you about Laurie, except that she's a Celtophile. Her specialty is trips to Ireland, Scotland, England, Wales, Australia and New Zealand. Whether it's helping folks get the most from their trip to "the Homeland" or accompanying them

11. Copy Laurie's frame and choose Edit>Paste in Place, then Shift-drag it into position for John's picture. Place the picture **john1.tif** into the copy of Laurie's frame and perform adjustments to fitting, offset, and size as you see fit. Reducing John to eliminate white space can result in a widow, so try enlarging him a bit:

John is our computer geek. He keeps track of all the best airfares and cruiseline fares, so we can pass them along to you. Like everybody else, he has a "life." In addition to living online, he's our resident expert on Florida theme parks

12. There isn't enough space left to place Glen's picture. Click the Type tool at the beginning of Glen's bio, and press Enter (on the numeric keypad) to force the paragraph to the next frame in the thread. This will leave some white space under John's bio, but that's OK, because there is more copy to put there later.

13. Copy and paste John's picture frame, and drag it into position next to Glen's bio. Place **glen.tif** into this frame, and use the functions you've learned to resize, fit, and position offsets to achieve a pleasing text wrap:

Glen is the person we all rely on to keep us together. He's the manager of the mailing list, keeper of the schedule — and all 'round expert on night life, concerts, and theatre. If you're planning an evening On the Town (New York, Chicago, San Francisco,

In this example, we fit the frame to the content, and then enlarged the frame and the content slightly by dragging the lower-right handle while holding Shift-Command/Control.

14. You have one more image to place on the first spread below Glen's bio. Make sure the proxy reference point is set to the upper left, then place the file **your_vacation.tif** into the third column, clicking the loaded pointer at X = 45p7, Y = 414 pt. No text wrap offsets are necessary. You want this image to span the column, so hold Shift-Command/Control and drag the upper-right handle until the image fills the width of the column.

15. Now the top of image cuts off the copy at the end of the story.

This is an easy fix. With the image selected, choose Object>Arrange>Send to Back.

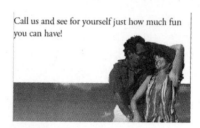

We've turned off frame edges here to show the result.

16. There's one more item you need to add, which is the copy under John's bio. Draw a text frame with the following specifications:

    X: 23p7   W: 19p1

    Y: 508 pt   H: 86 pt

17. Type the following, using a line break (Shift-Return/Enter) to separate the two lines:

    For your next vacation, call

    813/555-ATWV

18. Center the text horizontally with the Paragraph palette.
    Press Command/Control-B to open the Text Frame Options dialog, and center the text vertically.

19. Set both lines to Caflisch Script Pro, Regular, 18/18. You want the phone number to occupy roughly the same width as the first line, which means either enlarging the point size or tracking the type out. Enlarge the point size incrementally by selecting the second line, then pressing Command/Control-Shift-> until the type is about the same width as the first line.

    For your next vacation, call
    ## 813/555-ATWV

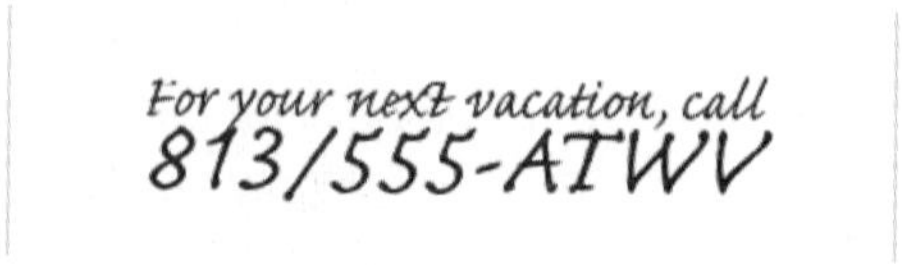

20. The spacing between the lines is a bit tight, so select the second line and set the leading to 22 pt.

    For your next vacation, call
    ## 813/555-ATWV

21. Select all of the text and set its fill to Paper.

22. Switch to the Selection tool and set the frame's fill to Dark Blue.

23. A colleague notices that the picture of John is the wrong John. Choose the Direct Selection tool, click the picture of the wrong John, then press Command/Control-D. Choose **john2.tif** in the Place dialog and make sure Replace Selected Item is checked. This action replaces the selected image with the new one, while maintaining any scaling or other transformations applied to the original image, but only if you start by selecting the original object with the Direct Selection tool.

John is our computer geek. He keeps track of all the best airfares and cruiseline fares, so we can pass them along to you. Like everybody else, he has a "life." In addition to living online, he's our resident expert on Florida theme parks — and has extended that expertise to cover other

Congratulations! You're more than halfway done. One side of the brochure down, and one side to go. Here's what the first side/spread should look like:

Your exact line breaks and text flow may differ somewhat from these images, due to the differences in type behavior between Mac OS and Windows.

24. Save the file and leave it open to continue.

Create the Special Offer Panel

The travel agency wants to give its customers something special to look for over the next few months. This Special Events panel requires some new styles, and you'll make it stand out with color too.

1. Go to the second spread by double-clicking the Page 2 icon in the Pages palette.

2. You want the leftmost panel to stand out against the other panels on this side of the brochure, so make it a shade of blue. Using the Rectangle tool, draw a rectangle with the following specifications (check your Fill and Stroke icons in the toolbox and set both to None if necessary):

   X: −0p9   W: 22p6

   Y: −9 pt   H: 630 pt

   This extends the panel beyond the page parameters and bleeds the color off the page so you will have no problems when the printed brochures are trimmed.

3. Deselect this new frame. Click the Light Blue swatch in the Swatches palette. From the Swatch menu, select New Tint Swatch. Set the Tint to 50% and click OK. Set the fill of the rectangle to the new tint.

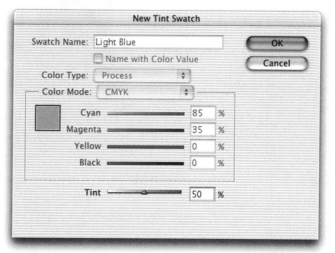

4. Make sure the stroke color of the frame is set to None.

5. With the Type tool, draw a frame with the following specifications:

   X: 1p6   W: 18p9

   Y: 18 pt   H: 576 pt

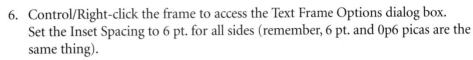

6. Control/Right-click the frame to access the Text Frame Options dialog box. Set the Inset Spacing to 6 pt. for all sides (remember, 6 pt. and 0p6 picas are the same thing).

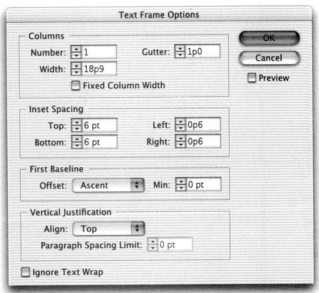

Justified text looks better in frames that have strokes around them and provides pleasing symmetry.

7. Choose the Selection tool and give the text frame a 1-pt. black stroke.

8. Switch to the Type tool and place **atwu_events.rtf** into the text frame.

9. You need to set up styles that are specific to this text. Create a new paragraph style named "BTS" (Body Text Special). Set the Basic Character Format to ATC Mai Tai, Normal, 9/11, with 3 pt. Space After, left justified. Click OK to save the style.

10. Duplicate the BTS style and name it "BTS2". Set its specifications to ATC Mai Tai Italic, 8/9, with 5 pt. Space After.

11. Duplicate the BTS style and name it "BTSH". Set its specifications to ATC Mai Tai Normal, 10/11, 5 pt. Space Before, and 5 pt. Space After. Set the fill to Dark Blue.

12. Duplicate the SH style and name it "SH2". Set its specifications as ATC Mai Tai Bold, 14/14, All Caps, with 14 pt. Space After, keeping the 10-pt. Space Before setting. Set the alignment to Center and the color to Dark Green.

13. Select the first paragraph — "Special Events" — and assign the SH2 style.

14. Select the second paragraph and assign the BTSH style. Highlight the words "Caribbean Sail and Dive" and change them from Normal to Bold.

15. Assign the BTS style to the next paragraph.

16. Assign the BTS2 style to the next paragraph.

17. Format the next two events the same way: the event name as the BTSH style, the description as the BTS style, and the prerequisite as the BTS2 style. Remember to set the event's name as bold.

18. Deselect the frame. Save the document and leave it open for the next steps.

Add the Mailing Panel

This brochure is designed to be a self-mailer. The middle panel in the spread is designated as the mailing panel. It needs to include the return address and the first-class permit stamp.

1. Place **atwv_logo_4c.eps** on the middle spread.

2. Hold down Command-Option-Shift (Macintosh) or Control-Alt-Shift (Windows) and scale the graphic so the width is 5p0 (or 60 pt.).

3. From the Transform palette, rotate the graphic 90°.

4. With the upper-left proxy reference point selected, position the logo at X = 23p3, Y = 477 pt.

5. Create a text box 14p0 wide and 50 pt. high. Select No Paragraph Style in the Paragraph Style palette, then type the following lines; use soft returns (Shift-Return/Enter) as line endings:

Around the World Travel

Surfside 6

Tampa, FL 35231

6. Format the text as ATC Mai Tai, Normal, 12/15, black. Set the alignment to Center.

7. Change to the Selection tool, rotate the text frame 90°, and, with the upper-left proxy reference point selected, position the frame at X = 29p0, Y = 426.

8. Create another text frame 6p0 × 72 pt.

9. Type the following lines, ending each line with Shift-Return/Enter.

Bulk Rate

U.S. Postage

PAID

Permit # 112

Tampa, FL

10. Format the text as ATC Mai Tai Normal, 10/12, with no additional space above or below. Set the alignment to Center.

11. Control/Right-click the frame and choose Text Frame Options from the contextual menu. Set the vertical justification to center, then click OK.

12. With the Selection tool active, set the stroke to 1 pt., and set the color to black.

13. Rotate the frame 90°.

14. With the upper-left proxy reference point selected, position the frame at X = 23p3, Y = 18 pt.

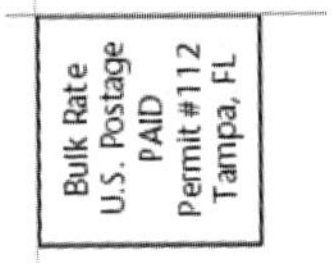

15. Save your document. Just one panel to go — the easy one.

Finish the Brochure

1. The right-hand panel, which is the "cover" or the first panel the recipient sees, needs an image on it. Using the Rectangle Frame tool, create a frame with the following specifications:

   X: 43p10   W: 22p10

   Y: –9 pt   H: 630 pt

2. Place **beach.tif** from the **RF_Intro_InDesign>Project_C** folder into this frame.

3. Click the beach image with the Direct Selection tool. This shows you the bounding box of the image, which is much wider than the frame, so you can choose exactly what part of the image to show. Position the tool over the image; when it changes to a hand icon, hold the Shift key, click and hold the mouse button, then move the image to left until you find a pleasing area of the image to show (a client would probably tell you what part of an image to use). A ghosted preview of the entire image helps you decide what part of the image to show.

When you're satisfied, release the mouse button and the Shift key.

4. Draw a frame at the bottom of the beach image with the following specifications:

X: 45p4   W: 19p2

Y: 454 pt   H: 102 pt

5. Set the frame's fill to Paper.

6. Switch to the Type tool and type "Around The World Travel" into the frame.

7. Select all of this text and format it to ATC Mai Tai, Bold, 32 pt., Auto leading, centered. Control/Right-click the frame, choose Text Frame Options, and set the vertical justification to Center.

8. Switch to the Selection tool and select the frame. Choose Object>Feather, and set the Feather Width field to 0p9.

The second spread should look like this:

9. Check your document for bad hyphenation or for kerning in headlines that you think should be repaired; fix any such problems.

Check Spelling/Find and Replace

1. Go to the first spread and click the text cursor at the beginning of the text. Choose Edit>Check Spelling, and click the Start button in the Check Spelling dialog. The first errors flagged relate to the drop cap you created earlier, because you forced a line break between the "W" and the rest of the word. Ignore these possible capitalization errors.

   The first misspelled word is "Americian," but an appropriate replacement doesn't show up in the Suggested Corrections list. When this happens, you have to edit the word in the Change To field, then click the Change button. Delete the last "i" in the word, and click Change.

2. The next misspelled word is "Chilian," and the correct replacement appears in the Suggested Corrections list. Click "Chilean" then click Change.

3. The next word, "Zeland," is clearly wrong. Click "Zealand" in the Suggested Corrections list, then click Change All to make sure there aren't any other occurrences. The next word, "max," is flagged as a possible capitalization error, but it's OK as is. Click Ignore.

4. The next word found, "Celtophile," isn't necessarily misspelled, but it's not in the default InDesign dictionary. Assume the word is correct as submitted by the client, and click Ignore.

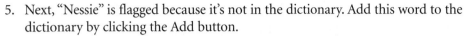

5. Next, "Nessie" is flagged because it's not in the dictionary. Add this word to the dictionary by clicking the Add button.

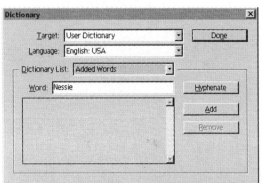

You don't want this word, a proper noun, to hyphenate, so just click the Add button, and then click Done.

6. The next two words, "Buckingham" and "geek," aren't found in the dictionary, so add them.

7. Change the next word, "cruiseline," to "cruise line."

8. The next word, "Williamsburg," is OK, but the one after it, "Fransisco," isn't. Choose the correct spelling from the list of suggestions then click Change. After this last change you should see a message stating that the spell check is complete. If you don't get this message, keep going with the spell check until it appears. If you stop or close the Check Spelling dialog in the middle of a spell check, you might not see the completion message after fixing "Fransisco."

9. Hidden on the back of the last page of the client's specifications is a sticky note directing that all em dashes be replaced with en dashes. While such a move isn't typographically correct, sometimes you have to do what the client wants even if it's not technically right. Better to do it than argue a point and lose an account. Press Command/Control-F and click the pop-up menu next to the Find What field. Choose Em Dash from the list of special characters, then press the Tab key to move the cursor to the Replace With field. Click the pop-up menu next to this field and choose En Dash. You could also enter a meta-character for each: for an em dash, type "^_" and for an en dash, type "^=".

10. Click the Change All button to perform the replacement. A completion dialog tells you how many replacements were made.

11. On the same hidden note (this sort of thing really happens, believe it or not) is an instruction to replace Max's name with her full name, Maxine. You could do this by hand, but using the Find/Change dialog to do the replacement ensures that you won't overlook any occurrences. Remember that the word "max" was also found during the spell check, so be sure to check the Case Sensitive check box in the Find/Change dialog. You should replace four occurrences of "Max."

12. Save and close the document.

Creating what looks like a simple brochure can be pretty demanding. Style sheets, however, can make a job much simpler. Using the techniques you have learned in the exercises and in this project will help you produce better-than-average publications.

While it's appropriate to bring spelling and grammatical errors to a client's attention, it is never appropriate to fix them without getting an approval from the client first, and it is probably not a good idea to argue with a customer over grammar and spelling. In this example, a customer could simply prefer en dashes rather than em dashes, so you should leave it at that and carry on.

Project D: Good Choices Newsletter

Many organizations produce newsletters to keep clients, customers, patients, and employees abreast of current events. Creating and producing newsletters is a very common design task that you'll probably be expected to do at some point in your career. Newsletters are generally informal, transient (meaning they're quickly read or thrown away), and produced with a minimum of inks on cheap paper stock. A newsletter rarely uses more than two inks, although there are exceptions; this example uses black and a Pantone spot ink.

For this project, you have been hired to take over the newsletter design for a local health organization. They want to maintain the same look and feel of their current newsletter, so they have provided you with a template from the previous designer.

Get Started

1. Open the InDesign template **newsletter_template.indt** from **RF_Intro_InDesign>Project_D**.

2. Because this is a template, when the document opens, "Untitled" will appear in the title bar. Save the file to your **Work_In_Progress** folder as "newsletter1.indd". The "1" in the file name refers to the fact that this is your first newsletter for this client. Alternatively, you could name it with the month, issue number, or a similar identifying code — what's important is using a consistent method for naming files so they are easy to locate.

Add Page Design Elements

1. Double-click Page 1 in the Pages palette. Four images will nestle into the checkerboard pattern on Page 1 and four different images on Page 2. Instead of sizing or cropping each image to fit the space, you'll first create a frame that fits within the guides, and then place the graphic into it; the frame will mask the edges of the graphic to ensure a perfect fit.

2. Zoom to the upper-left corner of Page 1. With the Rectangle Frame tool, drag a rectangle that snaps to the guides in the first white space down in the first column. Both stroke and fill should be None. With the upper-left proxy reference point active, the Transform palette should read:

X: -0p9	W: 5p3
Y: 0.75 in	H: 0.75 in

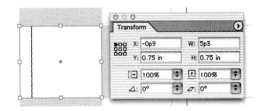

When positioning images for this newsletter, remember that 1/8" of the left edge will be trimmed off to create the bleed. The image should be positioned to the edge of the frame, but don't visually center it in the frame without considering the bleed cut off.

3. Place **cells.jpg** from the **RF_Intro_InDesign>Project_D** folder.

These images have a resolution of 225 ppi. The line screen for this document will be 133 lpi, giving the designer approximately 5–10% scaling flexibility.

Press Command/Control-; to show or hide guides. Press Command/Control-H to show or hide frame outlines.

4. Deselect the frame. Switch to the Direct Selection tool. Click the image and position it inside the frame as shown.

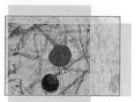

5. Deselect the cell's image and scroll down the page a few inches. Create a square frame in the third open space in the second column of blocks. (In other words, skip two rows of blocks.) Be sure to snap the frame to the guides. Place the image named **eye.tif** from the **RF_Intro_InDesign>Project_D** folder.

6. Deselect the frame. With the Direct Selection tool, select the image. In the Transform palette, reduce this image to 90% horizontally and vertically.

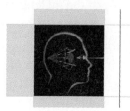

7. Deselect and switch back to the Selection tool. Select the cell's image (and frame) and Option/Alt-drag it to the first column white space that is approximately 5.25 in. down the page. With the frame still selected, place **veggies.jpg** from the **RF_Intro_InDesign>Project_D** folder. This image fits fine in the frame.

8. With the Selection tool, Option/Alt-copy the eye.tif image to the last white space in the second column. Place **moonlitjog.tif** from **RF_Intro_InDesign>Project_D**, replacing eye.tif. Do not scale this image, but move it straight up within the frame to show primarily the jogger and the sunrise.

9. Complete the images on Page 2 in the same manner and using the same pattern of white spaces. From top to bottom, place these images in order: **salad.tif** at 100%, **dna.tif** at 100%, **salmon.jpg** at 100%, and **brain.jpg** at 95%.

   Position the images to highlight each interesting, eye-catching section of the graphic. Your links palette should look like this when you've finished:

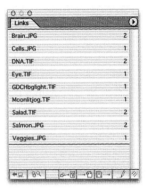

The graphic elements should look like this:

Picture placements for Page 1 (left) and Page 2 (right).

10. Save the file and continue.

Add a Masthead Gradient

1. Scroll to the upper-right corner of the first page. In the last column, create a 7p6 × 1.33-in. rectangular frame that extends from the top margin almost down to the top rule. Click the Fill icon in the toolbox.

2. The stroke and fill of this frame use a gradient. From the Swatches palette Options menu, choose New Gradient Swatch. Name this gradient "547 10-100/75". Choose Linear from the Type pop-up menu, and then click the left color stop. Choose Named Color from the Stop Color pop-up menu and select Pantone 547 U 10%.

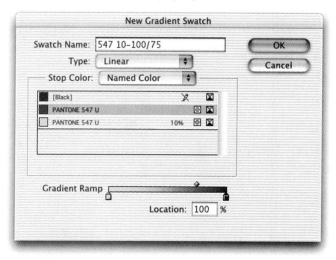

For the right color stop, select Pantone 547 U (100%). Drag the diamond to the 75% position and click OK.

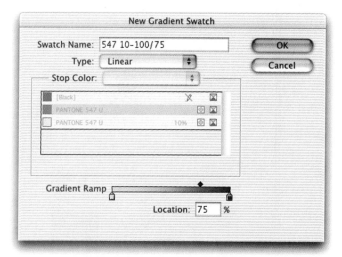

3. Because you already selected the frame and activated the Fill icon in the toolbox, the frame should fill with the new gradient. You're going to angle the gradient — select the Gradient tool and drag from the top right of the box to the lower left to direct the fill. Do not start or release very far from the frame boundary, because that would extend the lightest and darkest colors beyond the visible frame.

The Weight Changes Bounding Box option controls how an object's stroke spreads or doesn't as it gets thicker. With this option off, the stroke grows inward; with it on, the stroke expands outward and changes the size of the object's bounding box.

You may see a white background in placed EPS images on Windows computers. If this happens, right-click the image and set the Display Performance option to High Quality Display.

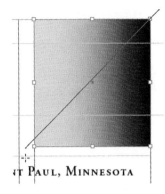

ıT PAUL, MINNESOTA

4. Switch to the Stroke icon and click the gradient swatch. Make certain the Weight Changes Bounding Box option is unchecked in the Stroke palette Options menu. Change the stroke weight to 4 pt. Select the Gradient tool and drag over the frame in the opposite direction, lower left to upper right.

ıT PAUL, MINNESOTA

Reversing the stroke gradient direction gives a three-dimensional appearance.

5. With the Selection tool, select the frame, place the image **yy.eps** from **RF_Intro_InDesign>Project_D** in the frame, and then deselect. Change to the Direct Selection tool and select the placed graphic. Drag the lower-right corner of the graphic to the lower-right corner of the frame to scale it; you can't use Object>Fitting>Fit Content to Frame because the thick stroke would cover up the edges of the graphic, so resize the graphic as shown.

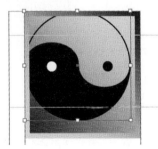

6. Control/Right-click the graphic, and choose Object>Fitting>Center Content.

7. Save the file and leave it open.

Format the First Article

1. The first page has two rules on it that are intended to frame the lead story. The first story fits in the first three columns in the top section defined by the rules.

Guides hidden for clarity.

Create a rectangular frame that fits inside that section and spans from the left margin guide to the right edge of the third column. Size the frame as X = 10p0, W = 24p6, Y = 2.25 in., H = 4.25 in. using the upper-left proxy reference point in the Transform palette.

2. Place **exercise.txt** from **RF_Intro_InDesign>Project_D** into this frame. Ignore the missing fonts warning, if one appears. Select all of the text and apply the 4-Column Body style.

3. Text flows across the entire frame, so you need to make columns to match the base template grid. Choose Object>Text Frame Options or press Command/Control-B. Enter "3" for the number of columns, and click OK.

4. Unfortunately a three-column format doesn't allow headlines to cross columns. Reduce the height of the three-column frame so it is at Y = 2.75 in., with a height of 3.75 in. Drag a new text frame above it that spans the three columns, then cut the title of the article, "A New Look at Exercise", and paste it into the new frame. Apply the Article Head style. This new frame's position and dimensions should be: X = 10p0, Y = 2.35 in., W = 24p6, H = 0.3 in.

5. Before applying further styling, you need to clean up each article by checking the spelling and replacing certain characters. First, delete the extra paragraph return at the very beginning of the story (turn on Show Hidden Characters to make this easier to see).

   With the Selection tool, click the text overflow symbol (the box with the red "X").

   With the loaded text icon, draw a text frame on the pasteboard. The text will flow into the frame, so all text in the article will be visible during cleanup.

6. You need to change every occurrence of the "%" symbol to the word "percent" with a space in front of it. With the Type tool selected, place the cursor at the beginning of the article (not the headline) and choose Edit>Find/Change.

   In the Find/Change dialog box enter "%" in the Find What field and "[space]percent" in the Change To field. (Don't type the word "space", just press the Spacebar.)

   Select Story in the Search pop-up menu.

   Click Find Next to locate the first "%". When it's highlighted, click Change All to replace every occurrence of "%" with " percent". At the message telling how many replacements were made, click OK.

7. This story contains two returns at the end of every paragraph, which is messy. The extra paragraph returns must be removed, but not every "¶" because that would run all the paragraphs together. If hidden characters are not already visible, select Type>Show Hidden Characters to reveal the paragraph returns.

   In the Find/Change dialog box, type "^p" in the Find What field to locate all paragraph returns. You only want to find instances of two returns together, though, so type another "^p" in the Find What field.

In the Change To field type "^p" to replace two paragraph returns (¶¶) with one paragraph return (¶). You could also use the pop-up menu next to the Change To field to select an End of Paragraph symbol if you forgot the "^p" meta-character.

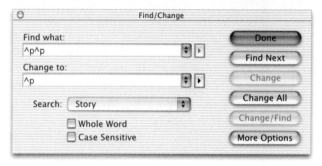

Click Find Next. When the cursor highlights the first pair of paragraph returns, click Change All. Click OK in the completion dialog, then click Done.

8. Select the last five lines of the article (one or more lines may still be flowed into the box on the pasteboard) and change the text formatting to 8-pt. ATC Flamingo, Bold, with 10-pt. leading.

9. Change the paragraph formatting to a left indent of 0p4, first-line indent of –0p4, with 0p2 space above each line. (InDesign converts these measurements to inches for you.)

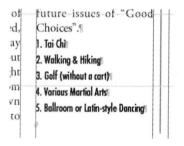

10. With these items still selected, choose New Style from the Styles palette Options menu. In the Style Options window, name the new style "Lists". Notice that the formatting you manually entered is copied to the new style sheet, but that the selected text shows as "4-Column Body+" in the Paragraph Styles palette. Click Lists in the Paragraph Styles palette to assign the new style to the selected text, and then click OK.

By now all of the text should have flowed back into the frame on the page, so you can delete the frame you made on the pasteboard.

The first page, so far:

A New Look at Exercise

In a poll taken over our web site we found out 98 percent of you "exercise regularly" but only 20 percent of you include aerobic activity twice a week or more. Over 40 percent of you rarely jog or participant in aerobics classes. So we asked 125 of you at an internet town meeting, "Why not?" and "What do you do?"

The responses to "Why not?" ranged from "it's boring" and "it's too expensive" to "my doctor recommends other forms of exercise for [my condition]". In fact, many of you discovered some qualified negatives to excessive aerobic exercise that make justified your claims. These are posted on the "Exercise" discussion at our site www.CPHR.org, but one quote deems publication here.

"Aerobic activity is important, but should not be used exclusively. Other forms of exercise, such as stretching, moderate strength building, muscle concentration, and mind and spirit enhancing exercises, should be part of a well balanced, active life." Dr. Hartlett, President of the Vienna School of Medicine. She continued, "strenuous exercise may prevent heart disease, but it can't guarantee weight loss or protect you from 70 percent of known cancers. It has proven to be a destabilizing force in behavioral disorders, as well. The best way to be healthy is to involve all aspects of your body and lifestyle."

Many of you sought and found alternative combinations of exercise that satisfy both your physical heart and your spiritual heart.

Five of the most popular activities are listed below. Special articles on each will be include in future issues of "Good Choices".

1. Tai Chi
2. Walking & Hiking
3. Golf (without a cart)
4. Various Martial Arts
5. Ballroom or Latin-style Dancing

11. Save the document.

Add More Text

1. Shift your view of the page to the right column. Select the Rectangle Frame tool and create a frame in the one-column space at the right of the page. Size it as X = 35p6, W = 7p6, Y = 2.35 in., H = 4.15 in.

2. Select the frame with the Selection tool. Check to see that its stroke and fill colors are set to None, and then choose Object>Content>Text.

3. Place the text file **multivariable.txt** from **RF_Intro_InDesign>Project_D** into the frame.

4. Select all of the text and apply the 4-Column Body style.

5. Select the headline "One just isn't Enough" and apply the Article Head style.

6. There isn't enough space between the headline and the body, and there's too much space at the bottom of the story.

One just isn't Enough

Researchers question why the same foods and activities do not uniformly produce similar results in people. A few studies provide a clue that makes statisticians "none too happy": Multivariable testing.

This method, being perfected by engineers at MIT, is now being applied to medical studies tracking more than one variable in the course of studying obesity, birth defects, fatigue syndrome. "This has never been done before, so finding data is difficult, but we think it will lead to solutions that have eluded medical science."

7. Double-click the style Article Head in the Paragraph Styles palette. Reset the leading to 26 pt., and the Space After to 0.125 in., then click OK. This opens up the spacing of the headline and adds some space below it.

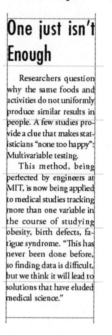

8. This article is complete. Save the file and continue.

Work with Threaded Text

1. Shift your view of the page so the four-column space remaining to fill is at the bottom of the screen. Instead of four narrow columns, you will build two text frames, each two columns wide, and thread the article text through them and to the second page. Drag a text frame with the Type tool starting at the horizontal 6.75-in. guide and spanning the left two columns. The Transform palette should read X = 10p0, W = 16p0, Y = 6.75 in., H = 1.8333 in.

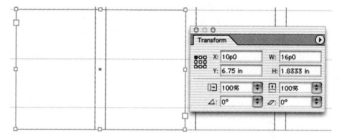

2. Place the text file **attitude_check-up.txt** from **RF_Intro_InDesign>Project_D** into this frame. Click the red overset text symbol at the right of the box with the Selection tool. Click with the loaded cursor and drag a two-column frame to the right, using the guides to match the height of the first column.

```
Attitude check-up¶
Thoughts are the blood stream
of the mind. That's the claim Dr.
Gunther Ancara pronounces in his
thesis, "Pump Up your Mind". Dr.
Ancara, Professor psycho-theism
at Yucatan University, has spent
25 1/2 years studying the medical
progression of two tribes: one, a
```
```
native culture in the mountains
of Brazil, the other, a small
neighborhood in Munich, Germany.
In an interview about his paper,
published by the American journal
of Psycho-health, Dr. Ancara stated,
"I set out to help others [in the
peace-corp] and ended up helping
myself." ¶
```

3. To thread the text file to the second page, click the plus symbol in this second frame and navigate to Page 2.

4. On Page 2, locate the guide that is 6 in. down the page. With the loaded cursor, click where that guide intersects the left side of the third text column and drag a one-column frame to the bottom page margin.

5. Thread that frame to the fourth and last frame. This frame should be the same height as the last, occupying the lower portion of the fourth column on Page 2.

```
Dr. Ancara
became
personally
enthralled with
the clinical
study when he
realized that the
thread which
resurfaced in
his study of
the two "tribes"
was how their
individual and
```
```
group attitudes
correlated to
overall health.
"More than
environment
or physical
conditions,"
he concluded,
"healthy, happy
members of
each tribe
practiced
hopeful, mature
```

6. Return to Page 1. Select the heading "Attitude check-up" and apply the Article Head style. Select all of the story text and apply the 2-Column Body Style.

7. Find the phrase "…has spent 25 1/2 years…" in the first paragraph. Select the characters "1/2" and apply the OpenType Fractions format command from the Character palette Options menu, and then delete the space between "25" and "1/2".

:ara, Professor psych

spent 25½ years stuc

vo tribes: one, a nati

8. Create a new character style from this selection and name it "OT Fraction".

9. These two columns don't align very well, because the spacing applied to the headline throws off the column balance and the 2-Column Body style has a Keep option applied to it.

Attitude check-up

Thoughts are the blood stream of the mind. That's the claim Dr. Gunther Ancara pronounces in his thesis, "Pump Up your Mind". Dr. Ancara, Professor psychotheism at Yucatan University, has spent 25½ years studying the medical progression of two tribes: one, a native culture in the mountains of Brazil, the other, a small neighborhood in Munich, Germany. In an interview about his paper, published by the American journal of Psycho-health, Dr. Ancara stated, "I set out to help others [in the peace-corp] and ended up helping myself."

Dr. Ancara became personally enthralled with the clinical study when he realized that the thread which resurfaced in his study of the two "tribes" was how their individual and group attitudes correlated to overall health. "More than environment or physical conditions," he concluded, "healthy, happy members of each tribe practiced hopeful, mature attitudes."

"Pump Up your Mind" studies the effects of anger and outbursts on progressive atherosclerosis, high cholesterol, and coronary heart disease. Hostility seems to release

To fix this, you can do one of several things: eliminate or reduce the space below the headline, align the text to the document baseline grid, or turn off the Keep With Next options in the style options. Eliminating the space below the headline is the easiest fix, but the line alignment between the columns is still off. Define the space after the headline to be 0 in.

Attitude check-up

Thoughts are the blood stream of the mind. That's the claim Dr. Gunther Ancara pronounces in his thesis, "Pump Up your Mind". Dr. Ancara, Professor psychotheism at Yucatan University, has spent 25½ years studying the medical progression of two tribes: one, a native culture in the mountains of Brazil, the other, a small neighborhood in Munich, Germany. In an interview about his paper, published by the American journal of Psycho-health, Dr. Ancara stated, "I set out to help others [in the peace-corp] and ended up helping myself."

Dr. Ancara became personally enthralled with the clinical study when he realized that the thread which resurfaced in his study of the two "tribes" was how their individual and group attitudes correlated to overall health. "More than environment or physical conditions," he concluded, "healthy, happy members of each tribe practiced hopeful, mature attitudes."

"Pump Up your Mind" studies the effects of anger and outbursts on progressive atherosclerosis, high cholesterol, and coronary heart disease. Hostility seems to release stress hormones into the blood which alleviates low-density cholesterol levels (LDL) regardless of diet. This

You could set the baseline grid to 11 pt. in the InDesign preferences, which is the leading value used in both of the body styles, then set the 2-Column Body style to align to the baseline grid, but this moves the bottom two lines of the first paragraph to the second column because of the Keep option defined in the style. Turning off the Keep option leaves a widow at the top of the second column, which you definitely don't want. So it looks like your only option is to make the columns a bit taller, move both of them (plus the rule above them) up slightly, and then apply a baseline alignment.

Using the Selection tool, move the rule up to Y = 6.5711 in., and then grab the top handle of each column frame and move them up to Y = 6.6806 in. The final height of the two frames should be 1.9028 in.

10. Press Command/Control-K and click Grids. In the Baseline Grid area, set the Increment Every value to 11 pt. (or 0.1528 in.), and then click OK.

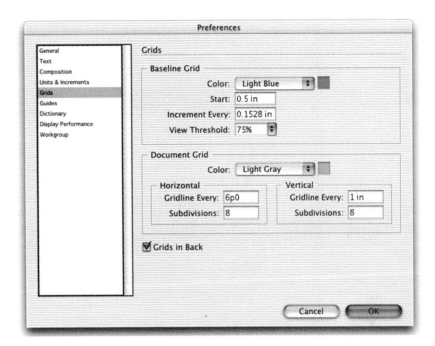

11. Double-click the 2-Column Body style and, in the Indents and Spacing pane, check the Align to Baseline Grid box. Check the Preview box to see how this will look. Click OK, and look at the area in question. The entire first paragraph should remain in the left column, and the lines in the columns should fall on the same baseline.

Attitude check-up

Thoughts are the blood stream of the mind. That's the claim Dr. Gunther Ancara pronounces in his thesis, "Pump Up your Mind". Dr. Ancara, Professor psycho-theism at Yucatan University, has spent 25½ years studying the medical progression of two tribes: one, a native culture in the mountains of Brazil, the other, a small neighborhood in Munich, Germany. In an interview about his paper, published by the American journal of Psycho-health, Dr. Ancara stated, "I set out to help others [in the peace-corp] and ended up helping myself."

Dr. Ancara became personally enthralled with the clinical study when he realized that the thread which resurfaced in his study of the two "tribes" was how their individual and group attitudes correlated to overall health. "More than environment or physical conditions," he concluded, "healthy, happy members of each tribe practiced hopeful, mature attitudes."

"Pump Up your Mind" studies the effects of anger and outbursts on progressive atherosclerosis, high cholesterol, and coronary heart disease. Hostility seems to release stress hormones into the blood which alleviates low-

12. Save the file and leave it open.

Create a Jump Line

1. You need to create a jump line — a line reading "continued on page 2" — to tell the reader where the story continues. Draw a small text frame under the right-hand "Attitude check-up" frame on the first page. The top of this frame should touch the bottom of the main text frame.

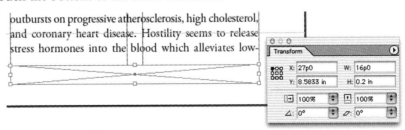

Choose No Paragraph Style before typing anything if you don't want the last style's attributes applied to the text.

Jump line frames must touch or overlap the frames they refer to. If you move the jump line frame away from the reference frame, the Next Page number changes to the current page.

2. Choose the Type tool, choose No Paragraph Style in the Style palette, and type "continued on page" (note the space after "page"). Control/Right-click the frame and choose Insert Special Character>Next Page to insert the page number where the story continues. Format this text as ATC Mai Tai, Italic, 8/10, right justified. Press Command/Control-B and set the vertical justification to Bottom. As long as the jump line frame is touching the referenced story frame, the page number is automatically updated, even if you move the next continued frame to another page.

"Pump Up your Mind" studies the effects of anger and outbursts on progressive atherosclerosis, high cholesterol, and coronary heart disease. Hostility seems to release stress hormones into the blood which alleviates low-

continued on page 2

This finishes the first page, which should look like this:

3. Save the file and continue.

Add Text and Build a Table

1. Shift your page view to see the top of Page 2. Choose the Rectangle Frame tool and draw a frame from the top-left margin guide across all four columns to the sixth guide down from the top (4 in.). Make sure that its stroke and fill are set to None.

2. Choose Object>Content>Text to convert it to a text frame.

3. Click in the frame with the Type tool and place **eastern_diet.txt** from **RF_Intro_InDesign>Project_D**.

4. Select all of the text in this frame and assign the 2-Column Body style.

5. You need to modify this frame so the text fits more logically. Resize the text frame to fit in the first two columns only, and lower the top edge to the first horizontal guide.

6. Create a second text frame in the other two columns, from the top guide down to the sixth guide.

7. Click the plus symbol at the bottom of the left frame with the Selection tool, then click in the right frame to thread text to it.

8. Now create the headline for the article. Delete the first line of the copy, "Eastern diet", and the return character below it. Drag a new text frame across all four columns between the margin guide and the top horizontal guide, and then type, "Is an Eastern diet infusion for you?"

9. Assign the Article Head style to this headline, then set the text to left justify.

10. Click the text cursor at the beginning of the line "Prep. Benefits" and type the word "Food". Position the cursor at the beginning of the line, and then press the Enter key on the numeric keypad to force the rest of the story to the next column.

11. Select all of the text in the right column and click the Don't Align to Baseline icon in the Paragraph palette. You need to do this because baseline alignment doesn't work very well in a table.

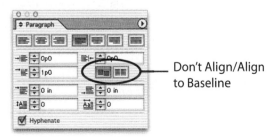

Don't Align/Align to Baseline

Now choose Table>Convert Text to Table. This makes a messy table, but you'll fix that. Note that the right-hand column is now overset. Your changes to the table will fix that problem.

12. Select the entire table by clicking at the top-left corner of the table with the Type tool (the cursor changes to a diagonal arrow pointing down and to the right).

Food	Prep.	Benefits
Artichokes	ST, RT	potassium, magnesium, copper, iron, A, C, iodine, fiber
Fennel, peppers	RT, R	potassium, A, C
Sweet potatoes	ST, BK	potassium, iron, A, C, fiber
Portobello Mushrooms	ST, RT	B, germanium, potassium, phosphorus, niacin, Oxygen
Spinach	ST, SD	Calcium, silicon, C, A, iron

13. Change the type to ATC Flamingo, Light. Leave the rest of the Character palette settings alone. Change to the Paragraph palette, set the First Line Indent to 0p0, and set the text to left instead of full justification.

14. Resize the first column of the table by dragging the column's right edge toward the left until the word "peppers" in the "fennel, peppers" cell breaks to two lines. Drag back to the right slightly and stop when the word "peppers" hops back into place.

| Fennel, peppers | RT, R | | | potassium, A, |

| Fennel, peppers | RT, R | | | potassium, |
| Sweet potatoes | ST, BK | | | potassium, |

15. Resize the second column and make it narrower. The bulk of the copy is in the third column, so you need to make as much room as you can for that one, but don't let the contents of the "Prep." column wrap.

| Portobello | | | |
| Mushrooms | ST, RT | B, germanium, potas- |

16. Resize the right edge of the third column by dragging it to the edge of the containing frame.

| Mushrooms | ST, RT | B, germanium, potassium, phosphorus, niacin, Oxygen |

17. Note that the word "Portobello" is alone in its row, and really belongs with the word "mushrooms" below it. Select "Portobello," cut it, then paste it into the cell below in front of the word "mushrooms." Type a space between the two words to separate them.

| Portobello Mushrooms | ST, RT | B, germanium, potassium, phosphorus, niacin, Oxygen |

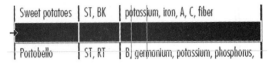

18. There are two empty rows in the table now: one where the word "Portobello" used to be, and another at the now-visible bottom of the table. Select each empty row and press Command/Control-Delete (or choose Table>Delete>Row) to remove it.

Sweet potatoes	ST, BK	potassium, iron, A, C, fiber
Portobello	ST, RT	B, germanium, potassium, phosphorus,

19. Select the first row (with the words Food, Prep., and Benefits) and change the type to ATC Flamingo, Bold.

The top of the page should now look like this:

Is an Eastern diet infusion for you?

Americans have the highest and best of everything, including levels of cholesterol, fat, sodium, and preservatives. We may be excellent at putting out, but we are terrible at putting in . . . to our bodies.
Years of demanding "fries with that" have put Ameri-

Food	Prep.	Benefits
Artichokes	ST, RT	potassium, magnesium, copper, iron, A, C, iodine, fiber
Fennel, peppers	RT, R	potassium, A, C

When text is aligned with the baseline, it doesn't move, even if its containing frame is moved vertically, until the frame is moved at least the distance specified in the Baseline Grid Increment preference — then it jumps to the next baseline.

20. The text at the left starts on the first baseline grid line, but the table doesn't, so it nudges up against the top of the frame. Select both frames with the Selection tool and press the Down Arrow key until the top of the table visually aligns with the top of the text. The text doesn't move, but the table does. If you press the Down Arrow key too many times, the text in the left frame jumps down an entire line.

Is an Eastern diet infusion for you?

Americans have the highest and best of everything, including levels of cholesterol, fat, sodium, and preservatives. We may be excellent at putting out, but we are terrible at putting in . . . to our bodies.
Years of demanding "fries with that" have put Ameri-

Food	Prep.	Benefits
Artichokes	ST, RT	potassium, magnesium, copper, iron, A, C, iodine, fiber
Fennel, peppers	RT, R	potassium, A, C

21. The lines in the table are a little distracting. Select the table and choose Table>Cell Options>Strokes and Fills. Change the stroke weight to zero, and click OK.

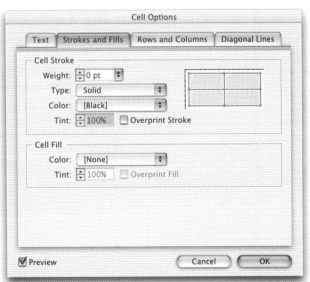

The lines are now gone, but it's a good idea to leave them on while you're formatting a table because they make it easier to see what you're doing.

	Prep.	Benefits
Artichokes	ST, RT	potassium, magnesium, copper, iron, A, C, iodine, fiber
Fennel, peppers	RT, R	potassium, A, C
Sweet potatoes	ST, BK	potassium, iron, A, C, fiber
Portobello Mushrooms	ST, RT	B, germanium, potassium, phosphorus, niacin. Oxygen
Spinach	ST, SD	Calcium, silicon, C, A, iron
Saltwater fish	RT, BK	phosphorus, omega 3 fatty acids. Lungs, lowers LDL, raises HDL
Rice, Pasta	ST	iron, phosphorus, NA2, complex carbohydrates. Sustained energy
Cardamom	BV, SP	digestion, general stimulant
Peppermint	BV, SP	stimulate central nervous system

22. Save the file and leave it open.

Add a Table Legend

Sometimes assigning No Paragraph Style can cause text to assume unpredictable attributes, such as size. If the text changes to a large size, select all of it and make it 12 pt.

1. Select the Rectangle Frame tool. Draw a frame under the table snapping to the horizontal guides and extending across the two columns.

2. Apply a 2-pt. dotted stroke, colored Pantone 547 U, to the frame.

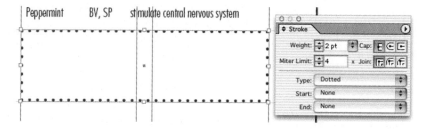

3. Place **legend.txt** from **RF_Intro_InDesign>Project_D**.

4. Using the Type tool, select all of the text in the frame and assign No Paragraph Style from the Paragraph Styles palette. Change the first-line indent field in the Paragraph palette to 0p0.

5. Choose Type>Tabs and set centered tabs at 3p1, 8p4, and 13p3. There are only two typed tabs in the story, so place a tab at the beginning of the first two lines to center the first elements, and type two tabs to center the single element on the third line.

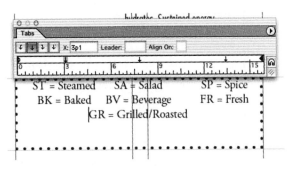

6. Select all of the text and apply ATC Mai Tai, Normal, 9/14. Press Command/Control-B and set the vertical justification to Centered.

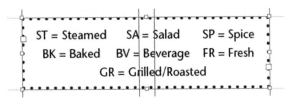

7. Save the file and continue.

Copyfit a Story

1. Now that you've added a legend, the story that goes with the table of foods should be the same height as the table. You have about a half-inch of space to fill.

   Select the four paragraphs in the left-hand column and examine the type specifications. The text is set at 9 pt., but you can make it a little bigger to fill the space, or you can open up the leading a little to do the same thing. It's probably better to adjust leading than type size so there's some visual uniformity. But to adjust leading, you need to turn off baseline alignment, so do that now in the Paragraph palette.

2. Set the leading of these paragraphs to 12 pt. It's still not enough, so try 13 pt. This is better, but not perfect. Instead, press Command/Control-B and set the Vertical Justification, Align pop-up menu to Justify. This fills the height of the text frame and overrides any leading values. Adjust the bottom handle of the frame with the Selection tool to align the text with the table and the legend, if necessary.

Never alter copy that you didn't write without first obtaining permission. It's OK to point out spelling errors (and to fix them once you obtain approval), but it's inappropriate to edit someone else's work unless it's an explicit part of your job.

Is an Eastern diet infusion for you?

Americans have the highest and best of everything, including levels of cholesterol, fat, sodium, and preservatives. We may be excellent at putting out, but we are terrible at putting in . . . to our bodies.

Years of demanding "fries with that" have put Americans over the top in obesity, heart disease, and hypertension. Starting to include ingredients and dishes from Eastern cultures may reverse all that.

The Journal of Heart Research reports that individuals who regularly ate foods similar to the native Mediterranean diet were 50 to 70 percent less likely to suffer second heart attacks than those who continued eating "meat & potatoes". How much and when they eat has also proven to be beneficial. Small, frequent meals maintain blood sugar levels, prevent over eating and unnecessary fat accumulation in the cells.

A completely new meal plan is not necessary to gain the benefits. Adding side dishes or including ingredients in your regular diet will help you feel better. Here are examples:

Food	Prep.	Benefits
Artichokes	ST, RT	potassium, magnesium, copper, iron, A, C, iodine, fiber
Fennel, peppers	RT, R	potassium, A, C
Sweet potatoes	ST, BK	potassium, iron, A, C, fiber
Portobello Mushrooms	ST, RT	B, germanium, potassium, phosphorus, niacin. Oxygen
Spinach	ST, SD	Calcium, silicon, C, A, iron
Saltwater fish	RT, BK	phosphorus, omega 3 fatty acids. Lungs, lowers LDL, raises HDL
Rice, Pasta	ST	iron, phosphorus, NA2, complex carbohydrates. Sustained energy
Cardamom	BV, SP	digestion, general stimulant
Peppermint	BV, SP	stimulate central nervous system

ST = Steamed   SA = Salad   SP = Spice
BK = Baked   BV = Beverage   FR = Fresh
GR = Grilled/Roasted

3. Save the file and continue.

Add the Last Story

1. Place **eat_together.doc** from **RF_Intro_InDesign>Project_D**.

   Click with the loaded text cursor in the first column at Y = 5.25 in. This creates a frame that continues to the bottom margin.

2. Select all of the text and apply the 4-Column Body style.

3. Using the Type tool, delete the first line of the text body ("Eat together") and the blank line below it.

4. Click the overset text icon at the bottom of the frame and place the remaining text in the second column.

5. Select both text frames; use the Transform palette to move them so the top edges are at Y = 5.0 in. Set the height of each frame to 3.5 in. Adjust the left-hand frame height manually with the handle, from the bottom, until the text in both columns is even. The frames may not have equal heights, but the text will be even.

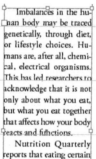

6. Make a new text frame with the Type tool that spans the two columns and type "What to Eat Together". Apply the Article Head style to this text.

The baseline grid should always be set to the leading value of the type that you want to align to it. If type is aligned with the baseline, and the leading of the type is changed, the type will have unsightly gaps between lines.

What to Eat Together

Imbalances in the human body may be traced genetically, through diet, or lifestyle choices. Humans are, after all, chemical, electrical organisms. This has led researchers to acknowledge that it is not only about what you eat, but what you eat together that affects how your body reacts and functions.

Nutrition Quarterly reports that eating certain foods together and avoiding other combinations will provide the greatest benefit to your health as well as your mental and physical performance.

This development is based on two related factors. Combining certain vitamin and mineral supplements boost the effectiveness of each other. In conjunction, the digestive system uses different chemistry to process different foods and some acids counteract another fluid's ability to break down and use food energy.

Foods that require different chemistry should be eaten separately otherwise parts will rot in your stomach and be flushed without benefit. Fruit is the best example requiring a unique processing acid. It should not be eaten within one half hour of eating meat, vegetables, or grains.

In the Transform palette, select the top-left proxy reference point. Position the headline block at Y = 4.644 in.

7. Deselect the headline frame and switch to the Pen tool. Click the Stroke icon in the toolbox. Choose Pantone 547 U in the Swatches palette, and 1 pt. in the Stroke palette. Click once to the right of the word "Together" in the headline, visually centering the click vertically. Hold Shift and click once more between the second and third columns. Hold Shift again and make the last click at the lower margin of the page.

What to Eat Together

Imbalances in the human body may be traced genetically, through diet, or lifestyle choices. Humans are, after all, chemical, electrical organisms. This has led researchers to acknowledge that it is not only about what you eat, but what you eat together that affects how your body reacts and functions.

Nutrition Quarterly reports that eating certain foods together and avoiding other combinations will provide the greatest benefit to your health as well as your mental and physical performance.

This development is based on two related factors. Combining certain vitamin and mineral supplements boost the effectiveness of each other. In conjunction, the digestive system uses different chemistry to process different foods and some acids counteract another fluid's ability to break down and use food energy.

Foods that require different chemistry should be eaten separately otherwise parts will rot in your stomach and be flushed without benefit. Fruit is the best example requiring a unique processing acid. It should not be eaten within one half hour of eating meat, vegetables, or grains.

8. Save the file and continue.

Finish the Layout

1. The last thing to do is place a recipe in the area between the table legend and the continuation of the story from the first page. Place **spcsalad.txt** and drag a text frame across the two column guides. The text is overset, but that's OK for now.

2. Choose the Selection tool, select both columns of the continued story, and set their height to 2 in. Move both so the bottom edges are on the bottom margin of the page.

3. Zoom in a bit on the continued story. Remember the jump line you made earlier? You're going to make another one, only this one will indicate that the story is continued from the prior page. Draw a text frame above the beginning of the continued story, the width of one column, at X = 27p0 and Y = 6.44 in. with a height of 0.1945 in. This should overlap the frame containing the continued story.

4. Type "continued from page " (note the space after the word "page"). Control/Right-click and choose Insert Special Character>Previous Page Number to insert the prior page number into the jump line. Set this line to ATC Mai Tai, Italic, 8/11, right justified, with no indents.

> *continued from page 1*
>
> density cholesterol levels (LDL) regardless of diet. This type of cholesterol results in blocked arteries. The other study showed that angry feelings seemed to produce a thickening of the carotid arteries.
>
> Dr Ancara's thesis also reviews ancient literature tying various maladies found in human organs
>
> to specific emotional tendencies. "Holding on to these emotions gradually drains the bodies ability to heal itself and eventually eats aware the related organs or prevents certain chemicals and hormones from being produced that are essential to life." His conclusion, "Think healthy thoughts."

5. Resize the frame containing the recipe so it fills the space between the legend and the continuation line that you just set. This frame should be about 1.8 in. high. Click the Fill icon in the toolbox and give the frame a fill of Pantone 547 U 10%. Press Command/Control-B and give the frame a text inset of 0p3.

6. Select all of the recipe text and apply No Paragraph Style. However, the text has probably picked up the last style used, so you'll need to reset the following:

   Font: ATC Flamingo, Bold, 7/9

   Left justified

   Indents: 1p0, left and right; no first-line indent

   Baseline Alignment: off

   Keep Options: off

7. Select the title of the recipe and set it to 12 pt., but leave the leading as is.

8. The continuation line looks more like it's part of the recipe. As an easy fix, select the frame containing the continuation line, set its vertical justification to Bottom, and then press the Up Arrow key once or twice.

9. A last touch would be a rule under the table heading. Draw a 1-pt. Pantone 547 U rule under the table heading that spans the two columns.

The finished second page should look like this:

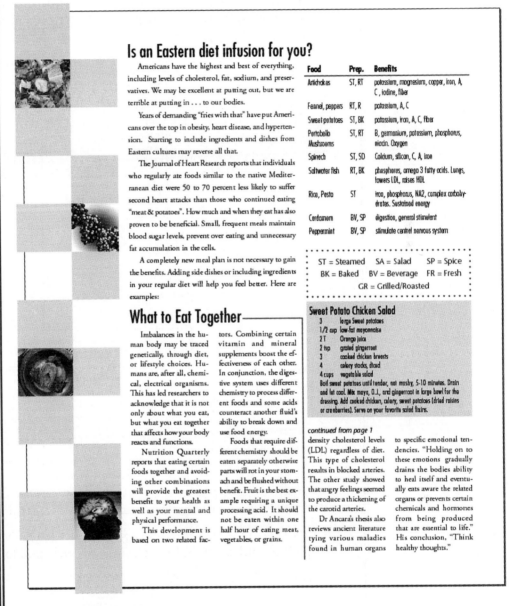

10. Save the file, and leave it open.

Print the Newsletter

1. Print some proofs for your files using the material you learned in Chapter 11. Check the Links palette to make sure all the placed images are linked correctly. Unlink all text files; you've made changes to them in InDesign, so there's no point in maintaining links to the uncorrected originals.

2. Choose File>Print and set up the options. This document should fit on a letter-size sheet even with printer's marks turned on in the Marks & Bleeds Section. Remember to set 1/8 in. of bleed all around.

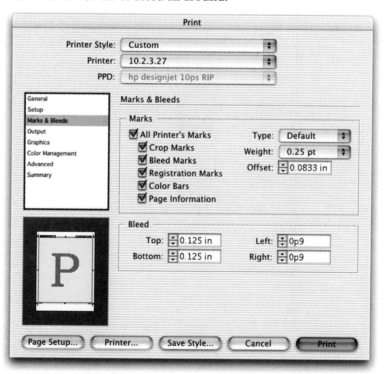

Package the Document

1. Assume the client loves the newsletter (although most clients make changes up to the last possible moment) and it's ready to send to a printer or service provider. Choose File>Package to prepare the job for hand-off. Remember to include all of the fonts, images, and links. Refer to Chapter 11, *Printing and Packaging*, for general information.

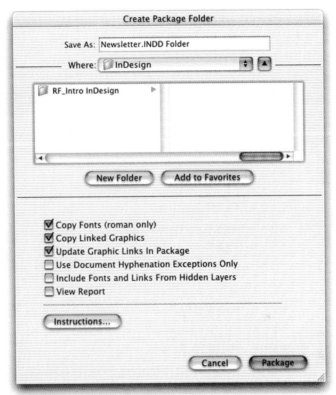

2. Save and close the file. You're done!

NOTES

Acrobat

Acrobat, from Adobe Systems, is an application supporting viewing, editing, printing, and annotation of PDF documents, which retains the page layout, graphics, color, and typography of an original document created in another application. It is widely used for distributing documents online because it is independent of hardware, software, and operating systems. The Acrobat Reader application is available for free from the Adobe Systems Web site (www.adobe.com) and offers a subset of the full Acrobat product's features.

Adobe Paragraph Composer

The text composition engine present in Adobe InDesign. Loosely based on Donald Knuth's TeX composition algorithms, this is the only desktop product that can perform text composition on multiple lines of text at a time, which produces excellent composition and color without unnecessary word breaks, excess white space, and rough justification. Most composition algorithms only consider one line of text at a time and cannot produce high-quality type composition without significant user intervention.

Adobe Systems, Inc.

This software developer invented the PostScript page description language (see *PostScript*) used in almost all graphic-arts environments. PostScript resides in a printer or Raster Image Processor (see *Raster Image Processor*) and is used to convert graphics from the screen to high-resolution output. Adobe also develops the popular InDesign, Photoshop, Illustrator, GoLive, and Premiere products along with a range of others.

Anti-aliasing

A feature that eliminates or softens the jaggedness of curved edges of raster objects or raster displays by introducing intermediate levels of gray or color between the light and dark edge.

Archiving

The process of storing data in a secure and safe manner. Archiving differs from backup in that it's meant to be used to restore entire systems or networks, rather than providing quick and easy access to specific files or folders. Archived data, recorded on tape or optical media, is typically stored offsite to prevent total data loss in case of a catastrophic event. See *Back Up*.

Artifact

A blemish or dust spot on a piece of film; unsightly pixels in a digital image; evidence of excessive compression that manifests as blotchy, rough areas in digital images.

Ascender

Part of a lowercase letter that exceeds the height of the letter "x." The letters b, d, f, h, k, l, and t have ascenders.

ASCII

Acronym for American Standard Code for Information Interchange, which defines each character, symbol, or special code as a number from 0 to 255 (8 bits in binary). An ASCII text file can be read by any computer.

ATM (Adobe Type Manager)

A system utility that smoothes the appearance of PostScript Type 1 fonts on screen at any point size. The Deluxe version can manage font libraries.

Back Up

The process of making copies of current work or work in progress as a safety measure against file corruption, drive or system failure, or accidental deletion. Backing up work in progress differs from creating an archive (see *Archiving*) for long-term storage or system restoration.

Baseline

The implied reference line on which the bases of capital letters sit.

Bézier Curves

Curves that are defined mathematically (vectors), in contrast to those drawn as a collection of dots or pixels (raster). Bézier curves and other vector elements can be enlarged or reduced without any apparent distortion or pixelization.

Bindery Marks

Marks that appear on a press sheet to indicate how the sheet should be trimmed, folded, collated, or bound.

Binding

In general, the various methods used to secure signatures or leaves in a book. Examples include *saddle-stitching* (the use of staples in a folded spine), *perfect-bound* (multiple sets of folded pages sewn or glued into a flat spine), or *case-bound* (sets of folded pages glued or sewn together, then taped into a book case; also called "hardcover").

Bit (Binary Digit)

A computer's smallest unit of information. Bits can have only two values: 0 or 1. This can represent the black-and-white (1-bit) pixel values in a line-art image. Or in combination with other bits, it can represent 16 tones or colors (4-bit), 256 colors (8-bit), 16.8 million colors (24-bit), or a billion colors (30-bit). These numbers derive from counting all of the possible combinations (permutations) of 0 or 1 settings of each bit: $2^4 = 2 \times 2 \times 2 \times 2 = 16$ colors; $2^8 = 2 \times 2 \times 2 \times 2 \times 2 \times 2 \times 2 \times 2 = 256$ colors; etc.

Bitmap

An image constructed from individual dots or pixels set to a grid-like mosaic. Each pixel can be represented by more than one bit. A 1-bit image is black and white because each bit can have only two values (for example, 0 for white and 1 for black). For 256 colors, each pixel needs eight bits (2^8). A 24-bit image refers to an image with 24 bits per pixel (2^{24}), so it may contain as many as 16,777,216 colors. Because the file must contain information about the color and position of each pixel, the disk space needed for bitmap images is usually quite significant. Most digital photographs and scanned images are bitmap images.

Black

The absence of color; an ink that absorbs all wavelengths of light.

Bleed

Page data that extends beyond the trim marks on a page. Illustrations that spread to the edge of the paper without margins are referred to as "bled off."

Body Copy

The text portion of the copy on a page, as distinguished from headlines.

Bullet

A marker, usually a solid dot, preceding text to add emphasis; generally indicates that the text is part of a list.

Byte

A unit of measurement equal to eight bits (decimal 256) of digital information, sufficient to represent one text character. It is the standard unit for measuring file size. See also *Kilobyte*, *Megabyte*, and *Gigabyte*.

Calibration

The process of bringing a device to a known, measurable, consistent state of operation.

Callout

A descriptive label referenced to a visual element, such as several words connected to the element by an arrow; an annotation.

Cap Line

The theoretical line to which the tops of capital letters are aligned.

Caps

An abbreviation for capital letters.

Caps and Small Caps

A style of typesetting in which capital letters are used in the normal way, while the type that would normally be lowercased has been changed to small capital letters. A true small-caps typeface does not contain any lowercase letters.

Caption

The lines of text that identify a picture or illustration, usually placed beneath it or otherwise in close proximity.

CD-ROM

An optical compact disc used to store approximately 600 MB of data. Files are permanently stored on the disc and can be copied to a computer's hard disk, but they cannot be altered directly.

CD-R/CD-RW

A development of CD-ROM technology, CD-R is a recordable CD disc and drive, also known as a "burner." A CD-R drive can write to a CD-R disc only once; afterwards, the disc cannot be erased or rewritten. CD-RW is the next generation of technology, and allows a CD-RW disc to be erased and rewritten. A CD-RW drive can also "burn" a CD-R disc.

Character Count

The number of characters (letters, figures, signs, or spaces) in a selected block of copy. Once used to calculate the amount of text that would fit on a given line or region when setting type.

Choke

See *Trapping*.

Clipboard

An area of computer memory that holds data that has been cut or copied. The next item cut or copied replaces the data already in the clipboard.

Cloning

Exact duplication of an element on a page; duplication of pixel data from one area to another in Adobe Photoshop.

CMYK

Acronym for cyan, magenta, yellow, and black, the four process-color inks that, when properly overprinted, can simulate a subset of the visible spectrum. These colors form the subtractive primaries. See *Color Separation*.

Color Balance

The combination of yellow, magenta, and cyan needed to produce a neutral gray. Determined through a gray balance analysis.

Color Correction

The process of adjusting an image to accommodate deficiencies in hue of CMYK inks. Not to be confused with the process of editing a scanned image to remove defects such as color casts.

Color Gamut

The range of colors that can be reproduced on a given device, such as a monitor, inkjet printer, or printing press.

Color Management System

A software system, such as Apple's ColorSync, that uses data contained in profiles to predict color appearance on varying devices.

Color Separation

The process of transforming color artwork (typically RGB images that have been scanned or digitally photographed) into four components corresponding to the four process colors. If spot colors are used, additional components may be created containing only those items that will appear in the corresponding spot-color layer. Each component is imaged to film or paper in preparation for making printing plates that correspond to each ink.

Column Rule

A thin vertical rule used to separate columns of type.

Comp

Comprehensive artwork used to present the general color and layout of a page.

Composite Proof

A version of an illustration or page in which the process colors appear together to represent full color. When produced on a monochrome output device, colors are represented as shades of gray.

Compression

A technique used to reduce the size of a file by analyzing occurrences of similar data. Compressed files occupy less storage space, and they copy and transmit more quickly. *Lossy* compression schemes such as JPEG can result in a loss of image quality and/or resolution because the technique throws away data considered to be unnecessary. *Lossless* compression does not discard any data and produces identical files when decompressed.

Compression Utility

A software program that reduces a file's size for storage on a disk. If a compressed file is too large to fit onto a single disk, the compression utility can create file segments that can fit on multiple disks.

Condensed Type

A font in which the width of the letters is narrower than that of the standard letters of the typeface, such as ITC Garamond Condensed. Condensed type can be drawn as such, or the effect may be poorly simulated by applying a percentage of width scaling to the normal font.

Continuous Tone

An image such as an original photograph in which the subject has continuous shades of color or gray tones through the use of an emulsion process. Continuous-tone images must be screened to create halftone images that can be printed. Also called "contone."

Contrast

The relationship between the dark and light areas of an image, dependent on the image content, context, and any artistic intent.

Copyright

Ownership of a work by the originator, such as an author, publisher, artist, or photographer. A copyright permits the originator of material to prevent its use without express permission or acknowledgment. Copyright may be sold, transferred, or given up contractually.

Crop Marks

Printed short, fine lines used as guides for final trimming of the pages within a press sheet.

Cropping

The elimination of parts of a photograph or other original that are not deemed necessary.

Crossover

An element in a book (text, line art, or other graphic) that appears on both pages of a reader spread crossing over the gutter.

Descender

The part of a lowercase letter that extends below the baseline (lower edge of the x-height) of the letter. The letters y, p, g, and j contain descenders.

Digital Proofs

A digital proof is created without the use of conventional film processes and is output directly from a computer to a digital proofing device, such as a calibrated inkjet printer or a sophisticated laser device such as the Kodak Approval© system.

Dingbat

A font character that displays a picture instead of a letter, number, or punctuation mark. The most commonly used dingbat font is Zapf Dingbats; others include Wingdings, Webdings, and Monotype Sorts. A printer's typographical ornament. Any pictographic element present as a character in a font.

Direct-to-plate

Producing printing plates or other image carriers from computer output, usually via laser exposure, without an intermediate film exposure.

Double-page Spread

A design that spans the two pages visible to the reader at any open spot in a magazine, periodical, or book.

Downloadable Fonts

Typefaces that can be stored on disk and then downloaded to a printer when needed.

DPI (Dots Per Inch)

The measurement of resolution for page printers, phototypesetting machines, and graphics screens. Currently graphics screens use resolutions of 60 to 100 dpi, standard desktop laser printers work at 600 dpi, and imagesetters operate at more than 1,500 dpi. Also, and more correctly, known as "pixels per inch" for displays and continuous-tone images, and "spots per inch" for imaging devices such as printers and imagesetters.

Drop Shadow

A gray duplicate of a shape placed behind and slightly offset from the original element, text, or graphic to give the effect of a shadow.

Duotone

The separation of a grayscale photograph into black and a second color having different tonal values and screen angles. Duotones are used to enhance photographic reproduction in two-, three- (tritone), or sometimes four-color (quadtone) work. The second+ ink can be black, gray, or any spot or process ink. Common two-color print jobs can often be improved by using a duotone instead of a plain gray image.

Embedding

1. Placing control codes in the body of a document. 2. Including a complete copy of a text file or image within a desktop-publishing document, with or without a link. See *Linking*.

Em Dash

A dash (—) that indicates the separation of elements of a sentence or clause. The en dash (–) has become an acceptable replacement for the em dash in recent years.

Em Space

A space that is of equal width in points to the point size. An em space in 10-point type is 10 points wide.

En Dash

A dash (–), half the width of an em dash, that often replaces the word "to" or "through," such as 9–5 or Monday–Friday.

En Space

A space that is equal to half the width of an em space.

EPS

Acronym for Encapsulated PostScript, a single-page PostScript file that contains grayscale or color information and can be imported into many electronic layout and design applications. An EPS file normally contains a small preview image that displays when placed in a layout or used by another program. EPS files can contain text, vector artwork, and images.

Expanded Type

Also called "extended type." A typeface in which the width of the letters is wider than that of the standard letters of the font. Expanded type can be a designed font, or the effect may be approximated by applying a percentage of normal width by a formatting command.

Export

To save a file generated in one application in a format that is readable in another application.

Extension

1. A modular software program that extends or expands the functions of a larger program. A folder of extensions to the Macintosh operating system is

found in the Macintosh System folder. QuarkXPress, InDesign, Photoshop, and other applications accommodate extensions written by third parties. 2. The characters following the filename and period in a complete file name, which indicates the file type and signals a computer operating system to open the file with a particular program. For example, the .eps in the file anyfilename.eps tells you and the operating system that the file is of type: Encapsulated PostScript, and that it can be opened with Adobe Illustrator (and other programs).

Film

In a graphic-arts context, the emulsion-coated polyester roll output of an imagesetter or phototypesetter that is developed like portrait film and used to expose printing plates or other image carriers.

Filter

In image-editing applications, a small program that creates a special effect or performs some other function within an image.

Floating Accent

A separate accent mark that can be placed under or over another character. Accented characters are usually available in a font as composite characters made of a letter and an accent mark.

Font Substitution

A process in which your computer uses a font similar to the one you used in your publication to display or print your publication. Although the substitute font may be similar to the original font, your publication will not look exactly as you intended; line breaks, column breaks, or page breaks may fall differently, which can affect the entire look and feel of the publication.

Force Justify

A type alignment command which causes the space between letters and words in a line of type to expand to fit within a line. Often used in headlines, and sometimes used to force the last line of a justified paragraph, which is normally set flush left, to justify.

FPO

Acronym of For Position Only, a term applied to low-quality art reproductions or simple shapes used to indicate placement and scaling of an art element in documents or camera-ready artwork. In digital publishing, FPOs can be low-resolution files that are later replaced with high-resolution versions. An FPO is not intended for reproduction but only as a guide and placeholder for the prepress service provider.

Frame

An area or block into which text or graphics can be placed.

Full Measure

A line set to the entire line length.

Gamma

A measure of the contrast, or range of tonal variation, of the midtones in a photographic image.

GIF

Acronym for Graphics Interchange Format. A popular graphics format for online clip art and drawn graphics. GIF images are suitable only for Web use and are unusable for print.

GIF, Animated

A series of GIF graphics that functions like a film loop, giving the appearance of animation.

Gigabyte (GB)

One billion (1,073,741,824) bytes (2^{30}) or 1,048,576 kilobytes.

Global Preferences

Preference settings that affect all newly created files within an application.

Gradient

An area in which two colors (or shades of gray or the same color) are blended to create a gradual change from one to the other. Graduated fills are also known as "blends," "gradations," "gradient fills," and "vignettes."

Grayscale

1. An image composed of gray tones ranging from black to white, usually using 256 different tones of gray. 2. A tint ramp used to measure and control the accuracy of screen percentages on press. 3. An accessory used to define neutral density in a photographic image.

Greeking

1. A software technique by which areas of gray are used to simulate lines of text below a certain point size. 2. Nonsense text use to define a layout before copy is available. Also called "placeholder text" in InDesign.

Grid

A division of a page by horizontal and vertical guides into areas into which text or graphics may be placed accurately.

Group

To collect graphic elements together so an operation may be applied to all of them simultaneously.

Gutter

Extra space between pages in a layout. Sometimes used interchangeably with "alley" to describe the space between columns on a page. Gutters can appear either between the top and bottom of two adjacent pages or between two sides of adjacent pages. Gutters are often used because of the binding or layout requirements of a job — for example, to add space at the top or bottom of each page or to allow for the grind-off taken when a book is perfect bound.

Hairline Rule

The thinnest rule that can be printed on a given device. A hairline rule on a 1,200-dpi imagesetter is 1/1200 of an inch; on a 300-dpi laser printer, the same rule would print at 1/300 of an inch.

Halftone

An image generated for use in printing in which a range of continuous tones is simulated by an array of dots that creates the illusion of continuous tone when viewed from a distance.

High-resolution File

An image file that typically contains four pixels for every dot in the printed reproduction. High-resolution files are often linked to a page-layout file, but not actually embedded in it, due to their large size.

Highlights

The lightest areas in a photograph or illustration.

HTML

Acronym for HyperText Markup Language. Content written in plain (ASCII) text can be marked up with HTML tags and commands, which Web browsers are designed to read and display. HTML focuses more on the logical structure of a page than its appearance, though appearance can be forced, and it includes provisions for creating links to other Web and Internet resources. HTML tags are usually simple on-off constructions; for example, the HTML fragment <bold>Hello</bold> will instruct a Web browser to display the word "Hello" in a bold font.

Hyphenation Zone

The space at the end of a line of text in which the hyphenation function examines the word to determine whether it should be hyphenated and wrapped to the next line. Generally used only when full justification is disabled.

Imagesetter

An expensive device used to output a page-layout file or composition at high resolution (usually 1,000–3,000 dpi) onto photographic paper or film, which is generally used to make proofs or printing plates. An imagesetter appears as a printer to a computer, and uses the PostScript language to generate the high-resolution image.

Import

To bring a file generated within one application into another application.

Imposition

The arrangement of pages on a printed sheet, which, when the sheet is finally printed, folded, and trimmed, will place the pages in their correct order.

Indexing

In desktop publishing, marking certain words within a document with hidden codes so an index can be generated automatically.

Initial Caps

Text in which the first letter of each word is capitalized.

Internet

An international network of computer networks, which links millions of commercial, educational, governmental, and personal computers.

Internet Service Provider (ISP)

A company that provides access to the Internet through a dial-up or broadband connection. Typically, ISPs charge a monthly fee and include an email account.

JPG or JPEG

Acronym for Joint Photographers Experts Group, an industry organization that created the standard compression algorithm that reduces the file size of bitmapped images. JPEG is a *lossy* compression method, and image quality is reduced in direct proportion to the amount of compression. High JPEG compression levels will produce visible artifacts in an image.

Justified Alignment

Straight left and right alignment of text — not ragged. Every line of text is the same width, creating even left and right margins.

Kerning

Moving a pair of letters closer together or farther apart to achieve a better fit or appearance.

Keyline

A thin, often black border around a picture or a box indicating where to place pictures. In digital files, the keylines are often vector objects while photographs are usually bitmap images.

Kilobyte (K, KB)

1,024 (2^{10}) bytes, the nearest binary equivalent to decimal 1,000 bytes. Referred to as "K" or "KB."

L*a*b* (Lab)

The lightness, red-green attribute, and yellow-blue attribute in the CIE color space, a three-dimensional color-mapping system.

Landscape

Printing from the left to right across the long edge of the page. A landscape orientation rotates a portrait (tall) page 90 degrees.

Layer

A function of graphics applications that isolates elements from each other, so a group of elements may be hidden from view, locked, reordered, or otherwise manipulated as a unit, without affecting other elements on the page.

Layout

The arrangement of text and graphics on a page, usually produced in the preliminary design stage.

Leading

Space added between lines of type. Usually measured in points or fractions of points. Named after the strips of lead that used to be inserted between lines of metal type. In specifying type, lines of 12-pt. type separated by a 14-pt. space is abbreviated "12/14," or "twelve over fourteen." Rhymes with "sledding," not "reading."

Letterspacing

The insertion or addition of white space between the letters of words.

Ligature

Letters that are joined together as a single unit of type (for example, æ).

Line Art

A drawing or piece of black-and-white artwork with no screens. Line art can be represented by a raster file having a bit depth of 1 (either on or off).

Line Screen

The number of lines per inch used when converting a photograph to a halftone. Typical values range from 85 for newspaper work to 150 or higher for high-quality reproduction on smooth or coated paper.

Linking

An association through software of a graphic or text file on disk with its location in a document. That location may be represented by a "placeholder" proxy image, or a low-resolution copy of the graphic.

Lossy

A data compression method characterized by the loss of some data.

LPI

Lines per inch. See *Line Screen*.

Luminosity

The amount of light, or brightness, in an image.

LZW

The acronym for the Lempel-Ziv-Welch lossless data- and image-compression algorithm. Often used for text, line art, and general data compression. Not very effective with raster data.

Macro

A set of keystrokes that can be saved. When the macro is invoked, the entire series of keystrokes will be performed in a single operation. Macros are used to perform repetitive tasks.

Mail Merge

The process of combining a data source with static text in a publication to print a batch of individually customized publications.

Margins

The non-printing areas of page, or the line at which text starts or stops.

Megabyte (M, MB)

One million (1,048,576) bytes (2^{20}) or 1,024 kilobytes.

Megahertz (Mhz)

An analog signal frequency of one million cycles per second, or a data rate of one million bits per second. Used in specifying computer CPU speed. A *gigahertz* represents one billion cycles per second.

Menu

A list of functions or items such as fonts. In contemporary software design, there is often a *menu bar* (fixed list of basic functions) at the top of a window or screen.

Metadata

Data that describes other data. For example, a file extension such as .eps or .tif is metadata that describes the file type to the user and to an operating system or application program.

Metafile

A Windows-only file type that combines the characteristics of raster and vector graphics formats; not recommended for high-quality output.

Misregistration

The unwanted result of incorrectly aligned process inks and spot colors on a finished printed piece. Misregistration can be caused by many factors, including paper stretch and improper plate alignment. Trapping can compensate for misregistration to an extent.

Modem

An electronic device for converting digital data into analog audio signals and back again (MOdulator-DEModulator). Primarily used for transmitting data between computers over analog (audio frequency) telephone lines.

Moiré

An interference pattern caused by the out-of-register overlap of two or more regular patterns such as dots or lines. In process-color printing, screen angles are selected to minimize this pattern. Pronounced "moray."

Monochrome

An image or computer monitor in which all information is represented in black and white, or with shades of gray.

Monospace

A font in which all characters occupy the same amount of horizontal space regardless of the character width. See also *Proportional Spacing*. Examples of monospace fonts are Courier, Monaco, and Lucida Monospace.

Montage

A single image formed by assembling or compositing several images.

Multimedia

The combination of sound, video images, and text to create an interactive document, program, or presentation.

Non-breaking Space

A typographic command that connects two words with a space, but prevents the words from being broken apart if the space occurs at the end of a line.

Object-oriented Art

Vector artwork composed of separate elements or shapes described mathematically rather than by specifying the color and position of every point. This contrasts to bitmap images, which are composed of individual pixels.

Oblique

A slanted character (sometimes backwards, or to the left), often used when referring to italic versions of sans-serif typefaces.

OLE

Acronym for Object Linking and Embedding, a data-sharing technology used in the Windows operating system. While OLE works well in office applications, it should not be used in any layout or illustration application. Import or place images and text rather than using OLE publishing functions.

OpenType

A modern font format developed by Adobe and Microsoft that (1) can be used on both the Windows and Macintosh platforms, (2) can contain over 65,000 distinct glyphs, and (3) offers advanced typographic features to applications such as InDesign. OpenType will eventually replace TrueType and PostScript Type 1 fonts.

Orphan

A single or partial word, or a partial line of a paragraph, appearing at the bottom of a page. See *Widow*.

Overprint

A printing technique in which one element prints over underlying elements (that is, one ink is printed on top of another ink). The overprinted inks can combine to make a new color. Often used with black type. The opposite of knockout.

Overset Text

Any text that does not fit within a text frame or container, usually indicated by a small icon at the bottom of the text container. Overset text is hidden and should be fixed when found.

Page Description Language (PDL)

A programming language that describes both text and graphics (object or bit-image) in mathematical form. A PDL makes the page content independent of the physical printing device. PostScript is a PDL, for example.

PageMaker

A page-layout application owned by Adobe Systems (7.0) and not being developed any further.

Palette

1. As derived from the term in the traditional art world, a collection of selectable colors. 2. Another name for a collection of (usually) related program commands and functions.

Panose

A typeface-matching system for font substitution based on a numeric classification of fonts according to visual characteristics. Supported in Adobe PageMaker.

PANTONE© Matching System

A system for specifying colors by number for both coated and uncoated paper; used by print services and in color desktop publishing to assure uniform color matching. One of the most widely used color-matching systems in commercial printing. Colors are chosen and specified from printed swatchbooks, which are available at most art-supply stores and graphic-arts dealers.

Pasteboard

In a page-layout program, the area outside of the printing page area, on which elements can be placed for later positioning. Items on the pasteboard do not print.

PDF (Portable Document Format)

Developed by Adobe Systems, this file format has become a de facto standard for document transfer across platforms. A PDF file usually contains all of the fonts, text, and images used in the originating document, and PDF is quickly becoming the file format of choice for sending completed pages to a service provider or printer.

Perfect Binding

A binding method in which the spines of signatures are ground off with a rough tool and then bound into a soft cover with adhesive. Each page is glued to the spine and to the adjacent pages.

Photoshop

The most popular image-editing and -creation application, developed by Adobe Systems. Currently at version 7.0.

Pi Fonts

A collection of special characters such as timetable and cartographic symbols, mathematical signs, and other specialized characters. Examples are Zapf Dingbats, Symbol, and Carta.

Pica

A traditional typographic measurement of 12 points, or approximately 1/6 of an inch. Most page-layout applications specify a pica as exactly 1/6 of an inch.

PICT

A once-common Macintosh file format that supports vector and raster data, comparable to a Windows metafile. The more recent PICT2 format supports 24-bit color. Should not be used for prepress.

Pixel

Abbreviation for picture element, one of the tiny rectangular areas or dots generated by a computer for the display of data on a monitor. If a pixel is active, it has color or shading. If it is inactive, it looks like a black space. Pixels can vary in size from one type of monitor to another. A greater number of pixels per inch of linear screen area results in a higher resolution on screen. Unlike printer dots, pixels typically represent eight or more bits of data; printer dots can only represent one bit of data and are either printed (on) or not (off).

PMS

See *PANTONE Matching System.*

Point

A traditional unit of measurement used to specify type size, rule weight, and other measures, equal to (approximately, in traditional typesetting) 1/72 inch. 12 points equal one pica. See *Pica.*

Polygon

A geometric figure consisting of three or more straight lines enclosing an area. Triangles, squares, rectangles, and stars are all polygons.

Portrait

Printing from left to right across the short edge of a sheet of paper. Portrait orientation on a letter-size page uses a standard 8.5-inch width and 11-inch length.

Positive

A photographic image made on paper or transparency film that is not a negative or inverted image.

PostScript

1. A page-description language developed by Adobe Systems that describes type and/or images and their positional relationships upon the page. 2. An interpreter or RIP (see *Raster Image Processor*) that can process the PostScript page description into a format for laser printer or imagesetter output. 3. A computer programming language.

PostScript Printer Description (PPD)

A text-only ASCII file that contains device-specific information enabling software to produce the best results possible for each type of designated printer.

PPI

Pixels per inch; used to denote the resolution of an image.

Preferences

A set of defaults for an application that may be modified.

Preflight Check

A final check of a page layout that verifies all fonts and linked graphics are available, that colors are properly defined, and that any necessary traps have been applied.

Prepress

Work done to prepare an electronic page layout for printing, typesetting, scanning, layout, and imposition.

Prepress Proof

A color proof made from electronic data or film images.

Primary Colors

Colors that can be used to generate secondary colors. For the additive system (i.e., a computer monitor), these colors are red, green, and blue. For the subtractive system (i.e., the printing process), these colors are cyan, magenta, and yellow.

Printer Command Language (PCL)

A language developed by Hewlett Packard for use with its own line of printers. Not suitable for prepress applications, though a PCL printer can be used for rough proofing.

Printer Driver

The software module that allows communication between an application, an operating system, and a printer.

Printer Fonts

The vector outlines of PostScript, TrueType, and OpenType fonts that are sent to the printer.

Process Colors

The four inks (cyan, magenta, yellow, and black) used in four-color process printing. A printing method in which a full range of colors is reproduced by combining four semi-transparent inks. Process-color printing is typically used when a publication includes full-color photographs or multicolor graphics. See *Color Separation, CMYK.*

Profile

A file containing data representing the color-reproduction characteristics of a device such as a monitor or printer, determined by a characterization process that is performed after a calibration; the calibration is done to bring the device to a known state of operation prior to characterization or profiling. Also called "ICC profile."

Proof

A representation of the printed job that is made from plates (press proof), film, or electronic data (digital proof). It is generally used for customer inspection and approval before mass production begins.

Proportional Spacing

A method of letter spacing whereby each character is spaced to accommodate the varying widths of letters or figures, thus increasing readability. With proportionally spaced fonts, each character is given a horizontal space proportional to its size. For example, a proportionally spaced "m" occupies more horizontal space than an "i."

Pt.

Abbreviation for point.

Pull Quote

An excerpt from the body of a story used to emphasize an idea, draw readers' attention, or generate interest.

QuarkXPress

A popular page-layout application.

Queue

A holding area on a client or server computer for jobs sent to a printer. Each job is sent to the printer as the printer finishes the prior job.

RAM

Acronym for Random Access Memory, the high-speed working memory of a computer into which the operating system and applications are loaded for execution by the processor. Also used to temporarily hold documents and data that are being edited or otherwise accessed. All information in RAM is lost when the computer is turned off, whereas files stored on a hard drive stay there until intentionally deleted.

Raster Image Processor (RIP)

That part of a PostScript printer or imagesetting device that converts the page information from the PostScript Page Description Language into a high-resolution bitmap pattern that is sent to the device's marking engine (laser, inkjet heads, etc.) for final output to the appropriate medium, such as paper, film, or a printing plate. The term "ripping" is also used to refer to the process of extracting audio data from a compact disc, though this is an incorrect colloquialism.

Rasterize, Rasterization

The process of converting vector data into pixels at the resolution of the output device. The process used by an imagesetter to convert PostScript files to high-resolution raster images before these are imaged to film or paper. See *Raster Image Processor.* Also known as "ripping" a job.

Registration Marks

Figures (often crossed lines and a circle) placed outside the trim page boundaries on all color-separation overlays to provide a common element for proper alignment.

Resolution

The density of graphic information expressed in dots per inch (dpi) or pixels per inch (ppi). Can also be expressed as a metric measure of dots/pixels per centimeter.

RGB

Acronym for red, green, blue, the colors of projected light from a computer monitor that, when combined, present a large subset of the visual spectrum. When a color image is scanned or digitally photographed, RGB data is acquired by the scanner or camera, and is usually converted to CMYK data later in the prepress process. Also refers to the color model of most digital artwork. See *CMYK.*

RIP

See *Raster Image Processor.*

ROM

Acronym for Read Only Memory, a memory chip in a computer, printer, and many other types of devices that permanently stores startup and hardware control information for use each time the computer is turned on. Usually contains a small, disposable operating system designed to read the main operating system from a disk.

RTF

Acronym for Rich Text Format, an ASCII text format that contains formatting tags and other styling information; requires an application capable of interpreting RTF data for proper display and editing.

Rules

Straight lines, often stretching horizontally across the top of a page to separate text from running heads.

Running Head

Text at the top of the page that provides information about the publication. Chapter names and book titles are often included in the running head. Also used in dictionaries, directories, and other reference works to inform the reader about the current page and/or section contents. Can also be used at the bottom of a page where it is called a "running foot."

Saddle-stitching

A binding method in which signatures are folded, stapled at the spine, then trimmed to the final publication size. It is not suitable for high page counts unless the paper is of a very light weight.

Sans Serif

Sans-serif fonts are fonts that do not have the tiny lines, knobs, and other ornamentation that appears on terminating strokes of serif letters.

Scaling

The means within a program to reduce or enlarge the amount of space an object will occupy by multiplying the data by a scale factor. Scaling can be proportional, or in one dimension only.

Scanner

A device that digitizes photographs, transparencies, drawings, and other media by illuminating the media and using special light-sensing analog or digital circuits to produce a digital image file, typically in TIFF or JPEG format. Color scanners will usually produce a minimum of 24 bits for each pixel, with 8 bits each for red, green, and blue.

Screen Angle

The angle at which the rulings of a halftone screen are set when making screened images for halftone process-color printing. The equivalent effect can be obtained electronically through selection of the desired angle from a menu.

Screen Tint

A constant halftone-screen pattern that creates an even tone at some percentage less than 100. Most printing presses can only reproduce screen tints ranging from 5% to 95%.

Serif

A line or curve projecting from the end of a letterform. Typefaces designed with such projections are called "serif faces."

Silhouette

To remove part of the background of a photograph or illustration, leaving only the desired portion. Usually created by drawing a path in Photoshop or another application that defines the area to be masked. Also called "clipping path."

Skew

A transformation command that slants an object at an angle to the side from its initial fixed base.

Small Caps

A type style in which lowercase letters are replaced by uppercase letters that have either been especially drawn for this purpose (known as "cut small caps"), or reduced artificially by a program to simulate cut small caps.

Smart Quotes

The opening/closing quotation marks (" " ' ') used by typographers, as opposed to the straight marks (" " ' ') on a typewriter. Automatic replacement of straight quotes with typographer's quotes is usually a setup option in a word-processing program or page-layout application. Automatic replacement will also apply to the apostrophe. Use straight marks as inch/foot symbols only.

Snap-to (Guides or Rulers)

An optional feature in page-layout programs that drives objects to line up with guides or margins if they are within a defined pixel range. This eliminates the need for very precise, manual placement of objects with the mouse.

Soft or Discretionary Hyphen

A hyphen coded for display and printing only when formatting of the text puts the hyphenated word at the end of a line.

Soft Return

A code that ends a line but does not apply a paragraph mark that would end the continuity of the style for that paragraph. Also called "line break."

Spine

The binding edge at the back of a book that joins the front and back covers and holds the pages in place.

Spot Color

Any pre-mixed ink that is not one of or a combination of the four process-color inks, often specified by a PANTONE swatch number in North America.

Spread

Two facing pages that can be worked on as a unit, and will be viewed side by side in the final publication.

Stacking Order

The order of appearance of overlapping elements on a page. Most elements can be moved in front of or behind other elements.

Stet

Used in proof-correction work to cancel a previous correction. From the Latin for "let it stand."

Stroke

The visible part of a vector line, curve, or outline.

Stuffit

A file-compression utility mostly used with the Macintosh, but also available for Windows. An analogous utility for Windows is WinZip.

Style

A set of formatting instructions for fonts, paragraphs, tabs, and other properties of text.

Style Sheet

A file containing all of the tags and instructions for formatting all parts of a document; style sheets create consistency between similar documents.

Subhead

A second-level heading used to organize body text by topic.

Subscript

Small-size characters set below the normal letters or figures, usually to convey technical information.

Substitution

Using an existing font to simulate one that is not available to the printer.

Superscript

Small characters set above the normal letters or figures, usually to identify a reference, and also for correct typesetting of ordinals (1st, 2nd, etc.).

Tabloid

Paper 11 inches wide and 17 inches tall. Also refers to a periodical produced at the same or a similar size, often containing scandalous and bogus content.

Tagged Image File Format (TIFF)

A common format used for scanned or computer-generated raster images.

Tags

1. The various formats in a style sheet that indicate paragraph settings, margins and columns, page layouts, hyphenation and justification, widow and orphan control, and other parameters. 2. Markup-control elements used in text-markup languages such as HTML, XML, and proprietary forms such as those created by QuarkXPress, PageMaker, and InDesign.

Template

A document file containing layout and styles by which a series of documents can maintain the same look and feel. A model publication that can be used as the basis for creating a new publication. A template contains some of the basic layout and formatting, and perhaps even some text and graphics that can be re-used in future publications.

Text Attribute

A characteristic applied directly to a letter or letters in text, such as bold, italic, or underline.

Text Converters/Filters

Tools that convert word-processing and spreadsheet documents created in other programs into files that can be imported into another program.

Thin Space

A fixed space, equal to half an en space, or the width of a period in most fonts.

Thumbnails

1. The preliminary sketches of a design. 2. Small images used to indicate the content of a computer file.

TIFF (.tif, .tiff)

Acronym for Tagged Image File Format. See *Tagged Image File Format.*

Tracking

Adjusting the spacing of letters in a line of text to achieve proper justification or general appearance. You may want to squeeze letters closer together to fit into a frame, or spread them apart for a special effect.

Trapping

The process of creating an overlap between abutting inks to compensate for imprecise registration in the printing process; extending the lighter colors of one object into the darker colors of an adjoining object. The color overlaps just enough to fill areas where gaps could appear due to misregistration.

Trim

After printing, mechanically cutting the publication to the correct final dimensions. The trim size is normally indicated by marks on the printing plate outside the page area.

TrueType

A non-PostScript outline font format used in both Macintosh and Windows systems; format invented by Apple Computer and licensed to Microsoft, but font data cannot be transferred from one platform to the other. TrueType fonts combine the outline data and screen font/font metrics into one file.

Type 1 Font

PostScript-based outline fonts; format invented by Adobe Systems. Can be used on Macintosh and Windows, but the font data is not cross-platform. Type 1 fonts require an outline file and either a screen font (Macintosh) or font metrics (Windows) file to operate properly. See *OpenType.*

Type Family

A set of typefaces created from the same basic design but in different weights, such as bold, light, italic, book, and heavy.

Typesetting

The arrangement of individual characters of text into words, sentences, and paragraphs.

Typo

Abbreviation for typographical error. A keystroke error in the typeset copy.

Uppercase

The capital letters of a typeface as opposed to the lowercase, or small, letters. When type was hand composited, the capital letters resided in the upper part of the type case, hence the name. Small letters were kept in the lower case.

Utility

Software that performs ancillary tasks such as counting words, defragmenting a hard drive, or restoring a deleted file.

Vector Graphics

Graphics defined using coordinate points and mathematically-drawn lines and curves, which may be freely scaled and rotated without image degradation in the final output. Fonts (such as PostScript and TrueType), and illustrations from drawing applications are common examples of vector objects. Two commonly used vector-drawing programs are Illustrator and FreeHand. A class of graphics that does not suffer the resolution limitation of bitmapped graphics; vectors can be scaled almost infinitely with no apparent loss of quality or detail.

Widow

A short line ending a paragraph appearing at the top of the page. Generally considered to be undesirable. See *Orphan.*

X-height

The height of the lowercase letter "x" in a given typeface, which represents the basic size of the bodies of all of the lowercase letters.